Davidson
2001

Catholicism, Controversy and the English Literary Imagination, 1558–1660

The Catholic contribution to English literary culture has been widely neglected and often misunderstood. Drawing on extensive original research, this book sets out to rehabilitate a wide range of Catholic imaginative writing, while exposing the role of anti-Catholicism as an imaginative stimulus to mainstream writers in Tudor and Stuart England. It discusses canonical figures such as Sidney, Spenser, Webster and Middleton, those whose presence in the canon has been more fitful, such as Robert Southwell and Richard Crashaw, and many who have escaped the attention of literary critics. Among the themes to emerge are the anti-Catholic imagery of revenge-tragedy and the definitive contribution made by Southwell and Crashaw to the post-Reformation revival of religious verse in England. Alison Shell offers a fascinating exploration of the rhetorical stratagems by which Catholics sought to demonstrate simultaneous loyalties to the monarch and to their religion, and of the stimulus given to the Catholic literary imagination by the persecution and exile which so many of these writers suffered.

Alison Shell is Lecturer in the Department of English Studies at the University of Durham. She has held a British Academy Post-Doctoral Research Fellowship at University College London, a visiting fellowship at the Beinecke Library, Yale University, and was formerly Rare Books Curator at the British Architectural Library of the Royal Institute of British Architects. She is co-editor of *The Book Trade and its Customers* (1997), and has published essays on Edmund Campion, Aphra Behn, conversion in early modern England, anti-Catholicism and the early modern English book trade.

CATHOLICISM, CONTROVERSY AND THE ENGLISH LITERARY IMAGINATION, 1558–1660

ALISON SHELL

PUBLISHED BY THE PRESS SYNDICATE OF THE UNIVERSITY OF CAMBRIDGE
The Pitt Building, Trumpington Street, Cambridge CB2 1RP United Kingdom

CAMBRIDGE UNIVERSITY PRESS
The Edinburgh Building, Cambridge CB2 2RU, UK http://www.cup.cam.ac.uk
40 West 20th Street, New York, NY 10011–4211, USA http://www.cup.org
10 Stamford Road, Oakleigh, Melbourne 3166, Australia

© Alison Shell 1999

This book is in copyright. Subject to statutory exception and to the provisions of relevant collective licensing agreements, no reproduction of any part may take place without the written permission of Cambridge University Press.

First published 1999

Printed in the United Kingdom at the University Press, Cambridge

Typeset in 11/12½ Baskerville   [CE]

A catalogue record for this book is available from the British Library

Library of Congress cataloguing in publication data
Shell, Alison.
Catholicism, controversy, and the English literary imagination, 1558–1660 / Alison Shell.
p. cm.
Includes bibliographical references and index.
ISBN 0 521 58090 0 hardback
1. English literature – Early modern, 1500–1700 – History and criticism.
2. Catholic Church – Controversial literature – History and criticism.
3. English literature – Catholic authors – History and criticism.
4. Christianity and literature – England – History – 16th century.
5. Christianity and literature – England – History – 17th century.
6. Christian literature, English – History and criticism.
7. Catholics – England – Intellectual life.
8. Anti-Catholicism in literature.
9. Catholic Church – In literature.   I. Title.
PR428.C3S54   1999
820.9′9222′09031 – dc21   98–35135   CIP

ISBN 0 521 58090 0 hardback

Contents

Acknowledgements vi
List of abbreviations ix
Note on the text xi

Introduction 1

PART I CATHOLICS AND THE CANON

1 The livid flash: decadence, anti-Catholic revenge tragedy and the dehistoricised critic   23
2 Catholic poetics and the Protestant canon   56

PART II LOYALISM AND EXCLUSION

3 Catholic loyalism: I. Elizabethan writers   107
4 Catholic loyalism: II. Stuart writers   141
5 The subject of exile: I   169
6 The subject of exile: II   194
   Conclusion   224

Notes   228
List of works frequently cited   300
Index   303

Acknowledgements

This book is all about how early modern Catholic literature and history is an undervalued topic: true now, still truer in the days when I was an Oxford D.Phil student. I was extraordinarily lucky in having supervisors who didn't want just to supervise theses on subjects they knew about already – Nigel Smith, on whose shoulders the main administrative burden fell, Edward Chaney and J. W. Binns – and I count myself more fortunate still that they continue to care about my scholarly and personal progress. Julia Briggs provided valuable preliminary help. T. A. Birrell, Charles Burnett, Victor Houliston, Doreen Innes, Sally Mapstone, D. F. McKenzie, Ruth Pryor, Masahiro Takenaka, Gwen Watkins and Karina Williamson were of enormous help to the first incarnation of this book as a doctoral thesis, and I should also like to thank Conrad Arnander, Rachel Boulding, Andrew Cleevely (Bro. Philip), Christopher Collins, The Rev. Kenneth Macnab, Joanne Mosley, The Rev. Dr. Michael Piret, Tim Pitt-Payne, Richard Thomas and The Rev. Robin Ward for reading portions of that thesis, and contributing some wonderfully unexpected insights. Patricia Brückmann was a sharp-eyed reader at proof stage.

My husband, Arnold Hunt, is another early-modern specialist, and if this book is any good, this is due in large part to his analytical mind and his unparalleled gift for finding exactly the right reference. Both I and the book have benefited enormously from the polyglot learning and baroque hospitality of Peter Davidson and Jane Stevenson. Michael Questier has been learned and consoling, as well as reading the whole typescript. I would like, as well, to thank him for being my co-organiser for the one-day conference 'Papists Misrepresented and Represented', held at University College London in June 1997. Martin Butler valuably commented on chapter 4 of this book. I have bothered many experts in my attempt to pull a wide-ranging argument together, and would particularly like to thank John Bossy, Patrick Collinson, David Crankshaw, Eamon Duffy, Katherine Duncan-Jones, Julia Griffin, Nigel Griffin, Brian Harrison, Caroline Hibbard, Michael Hodgetts, Victoria James, Peter Lake, Michelle Lastovickova, Giles Mandelbrote, Arthur Marotti, Steven May, Martin Murphy, Graham Parry, J. T. Rhodes, Ceri Sullivan, Joanne Taylor, Dora Thornton and Alexandra Walsham as well as all those acknowledged in the notes, and those who, to my embarrassment, I will have forgotten. Alan Cromartie, Seán Hughes, Mary Morrissey and Jason Scott-Warren have engaged in stimulating conversations on the topic. Dominic Berry, J. W. Binns, Martin Brooke, Robert Carver, Doreen Innes, Christopher Shell and Jane Stevenson have helped me in translating the Latin. Robin Myers has informed this, and every piece of scholarly work I have ever done, with an urge to get things right bibliographically. Stella Fletcher kindly undertook a last-minute check of manuscripts in the Venerable English College, Rome. John Morrill was a judicious and warmly encouraging reader for Cambridge University Press; Josie Dixon continues a most supportive editor, and I would also like to thank my copy-editor, Andrew Taylor, and the production controller, Karl Howe.

Having once been a librarian, I know that the profession is often forgotten in acknowledgements, and so I am pleased to thank those whose faces I got to know well but whose names I often never learnt: in the Bodleian; the University Library, Cambridge; the Senate House and Warburg Institute, University of London; the libraries of the University of Durham; and the North Library and Manuscripts Department of the old British Library. The great Catholic libraries in England and abroad were an indispensable resource, and I have greatly benefited from the expertise of The Revd. F. J. Turner, S.J., at Stonyhurst; The Revd. Geoffrey Holt, S.J., at Farm Street; The Revd. Ian Dickie, at the Westminster Catholic Archives; Sister Mary Gregory Kirkus I.B.V.M. of the Bar Convent, York; Fr Leonard Boyle, O.P., at the Vatican archives; successive student archivists at the Venerable English College, Rome; various correspondents at the English College, Valladolid; Bro. George Every at St Mary's College, Oscott; and Dom Daniel Rees, O.S.B., at Downside Abbey. No book can happen without practical help. Laura Cordy kindly resurrected my files from software nobody had ever heard of, and edited them into the bargain; the late Henry Harvey chauffeured me on many research trips; my parents-in-law, Bryan and Fiona Hunt, have been a prop in all sorts of ways.

St Hilda's College, Oxford, was a lovely place to spend both my undergraduate and postgraduate years, and I am grateful to the College for having elected me to a senior scholarship running from 1987 to 1990. It is a pleasure to acknowledge the kindness and scholarly support of many of my ex-colleagues in the English Department at University College London, where I held a British Academy Post-Doctoral Fellowship between 1994 and 1997: in particular, John Sutherland, David Trotter and Karl Miller, and Helen Hackett and Henry Woudhuysen, who made time in busy schedules to read and make detailed comments on large portions of the book. Kenneth Emond at the British Academy was sustainedly kind; and since it has not only been in this connection that the British Academy has helped me financially over the years, I would like to acknowledge my other debts to them here. Another travel grant came from the Una Ellis-Fermor Travel Fund, administered by Royal Holloway and Bedford New College, London. I am pleased, too, to thank those responsible for awarding me the James M. Osborn Fellowship at the Beinecke Library, Yale University, in September 1996; while I was there, I benefited from Stephen Parks's generous hospitality and knowledge of the collections. Finally, I am profoundly grateful to the English Department at Durham University, and especially its Head of Department, Michael O'Neill, for appointing me to a lectureship in October 1997 – at a time of real despair about jobs – and converting my temporary post into a permanent one as the last part of this book was being written.

As I was correcting these proofs, news came of the sudden death of Jeremy Maule. This book could not possibly go into the world without a tribute to his scholarship, his wit, and his inimitable kindness, especially as it was he who suggested, in the first instance, that Cambridge University Press publish it. There are scarcely any pages of this book that do not show his benign influence.

Finally, I dedicate this book to my parents: thanking them for everything, but in particular for all the sacrifices they made for me over my childhood, and over the doctoral student's characteristic prolonged adolescence.

Abbreviations

ARCR	Anthony Allison and D. M. Rogers, *The Contemporary Printed Literature of the English Counter-Reformation Between 1558 and 1640*, 2 vols (Aldershot: Scolar, 1989–94)
Beinecke	Beinecke Library, Yale University
BL	The British Library, London
Bod.	Bodleian Library, Oxford
CRS	Catholic Record Society
CSPD	Calendar of State Papers, Domestic
DNB	*Dictionary of National Biography*
EHR	*English Historical Review*
ELH	*English Literary History*
ELR	*English Literary Renaissance*
Folger	Folger Shakespeare Library, Washington, D.C.
HJ	*Historical Journal*
HLQ	*Huntington Library Quarterly*
HMC	His/Her Majesty's Commission for Historical Manuscripts
JEH	*Journal of Ecclesiastical History*
JWCI	*Journal of the Warburg and Courtauld Institutes*
Lewis & Short	Charlton T. Lewis and Charles Short, *A Latin Dictionary* (Oxford: Clarendon Press, 1980 edn.)
LPL	Lambeth Palace Library, London
MLQ	*Modern Language Quarterly*
MLR	*Modern Language Review*
MS	manuscript
N & Q	*Notes & Queries*
NAL	National Art Library, London
NLW	National Library of Wales, Aberystwyth
OED	*Oxford English Dictionary*

P & P	*Past and Present*
PMLA	*Proceedings of the Modern Language Association*
RH	*Recusant History*
SPC	Robert Southwell, *Saint Peters Complaint*
STC	A. W. Pollard and G. F. Redgrave, comp., *A Short-Title Catalogue of Books Printed in England, Scotland, and Ireland, and of English Books Printed Abroad, 1475–1640*, 3 vols, 2nd edn., rev. W. A. Jackson, F. S. Ferguson and Katharine F. Pantzer (London: Bibliographical Society, 1976–91)
TLS	*The Times Literary Supplement*
VEC	The Venerable English College, Rome
Wing	Donald Wing, *et al.*, *A Short-Title Catalogue of Books Printed in England, Scotland, Ireland ... and of English Books Printed in Other Countries, 1641–1700*, 3 vols, 2nd edn. (New York: MLA, 1972–88)

Quotations from unpublished manuscripts are reproduced by kind permission of the following: the Archives of the Archbishops of Westminster, with the permission of His Eminence the Archbishop of Westminster; the Bodleian Library, Oxford; the British Province of the Society of Jesus; Lambeth Palace Library; the National Art Library, Victoria and Albert Museum; the National Library of Wales; the Stonyhurst Library; the Board of Trinity College, Dublin; the Beinecke Library, Yale; the Folger Shakespeare Library; and the Venerable English College, Rome. The quotation on p. 23, from Donna Tartt, *The Secret History* (this edition, London 1993), p. 646, copyright © Donna Tartt, 1992, is reproduced by kind permission of Penguin Books Ltd.

Note on the text

In transcribing from sixteenth- and seventeenth-century documents, i/j and u/v have been normalized; superscript and subscript have been ignored, as have underlining and italicisation except where essential for the sense (e.g. to denote a refrain in a ballad); contractions have been expanded; and punctuation has been omitted before marks of omission except where it makes better sense to retain it.

Where a modern book has double imprints (e.g. London and New York), only the first has been given.

For the reader's convenience I have cited English translations of Latin works in the main body of the text, keeping the Latin to footnotes. Except where otherwise credited, I have translated all the Latin myself (with much-valued assistance, as recorded in the acknowledgements).

Introduction

My doctoral thesis on Catholicism in Tudor and Stuart drama, written between 1987 and 1991, was supervised jointly by a literary critic, a historian and a neo-Latinist – a state of affairs which, as I came to see, epitomised a deep uncertainty in early modern studies over the status of English Catholic writing. This book grew out of that early research; and as I write the introduction in the spring of 1998, Cambridge University Press is discussing how best to market the book to an audience divided between historians and literary critics. Not much has changed.

This is not a survey of Tudor and Stuart Catholic literature; such a book is badly needed, but for many aspects of the topic, far too little work has been done to make an adequate overview possible. My subject is a more specific one, the imaginative writing composed between the death of Mary I and the Restoration, which takes as its subject, or reacts to, the controversies between Catholics and Protestants or the penalties which successive Protestant governments imposed upon Catholics. This book comprises four essays, two subdivided, on aspects of this topic, with a bias towards poetry, drama, allegory, emblem and romance – though sermons and devotional and controversial religious prose have also been referred to on occasion.

It concentrates on imaginative writing, and also on writing where the internal logic of an argument is suborned to formal considerations, or considerations of genre: not necessarily decreasing its effectiveness, but enabling it to be effective in ways which have less to do with controversial rhetoric than with the expectations aroused by genre, or the mnemonic efficiency of a rigidly structured literary form. The idea of imaginative literature defines this book's main area of interest; but it is more of a convenience than a category, since many of the qualities one associates with imaginative writing – and, indeed, the lack of them – can operate quite independently of genre. Sermons can be full of extraordinary metaphor, didactic verse can be prosy. More generally, this book takes as its subject the literary response to an agenda set by theologians on both sides of the Catholic-Protestant divide. Sometimes the theologian and the agent of response are one and the same, sometimes they are far apart; but the poets, dramatists, emblematists and allegorists below were all dependent on polemical theology for their inspiration. A poem may transcribe doctrine, reflect doctrine or reflect upon doctrine; in odd cases, like that of Thomas Aquinas, a poem may crystallise a writer's theological formulations; but definitive theological argument is always in prose. Imaginative responses to theological agendas could be undertaken for mnemonic purposes, or to popularise, or to sweeten, or to complain – or simply because religious controversy so often results in the protracted demonisation of the other side, and demonisation is an imaginative process.

Imaginative writing has tended to be the province of the literary critic rather than the historian; and where historians do look at it, their use tends to be illustrative rather than analytical. To some extent the subject-matter of this book has been defined by former omissions: material that has not been felt to be the province of the church-historian, and about which, except in a very few cases, literary critics have been less than loquacious. This is hardly surprising, because Catholic imaginative writing, even in the case of important individuals like Southwell, Crashaw and Verstegan, is currently only available to the persevering, through facsimilisation and the second-hand academic bookseller. L. I. Guiney's *Recusant Poets* (1938), of which only volume I was completed,[1] remains the only substantial anthology for the topic. Literary-critical concern with Catholicism, as I comment in chapter two, has not been entirely absent; but it has centred around two areas, and tended to ignore the wider prospect.[2] The first of these areas is meditative verse: a phrase given wide currency in Louis Martz's *The Poetry of Meditation* (1954) but stalemated when critics recognised – quite correctly – that it was very difficult to identify a number of meditative techniques as being exclusively Catholic or exclusively Protestant. Secondly, the perceived necessity to say something new about canonical favourites has resulted in literary claims, of varying merit, being made about the permanent, temporary or possible Catholicism of Ford, Jonson, Shirley, Donne, and currently – again – about Shakespeare. But to identify Catholic elements in a writer's biography is one thing, and to use them to formulate a Catholic aesthetic, quite another; sometimes it has been well done, sometimes not. This book has largely bypassed those arguments – though they come from an attic which could do with spring-cleaning.[3]

History has covered a much broader range of Catholic material than literary criticism, and if this introduction says more about recent Catholic history than about Catholicism in English studies, it is partly because there *is* more to say. Perhaps church-historians are, by training, better equipped than literary critics to deal with the main preoccupation of this book, which can be defined – in distant homage to Max Weber – as the unintended *imaginative* consequences of religious controversy; certainly, literary critics discussing this material need to borrow from the nuanced appreciation of early modern polemical theology which history departments have formulated in recent years. But interdisciplinarity is a wholesome fashion, and it can work two ways. It can, as I argue in my first chapter, involve the forcible rehistoricising of canonical texts which have proved rather too successfully that they are for all time: texts where one needs to saw through the nacre of commentary to find the original stimulus, the grit of anti-Catholic prejudice. As the rest of the book goes on to contend, interdisciplinarity can also aid the thorough recovery of texts that have been neglected by the architects of the canon. In an age of spectacular confessional fragmentation it is sometimes easy to forget how much of what we take for granted in late twentieth-century England is built on an Anglican infrastructure. And within the academy, one needs to ask whether the criteria that cause some religious groups to be privileged in research terms, and others neglected, are protestantised in origin.

Though Tudor and Stuart Catholic history is only fitfully visible in university curricula, Catholics themselves have been interested in their ancestors for a very long time. From the beginnings of Catholic oppression in Britain, a genre existed which Hugh Aveling has called 'holy history' or 'salvation history'.[4] Based on collections of anecdotes including eye-witness accounts, exemplary tales and memoirs, and letters of confessors and martyrs, they were written to show the hand of God in the sufferings and martyrdom of their subjects, and in the deaths of the persecutors. There was also a concern to save biographical data for its potential usefulness in pressing the causes for canonisation of various English martyrs, a phenomenon which existed side by side with official and quasi-official veneration of them. This aim dominated the Collectanea of Christopher Grene, now preserved at Stonyhurst and Oscott, and, in the eighteenth century, the *Church History* of Charles Dodd (1737–42) and Bishop Challoner's biographical dictionary of missionary priests (1741–42).

With the nineteenth century, the era of Catholic emancipation and then of triumphalism, Catholic historians were given more public licence to plead their cause; and as so often, celebration was accompanied by stridency. Titles such as John Morris's *The Troubles of Our Catholic Forefathers* (1872–7) and Bede Camm's *In the Brave Days of Old* (1899) – with its shades of Horatius keeping the bridge – have unfairly invited some historians to conclude that the contents of many of these books are without objective value. Multi-volume biographical dictionaries, building on their forebears, characterised late-Victorian Catholic scholarship: Henry Foley's *Dictionary of the Members of the Society of Jesus* (1877–83), Joseph Gillow's *A Bibliographical Dictionary of the English Catholics* (1885–1902). The Catholic Record Society, founded in 1904, started publishing its invaluable editions of primary sources in 1905, and its periodical *Recusant History* has been counterparted by the *Innes Review* in Scotland. Catholic history has been unusually well-served by regional societies, illustrating the truth that academic historians ignore local ones at their peril.[5] Bio-bibliographical studies such as A. C. Southern's *English Recusant Prose*[6] (1950), Thomas Clancy's *Papist Pamphleteers* (1964) and Peter Milward's two-part *Religious Controversies of the Elizabethan (Jacobean) Age* (1968–78) have helped to clarify the complex, often dialogic nature of religious writing at this date. T. A. Birrell's inspirational presence at the University of Nijmegen lies behind much of the most fruitful post-war work on Catholic studies.[7]

The majority of twentieth-century English historians of post-Reformation English Catholicism have been Catholics themselves, or at least received Catholic education. Some have already been mentioned; but the list is long, encompassing Jesuits like Philip Caraman, Francis Edwards and Thomas McCoog, scholar-schoolmasters like J. C. H. Aveling and Michael Hodgetts, and the university academics J. J. Scarisbrick, Eamon Duffy, Brendan Bradshaw and Richard Rex. Within the last fifteen years Scarisbrick and Duffy, in particular, have mounted a high-profile revisionist critique of Reformation history in *The Reformation and the English People* (1984) and *The Stripping of the Altars* (1993), suggesting that the abuses that prompted the Continental Reformation were not characteristic of Britain, that Protestantism was not a popular movement but one imposed from above by Henry VIII and his ministers upon an unwilling populace, and that indigenous religious traditions were far more impoverished after the Reformation than before it.[8] Here the Catholicism of the historian has acted as a stimulus to fresh analysis in much the same way that gender studies or post-colonialism have done to others: an academic exploration of why one has the right to be aggrieved.[9]

But even though there are many ways that Catholics have an advantage in writing about Catholic history, non-Catholics are privileged in other respects: for one thing, they are not perceived as hagiographers. While there is nothing wrong with hagiography which is clearly signalled as such, most Catholic historians would be the last to deny that hagiography has sometimes resulted in an unnecessarily narrow and fictionalised scholarship. But there is a lingering feeling, among non-Catholics, that Catholic history by Catholic writers is bound to be hagiographical to some degree: a suspicion not helped by the way in which imprints on Catholic books, to this day, serve to reinforce an impression of marginality. Perhaps the proud imprimaturs on Victorian works of Catholic scholarship, and even a good number of twentieth-century ones, may still have power to kindle a residual anti-popery. But scanning the footnotes of this particular book will confirm that some things have still not changed about Catholic books and the English; Catholic scholarship, now as then, has a stronger association with Catholic presses in England and publishers on the Continent than with publishers like Cambridge University Press.

Christopher Haigh makes two necessary points in the preface to *English Reformations* (1993): that the link between Catholic research and Catholic conviction is not invariable, but that it is strong enough for other academics to assume that only Catholics are interested in Catholics. One historian, hearing that Haigh was not a Catholic, exploded 'Then why does he write such things?'[10] Like Haigh, I am not a Catholic myself. Throughout my research life, people have usually assumed otherwise; and whilst I have found it flattering to be linked – however spuriously – with a grand past and present tradition of Catholic scholars, the assumption has not always been voiced neutrally. One can understand why the dust-jacket of Mary Heimann's fine study *Catholic Devotion in Victorian England* (1995) carries the message that the author is 'neither English nor a Catholic'. Yet it is true that she and I are slightly unusual, as non-Catholics who find Catholic matter significant and engaging enough to read up on. The idea that research on Catholics is inseparable from Catholic conviction may seem a minor social confusion, but it matters a great deal. Because of another fallacy still, that only paid-up members of religious or political bodies have an axe to grind, it is where prejudice can begin. Most academic books on literary history assume the reader is agnostic even where the subject is religious, since this is presumed to be the least offensive stance – or the most convertible academic currency, at least. This study tries to recognise that its likely audience is pluralist, more ideologically heterogenous than the Reformation by far: Catholics, Protestants, ecumenists, members of other world religions, the atheist, the agnostic, the adiaphorist and the uninterested.

Catholics, especially Elizabethan and twentieth-century ones, are often called religious conservatives; and sometimes this is true. It is no reason to ignore them; in a plea for the acknowledgement of contrast and opposition within literary history, Virgil Nemoianu has written that 'A "politically correct" attitude, honestly thought through to its true ends and complete implications, will result in a careful and loving study of the reactionary, not as an enemy but as an indispensable co-actor.'[11] And a further caution is necessary. This book does not use the case-history of Catholicism to figure reactionariness in general, which would misrepresent a good many Catholics, then and now; it suggests instead, less judgementally, that the experience of early modern English Catholics, and consequently their main modes of discourse, are comparable to the experience and writing of other types of dissident. It attempts to discuss Catholics on their own terms, but its definition of a Catholic is broad – one who frequented secret or illegal Catholic worship or practised specifically Catholic private devotion, with or without attendance at the worship of other denominations – and will be too broad for some.[12] Yet it is crucial to the distinction that I wish to draw between the heroic Catholic – the recusant, the confessor, the exile, the martyr, even, perhaps, the conspirator – and the Catholic pragmatists, the occasional conformists and the crypto-Catholics. Neither is more real or more typical than the other, and both are discernible as part of the implied audience in Catholic and anti-Catholic discourse. But with imaginative literature, the gap narrows;

English Catholic imaginative literature in this period is extraordinarily interactive, and powerfully concerned with the didactic and autodidactic processes of creating heroes out of its readers.

Like many other, more fashionable modes of academic discourse in the past twenty years, Catholic analysis of English history borrows from apologia; but unlike them, it has acquired no substantial band of university camp-followers aiming to right historical wrongs. To point to the fact that Catholicism is an unfashionable minority study is not necessarily to praise it in a young-fogeyish manner, nor to denigrate the legitimacy of those minority studies that are currently fashionable, but it needs a little explanation. The twentieth-century historian sees a crucial difference between the unchosen cultural handicaps of race or gender, and those brought upon the individual by religious or political affiliation. With regard to the latter, sympathy is likely to vary widely according to whether the body in question is perceived as having been oppressive in other contexts; and between Marxist and neo-Marxist hostility, humanist embarrassment and feminist complaint, all churches have suffered. This is not the place to analyse the justice of the dismissal, but two points are worth considering: firstly, whether it is appropriate to the period and the country, and secondly, whether the effect it has had of driving the present-day Catholic hermeneutic underground has been conducive to academic fairness.

Equally irreducible, equally awkward, is the fact that some academics still refuse to acknowledge that the late twentieth century is supposed, in the West, to be post-Christian. Old-style, 'objective' academic discourse – in fact, a twentieth-century development that was never subscribed to by every academic – was less a declaration of open-mindedness or agnosticism than a gentleman's agreement to stop short of disputed territory. Now we can see that it was not invulnerable to the infiltration of received ideas: hence deconstruction, a radical shifting of the sites of controversy, and the jubilee spirit of revisionism. But any historian who acknowledges in print that membership of an exclusivist religious body has suggested his or her lines of research breaks a taboo, agitating the smooth waters of academic agnosticism. Duffy and Scarisbrick are well-known commentators on Catholic affairs, and one can infer from their writing in general that Catholic indignation goaded them to formulate their revisions of the English Reformation; but in their historical works, their Catholicism is not explicitly stated. Where a historian is a practising Christian of any denomination, there can arise a two-tier system of interpretation, where colleagues or students are familiar with the writer's convictions but the wider reading public need not be. Such historians often write with a powerful chained anger, utilising the insights of historical oppression but unable to admit to doing so. Coding and censorship are still with us, and necessitate an academic discourse which conceals religious belief as well as Catholicism.[13]

Catholicism, besides, is perhaps unique in the strength of the identification it demands between the Reformation and now. The Church of England has only ever made partial claims to universality, and was so clearly a state construct that historians indifferent or hostile to its claims can dismiss it easily, or discuss it simply as an instrument of authority. Conversely, to call someone a puritan now is a judgement, not a plain description. The capacity of Protestant Christianity for spontaneous re-invention has resulted in different names for similar movements: one reason why the idea of a Puritan has been so open to reductive redefinition by Christopher Hill and others.[14] Besides, there is something about the notion of Protestantism – certainly not always the same as Protestantism itself – which makes it especially acceptable to the academic mind: the sceptical, the enquiring, as against the authoritarian, the dogmatic and the superstitious.[15] But Catholicism, despite the differences between its manifestations in the sixteenth century and the twentieth, places such emphasis on tradition that it cannot be read as anything other than itself; and so, responses to current Catholicism have seemed to determine whether one welcomes or shuns it as a subject for historical enquiry. If one thinks of it as inordinately powerful and unconscionably conservative under John Paul II, one's sympathy for its persecuted representatives in early modern Britain is likely to be diminished; and thence there arises a secularised anti-popery.

Part of the reason Puritans have been more studied than Catholics by university historians is that, while there are several twentieth-century Christian denominations which have Puritan characteristics, none call themselves Puritan; there are certainly Nonconformist historians of Puritanism, but none are denominational historians in the Catholic, or Methodist, or Quaker sense. There is still a dangerous myth abroad that denominational historians are an unscholarly breed, prone to hagiography, and quick to take offence at anyone coming from outside the fold. Puritanism, on the other hand, is a vacated name bright with suggestions of revolution: excellent material for scholarly empathy. And something of the same phenomenon is observable with the study of seventeenth-century radical religionists, the Ranters and their kindred. Both have demonstrated a remarkable ability to metamorphose with the times – Christopher Hill's *The World Turned Upside Down* (1978) tells one a good deal both about the 1640s and the 1960s. But when non-Catholics consider early modern Catholicism, their attitude is inevitably coloured by their views on Catholicism now. They may have an explicit or residual Protestant distaste for what they perceive as Catholic superstition or the commercialisation of miracles. They may have a twentieth-century anger at the Catholic position on women priests, or divorce, or contraception and the Third World. They may feel about all organised religion as Milton did about Catholicism: that it is the only kind of unacceptable creed, because it tries to impair the freedom of others. More mildly, as commented above, they may associate it with conservatism.

Historians' Athenian anxiety to identify newness has also led to the under-representation of Catholics. Study of the mutations of conservatism tends to characterise the second, corrective stage in any given historical debate. But even revisionism, like any corrective historiography, has had its terms defined by what came previously. There is no necessary connection at all points between Catholics and the conservative spirit – historians have always admitted that the English Jesuits attracted opprobrium for their newness – but because Catholicism prevailed in medieval England, the two have tended to be handcuffed together in discussions of Catholicism under the Tudors and Stuarts. And, undoubtedly, there is plenty of literary evidence indicating that some Catholics eschewed Protestantism for its novelty. But Protestants became Protestants not because the doctrinal changes were new, but because they were convinced of their efficacy; similarly, one should not assume that Catholics remained or became Catholics only out of conservative prejudice, not because they identified truth. The argument from visibility, how the Church had always been identifiable as such, was necessarily a conservative one; but it was only a part of the Catholics' polemical armoury, and not automatically convincing.[16]

As historians have recently reminded us, the brevity of Mary I's reign, and the timing of her death, show how much the Protestant consensus in England was dependent on chance: but it was a chance that muted the articulacy of English Catholics for the next century.[17] There is literary evidence that the reign of Edward VI was regarded as an aberration, not only by those hoping for royal patronage, but among publishers of popular verse whose trade depended on identifying common sentiments.[18] Panegyrists exploited the coincidence of Mary's name with the Virgin's, sent to re-evangelise England: Myles Hogarde, the best-known of them, related how 'Mary hath brought home Christ againe' to a realm filled with 'frantike infidelitie'.[19] In his poem presented to Mary I, William Forrest looked back with what now reads as a combination of prescience and unconscious bitter irony.

> So was ytt, It ys not yeat owte of remembraunce,
> moste odyous schysmys / this Royalme dyd late perturbe:
> Almoste, the moste parte / geavynge attendaunce:
> (aswell of Nobles / as the rustycall Scrubbe:
> withe Thowsandys in Cyteeis / and eke in Suburbe)
> to that all true Christian faythe dyd abhore:
> Receavynge plagys not yeat extyncte thearfore ...[20]

But laments had characterised the Catholic voice during the reformers' depredations, during specific events like the Pilgrimage of Grace, and as a more general expression of dissension and despair; and lament was again, all too soon, to become a dominant Catholic genre. The period of this study covers the century which elapsed between Elizabeth I's Act of Uniformity and the Restoration: not because it is the only period in which interesting Catholic writing can be found, but because – taken as a whole – it was the period which most obviously encouraged the formulation of a various and distinct Catholic consciousness. Chapters three and four, chronological in arrangement, have more to say about this; yet, while they try to emphasize Catholic mental distinctiveness, they concentrate upon Catholic loyalism. Distinctiveness can be both oppositional and eirenical, and loyalism problematises any simple idea of Catholicism as an opposition culture.

The final success of the Protestant Reformation obviously had a lot to do with the fact that Elizabeth lived where Mary had died, but it was Elizabeth's positive actions which re-imposed it with an early decisiveness. The 1559 Act of Uniformity reinstated the 1552 Prayer Book, and the episcopal visitations of the same year saw to it that the royal supremacy and recent Crown injunctions were established across the country. Religious conservatism was so firmly set at the parochial level that it took a long time to die, and the picture is complicated by the fact that certain features of it soon began to be exploited as an anti-Puritan statement.[21] Catholic writers, of course, necessarily continued to refer to the past. But forty-five years is a long time, and during it, the sustained application of a Protestant order made it possible to distinguish conservative from Catholic.

Survivalism, the retention of pre-Reformation religious practices beyond the date of the Elizabethan Settlement, has become a constant element in historians' discussion of the period.[22] But it is not intended here to go into much detail about the varying definitions of Catholic survivalism; clearly it existed, clearly it does not explain all elements of post-Reformation English Catholicism. Though individuals may disagree on when Catholic revivalist influences reached England, or the kind of effects they had, it is universally acknowledged that the picture of post-Reformation English Catholicism is not complete without them. The English Counter-Reformation is a phrase with some meaning – distinct though it is from Catholic revivals in Italy or Spain.[23] In addition, the history of Catholic texts, particularly those associated with oral tradition, is a way to trace not only survival and revival but re-affirmation of the Catholic heritage, definable by a process which it is easier to postulate than to identify in specific instances. During England's period of transition from a near-uniformly Catholic to a largely Protestant society, the popery or the catholicity of a previously existing Catholic text depended not on its contents, but on the individual recipient's degree of ideological awareness. At some irrecoverable point, a medieval celebration of Corpus Christi or a folk carol about the Virgin would have *become* a Catholic text to a singer or copyist, not simply a religious one. Where such texts survive long past the Reformation, one can often assume that this has happened.

The shift in attitudes towards pre-Reformation texts and practices was particularly important over the length of Elizabeth's reign. Where a status quo becomes outlawed, there is always the danger – especially in remote parts of the country – of confusing deliberate defiance with custom; and because Elizabeth's reign was so long and policies towards Catholics grew stricter towards the middle and end of it, one recognises the presence of pre-Reformation texts and ideas throughout it, but sees emerging a change in attitude. Notwithstanding this, a greater awareness of the Catholic contribution to English culture would result in some important modifications to received ideas of when medievalism ended in the British Isles. Medieval patterns of life, religious and social, were sustained on the Continent by English Catholic religious orders – in some cases to this day – and continued, as far as was practicable, within many Catholic households. These are shaken traditions, because of secrecy and geographical dispersal; nevertheless, it is remarkable how long they survived.

Texts, like customs, can acquire defiance; and Catholic manuscript culture tells a tale of continuance modulating into a deliberate stylistic and confessional choice. A manuscript in the National Library of Wales, covered with a leaf from an English breviary, copies out a number of medieval saints' lives in a style designed to recall pre-Reformation precedent; Thomas Jollet's theological manuscript in the Bodleian is full of decorative initials cut out from medieval manuscripts and re-used; a manuscript of Catholic devotional material in the Folger Library is partly copied out in a quasi-medieval script.[24] This kind of self-conscious medievalism is further set in context by the provenance-history of many pre-Reformation manuscripts; the decisive resurgence of an enthusiasm for the medieval at the beginning of the nineteenth century proved how many important manuscripts had survived in the libraries of Catholic families.[25] As discussed in chapter five, Catholicism or pro-Catholic sympathy was often a stimulus towards antiquarian interests; which is hardly surprising, since Catholics had a religious stake in preserving the antique.[26]

But identifying the Catholic text is not a simple process. Preserving a pre-Reformation manuscript through the Tudor and Stuart period did not necessarily indicate endorsement of the contents; and even when a manuscript is clearly post-Reformation, it is still no easy matter to establish whether it is Catholic or not. Throughout this study, the methodological problems of determining the Catholic text have been in the forefront of my mind, and the problems posed by individual texts have – where appropriate – been explained.[27] A manuscript can be identified as belonging to a Catholic family; yet families were often not religiously uniform. Verses on Catholic doctrinal topics, or about Catholic martyrs, or by known Catholic authors, or extracts from Catholic devotional books, may characterise a Catholic manuscript; yet they could also be copied by non-

Catholics.[28] Catholics may even have used, or at least not objected to, the word 'papist' to dissociate themselves from other Catholics with whom they disagreed.[29]

Here, an account of a recent methodology used to define the Catholic text may be instructive: that applied by Anthony Allison and D. M. Rogers in their awesome two-part bibliography *The Contemporary Printed Literature of the English Counter-Reformation* (1989–94). It would be hard to overemphasize the importance of a book which has defined so many areas demanding future study, as well as tidying up the confusions that have proliferated around a body of literature produced by groups obliged to publish abroad or from secret presses in England, and who relied on elaborate multiple anonymities.[30] Many books are included in Allison and Rogers that do not figure in the *Short-Title Catalogue (STC)*, the most comprehensive record of English books to 1640: most commonly books written by Catholic Englishmen in some language other than English – usually Latin – and published overseas. Bibliographies are the least judgemental of catalogues, yet the exclusions of the *STC* are a chastening reminder of how even the most generous boundaries of comprehensiveness can exclude, perhaps unwittingly, an important part of the output of certain dissident or minority groups: in this case, Catholics writing for the general market of the European intelligentsia, or in the language of the country playing host to them. To their actual deracination has been added bibliographical.[31]

Though Protestants liked to think that they had a special relationship with the printing-press, and books like Elizabeth Eisenstein's highly influential *The Printing Press as an Agent of Change* (2 vols, 1979) have taken their word for it, Allison and Rogers have proved unanswerably that English Protestant printing initiatives stimulated a formidable degree of Catholic retaliation. This sometimes took the form of consolidating the continued strength of Catholicism in outlying areas of the British Isles, where the language difficulty was greater, resulting in some bibliographical firsts: the first legitimate printed Irish letter, and *Y Drych Cristianogawl*, the first book printed in Wales, as well as the first to be printed in Welsh.[32] But Catholic printing in Britain was hindered because presses were clandestine, while printing abroad was made more difficult by the fact that the compositors often did not know English well. *The Reply of the ... Cardinall of Perron, to the ... King of Great Britaine*, published from Douai in 1630, is prefixed by a weary apology that can be paralleled elsewhere. 'The printers being Wallons, and our English strange unto them it was incredible to see how may [sic] faults they committed in setting; so that in overlooking the proofes for the print, the margins had not roome enough to hold our corrections: and do what we could ... a great many of them remayned uncorrected by the fastidious fantasy of our workman' (ëib).[33]

Yet Allison and Rogers applied some severe criteria of orthodoxy to arrive at their final list of books and writers. Editions of Catholic writers from mainstream presses are explicitly excluded; and, unless read in careful conjunction with the *STC*, this can result in a minimising of the importance of writers like Robert Southwell. Nor – unlike, for instance, the Backer-Sommervogel bibliography of the Jesuit order – do they list books by Catholics that are not clearly on religious topics; and this has the effect of excluding some imaginative works where response to the Catholic condition is only implicit. The vast literature spawned by apostates from Catholicism is largely absent, and where apostates are included – William Alabaster being an example – it is only by virtue of the books they wrote as Catholics. In effect, then, Catholic orthodoxy is demanded both of writer and of publisher, if a work is to be included: criteria which are also evoked by the title – if not necessarily by the editorial choices – of the Catholic Record Society's journal, *Recusant History*.[34]

Recusant history, as commented earlier in this introduction, has had a long, famous and instructive past; for the Catholic, it is uniquely important to know who one's saints are. The term has the merit of chronological precision, as a means of defining English Catholic history from the Reformation to the Emancipation, and highlights how the idea of exemplarity is crucial for the understanding of English Catholics at this date; but, all the same, thinking of Catholics too narrowly in terms of recusants has had the effect of encouraging the continued underestimation of Catholic population, influence and importance. As research continues, use of a term which presupposes that non-recusant Catholics were hardly Catholics at all is growing increasingly problematic. A good case can certainly be made for employing 'recusant' to designate the Catholic who refused to come to church – despite the fact that defaulting puritans were also called recusants – and for seeing recusants as the nucleus of what is commonly meant by the post-Reformation English Catholic community; but future estimations of English allegiance to Catholicism can only be made more plausible by employing, together with the idea of recusancy, a broader designation which acknowledges that not all Catholics were exemplary, or conspicuously dissident and heroic.[35]

John Bossy, in his landmark study *The English Catholic Community* (1975), emphasised the importance of non-recusants and recusants who avoided the statutory penalties, and one can single out two more recent books as having further changed the academic landscape. Alexandra Walsham's *Church Papists* (1993) is the first full-length study of the Catholics who chose also to attend church, reluctantly or otherwise, in order to evade recusancy fines and other forms of persecution. Michael Questier's *Conversion, Politics and Religion in England* (1996), which discusses apostates to and from Catholicism, has highlighted the importance of the category of convert, as illustrating the fluidity and dynamism of denominational membership. Not all conversions were instantaneous, unrepeatable road-to-Damascus experiences. The serial convert who might alternate between Catholicism and Protestantism twice, three times and more during a lifetime, and the near-convert who might hesitate between denominations for decades, both need to be allowed for in any estimate of Catholic or pro-Catholic sympathy at this time: a point which is discussed in chapter two with reference to one of the most famous literary converts of the seventeenth century, Richard Crashaw.[36]

This book discusses the writing of many types of Catholic: male and female, clerical, religious and lay, identifiable and anonymous, resident in Britain and exiled on the Continent. But though so many of them were widely scattered, across the Continent and barely-accessible parts of England, the whole notion of an English Catholic *community*, which takes its bearings from John Bossy's formulation, is a helpful one which needs to be borne in mind when looking at literary texts. The swift, reliable, controllable operation of information networks was essential to the effective functioning of this community: both because masses and other illicit gatherings were selectively publicised in this way, and because they could serve for the more general gathering and dissemination of news. Definitions of a news item's relevance to Catholics could be wide, and Richard Verstegan, the English Counter-Reformation's most tireless publicist, is also an unignorable figure in the prehistory of the English newspaper.[37] But English Catholics needed emotional information about the state of Catholicism, as well as factual; and literary texts, best-suited to deliver that information, could be communally performed as well as read in private. Ballads, protest-songs and the imaginative liturgies of John Austin are only a few examples of the way that verse could define a community, contribute towards its sense of solidarity or unite the literate with the unlettered.[38]

On an interpersonal level early modern Catholicism was a catacomb culture, defined by secret or discreet worship; but Catholics did not spend all their lives underground, and their visibility had complex effects. While pointing to communities of Catholic Englishmen, in England and outside, one needs also to acknowledge two further points which affected the relationship of Catholics with other Englishmen. Firstly, there was considerable personal and literary interaction between individuals of opposing religious views. Catholics and Protestants often lived side by side, sometimes spoke to each other without quarrelling, and read each other's books.[39] Textual evidence can figure what happened to people; devotional writing, in particular, demonstrates how very little *real* difference there was between Catholic and Protestant spirituality, since it is often hard to tell the denominational allegiances of the authors of devotional tracts where they are not demonstrable from outside evidence. This, indeed, was one of the factors that contributed towards a long-standing debate over whether it was possible for Catholic devotional texts to be appropriated by Protestants. William Crashaw thought it 'no small point of wisdom, to seeke out gold out of mire and clay', but Luke Fawne, retorting to a similar argument, pointed out how necessary it would be to 'throw away a whole gile of beer that hath a gallon of strong poyson in it'.[40]

Secondly, debates like these demonstrate how interaction between Catholic and Protestant could never occur without, at the very least, some awareness of anti-Catholicism. With its call to arms against Catholic Babylon on the European stage, anti-popery was a shaping factor to domestic and foreign policy throughout this period, stimulating precautions which at least one historian has argued were out of all proportion to any real threat that Catholics could have posed;[41] and, to a degree that is still not fully recognised, it was a stimulus to imaginative writers. These two manifestations of prejudice are inseparably and symbiotically linked. Because of its quest to make differences clear and suppress similarities, religious polemic thrives on distortion;[42] its generic links with satire are a commonplace, but more generally, it is perhaps nearer to imaginative writing than any other theological mode. It creates, but also acknowledges, an other.[43]

Both anti-Catholicism and the interaction of Catholic and Protestant can be seen in the large category of Catholic texts which were read by both sides and altered by Protestants. This could be achieved by expurgation,[44] or even the innocent signs of punctuation could be used to reform a text. Lines 9–10 of Henry Constable's poem 'Sweete hand the sweete, but cruell bowe thou art' reads in the original, 'Now (as Saint Fraunces) if a Saint am I, / the bowe that shot these shafts a relique is ...'; but in one manuscript copy the brackets have been placed instead round '(if a Saint)', injecting Protestant scepticism while leaving the comparison intact.[45] More puzzling is the occasional phenomenon of texts attributable to outlawed Catholic Englishmen or containing unmistakably Catholic sentiments, issued by mainstream presses without comment. Chapter two will discuss this phenomenon of Catholic seepage, in relation to Robert Southwell. Sometimes, as with poems which copy Southwell's *Saint Peters Complaint*, this appropriation could take the form of imitation: but it was an imitation that did its best to downplay the importance of the text that inspired it.

In this as in so many other respects, an historical wrong has been done to Catholics; but English departments are good at being offended. The unmasking of prejudice, and the dissection of its imaginative complexities, have been central to post-war study within the humanities; and many of the best scholars have also tried to go outside the literary canon, respecting and recovering cultural traditions, texts and histories which earlier generations, influenced by prejudiced hierarchies of taste and importance, have buried, forgotten or despised. Historians, by the nature of their trade, are readier to confound what E. P. Thompson famously called 'the enormous condescension of history' by recovering primary sources. Literary criticism, on the other hand, is particularly well-fitted to analyse the imaginative techniques of despite: through recognising and utilising the hermeneutics of suspicion, and through setting out the phenomenology of the other. There is no area of academic study where deconstruction, so often criticised as being of wanton effect, has been deployed more seasonably in the cause of social justice; yet as often, and perhaps as effectively, the inspiration has been an untheorised anger.

There would be a good case for including the Elizabethan or

Stuart Catholic alongside women, racial minorities, Jews, homosexuals and the common sort in lists of the historically downtrodden. The provisos are obvious: these lists vary from era to era and from country to country; some individuals who fall into these categories were also the recipients of enormous privilege; and no-one in the late 1990s would be naive enough to assert that the grievances of all non-élite or victimised groups are the same, or even particularly similar. But one is also entitled to ask, at this point, how *different* Catholics are from the others. To differentiate between those whose disadvantage is innate, and those who bring their troubles upon themselves by opting for an outlawed faith, makes a very dubious assumption: which is that, at all dates, one can *help* one's religion. Even non-believers in predestination should be willing to accept that psychological, social and familial reasons to adhere to one's faith, or to change it, could be compelling in Tudor and Stuart England – or at any other date. Recovering the voices of the silenced has been an extraordinarily fashionable academic pursuit for the last few decades, but also a conscientiously engaged and successful one. Not everyone has been pleased, even among the plaintiffs; feminist criticism, notoriously, has been split into many sects almost from the beginning, and given the resilience of the literary canon, the demands of the more radical of these may never be widely met. Yet there has been solid victory, irreversible change, and prominence newly accorded to women's writing, homosexual writing, popular culture, anglophone literatures and the writing of ethnic minorities. The high quality of so much Catholic writing ought to make similar reparations pleasurable and easy to accomplish.

This book is divided into four chapters. Chapter one addresses the anti-Catholic revenge tragedies of Webster and Middleton, the manner in which their imagery took its bearings from anti-Catholic polemic, and how since the plays came back into mainstream fashion in the late nineteenth century, this inspiration has not been recognised. Without wishing to denigrate either writer, it argues that their plays have taken on a fortuitous enigmatism because the tropes of anti-Catholic polemic are no longer part of most people's frame of reference; yet that, because those controversial tropes have contributed to a stereotype, this very enigmatism can, in turn, encourage an unconscious re-association of Catholicism with evil. Against the background of an anti-Catholic norm within the mainstream imaginative discourse of Tudor and Stuart England, the remaining chapters discuss Catholic writing, and – to some degree – the surprisingly large quantity of it to be found within the mainstream. Chapter two addresses, with particular reference to Southwell and Crashaw, the issue of why Catholic religious poetry has been so marginal a presence within the canon. Chapters three and four look at the imaginative preoccupations of Catholic loyalists, those who had allegiances both towards the monarch and towards the Catholic hierarchy. Chapters five and six examine the imaginative transmutations that Catholics – some actually exiled, some not – gave to the topic of physical and spiritual exile from one's native land, while admitting that for those who wanted to write and perform plays about English heresy and schism, there were practical advantages to geographical removedness from England. The preoccupation with conversion, marginality, deracination and hatred which runs throughout the book is perhaps summed up in the common equation between Catholicism and foreignness. As within the embassy chapels, and Henrietta Maria's francophile circle in the Caroline court, this sometimes meant that Catholicism was tolerated to an unusually high degree; but more often it added xenophobic epithets to the bulging linguistic arsenal of anti-Catholic prejudice. Southwell was not unique in losing fluency in his mother-tongue while abroad; Crashaw wrote in the baroque idiom, so often thought of as un-English; but, as chapter two argues, they should not for that reason be dropped from the English canon.

A monograph has more freedom with its emphases than a survey, and this one has been planned to counteract the controversial distortions of the past: if – for instance – Catholic loyalists figure more largely than angry Catholics, it is because they have attracted less interest hitherto. For reasons of length many topics had to be left out or abbreviated, and others, for reasons of practicality, were never included within the design. The decision had to be taken not to write copiously on devotional poetry, apart from Southwell's *Saint Peters Complaint*; but it is an area which badly needs reassessment in the light of recent scholarship on early modern manuscript culture. As commented above, there is no detailed consideration of major canonical figures who are known to be Catholic, or whose name has been linked with Catholicism. Martyrologies, Jesuit drama, emblematics and Catholic historiography, topics which have all been alluded to briefly, could each do with book-length treatment.[46] I hope to address some of them in future work, and a follow-up study to this will deal with Catholics and orality, but my chief aim is to urge others to join in the task of reclamation. Historians usually end their introductions with the hope that their work will be superseded, and so shall I; for, as early modern Catholics knew so well, pious formulae can also be sincere. If this book is read, responded to and even disagreed with, and if it helps to put Catholic writing back on the mainstream agenda while alerting scholars to the complexities of anti-Catholic prejudice in Protestant imaginative writing, it will not have been useless meanwhile.

PART I

Catholics and the canon

CHAPTER I

The livid flash: decadence, anti-Catholic revenge tragedy and the dehistoricised critic

Nauseated with murder and steeped in unspoken guilt, the protagonist at the end of Donna Tartt's *Secret History* finds that only one fictional genre speaks to his condition.

I spent all my time in the library, reading the Jacobean dramatists. Webster and Middleton, Tourneur and Ford. It was an obscure specialisation, but the candlelit and treacherous universe in which they moved – of sin unpunished, of innocence destroyed – was one I found appealing. Even the titles of their plays were strangely seductive, trapdoors to something beautiful and wicked that trickled beneath the surface of mortality: *The Malcontent*, *The White Devil*, *The Broken Heart* ... I felt they cut right to the heart of the matter, to the essential rottenness of the world.[1]

Like many previous literary critics, he enshrines these thoughts in a dissertation on *The Revenger's Tragedy*. It might have read something like an academic book, also published in the early 1990s, which sees Webster's tragedies as 'lit only by the flickering and insubstantial pageants of worldly pomp, and the brief pale fire of diamonds cut, like sinners, with their own dust'.[2]

This chapter is designed to expose the history of a critical imperception. All critics are agreed that the strobe-like imagery of Italianate revenge-tragedy lights up the corrupt world inhabited by the speaker and the other characters; none has demonstrated an awareness that both the corruption of that world, and the means of its illumination, are conceived in specifically anti-Catholic terms. In fact, there are innumerable parallels between the imagery of Webster and Middleton and the apocalyptic image-clusters of sixteenth- and seventeenth-century anti-Catholic polemic, and the former is designed to evoke the latter. But critics of these plays have tended to impute a false universality to the playwrights' conception of evil, and, as a result, criticism has suffered over several generations from a lack of historical locatedness, and from an unconscious entrenched anti-Catholic bias.

This is particularly remarkable because, in some ways, the role of anti-Catholicism in determining the imaginative milieu of Italianate revenge tragedy is very obvious, and has long been recognised. But this chapter tries to avoid re-rehearsing what the genre owes to parodies of Catholic liturgy, or to anti-Italian xenophobia and debased Machiavellianism.[3] The difference between the two kinds of anti-Catholicism is that between the obvious and the omnipresent, and the critic – on a limited scale – has to try and reproduce the kind of leap which feminist literary critics made when they moved from specific instances of fictional sexism to thoroughgoing critiques of patriarchal epistemology.

The focus is on canonical plays – *The Revenger's Tragedy*, and Webster's *The White Devil* – partly because these have inspired most criticism. I have devoted more space to a collage of unfamiliar texts than to a close reading of familiar ones; nevertheless, my aim is not to collapse the difference between text and context, but to emphasise it. One test that has been used to define a canonical work is its relevance to readers of many different eras: in other words, its potential to be dehistoricised. And a critic has an obligation to accept this canonicity: sometimes, indeed, to be alarmed by it.

APOCALYPTIC DISCLOSURES

At a philological or conceptual level, an apocalypse is an uncovering or a disclosure. Davis J. Alpaugh has said, 'In a world charged with meaning by the Creator, the elect are distinguished by their accurate sense of vision, and this in turn involves not only seeing but interpreting correctly.' Ronald Paulson, commenting upon this, adds that 'The Puritan's was a world of *seeing*, which meant to see not only literally but to sense the unseen reality within natural objects as well.'[4] There was thought to be a particular obligation to discern eschatological signs, and it was not just Puritans who were urged to scrutinise the world for these, but Protestants in general. Just as the temple veil was rent in twain at the Crucifixion (Mark 15.38) so the mysteries of creation, redemption and judgement were thought to have been allegorically foretold in the Apocalypse, or the Book of Revelation.[5] Individual acts of ontological disclosure were seen as meritorious, proving the common man's ability to unravel scriptural mysteries; yet the disclosures of the Book of Revelation were conventionally predetermined for the non-elite who nevertheless had access to sermons, commentaries and controversial literature. Only an elite group could make convincing and widely disseminable attempts to unravel allegory, and they were governed by the topical demands of orthodoxy. Allegory, thus, was potentially more open than any other literary convention to topical or polemical interpretation.

Richard Bernard's *A Key of Knowledge for the Opening of the Secret Mysteries of St. Johns Mysticall Revelation* (1617) explained that 'as it is composed of such similitudes, so the words are figurative, the whole prophecie full of Metaphors, and almost altogether Allegoricall; so as we must take heede, that we looke further then into the letter and naked relation of things, as they are set downe' (p. 130).[6] This was partly to be done by observing similitudes between everyday incidents and apocalyptic signs. Bernard in his prefatory epistle stresses the importance of familiarising oneself with history and contemporary politics, and knowing the direct relation of the Apocalypse to the law of the land. Among much else, Webster and Middleton's public were well used to finding Rome behind figurations of southern European decadence. It is a commonplace that certain features of the Book of Revelation lent themselves to anti-popery.[7] The Pope was identified with Antichrist, since his kingdom of Rome was on seven hills and his doctrines and hierarchies perverted true religion while maximising worldly power.[8] Numerological exegeses also identified various popes with the Beast, whose number was 666. From after England's break with Rome to well into the nineteenth century, it was commonplace for the orthodox English Protestant to identify the Pope as the Whore of Babylon: at times an article of faith, and at all times tenacious at the popular level.[9] In popular engravings and woodcuts throughout Protestant Europe, it is very common indeed for the Pope to be depicted astride the seven-headed beast, and for the Whore of Babylon to have the head of a pope or to be wearing a papal tiara.[10] Nevertheless, it is usually more helpful to see the Whore of Babylon as the personification of the false church of which the pope is the representative.

Allegory is traditionally conceptualised as veiling and clothing, and so the allegorical conception of the Apocalypse created a veil that it was the duty of true believers to penetrate by the act of interpretation.[11] In Bernard, the book and the acts of reading and understanding it are referred to as an unsealing, alluding to the

Seven Seals and a 'discovering and making manifest of secret . . . things' (p. 85) which the reader, in a conflation of the intellectual and the visual, is asked to 'look upon and behold' (p. 108). There is nothing god-given about this velar conceptualisation of discovery, but – given the extent to which the metaphors of the Bible dictated hermeneutical technique in the seventeenth century – there might as well have been.

Disclosure implies concealment, and metaphors of concealment have a long history in anti-Catholic polemic. The role of visual beauty in the Catholic church – pictures, images, vestments and liturgy – was held to have a concealing function; it was superficially enticing but rotten beneath. Radford Mavericke's *Saint Peters Chaine* (1596) is typical in visualising idolaters as wearing the 'cloak of hipocrisie' (p. 65). They take their cue from proverbial visualisations of hypocrisy, many of which depend on the idea of an alluring, a pure or a glorious outside concealing an inside that is corrupt: the most famous Biblical example being the whited sepulchre, 'beautiful outward, but . . . within full of dead men's bones, and of all uncleanness'.[12]

Other manifestations of the topos, relying on a prejudice against ornament rather than a deceptive appearance of purity, include ornamental paint on any surface, cosmetics on an old or diseased face or a death's head and fine clothes or draperies concealing a sick or dead body, wood or stone.[13] They are schematically identical, exploiting the prejudice against the 'intervening medium'.[14] Morally speaking, they all convey the same message: the outside is what attracts the eye, yet it is nothing more than a skin or a veil concealing what is not fit to be looked on. The object is not what it is, and the tighter the skin or veil that clings to it, the more culpable is its hypocrisy. The veil gives the appearance of health, beauty and life, the object is death itself. Its two states juxtapose in space, outraging time and defying dualism; and the Protestant who flays hypocrisy of its pretensions is obliged to adopt a dualistic habit of thought.

One cannot overemphasise the *closeness* of negative and positive images. Catholicism could be seen as the intaglio of the true church, with the true church defining itself in the process of establishing an other. Dualism is crucial to any understanding of anti-popery, whether image-oriented or political. Popery was regarded as the debasement and perversion of Christ's teaching, with Antichrist, the

Pope, being the negative image of Christ.[15] Peter Lake has spoken of a 'process of binary opposition, inversion or argument from contraries' as characteristic of both learned and popular culture in early modern Europe, and especially conspicuous in anti-Catholicism: popery was an 'anti-religion, a perfectly symmetrical negative image of true Christianity', with much anti-Catholic writing pervaded by 'an inverted, hall-of-mirrors quality'.[16] While there are many genres of theological writing for which this judgement could be modified, it exactly describes the world of polemic.

The concept lent itself well to visual realisation, and superimposition upon other commonplaces. Fruit, to take one extended example, was an especially powerful emblem of how beauty could be juxtaposed with disease, emptiness or ashes. The origin of the topos is twofold: the verses in the Gospels where good and evil men are identified by the spiritual fruits they bring forth, and the legend of the Apples of Sodom by the Dead Sea which are alluring without, but dust and ashes within (Matthew 7.16–20). Richard Carpenter's sermon *Rome in Her Fruits* (1663) punningly refers to Catholicism's 'salt-peter fruits' (p. 9) enclosing gunpowder. In Middleton's anti-Catholic allegory *A Game at Chess* (1624) it could be simplified into rotten fruit: the White King asks the White Knight's pawn, who has just been revealed to be black underneath, whether he falls 'from the top bough by the rottenness / Of thy alone corruption, like a fruit / That's over-ripened' (III i, ll. 269–71).[17] In *Reflections Upon the Murder of Sir Edmund-Bury Godfrey* (1682) the interlocutor says to his fictional pro-Catholic audience: 'Since you have been picking and eating the Strawberries of your Religion, what think you of the poysonous Mandrake-Aples that follow?' (p. 31).[18] A variant on this, which the above quotation also alludes to, emphasises the sweets of sin. Here a temporal skin replaces the spatial, with a quantifiable moment between tasting sweetness and apprehending bitterness.

The conceptualisation of a deceptive covering had especial force when that covering already had implications of sin. Fine clothes, given their high relative cost in relation to other consumer goods, were an emotive subject to the Elizabethan and Jacobean pamphleteer.[19] Charles Bansley's *A Treatyse Shewing and Declaring the Pryde and Abuse of Women* (ca. 1550) contains lines on light raiment, which – like a veil – conceals and reveals at the same time; and this is unequivocally related back to Catholicism:

> From Rome, from Rome, thys carkered pryde,
> from Rome it came doubtles:
> Away for shame wyth soch filthy baggage,
> as smels of papery and develyshnes! (p. 8)[20]

Cosmetics – and, by transference, all other paint – had similar implications of wanton luxury. Painting the face was a hypocritical act, while the representative function of paint deceived the beholder into believing falsity. The metaphor is complicated by the fact that Renaissance pigments were frequently obtained by crushing precious stones.[21] Pulverisation of precious substances for alchemical, medical or painterly purposes fascinated the early Jacobeans – the dramatic *locus classicus* of this fascination is *The Alchemist* – and it could easily be employed to anti-Catholic ends: either Rome's Cleopatrean dissolution of pearls in wine or the Protestant act of iconoclasm performed on worldly glory and pernicious beauty, proleptic of the dust to which these things would come. In Barnabe Barnes's anti-Catholic play *The Divils Charter* (1607) Lucretia Borgia is poisoned by a corrosive in her cosmetic (IV iii).[22]

Apocalypse declared an end to hypocrisy, rending the veil, cracking the rind and stripping away pigment; and the act of interpreting allegory, a penetration to the inner meaning, required a similarly aggressive disclosure. A recent discussion of inwardness in the Renaissance has compared the errors inherent in the inductive process of reading personality – possible discoveries of rottenness under beauty – with the unveiling or dehusking process of biblical interpretation. Drama subjects personality to exegesis;[23] and when the veil of obscurity is penetrated, the hinderers of the true light are disclosed in all their specious glory, and become a target for iconoclastic acts. One must remember that the process of disclosure was intended to be entertaining. Popular commentators on the Apocalypse stressed its appeal to the imagination; Bernard argued that 'here are manifold visions and similitudes; the Lord by certain formes, shapes, and figures, as it were Images and pictures, did lively represent the whole Comicall tragedie, or tragicall Comedie, that was from the time of the revealing of the Revelation, to be acted upon the stage of this world' (p. 130). It was an obvious way of making allegory attractive rather than difficult, sweetening the necessity of continuous study.[24]

An element of intense light, or of dazzle, is important in the moment of revelation. It can be taken as a disclosure of bright intellectual truth, or as the rays thrown off by the attributes of the object, designed to attract the unwary beholder by their glitter: either a dazzling revelation of corruption or a revelation of dazzling corruption.[25] The subtitle to John Mayo's *The Popes Parliament* (1591) promises that in the book there are 'throughly delivered and brightly blazed out, the paltry trash and trumperies of [the Pope] and his pelting Prelats'. The idea of an *ignis fatuus*, promising guidance and revelation while leading the traveller into swamps, figures the notion of theological error. Jewels figure as part of the dazzle of corruption, as tokens of wealth and power, as aids to beauty and sexuality, and as lucent objects that blind the unwary. As with paint, the evocation of colour can often be pejorative: Stephen Batman's *A Christall Glasse of Christian Reformation* (1569) contrasts in its title the clear jewel of reformed Christianity with the 'coloured abuses' of the Roman church.

Finally, the essence of a veil is that it is impermanent; as an illusion, it has only a limited life. Mortality is a veil, with disclosure bringing immortality or death; John Owen in *The Chamber of Imagery in the Church of Rome Laid Open* (1682) says that Catholics have placed their image 'behind the Curtain of Mortality, that the cheat of it might not be discovered' (p. 69).[26] It is the duty of the believer to hasten the disappearance of the veil, since this brings about the kingdom of heaven; but, since the whole merit of Rome consists in its outside, it offers its flock no salvation when that outside passes away.

THE THING DISCLOSED

There is a double layer to apocalypse: the first, when the veil of clouded perception is torn down, and the second, when the cosmetic layer of an idol is damaged to reveal its hideous inside. Rhetorically speaking, the two acts can be described in much the same language, and often both are simultaneously implicit in one action; but morally speaking, they can be distinguished as the apprehension of truth and the destruction of falsity. In the last scene of *The Divils Charter*, Pope Alexander VI draws back the curtains of his library to expose the devil sitting there in papal pontificals; and on the engraved title-page of Thomas Robinson's *The Anatomie of the English Nunnery at Lisbon* (1623) the author is shown in the act of drawing a curtain to disclose a lewd embrace between monk and nun.[27] The staging of *The Divils*

Charter and the conceptualisation of Robinson's title-page both arrest the process of apocalypse, enlisting the viewer to help bring about exposure. Behind each curtain an epitome of corruption is disclosed, an abstract concept commonly given human iconographical form. On Robinson's title-page, truth is apprehended and falsity destroyed by the single act of drawing the curtain, and the revelation is simply obscene; but Barnes's devil in vestments presents again the apocalyptic necessity to strip.

It also fulfils an iconographical commonplace, since in medieval iconography images were considered memorable insofar as they were either beautiful or monstrous. The two were juxtaposed long before the Reformation.[28] In a *memento mori* the combination of the two states was iconographically appropriate; diptychs on the theme might have maidens juxtaposed with hags, attractive and repugnant subjects on facing panels. With images of Vanitas, often a beautiful and richly dressed woman gazing into a mirror, the beholder was invited to read moral depravity into a superficially attractive subject.[29] The iconographical associations were overpoweringly female, with a misogyny too obvious to need labouring. The related topos of cosmetics concealing a ravaged face or a death's head is ubiquitous throughout the period, and has many variations. Medieval Catholic churchmen, following Tertullian, had perceived the use of cosmetics as implicitly idolatrous.[30] The common seventeenth-century genre of poems purporting to advise a painter lent themselves especially well to this combination of anti-Catholicism and misogyny; their presumption is that the painter shows Catholicism in its true colours, employing in the cause of exposure the same methods of pigmentation that popery uses to deceive.[31] Finally, cosmetics in a polemical religious context are equated with the paint that beautifies an idol of wood or stone, or the drapery that conceals it.[32]

The contradictions inherent in imposing beauty and monstrousness upon a female iconographical figure invite two reactions from the beholder, one moralistic and one not: firstly, that her beauty makes her monstrousness all the more reprehensible, and secondly, that her monstrousness adds to her beauty. The first reaction is the one ostensibly intended by the controversialists, and it leads naturally to the pronounced anti-aesthetic bias that has always been recognised as a common characteristic of puritanism; but it would be disingenuous not to admit that the second reaction, that which interested the nineteenth-century Decadents, is also invited by the visual and verbal language of anti-Catholic controversy. The vivid imaginations and the vicarious – even prurient – pleasures of Protestant imagination served an urgent cautionary function, by showing how temptation could be tempting. As Carol Weiner has said, one of the ways in which Protestants expressed fears about losing their self-control was by portraying the enemy as unusually persuasive.[33]

Female beauty and horror culminated in the Whore of Babylon, the most powerful anti-Catholic icon of all.

And I saw a woman sit upon a scarlet-coloured beast, full of names of blasphemy, having seven heads and ten horns.
And the woman was arrayed in purple and scarlet colour, and decked with gold, and precious stones, and pearls, having a golden cup in her hand full of abominations and filthiness of her fornication:
And upon her forehead was a name written, MYSTERY, BABYLON THE GREAT, THE MOTHER OF HARLOTS AND ABOMINATIONS OF THE EARTH.
And I saw the woman drunken with the blood of the saints, and with the blood of the martyrs of Jesus: and when I saw her, I wondered with great admiration. (Revelation 17.3–6)

For a certain cast of Protestant, the Whore of Babylon was inherent in all images and posed a perennial threat to one's spiritual chastity. She epitomised the favourite Protestant theme of how idolatry was akin to spiritual whoredom (Jeremiah 3.9); and it is almost impossible to overestimate her ubiquity and her synonymousness with the Catholic Church during the English Reformation and its aftermath.[34] With the hieratic quality of an icon, and the beauty and monstrousness of a mnemonic image, she represents icon made idol.

Within drama, her presence is ubiquitous. She appeared on stage in many Tudor anti-Catholic interludes and in Dekker's *The Whore of Babylon* (1606),[35] but she is also invoked by much of the language of decadence and feminine depravity typical of Italianate tragedy, and that invocation, sometimes only an innuendo, is enough to spark off a gunpowder-train of pre-existing association. Within a context of anti-Catholicism, an anti-Catholic frisson is potentially inherent in any mention of hypocrisy, cosmetics or deceit. The idea of idolatry is central to this; idolatry was held to be the Romish church's greatest sin, and is of all sins most appropriately conceptualised by the techniques of iconography.

Having identified the idol, iconoclasm has to be the automatic reaction. Iconoclasm comprises a tearing down followed by a breaking apart: whether by the active agency of the iconoclast observer, or in passive mode by watching it collapse under disease. It has often been argued of the iconophobic mode of thought in late Tudor and early Stuart England that it deliberately stunted the visual sense. The imagery of breaking challenges this; paradoxically, it yields plentiful evidence of the Protestant visual imagination. Protestants borrowed it from the very ecclesiastical traditions they were condemning, since medieval manuscripts show enormous pictorial fascination with the breaking of idols; images survive of their symbolic execution, amputation of their hands and limbs, their automatic shattering in the presence of holiness or their explosion on the expulsion of the resident evil spirit.[36] Both tearing down and breaking apart may operate on the same figure: exposition followed by an inevitable, almost mechanistic self-exposure.

ORNAMENT AND HYPOCRISY

History has moved on from assuming that Tudor and early Stuart England was free of religious imagery, or even that the reluctance of the clerisy to condone it was systematic. But even to the moderate iconophobe, anti-Catholic imagery occupied an ideologically unique position: visualisation of it could be argued to be acceptable, since to visualise it was to condemn it in its own terms. There were also positive polemical benefits to visualisation. As Kenneth Clark has pointed out, there is a need for religious iconography in order that theological concepts may be crystallised and retained; and there is a corresponding need for an iconography of religious polemic to give imaginative substance to hatred.[37] This iconography was perpetually subject to addition and change, forming a capacious repository which could be drawn on for images of hate. Peter Lake has said: 'The Protestant image of popery allowed a number of disparate phenomena to be associated to form a unitary thing or force [which] could then be located within a certain eschatological framework.'[38]

The habit of extrapolation from an icon, using reflection upon it to lead the mind onto a number of moral messages, could bring about an accretion of attributes centring around the iconic figure, or loaded onto it. This is nowhere more pronounced than in anti-Catholicism. Protestant criticism of popery often concentrated on its elevation of the unnecessary, claiming that its accretion of objects and rituals had narrowed the arteries from God. Iconographical criticism was loaded, indeed overloaded, with this message, and in anti-Catholic visual narratives many Catholic objects are depicted where one would be sufficient to establish the point. In *A Christall Glasse of Christian Reformation*, Pride is depicted as a monster with a crest and a peacock's tail, shooting from a gun a crozier, an asperges bucket, a candle, a crucifix, a chalice, a rosary and a skull; the effect of visual confusion is quite deliberate. The common medieval depiction of idols with shields made in the form of a mask indicates that, even for previous ages, to think in terms of idolatry involved a sense of the multiplication of horrors.[39]

Much of this imaginative accretion one can describe as a highly ornamental criticism of ornamentation. Like Babylon, Rome was a city of consumer non-durables.

And he cried mightily with a strong voice, saying, Babylon the great is fallen, is fallen, and is become the habitation of devils, and the hold of every foul spirit, and a cage of every unclean and hateful bird.
For all nations have drunk of the wine of the wrath of her fornication, and the kings of the earth have committed fornication with her, and the merchants of the earth are waxed rich through the abundance of her delicacies . . .
And the merchants of the earth shall weep and mourn over her; for no man buyeth their merchandise any more;
The merchandise of gold, and silver, and precious stones, and of pearls, and fine linen, and purple, and silk, and scarlet, and all thyine wood, and all manner vessels of ivory, and all manner vessels of most precious wood, and of brass, and iron, and marble.
And cinnamon, and odours, and ointments, and frankincense, and wine, and oil, and fine flour, and wheat, and beasts, and sheep, and horses, and chariots, and slaves, and souls of men.
And the fruits that thy soul lusted after are departed from thee, and all things which were dainty and goodly are departed from thee, and thou shalt find them no more at all. (Revelation 18.2–3, 11–14)

Babylon was compared with the numerous decorative ceremonies and artistic trifles that the Church of Rome had accumulated over time. Pamphleteers played up to this in such titles as Anthony Egan's *The Book of Rates Now Used in the Sin Custom-House of the Church and Court of Rome* [1670] and Titus Oates's *The Pope's Ware-House* (1679).[40] The figure of a mountebank, purveying worthless wares and unreliable medicaments while indulging in shameless rhetorical advertisement, epitomises the notion of Catholicism as weighed down with the unnecessary. Iconic overload meets iconoclasm in the actions of stripping and of disclosure. Ideas on the perniciousness of ornament would have influenced Protestant reaction to such Catholic subterfuges as rosaries disguised as rings, and the fusion of ornament with hideous inside may also have been reinforced by the popish caches of vestments, rosaries and books found when pursuivants ransacked Catholic houses.[41] In plays, the trope often appears in the compressed form of the sick jewel. The Duchess of Malfi visualises herself as having her 'throat cut with diamonds' or 'shot to death, with pearls' (IV ii, ll. 203–5) and in the final scene of *The White Devil*, Flamineo exits to find 'two case of jewels' (l. 20) which prove to be pistols.[42]

The trope permeated plays and poetry, popular writing and elite. In the Spenserian Phineas Fletcher's didactic allegorical poem *The Purple Island* (1633) the images of anti-Catholicism are iconographically displayed in a manner that emphasises their complexity and accretiveness. In canto seven, which discusses sins and personifies them, the reader is introduced to Asebie, who represents irreligion, and her four sons Idolatros, Pharmacus (Witchcraft), Haereticus and Hypocrisie; their nurse, Ignorance, has a number of daughters, among whom Errour is the most prominent, and the family is accompanied by Dichostasis (Sedition), who has many heads, bears armour and a shepherd's crook and wears a triple crown.

Idolatros is conceived along traditional mnemonic lines, attaining monstrousness from a multiplicity of borrowed, disparate bodily elements: 'For to his shape some part each creature lent, / But to the great Creatour all adversly bent' (p. 91). He is of gigantic stature, oppressing the world, and bears the golden calf idolised by the Israelites; his anti-Catholic nature and that of his family is made explicit by the fact that he wears a 'bloudie Crosse' on his breast, 'but the Christ that di'd / Thereon, he seldome but in paint ador'd' (p. 92). Hypocrisie masks 'a rotten heart . . . with painted face' (p. 93) and elicits from the poet a catalogue of comparisons that is worth quoting in full:

> So tallow lights live glitt'ring, stinking die;
> Their gleams aggrate the sight, steams wound the smell:
> So Sodom apples please the ravisht eye,
> But sulphure taste proclaims their root's in hell:

So airy flames to heav'nly seem alli'd;
But when their oyl is spent, they swiftly glide,
And into jelly'd mire melt all their gilded pride.

So rushes green, smooth, full, are spungie light;
So their ragg'd stones in velvet peaches gown:
So rotten sticks seem starres in cheating night;
So quagmires false their mire with emeralds crown:
Such is *Hypocrisies* deceitfull frame;
A stinking light, a sulphure fruit, false flame,
Smooth rush, hard peach, sere wood, false mire, a voice, a name.

Such were his arms, false gold, true alchymie;
Glitt'ring with glassie stones, and fine deceit:
His sword a flatt'ring steel, which gull'd the eye,
And pierc't the heart with pride and self-conceit:
On's shield a tombe, where death had drest his bed
With curious art, and crown'd his loathsome head
With gold, & gems: his word, *More gorgeous when dead.*   (p. 94)

All the proverbial characteristics of hypocrisy are illustrated here: an outside that belies the inside, unreliability as a guide, a state of decay. The description of the family group as a whole and of Hypocrisie in particular is a paradigm of anti-Catholic iconographical discourse, and demonstrates how such a discourse can be constructed out of pre-existing topoi. Certain elements of it – the luminous decayed wood, for example – can be paralleled elsewhere: in Walter Raleigh's 'Say to the court, it glows / And shines like rotten wood', and in other poetic contexts where no religious comment is intended.[43] Within this context, however – and context is all-important in establishing the presence of anti-Catholicism – it echoes the wood worshipped by Idolatros with its alluring glitter and collapsible rottenness. Mutability and deceit is further signified by the *ignis fatuus*, and the corrupt jewels of idolatry by the emeralds over quagmires.[44] One image of deceit is tied to another till all are given focus in the description of Hypocrisie himself, enclosed in the hieratic gold and jewelled armour of an idol, with an idol's shield of horrors;[45] this in turn has the dual significance of tyranny, and of a splendid skin concealing a loathsome inside. The tomb on the shield is the final paradox, since Hypocrisy is dead by definition, employing outward show to conceal the fact that it has perished.

Tropes of hypocrisy – rotten wood, false lights, the apples of Sodom – combine with evocations of idolatry and with specifically anti-Catholic satirical references, such as Dichostasis's triple crown; and the poem speaks an anti-Catholicism which seems all the truer because it is capable of being couched in proverbial images. This passage towards overt and specialised polemic, from the proverbial through the theological to the satirical, can be paralleled in Italianate tragedy by the procession of image, moral environment and historical or topical comment; if the third makes use of anti-Catholic reference, and the second is suggestive of depravity, then the imagery too takes on an anti-Catholic cast. A further point, so obvious that it tends to be neglected, is that if a play is set in Southern Europe its characters are Catholic, and it makes sense in the context of seventeenth-century England to identify Catholicism as inspiring its rhetoric of evil. The language of English domestic tragedy is very different.

The personifications of *The Purple Island* also prompt a new – or rather, an old – way of looking at Renaissance drama in which the language of evil is dense and packed with images. If some of those images are identifiably tied to one individual – as in *The White Devil*, where the language of glitter is attached to Vittoria and that of disease to Brachiano – it seems clear that some effect of the specific iconographical attribute is intended: the attribute may, in some degree, even serve to represent the person when the person is absent. Where the imagery is less attributable and more diffuse, the effect is twofold: it affects the audience's perception of the environment of the play, and it tends to give a family resemblance to all the characters affected by corruption. Like the family of evil personifications in *The Purple Island* they share common traits, with each highlighting some aspect of evil in individual character. Even if a play is not allegorical, the characters may sometimes walk in allegory; and an image is a moment of insight and therefore of revelation.

MIDDLETON'S MANIFESTO

The idea that to know idolatry was to know all ill, Margaret Aston has argued, gave a new, explicitly Protestant emphasis to popular theology. 'Sometimes it seems as if all the major sins a Protestant could catalogue came under the umbrella of this damning offence.' All Protestants who believed in idolatry thought that it was the distinguishing stain of Catholicism.[46] The medieval interest in idolatry, centred round pagans and Mahometans, had collected an iconography and inculcated an atavistic horror which was then, like a burning-glass of damnation, redirected towards Rome. Though something has been said of the idol's characteristics, it is now time to consider its effect: an effect that was described in the first piece of writing ever completed by Thomas Middleton.

Critics have tended to ignore *The Wisdom of Solomon Paraphrased* (1597), which Middleton published when he was seventeen.[47] Yet the sixteenth and seventeenth centuries frequently used translations for personal and contentious ends; a paraphrase is more copious than a translation; and, as with John Bale's *The Image of Both Churches* [1545], which paraphrases Revelation, the form can offer considerable scope for anti-Catholic inventiveness. Every Bible verse in the poem corresponds to either one or two of Middleton's six-line stanzas; it would tax ingenuity to spin the text out this long, and so Middleton frequently departs from the text altogether and writes according to the perceived spirit rather than the letter. It is one of the characteristics of paraphrase that it has the authority of the original, but serves the personal function of interpretation and exegesis.

In Middleton's case, this is combined with a nascent creative gift.[48] Within and even outside the strict limits of a paraphrase, Middleton's poem combines present creativity with statement of future creative intention, and sheds considerable light on the plays he was later to write. Beginning his career as a Protestant writer with a piece of Protestant extrapolation, and sheltering his creativity under the authority of the Apocrypha, may even have allowed him an imaginative freedom.[49] Reading *The Wisdom of Solomon* in its early modern English translations, it is easy to see what attracted the young Middleton. Its vigorous sententiousness offers admirable scope for inkhorn rhetoric, which he did not fail to deploy; and, more importantly from the present point of view, it is a Biblical *locus classicus* for the condemnation of idolatry. Middleton finds himself here in a tradition of Protestant writers, canonically exemplified by Spenser and *The Faerie Queene*, who explored the perniciousness of idolatry in imaginative verse. By looking at verse and drama together it is possible to discern the theme as common to both; but whereas the verse is explicit and didactic, the greater suggestiveness and impersonality of the dramatic medium renders it more capable of being dehistoricised by readers many centuries later. If *The Wisdom of*

Solomon sets Middleton's plays in context, it must itself be set in the wider context of contemporary verse.

Though idolatry did not inspire poetic genres, it made a regular intrusion into genres already existing, and often dictated subject-matter that offered scope for reflection on the image. This, for instance, is Marston in his epyllion *The Metamorphosis of Pygmalion's Image*:

> Look how the peevish Papists crouch and kneel
> To some dumb idol with their offering,
> As if a senseless carved stone should feel
> The ardour of his bootless chattering,
> So fond he was, and earnest in his suit
> To his remorseless image, dumb and mute.[50]

Tourneur's poem *The Transformed Metamorphosis* shows the same preoccupation in its title, but unlike the story of Pygmalion's statue, change here is for the worse. Marston emphasises the vanity of idolatry and Tourneur its perniciousness, while both join in condemning the idol's lack of signification.[51] The poem begins by describing changes in the earth which herald darkness and apocalypse, and it is soon clear that Rome is the cause.

> See, see, that mount that was the worldes admire,
> The stately Pyramis of glorious price;
> Whose seav'n hill'd head did over all aspire,
> Is now transform'd to Hydra-headed vice:
> Her hellish braine pan of each enterprice . . .   (p. 59, ll. 57–61)

Tourneur proceeds to compare this pyramid to the Tower of Babel – that is, of Babylon – and contrast its shifting structure with the firm foundations of the godly. He begins his exposition of the metamorphosis of the True Church of Revelation, clothed with the sun, the moon and twelve stars, into the Whore of Babylon:

> Her robe, that like the Sun did clearly shine,
> Is now transform'd unto an earthy coate,
> Of massive gold: because she did combine
> Affection with the Moon; and did remote
> Her heart from heav'ns book where her name was wrote.
> The globe takes head, that was her footstoole set:
> And from her head doth pull her coronet.
>
> Her twelue starr'd glorious coronet, (which Jove
> Did make her temples rich environrie:
> And for the more to manifest his love,

> Encircled them with faire imbroderie,
> Of sacred lights in ayre-cleare azurie.)
> She is deprived off: and doth begin,
> To be the coverture of laethall sin.   (p. 61, ll. 134–147)

Tourneur emphasizes the woman's seductiveness as the cause of her danger; she is compared to Circe, the enchantress and creatrix of metamorphosis, and then – perhaps alluding to the Protestant poetics of Spenser – to a serpent in female shape enticing the human soul into a bower of bliss.[52] Her opponent is Pan the pastor, the Church of England in its uncorrupted state; his saviour is Elizabeth I, and the poem ends with her apotheosis as head of the church:

> Come, come, you wights that are transformed quite,
> Eliza will you retransforme againe;
> Come star-crown'd female and receive thy sight,
> Let all the world wash in her boundlesse maine,
> And for their paine receive a double gaine.
> My very soule with heav'nly pleasure's fed,
> To see th'transform'd remetamorphosed.   (p. 74, ll. 596–602)

Though he ends on an optimistic note, the predominant impression left by Tourneur's poem is that of his fear at change and decay; and he takes as many pains as a polemical pamphleteer to equate this with the ecclesiastical innovations that have rendered Rome poisonous. This is where the poems differ: whereas *The Wisdom of Solomon* presents us with a *fait accompli*, a damned world which seems predestined to damnation, *The Transformed Metamorphosis* shows the process of transformation and demonstrates that it can be reversed. Solomon's and Midleton's idols are dead and useless; Tourneur's is a living church who has fallen through Luciferean pride, rendering herself an idol and her devotees idolaters. Idolatry may be conceived as worshipping either something dead or something degenerate; degeneracy of an idol leads to its eternal death, and the worshipping of dead idols to human degeneracy.

Middleton's presentation of the latter idea occurs in chapters thirteen, fourteen and fifteen of *The Wisdom of Solomon*. He adheres, in keeping with the poem's genre of paraphrase, closely to the structure of the Apocrypha book. Both chapters thirteen and fifteen are concerned to demystify idols, and this they do by showing how they are constructed. In chapter fifteen the craftsman who makes the idol is a potter, a typological parallel to the New Testament verses (Romans 9.20–3) interpreted within much Protestant theology as expounding the Divine potter's predestinatory power over human clay. The potter is shown defying God in his craft, using his own image of deceit to deceive, but being deceived by it in turn. Solomon and Middleton stress that other deceits necessarily follow, and from them misery.

In chapter thirteen the craftsman is a carpenter, and the idol made of wood.[53] It is here, for those who care to compare paraphrase with original, that Middleton's creativity takes off; his version bears very little relation to the text, as the idol that Solomon describes is re-rendered in contemporary terms. Protestants had an aesthetic focus for their theological condemnation of Catholic iconodulia. Those who abhorred the practice of worshipping a breaden god, venerating images or paying homage to the Pope had their loathing exacerbated by the visual opulence associated with these offices and ceremonies: precious monstrances, draped and bejewelled statues and papal pontificals. Margaret Aston stresses that precious images were considered especially dangerous.[54] These are the ideas that Middleton transposes into Solomon's text.

> Golde was a God with them, a golden God,
> Like children in a pageant of gay toyes,
> Adoring images for saints abode,
> Oh vaine vaine spectacles of vainer joyes:
> Putting their hope in blocks, their trust in stones,
> Hoping to trust, trusting to hope in mones. (ch. 13, f.Q3a)

Chapter fourteen, which these two accounts of the beginnings of idolatry frame, describes the miseries and sins of those who live in an idolatrous world; the idol becomes both the genesis and the symbol of all other evil. Tyranny in the medieval world was thought to be directly related to idolatry, and this is stressed with regard both to the tyrant and to his subjects; idolatry promotes both servility and rebellion.[55] If the carpenter in chapter thirteen is demonstrated 'To be the authour of his own lives paine, / To be the tragick actor of his will' (f.Q4a) then chapter fourteen describes the behaviour of a whole cast of tragic actors; and though paraphrase here is reasonably close to original, the play they are acting in could well be an Italianate tragedy. Samuel Harsnet's coinage *daemonopoiia*, referring to diabolical Catholic actions, is the most appropriate word to employ:

> For either murders pawe did gripe their harts,
> With whispring horrors drumming in each eare,
> Or other villanies did play their parts,
> Augmenting horror to newe strucken feare:
> Making their hands more then a shambles stall,
> To slay their children ceremoniall.
>
> No place was free from staine of blood or vice,
> Their life was markt for death, their soule for sin,
> Marriage, for fornications thawed ice,
> Thought for despaire, body for eithers gin:
> Slaughter did either end what life begunne,
> Or lust did end what both had left undone . . .
>
> O idoll-worshipping, thou mother art,
> Shee procreatresse of a he offence,
> I know thee now, thou bearst a womans part,
> Thou nature hast of her, shee of thee sence:
> These are thy daughters, too too like the mother,
> Black sins I dim you all with inckie smother[.]   (f.R4b-S1a)[56]

The particles of Catholic generation are loathsome because permeated by idolatry. Though Middleton's idols may be dead ones, the idol-worshipping that he describes as 'shee procreatesse of a he offence' has a supernatural reality. Were it not so, the worshipping of idols would be merely futile; her presence makes it simultaneously futile and pernicious. She is an abstract version of the Whore of Babylon, as against Tourneur's concrete one. Both are fecund of monsters: in Tourneur they are generated from her blood and 'noysome steeming breath' (p. 69, l. 417), and in Middleton they are the 'black sins' which spring from idolatry. The whole passage is comparable to Rupert Brooke's description of Webster's world, one of the phenomenological criticisms of revenge-tragedy identified later in this chapter: 'life . . . seems to flow into its forms and shapes with an irregular abnormal and horrible [sic] volume . . . It fills one with the repulsion one feels at the unending soulless energy that heaves and pulses through the lowest forms of life . . . A play of Webster's is full of the feverish and ghastly turmoil of a nest of maggots.'[57] Though Brooke describes without analysing, what he says is relevant here: Webster and Middleton share a fear of the autonomous energy of the idol.

In one of the most perceptive pieces of revenge-tragedy criticism in recent years, Norma Kroll has analysed what Webster's dramatic view of the universe owes to Lucretius's *De Rerum Natura*.[58] She points to his use of Lucretian *imagines* to describe dreams, and her insight is capable of much wider application. *Imagines* are the images of things, sometimes translated as 'idols'; and though Lucretius uses the term *imago* non-judgementally, it had idolatrous connotations to Protestant England.[59] Like idols, *imagines* have dynamic powers of their own: 'like films peeled off from the surface of things, [they] fly to and fro through the air', and 'the outermost surface is ever streaming off from things'. They appear as composite figures in dreams, wandering about 'in all directions ... extremely thin; and these when they meet, readily unite, like a cobweb or piece of gold-leaf ... enter in through the porous parts of the body and stir the fine nature of the mind within and provoke sensation'.[60] Lucretius's omnivagant *imagini* must certainly have influenced imaginative conceptions of idolatry: sometimes directly, as with Webster, but more often *via* the imprint Lucretius left on later commentators.

Middleton adds to this an intuition that there exists a symbiotic mutual infection between creator and created, with terrible implications of sexual congress. With a distinction that has no basis in Solomon, he is careful to differentiate between the male and female elements in idolatry. Idol-worshipping is a she-procreatress, like the Whore of Babylon, and gives birth to the active he-offence as the corrupt church does to churchmen. As a very general rule – but one that is often broken by the major playwrights – the Whore of Babylon is suggested most insistently by the imagery surrounding the female characters in a drama, while her masculine counterpart, the churchman, figures in the plot and promulgates the idea of plotting. She is the procreatress, he the offence; but *The Wisdom of Solomon* emphasises her dependence on a male agent, to the extent that he is, in turn, perceived as creating her. In chapter thirteen the male carpenter carves an image referred to as 'she', becoming thus a 'substantive, able to beare it, / And she an adjective, nor see, nor heare it' (f.Q3b). The masculine noun defines, and the female adjective decorates: 'His sin deceiveth him, and he his sin' (f.T2a). As craftsman he may carve her; as procreatress, she begets him. As an object of worship she is barren, as a mother of mischief fruitful.

Solomon sums up his message in chapter 14.27: 'For the worshipping of idols not to be named is the beginning, the cause, and the end, of all evil.' Middleton, in contrast, uses this point in his narrative to declare a manifesto:

> My pen shall be officious in this scene,
> To let your harts blood in a wicked veine,
> To make your bodies cleare, your soules as cleane,
> To cleanse the sinkes of sin, with vertues reine:
> Behold your cole-blacke blood my writing inke,
> My papers poysoned meate, my pens fowle drinke.   (f.S1b)[61]

But though Middleton then proceeds to announce that the idolaters have been convinced of their error and that his castigation has worked, the recurrence of the idolatrous craftsman in chapter fifteen has a cyclical effect that he does not trouble to counteract. The abiding impression is of a damned world, the damnation of which is informed and voluntary, ignoring such moral outbursts as Middleton's.

The Wisdom of Solomon is an explicit manifesto to justify creativity, the most explicit that we have from Middleton's pen. In the following discussion of *The Revenger's Tragedy*,[62] the hypothesis is put forward that the conception of idolatry formulated in *The Wisdom of Solomon* is central to an understanding of the damned world of Middleton's plays, and that a similar intuition directs Webster.[63] An idol is static, just as imagery freezes action and the onrush of plotted language, not advancing the plot but giving one an insight into it.[64] Though immovable in itself, it compels drama. Its aspect is fascinating, demanding sacrifices, genuflexions and prostrations; action is dictated by the image, and rays out from it. There is both an ambivalence and an appropriateness about idolatry in the theatre.

REVENGE AND TRIAL

The iconographical focus of *The Revenger's Tragedy* is the richly caparisoned skull of Gloriana.[65] Vindice tells the audience that she was virtuous during her life, and that this was why she died at the hands of the lascivious and frustrated Duke. But having been ravished by death she is a whore, and the Duke dies when he kisses her. The Duke himself invites religious comparisons for her: 'Give me that sin that's rob'd in holiness' (III v, l. 138).[66] Vindice is the procurer or masculine substantive; she is the adjective whose decorative capacity is evident from the point of view of stagecraft. She is at once a dead virgin and the icon of whoredom. This is a whoredom arrived at through the degeneration of death, a transformed metamorphosis; and the Duke who has crafted her by murdering her is, like an idolater, undone by his own creation. She has potential to make a man 'falsify highways, / And put his life between the judge's lips /To refine such a thing' (III v, ll. 75–7). As has frequently been recognised, these lines refer not only to highwaymen but to those who pervert obvious rules of conduct, with the judge in question being both human and divine.[67] There is a parallel between the manner of the Duke's death, poisoned by a kiss of Gloriana's skull, and a passage in *The Wisdom of Solomon*:

> Narcissus fantasie did die to kisse,
> O sug'red kisse dide with a poisoned lip . . .   (ch. 13, f.Q2b)

Narcissus is being used as an exemplum of the idolater who worships himself in his own creation.[68] Middleton's embroidery in the second line, which is not in the Apocrypha text and has no literal basis in the watery grave of the mythical Narcissus, intrudes the sweets-of-sin topos into the text.

The explicit language of iconography and emblem pervades *The Revenger's Tragedy*, from the type-names of the characters onwards. The pictorial conceit that Vindice presents to Lussurioso in IV ii, depicting 'a usuring father, to be boiling in hell, and his son and heir with a whore dancing over him' (l. 85) elicits an objection from Lussurioso, and Vindice's response that 'some . . . had rather be damn'd indeed than damn'd in colours' (ll. 99–100), making overt the play's intention to utilise iconography for polemical and condemnatory purposes. On another level an army of conventional personifications is invoked, Law, Opportunity and Nudity, the last conventionally equated with simplicity and truth (I i, l. 55, 115): Vindice describes bashfulness as 'that maid in the old time, whose flush of grace / Would never suffer her to get good clothes' (I iii, ll. 13–14). The skull in its unadorned state serves a similar iconographical function, with that of *memento mori* added: Vindice apostrophises its eye-sockets as 'able to tempt a great man – to serve God' (III v, l. 55).

The eye itself sees best when about to be blinded. Spurio asks 'Is the day out o'th' socket, / That it is noon at midnight?' (II iii, l. 45) and Vindice, having torn off the Duke's eyelids, wishes to 'make his eyes like comets shine through blood' (III v, l. 198).[69] Weather adds to the apocalyptic sense of doom: comets and thunderclaps punctuate the revelatory masque-scene, while in the lodge where the Duke makes his assignments it is 'night at noon' (III v, l. 19). Vindice sees

The livid flash

Night as associated with the hangings of deceit, but threatens it with disclosure:

> Night! thou that look'st like funeral herald's fees [i.e. frieze]
> Torn down betimes i' th' morning, thou hang'st fitly
> To grace those sins that have no grace at all.   (II ii, ll. 132–134)

Light, like fire, can be hidden within: Vindice, as vigilante, adjures his followers that they must 'let . . . hid flames break out, as fire, as lightning, / To blast this villainous dukedom vex'd with sin' (V ii, ll. 5–6).

Other metaphors of concealment and apocalypse are frequent, giving a specific volumetric substance to secrecy, hypocrisy, evil and death. Oaths which can be bought by bribery are 'but the skin of gold' (III i, l. 7), and Vindice denies that his 'outward shape and inward heart / Are cut out of one piece' (III v, ll. 9–10). Visualisations of the process can be conflated: offences 'gilt o'er with mercy' are compared to women 'good only for their beauties, which wash'd off, / No sin is uglier' (I ii, ll. 29–31). Hippolito says of Lussurioso that he 'began / By policy to open and unhusk me' (I i, l. 69) and, of the concealment of the duke's death, Vindice warns that 'murder will peep out of the closest husk' (IV ii, l. 202). Gloriana's skull is a 'shell of death' (I i, l. 15), and, in addressing it, Vindice equates reputation's fragile, enclosing nature with the substance of the skull: 'Known? / Few ladies respect that disgrace: a poor thin shell!' (III v, ll. 45–6).

The substance of reputation is specifically related to the loss of virginity, in Vindice's description of how a virgin becomes a prostitute: 'Break ice in one place, it will crack in more' (IV iv, l. 81). Vindice reproaches Gratiana that 'in that shell of mother breeds a bawd' (IV iv, l. 10). In terms of garments, 'the faults of great men through their cerecloths break' (I ii, l. 16) while the Duke specifies 'Give me that sin that's rob'd in holiness' (III v, l. 138). Vindice loathes his inside when he is engaged in corrupting Gratiana: 'turn the precious side / Of both mine eyeballs inward, not to see myself' (II i, ll. 127–8). But the contradiction of outside and inside is fully exemplified in the supposed diabolical possession of Gratiana. She is proleptic of endless maternal shame and deceit: 'All mothers that had any graceful hue / Would have worn masks to hide their face at you' (IV iv, ll. 65–6).

The loathsomeness of the inside is further suggested by metaphors of disease: Vindice tells the poisoned Duke 'Now I'll begin / To stick thy soul with ulcers' (III v, ll. 171–2). These are reminiscent of the metaphors of disease surrounding Brachiano in *The White Devil*.[70] Muriel Bradbrook points out that the three chief clusters of metaphor in *Women Beware Women* are plagues and diseases, treasure and jewels, and light and darkness; and all of these have an anti-Catholic significance.[71] And whereas *The Revenger's Tragedy* is replete with metaphors of concealment and revelation, Webster adopts the slightly different emphasis of the sweets of sin: what Vittoria tells Francisco, 'I discern poison / Under your gilded pills' (III ii, ll. 190–1) can be paralleled at a number of points in his oeuvre.[72]

Perfumes as well as tastes convey the synesthaesia of Catholic sin. Hypocrisy and the sweets of sin are again conflated in the exchange between Spurio and the Duchess:

SPURIO   Had not that kiss a taste of sin, 'twere sweet.
DUCHESS Why, there's no pleasure sweet, but it is sinful.
SPURIO   True; such a bitter sweetness fate hath given,
         Best side to us is the worst side to heaven. (III v, ll. 201–4)

In these intensely condensed lines, the gap between tasting sweetness and apprehending bitterness is compared to the thickness of the veil of deception: for the jaded sensualist, the core of the pleasure is the shameful inside that heaven condemns. Sweetness can even be a skin to loathsomeness: Lussurioso inquires whether Vindice, in procuring him a new mistress, has 'rubb'd hell o'er with honey' (II ii, l. 22).

The antitheatrical writer William Rankins described Impudence as the presiding goddess of both Catholics and players.[73] Certainly, the personification is invoked in connection with images. Vindice, addressing Impudence with the litanic titles of 'goddess of the palace, mistress of mistresses' asks her to strike his 'forehead into dauntless marble' and his 'eyes to steady sapphires' (I iii, ll. 6, 8–9) and again, in the aftermath of the bloody masque, he exclaims 'O marble impudence!' of Lussurioso (v iii, l. 68). In her resolution to prostitute herself to Lussurioso, Castiza declares to Gratiana that 'I am, as you e'en out of marble wrought' (IV iv, l. 108). The impudent Lussurioso is seen as courting an idol's fate:

                'Tis my wonder
     That such a fellow, impudent and wicked,
     Should not be cloven as he stood,
     Or with a secret wind burst open!   (IV ii, ll. 189–92)

In Act II ii, Vindice comments of Castiza's constant chastity that 'many a maid has turn'd to Mahomet / With easier working' (ll. 28–9).[74]

Within *The White Devil*, the impudent Vittoria is cast as idol, and the scene of her trial is a prolonged apocalypse that exposes not only her, but those who are impeaching her.[75] Monticelso's famous speech on whores is exceedingly productive of anti-Catholic topoi that identify her with the Whore of Babylon:

> Shall I expound whore to you? sure I shall,
> I'll give their perfect character. They are first,
> Sweetmeats which rot the eater; in man's nostril
> Poisoned perfumes; they are coz'ning alchemy...
> They are the true material fire of hell...
> Take from all beasts, and from all minerals
> Their deadly poison...
> I'll find in thee a pothecary's shop,
> To sample them all.   (III ii, ll. 78–81, 85, 103–4, 105–6)[76]

Vittoria is portrayed as the quintessence of all poisons, a cup of abominations and the epitome or Theophrastan character of whoredom: thus, she is pressed to death by a configuration of anti-Catholic topoi. Deadly to consume, she invites both the Protestant interpretation of the Mass as whore, and, earlier in Monticelso's speech, the inevitable comparison with the Apples of Sodom:

> You see my lords, what goodly fruit she seems;
> Yet like those apples travellers report
> To grow where Sodom and Gomorrah stood,
> I will but touch her and you straight shall see
> She'll fall to soot and ashes.   (III ii, ll. 63–67)[77]

The clinching irony, inexplicable if an apocalyptic reference were not intended, comes at the end of his description of Vittoria's delicious living with his declaration: 'This whore, forsooth, was holy' (III ii, l. 77).

Vittoria proclaims her innocence with a constellation of images invoking light and diamonds, invocative of the superstition that Catholics engaging in necromancy enclosed spirits in crystal. Samuel Harsnet's remark in *A Declaration of Egregious Popish Impostures* that Catholic magicians are reputed to carry around with them 'their familiars in rings, or glasses' (p. 13) penetrates to the heart of this sick jewel. The imagery, because of and despite its simpler associations with good, serves to portray Vittoria as 'a white devil, and to define the concept of a white devil as such'.[78] The hypocrisy and dazzling corruption of the Romish church are among the complex associations which it invites; and the term itself, as has frequently been pointed out, is one used by Protestant polemicists to refer to the Catholic church. Thomas Adams used the phrase for his anti-Catholic sermon *The White Devill* (1st edn. 1613), and a pamphlet narrating the discovery of seven Catholic prostitutes in Covent Garden seems to be alluding to Webster and to Vittoria in its title: *The Seven Women Confessors, or a Discovery of the Seven White Divels* (1641).[79]

In the phrase 'women confessors' there appears a familiar fusion of whore and churchman, made more potent through the personification of the church as Christ's bride, and by the scandalous associations of confession with sexual union. This fusion also appears in the trial scene, in the interplay between Vittoria and Monticelso. The latter is the other main critical candidate for white devil-hood, self-consciously so in recognising how he represents a corrupt church.[80] In Act IV i he comments that his black book of offenders could potentially contain divines 'But that I slip them o'er for conscience' sake' (l. 60) while in Act III ii he accepts that preachers are 'charm'd silent' by the power of the vicious (l. 251). The double-edged power of a trial-scene in which a corrupt Catholic churchman condemns the Whore of Babylon would certainly have been augmented by the simple association of visual imagery with its speaker. Vittoria, in her defence, drives home by dialectic the point that he is characterising himself, and the church for which he stands, quite as much as he is talking about her; and, from the beginning of III ii, she draws attention to the vestments that show his allegiance and, by their colour, symbolise whoredom: 'O poor charity! / Thou art seldom found in scarlet' (l. 71). If he is not to be identified as the personification of charity, the question remains as to what exactly he does personify; and as Vittoria says, the insults which are directed against her but fail to describe her reflect more on the prosecutor than on the defendant:

> These are but feigned shadows of my evils.
> Terrify babes, my lord, with painted devils,
> I am past such needless palsy. For your names
> Of "whore" and "murd'ress", they proceed from you
> As if a man should spit against the wind,
> The filth returns in 's face. (ll. 146–51)

The blurring of gender is deliberate, and echoed at other points in the play: for instance, when Monticelso says of Vittoria 'If the devil / Did ever take good shape, behold his picture' (III ii, ll. 216–17) and when Lodovico compares Monticelso to a secretly lustful bride (IV iii, ll. 142–8).[81] If one identifies Monticelso with Paul IV, the title he assumes in the play at the papal election, rather than with Sixtus V, whom his real-life counterpart became, there appears yet another link between whore and churchman; the real Paul IV conducted a drive against courtesans in Rome, and was a man of whom a speech against whores would be most characteristic.[82]

THE DECADENT IMAGE

Inevitably, many of the above quotations are over-familiar; for the imagery of Jacobean Italianate tragedy, though not currently a fashionable topic, has in the past been discussed again and again. As Jack Landau has said, 'Webster's imagery – how many graduate theses?'[83] But the topic has inspired famous critics to fine confessional writing, scaling heights of finely wrought suggestiveness which would not seem out of place in the plays themselves. Swinburne and Eliot brought to it the subjective insight of the creative writer. Swinburne, commenting on Webster's ability to express 'the latent mystery of terror that lurks in all the highest poetry and beauty', quotes – as many do – a nineteenth-century Frenchman: in this case Victor Hugo.[84] Eliot speaks of Tourneur's 'intense and unique and horrible vision of life' and the 'characters which seem merely to be spectres projected from the poet's inner world of nightmare, some horror beyond words'.[85] The idea of a horror beyond words presupposes an ineffability that is more of a Romantic than a Renaissance idea. But critics have, to an extent, been right to describe their reactions to so suggestive a medium as Jacobean Italianate tragedy, if only to testify that it is suggestive. Typical of the flavour of this fantasy is a phrase of Marcel Schwob's quoted at the beginning of Allardyce Nicoll's edition of Tourneur: 'Cyril Tourneur naquit de l'union d'un dieu inconnu avec une prostituée' (p. 1).[86]

In *Radical Tragedy*, perhaps the most influential recent discussion of the genre, Jonathan Dollimore calls *The Revenger's Tragedy* 'camp'. This manifests an irresponsibility common to many critics of Jacobean tragedy: a willingness to describe a phenomenon without accounting for it, and to be titillated by, rather than analysing, the *frisson* it gives.[87] His is an 1890s interpretation of the play, equating homosexuals and Catholics as groups which dare not speak their name, but which delight in shared mannerisms of concealment and revelation. Though the equation of homosexuals with Catholics is as old as anti-Catholicism, the assumption that ritualism is a distinctively homosexual mode of behaviour belongs not to the Renaissance, but to the eras of Gautier, Huysmans and Wilde.[88] One can see, though, how the confusion has arisen. Canonical purging results in loss of context, and therefore in reinterpretation; thus, Jacobean Italianate tragedy has provided a dehistoricised metaphor of cosmic horror for many generations. For Decadents, it has also contributed to a language.

The rhetoric of French Romanticism and Decadence, tinctured by the anticlericalism of the French Revolution, associated Catholicism with gorgeous corruption.[89] A recent study of the Decadent imagination emphasises its idea of Christianity as exemplifying mystical rottenness and its use of Catholic themes for sacrilegious intentions; moreover, it identifies a number of the topoi identified above and below as anti-Catholic, such as the inherent evil of precious stones, the perversion of the natural world, cosmic misogyny and monstrous fruits.[90] The decorative, violent and sacrilegious language of Jacobean tragedy was found congenial by Decadent writers: Ronald Firbank's Artificial Princess quotes from *The Duchess of Malfi* after displaying a Felicien Rops Crucifixion to her visitors, whilst a line like 'Miss Compostella swept by them, in some jewelled hades of her own' has an unmistakable parodic kinship with both Jacobean drama and Jacobean dramatic criticism.[91] Like Webster, Firbank hints at more than he says, but unlike Webster, these hints are suggestive above all of a deviant sexuality. It is an inescapable irony that the aesthetics of Puritan warning re-emerged in camp Catholicism.

Allardyce Nicoll's relish in describing the imagery of *The Revenger's Tragedy* owes something to the Decadents. Part of his effusion is quoted below: at length, because it exemplifies two trends in revenge-tragedy criticism. Though it rivals the tragedy itself in horrid suggestiveness, it also shows how the *belle-lettriste* tradition often gave rise to commentaries which, even though quite without technical vocabulary, were phenomenologically accurate.[92]

Sometimes, the images which constitute the truly cardinal quality of Tourneur's verse merely thrill by their precision and insight . . . More commonly, these images are so composed of light in darkness or of darkness in light that they sear the spirit, they wound, they terrify; there is here a kind of translucent quality which pierces through the worldly veil, which throws the glare of eternity on the dark courts of the palace or creates spiritual figures who move and have their spiritual being beside the all too fleshly denizens of the earth. Examples throng upon us as we read these plays. Now it is Vindice's

> The Dukes sonnes great Concubine:
> A drab of State, a cloath a silver slut,
> To have her traine borne up, and her soule traile i'th durt.
>
> (*Revenger's Tragedy*, IV iv)

Now it is Castiza's

> Are not you she
> For whose infect persuasions I could scarce
> Kneele out my prayers, and had much adoo
> In three houres reading, to untwist so much
> Of the black serpent, as you wound about me?
>
> (*Revenger's Tragedy*, IV iv)

Or else,

CASTIZA I have endur'd you with an eare of fire,
       Your Tongues have struck hotte yrons on my face;
       Mother, come from that poysonous woman there.
MOTHER Where?
CASTIZA Do you not see her? shee's too inward then.   (*Revenger's Tragedy*, II i)

The phrases lacerate and scorch, and all are symbolic of the general mood of the tragedies – a mood through which the poet tears back the dark tapestried veils from villainy 'When torch-light made an artificiall noone' (*Revenger's Tragedy*, I iv).

    Nicoll identifies as most characteristic the quotations that combine, in various ways, the characteristics of metaphorical apocalypse and idolatry. In the first, the hypocritical contrast between state position and sexual immorality is emphasised by close juxtaposition ('drab of State', 'cloath a silver slut') with the adjectival phrase 'cloath a silver' providing the element of dazzle, and the parting 'her soule traile i'th durt' the moral and religious dimension. In the second, Gratiana in her role as bawd to Castiza is seen as imposing the iconic attribute of a monster – a snake recalling the corruption of Eve[93] – onto Castiza; and she, though recalling herself at her prayers, has been demonstrated as having taken readily to the role of a prostitute. In the third, the outward and the inward Gratiana are perceived as fitting closely together to make a hypocrite, and the inward 'poysonous woman' is accorded, through linguistic compression, the bestial and serpentine attribute of several 'Tongues'; Castiza's evocation of 'fire' and her question 'Do you not see her?' suggest the obligation to perceive evil, while calling up the dazzle that prevents perception. Nicoll's view of the poet's role recalls the vows of the young Middleton in *The Wisdom of Solomon* to become a vigilante against idolatry; and, in describing 'spiritual figures who move and have their spiritual being beside the all too fleshly denizens of the earth' Nicoll chances on an important truth. The spiritual figures can be demonstrated to be iconic: they 'move . . . beside' the play's characters because iconic language is used at heightened moments to set those characters within a wider frame of reference, linking one attribute of decadence to another, within language and beyond. Given what has been said about the function of gender within anti-Catholic drama, it is especially noticeable that Nicoll's quotations all refer to female characters.

Most suggestive of all, perhaps, is Nicoll's own unconscious use of the topoi of apocalypse: the 'light in darkness or darkness in light' that may 'sear the spirit, . . . wound [and] terrify', and the worldly veils that are either pierced through by the images' 'translucent quality' and 'glare of eternity', or the dark tapestried veils which are torn down by the poet to expose villainy under the artificial dazzle of torchlight. It finds an echo in Swinburne, whose essay on Tourneur begins with a long unattributed quotation: 'For while they supposed to lie hid in their secret sins, they were scattered under a dark veil of forgetfulness, being horribly astonished, and troubled with sights . . . Sad visions appeared unto them with heavy countenances. No power of the fire might give them light . . . Only there appeared unto them a fire kindled of itself, very dreadful: for being much terrified, they thought the things which they saw to be worse than the sights they saw not.'[94] As the first paragraph of this chapter demonstrates, the tradition of chiaroscuro criticism continues.

CONCLUSION: A DAMNED WORLD?

The perennial commonplace in Webster and Middleton criticism, most important in a Websterian context, is that the imagery of both writers illumines a fated and damned world, where humanity is seen to be 'irretrievably prone to corruption and error'.⁹⁵ Nature, too, is infected by the sinfulness of man. Like the wood made evil by its fashioning into an idol, the husbandry performed on nature denatures and poisons it: Vittoria, for instance, is compared to a vine manured with warm blood and bearing 'unsavoury fruit' (III ii, l. 187). This corruption of nature finds many analogies in anti-Catholic pamphlets: John Gee's *The Foot Out of the Snare* (2nd edn. 1624) accuses Catholic pastors of leading their sheep to drink at the poisoned fountain of erroneous doctrine (p. 23), while at the beginning of *The Duchess of Malfi*, Antonio invokes the emblem of a fountain for the example of a prince's court:

> whence should flow
> Pure silver-drops in general. But if 't chance
> Some curs'd example poison't near the head,
> Death and Diseases through the whole land spread.
>
> (I i, ll. 12–15)⁹⁶

Nature is as susceptible to Catholic corruption as artifice; when metaphor burgeons with weeds on dunghills, rotten fruit and poisonous waters, a damned world can be a blighted natural world.⁹⁷

Antonio's similitude comes at the beginning of the play, and beginnings and ends have weighty interpretative implications within a play's hermetic moral message. At the end of *The Changeling*, while De Flores compares Beatrice-Joanna to Eve, 'That broken rib of mankind' (V iii, l. 146), Alsemero pushes her sin on to an apocalyptic time-scale:

> Rehearse again
> Your scene of lust, that you may be perfect
> When you shall come to act it to the black audience
> Where howls and gnashings shall be music to you.
>
> (V iii, ll. 114–17)

In Beatrice's and De Flores's unholy union, it is made clear that they are but two elements in a damned world:

DE FLORES Yes, and the while I coupled with your mate
   At barley-break; now we are left in hell.
VERMANDERO We are all there, it circumscribes us here. (V iii, ll. 162–4)

Various reasons and various *mentalités* are invoked to explain the damned world. Speaking of the nightmare oppressiveness of a 'hideously deformed universe', John Wilks describes the 'Websterian cosmos in which a womanish and fearful mankind gropes blindly towards a necessary fate it can neither see nor avoid' as being 'a . . . testament . . . to the sceptical and nominalist temper of the age'. L. L. Brodwin believes that Webster thought the efficacy of Christianity 'a delusion, a subject for pathos or bitter satire', and the only moral alternative a 'stoic adherence to personal integrity'.[98] Muriel Bradbrook has observed that 'Webster's God, unlike his devil, is a hidden one', and Roma Gill, that without the bloody masque at the end of *Women Beware Women*, the characters would be 'trapped without salvation in an infinity of soulless intrigue'.[99] More recently – and with more relevance to an anti-Catholic interpretation – it has been commented that the opening speeches in many revenge-tragedies locate the horrors to come in the specific conditions of an Italian city-state.[100] But all these varied causes – a medieval *contemptus mundi*, a deterministic and fatalistic Augustinian Calvinism, scepticism, proto-nihilism, and an 'existential metaphysic of anguished agnosticism' – attribute to the authors of these dramas psychological, philosophical and spiritual motives as contorted as Ferdinand's and the Cardinal's plottings in *The Duchess of Malfi*.[101] It is not to deny the revenge-tragedians' medieval inheritance, nor that they have lent themselves to powerful anachronistic interpretations, to comment that the idea of a damned world has an obvious inspiration in contemporary anti-Catholicism, which commentators have sometimes been too subtle to see.

In discussing the fatalistic element in the plays of Webster and Middleton, critics have most often called the playwrights Calvinist. If this epithet is to continue, its use needs to be substantially modified, stressing – insofar as the two can be separated – polemical rather than doctrinal Calvinism, less the sorrows of predestination than the inevitable damnation of the papist; though since Calvinists were not unique in their emphasis on predestination, and most Protestants, Calvinist or not, would have felt able to assent to imaginative anti-Catholicism, it is perhaps more advisable to stretch the idea, and the phrase, of Protestant poetics to accommodate the livid flash. But the term 'Calvinist' has certainly been preferable to vagueness in using the term 'religion', or the common imprecision of mixing up Catholicism with Christianity. Thus L. L. Brodwin described the liturgical parody at Brachiano's deathbed in *The White Devil* as being a 'final mockery of Christian consolation', and commented: 'Though the word "charity" appears throughout the play, it is only in connection with this black mass that the phrase "Christian Charitie" is used. Christian charity can only be a perversion "when Churchmen stagger in't."'[102] G. Wilson Knight interpreted Act v iii of *The Duchess of Malfi*, set among the Abbey ruins, as externalising the decay of medieval religion – though not explaining whether he meant religion in general or Catholicism in particular.[103] The sympathetic characters have been categorised as sceptics or – more anachronistically – agnostics struggling for ethical standards outside religion, somehow proleptic of the modern condition.

Webster as sage of transgressiveness has perhaps been most characteristic of recent criticism. In an appraisal of their own criticism in their edition of Webster's plays, Jonathan Dollimore and Alan Sinfield assert that the 'discontinuity of character and form' in *The White Devil* 'works to demystify and so challenge the power structures of religion and the state', and that Webster is to be placed in the context of 'the problematic and provocative doctrines of contemporary Protestantism'.[104] Perpetuating the old confusion of religion with Catholicism, their argument demonstrated for the 1980s that the plays can still serve as a metaphor for state evil: coupled, in their case, with a teleological interpretation of Protestantism as hardly religion at all, a kind of anti-Christian benign anarchy. Neither seem aware of the fact that the Protestant establishment in England erected the imaginative structure of a corrupt, politicised Catholic church for reasons far from radical, and only oppositional on the international level; but they show how, in a secularist age, the myth of anti-Catholicism may serve as a flail for Christianity.

But without some degree of affirmative action on the part of the critic, this kind of misreading is likely to continue. To quote Robert N. Watson, the 'multivocal and indeterminate' nature of the tragedies of Webster and Middleton makes them endlessly susceptible to interpretative criticism in a way which overtly polemical drama is not.[105] Prejudice is obvious in the one case, while in the other it is given a spurious universality. Critics unhappy with othering, or even Catholic critics, should perhaps object more to criticism which fails to engage with these phantoms of prejudice. But the task of this chapter ends here: to give a name to the nameless horror of Jacobean tragedy.

CHAPTER 2

Catholic poetics and the Protestant canon

The last chapter posed a very simple question: why it is that literary critics have been largely unconscious of the anti-Catholic prejudice which structures a Websterian or Middletonian vision of evil, and so have performed the illiberal act of perpetuating it. This chapter begins in a similar manner, asking why in university bookshops, in the year 1998, Crashaw is absent from shelves where cheap editions of Donne, Herbert, Vaughan and Traherne are easy to find. Within the critical *consensus fidelium* Crashaw has generally been regarded as a leading poet of the period; and he has never disappeared from anthologies, itself a sign that he is an unignorable presence. But despite some eloquent recent defenders, to whom this chapter owes a debt,[1] reading the unanthologised Crashaw is still felt to be supererogatory. He is called an isolated figure in English poetry: as recently as 1993, the sixth – revised – edition of the *Norton Anthology of English Literature* declared that 'Richard Crashaw is a phenomenon unique in Anglo-Saxon taste ... his roots seem to be sunk less in English literature than in Italian, Spanish, and neo-Latin writings', and questioned whether it was worth importing the term 'baroque' into English literature 'to take care of a largely isolated figure like Crashaw'.[2]

When Spenser writes in Italian fashions, it enriches English culture and helps to make Spenser a major poet; when Crashaw does the same, he is called foreign. The difference – an ideologically loaded one, which continues to affect critical judgement – is in the type of fashion being imported. Crashaw is a baroque poet; though post-war art-historians have problematised the traditional connection of baroque styles with Catholicism, and though recent literary criticism has arrived at the idea of Protestant baroque through Milton, the equation was simpler for critics in the more distant past.[3] To them, the baroque was a Catholic fashion; and for many of them

– in a symbiosis of religious and aesthetic prejudice – the baroque equated to blowsy emotionalism and dropsical bad taste. Half-buried, this is a prejudice which continues to affect the reputation of baroque writers who are known to be Catholic.[4] The suggestion that Crashaw is best understood in the context of the literature of other countries may seem, by comparison, a mild and non-judgemental one; yet it can result in a kind of critical customs control where desirable continental goods are waved through, and the purveyors of undesirable ones deported. One could extend the analogy further: because Crashaw himself left England when he converted to Catholicism, he has been refused a re-entry visa. It is hard not to see in this an outcrop of unconscious anti-Catholic prejudice.

But though Crashaw has been deracinated by the nineteenth and twentieth centuries, he was certainly not isolated at the time. Among his countrymen, he was influential; plenty of English poetry is Crashavian, both in print and – as so often with Catholic verse – in manuscript, and some of it is discussed in this chapter. More influential still was his predecessor, Robert Southwell, to whom the largest portion of this chapter is devoted; if Crashaw has received more praise for his aesthetic merits, Southwell's verse was the more powerfully infectious, to a degree that – depite the powerful claims for it made by Pierre Janelle in the 1930s and Louis Martz in the 1950s – is still not adequately recognised. Beginning with Southwell and ending with Crashaw, two poets who have strong claims to canonicity, this chapter asks for a wide acknowledgement of the tradition which they embody: a tradition that, in defiance of the *Norton Anthology*, one could term the English Catholic baroque.[5]

One manifestation of that tradition is their work within the genre of tears-poetry. The poetry of tears was inaugurated far earlier than the Reformation,[6] and was not exclusively Catholic afterwards; but it was highly visible within Counter-Reformation poetics, and repentant devotional weeping was strongly and overtly associated with both Catholicism and conversion at the period when Crashaw was writing.[7] Through Catholic influence, it also became common in mainstream poetic discourse. Though it would be a mistake to claim that Southwell single-handedly re-introduced imaginative religious poetry to England after the Reformation, the posthumous publication in 1595 of his collection *Saint Peters Complaint* gave sacred verse a definitive new direction, and helped to create a climate in which non-biblical religious poetry became increasingly acceptable.

The title-poem in particular inaugurated a publisher-led trend, while the collection as a whole was one of the most important stimuli to the urgent moral debates conducted by English poetic theorists of the later 1590s. But as often with xenophobic prejudice, foreignness could be ignored for long periods of time and re-imputed at times of crisis; the topos was still sufficiently identifiable as Catholic to attract criticism for popery. This liminal quality inspired two distinguished poetic converts from Protestantism, Alabaster and Crashaw, to conceptualise repentance and conversion as a dissolution into tears.

THE INVISIBLE INFLUENCE: ROBERT SOUTHWELL

First, though, comes Southwell; and again, a certain invisibility. Though his lyric 'The Burning Babe' is regularly anthologised, Southwell's collected poems, like Crashaw's, have long been out of print; extended studies of his work are rare;[8] he seldom appears on the undergraduate curriculum; and when general studies are written of the religious poetry of the Tudor and Stuart eras he tends to be left out. The reason is partly one of terminology. In the last few decades, critics have sought alternatives to phrases like 'metaphysical poetry', and the formulations 'seventeenth-century lyric' and 'seventeenth-century religious poetry' have gained wide currency. Though they avoid value-judgement, and the implication that certain mental habits can be imputed with little variation to a heterogeneous group of poets, they should, nevertheless, be treated with caution. Southwell was executed in the last decade of the sixteenth century, in 1595; had he been thought to be an important poet, they would never have been coined, and with the persistent use of these terms, he continues to be written out of the canon. But Southwell is important on the canonical level: for the quality of what he wrote, and even more for his influence on the poets immediately succeeding him.

The latter may not seem a particularly novel claim. Southwell's significance as a precursor of Herbert and other seventeenth-century practitioners of the religious lyric is, after all, a commonplace, and has inspired a number of critics to explore the relationship between devotional poetry and Ignatian meditation. This is a debate that has taken its post-war bearings from Louis Martz's *The Poetry of Meditation*, which argued that English poetry was greatly influenced by Ignatian imaginative habits. Martz's book contains a prolonged discussion of Southwell himself, a lead which has been followed up by few of his successors;[9] it is as if Southwell's importance ends with his being a harbinger, and the tendency is towards impatience until critics reach the home-territory of Herbert and Donne. Though this study does not aim to cover meditative verse in general, the following chapter makes a claim supplementary to Martz's: that the publication and immediate, sustained popular success of *Saint Peters Complaint* after Southwell's martyrdom in February 1595 prompted a sudden large-scale reaction from both elite and non-elite poets, partly imitative and partly agonistic.

Martz's study was important because it helped to establish the *scale* of Southwell's influence, an influence which is much more discernible from internal than external evidence. Simply from reading what Elizabethan poets have to say about their mentors, one would assume that the turn towards religious poetry at this date was spearheaded almost entirely by Edmund Spenser, Guillaume Salluste du Bartas and the spirit of Sir Philip Sidney.[10] It is not that Southwell is never mentioned at all, since a number of contemporaries praise his style; and much of this chapter is dedicated to proving how widely he was read. But it is as if a martyred Catholic could not escape an ideological miasma of a kind which did not prevent his being read or imitated by non-Catholics, but which may well have impeded their overt acknowledgement of him as an exemplar.

Two examples may serve. Book III of Giles Fletcher's long poem *Christs Victorie* (1610) is strongly influenced by *Saint Peters Complaint*, and the book's preface, while owing something both to Southwell and du Bartas in its discussion of the relationship of poetry to religion, echoes the Englishman's conclusions more than the Frenchman's; yet neither Southwell nor his works appear in Fletcher's impeccably Protestant list of mentors, including Spenser, du Bartas and James I.[11] Forty-five years later, Henry Vaughan's preface to the 1655 edition of *Silex Scintillans* spoke of the long-continued war in England between religious and secular poetry, and of George Herbert as 'the first, that with any effectual success attempted a diversion of this foul and overflowing stream'.[12] Southwell, of course, is not the only poet which this judgement ignores; but the poetic theories of Southwell, Herbert and the later Vaughan share a distinctive intolerance of secular verse, which Vaughan's mentor Herbert largely derived from Southwell.[13] Vaughan's judgement may reveal an ignorance of Southwell's part in this, or a view that Herbert's was by far the more important articulation of the idea; but the wording of the preface is precise, and seems designed to imply that for poetry to be truly effective, religious fervour needed to accompany right belief. Southwell could be conceded a certain measure of success; but for *effectual* success, it may have been important to be a member of the Church of England.

Given suppressions like this, it is hardly surprising that Southwell has been largely invisible to literary critics looking for a great acknowledged tradition; yet even plaudits on Southwell can show why his influence is still underestimated. In *Hypercritica*, Edmund Bolton demonstrates how a dissident's anonymity could lead to uncertainty in attribution – strikingly, since Bolton was a Catholic himself. 'Never must be forgotten *St Peters Complaint*, and those other serious Poems said to be father Southwell's; the English whereof, as it is most proper, so the sharpness and Light of Wit is very rare in them.'[14] More commonly, Southwell's poems are definitely identified as his. Ben Jonson's tribute is well-known: 'That Southwell was hanged; yet so he had written that piece of his "The burning babe", he would have been content to destroy many of his.'[15] But the judgement seems framed to display Jonson's own discernment as much as to praise Southwell; it implies that less perceptive critics might not see that a Catholic traitor could write well. Conversely, it was sometimes admitted that an author could write well, even though he was a Catholic traitor: Francis Bacon commented of Southwell's *A Humble Supplication to Her Majesty* that 'it is curiously written, and worth the writing out for the art; though the argument be bad'.[16]

Marginalisation began in Southwell's lifetime, since the very factors which inspired his poetic theory, his Catholicism and his missionary endeavour, set him at odds with the literary fashions which prevailed in England during the period of his ministry. Counter-Reformation Catholicism, as well as encouraging the use of the imagination by dint of meditative techniques, favoured a wide range of religious poetry; and Southwell's importation of continental trends, discussed below, is marked by an untroubled use of verse for devotional ends which, at this date, is more characteristically Catholic than Protestant. As another English Catholic poet, F.W., put it eloquently some decades later in the preface to his manuscript sonnet-sequence on the joys of heaven,

It seemethe verie conforme, to reason, that poetrie and divinitie shouldbe matched together, as soule and bodie, bodie and garment, substance enwrapped withe hir accidents ... for if poetrie be an arte apte to depainte most livelilie, the conceite of o[ur] mind ... who then will not judge poetrie best applied to the misteries of o[ur] faithe: the whiche for theire p[ro]fundnes deterr most men from understandinge them: yet all are bound to know them, and withe most pure and sincere affection accept and imbrace them.[17]

It is here that clues may be found to Southwell's popularity in print. Scholarship has tended to concentrate on the influence of Southwell's short poems upon the religious lyricists of the next generation: naturally enough, given how firmly literary studies are still tied to anthological familiarity. But a wider view of Southwell's influence – on the longer religious poem, and on private meditations – indicates how he met a common devotional need which, in Protestant circles, was only just beginning to be acknowledged again. His sententious verse would have looked very dated towards the end of his life, which must have lessened still further the willingness of elite poets to acknowledge him as a forbear; but it was exactly the kind of moral verse which was popular with non-elite audiences. Though Southwell only circulated his poems in manuscript during his lifetime, they became – with some deletions to suit a Protestant audience – a very popular and valuable commodity to the London book trade after his death.

They were published soon after his execution in 1595; and while their popularity must initially have owed much to topical interest, they continued to sell well up to the Civil Wars.[18] They inspired imitations and appealed to a wide readership, socially and religiously heterogeneous; and with a publishing record that rivals many popular prose works of religious devotion, they succeeded in pleasing both Catholics and Protestants for just under half a century. *Saint Peters Complaint* ran through thirteen mainstream editions between 1595 and 1640, and two printed by clandestine Catholic presses – given how often Southwell is merely considered a recusant poet, the imbalance is worth noting. Its supplement *Mœoniæ* ran through three mainstream editions, all dated 1595, before being appended to *Saint Peters Complaint* in 1620.[19] The economics of publishing make it clear that the promulgators of Southwell in the mainstream of the London book trade, and Southwell's later imitators within that mainstream, were mainly catering for the non-elite reader. This is a group best definable by a negative: those who were able to read, to pay for books and to utilise printed sources for their religious devotions, but who, for whatever reason, did not have access to the systems of scribal publication prevailing in court, university and aristocratic circles. For such readers, a book's didactic usefulness would often have dictated whether they could justify buying it; and the longer poem might have been attractive for its greater expository possibilities.

But, this consideration apart, the editors' choice of title-poem was apt. Though Southwell is now thought of principally as a lyric poet, it was his long lachrymal elegy that had the greatest effect upon contemporary writers. Strongly influenced by Luigi Tansillo's *Le Lagrime di San Pietro* (1st edn. 1560), it comments on the Passion by means of the dramatic contrition of the narrator, St Peter.[20] As with Tansillo, the rhetorical drama of *Saint Peters Complaint* makes constant participatory demands on an audience. Joan Grundy has said that tears-poetry pushed to the limit the tendency towards apostrophe, exclamation and other rhetorical incarnations of excitement which the Passion had always inspired in devotional writers, 'by making the rhetoric predominate and by dissolving narrative, very largely, into declamation'.[21] The emphasis on dissolution is one that will recur.

Saint Peters Complaint was issued shortly after Southwell's execution, and was designed to capitalise upon it. Three editions appeared in the first year, two published by John Wolfe and one by Gabriel Cawood, with the first to appear being issued by Wolfe.[22] Southwell's bibliographers agree that there was a race to get the book out.[23] Unusually for English mainstream publications of a Catholic text, both men eschew the various strategies of maintaining ideological distance from it: the condemnatory or regretful dedication or epistle, or the systematic parody.[24] Other than Southwell's own apologia for religious poetry, the text is presented without apology or explanation, and as far as internal evidence goes, there is nothing to suggest that there might be a need for either. This is clearly not because the publishers were unaware of the dangers; despite the possibility of their being in manuscripts from which the printers were working, Southwell's most obviously Catholic poems are not included.[25] A number on the Virgin Mary were issued later in *Mœoniæ*, a supplementary volume to *Saint Peters Complaint* issued by John Busby, while others had to wait until the nineteenth century to be printed.

The appropriate official sanctions were obtained early on, when

Gabriel Cawood entered it in the Stationers' Register on 5 April 1595.[26] Previously to that, either he or Wolfe had secured an ecclesiastical licence,[27] notwithstanding the fact that in the previous year, 1594, a manuscript copy of *Saint Peters Complaint* was presented as evidence of recusancy in the examination of John Bolt.[28] The official attitude is certainly a little inconsistent: perhaps this is evidence of inefficiency, but more likely it reflects an acknowledgement that there was nothing in the poems as printed that a Protestant could not read with profit. Censorship is not just a matter of text, and the disciplining of Bolt penalised not merely a poem, but that poem's connection to a suspected individual and the clandestine manner of its distribution.

Southwell is no exception to the rule described in the introduction, that most religious poems written by Catholics could have been read – though often differently interpreted – by Protestant and Catholic alike. With Southwell, the real question is different: given the notoriety of their author, how could Protestants buy and read him? Many of the first purchasers must have been curious or voyeuristic, and conversely, ignorance of the author's identity must also have played a part.[29] Catholics, too, would not have confined their purchasing to editions of Southwell produced by clandestine presses. But the majority of Southwell's large audience, certainly at the beginning, must have been Protestants aware of Southwell's religious persuasions and Southwell's fate; and the poems' instant and continued popularity argues that a large section of the reading public was prepared to buy, and to go on buying, the works of a papist who had died a traitor's death. The book's popularity with the public may be evidence of sympathy for Southwell in particular, even if not for Catholics in general; but the publishers' style of presentation must have made it easier to justify buying the book. It may be possible to see the semi-anonymity and continued popularity of Southwell's poems as a collusion between officialdom, publisher and public.

SOUTHWELL AS POETIC THEORIST

It was a collusion worthwhile because Southwell's poems met a need for imaginatively engaging religious verse, different from mainstream English religious poetry of the 1590s. This was probably due, in large part, to the inhibiting effects of Protestant nervousness; treatments of the New Testament, particularly the Gospels, were still a subject-area where accusations of idolatry could be upheld.[30] In relation to drama, Murray Roston has postulated a 'ladder of sanctity', whereby the Reformation rendered first the New Testament, then the Old Testament and the Apocrypha, too sacred for imaginative treatment.[31] But nothing so schematic is necessary to imagine ways in which Southwell's poems might have incurred disapproval. Southwell uses two New Testament characters as narrators, St Peter and Mary Magdalen, and their long meditations could have been read as illegitimate embroidery of the Gospel, supplanting God's Word by the fruits of fallible human imagination; in fact, they could have been read as popish. As various critics have noted, English Calvinist piety did not tend to encourage passion narratives.[32] But Southwell's emphasis on repentance may have had the effect of claiming the moral high ground and disarming Protestant criticism.

Though striking, the novelty of Southwell's product on a public level should not be over-emphasised; it came into a market prepared to welcome something new in a recognised field, rather than one where there was a complete lack of divine verse. Religious poetry in certain genres was already part of the repertoire of the English Reformation publisher. Polemical anti-Catholic verse was, of course, ubiquitous; prayers were sometimes versified; Biblical paraphrases were not uncommon;[33] metrical psalms had been advocated by the reformers, welcomed by Catholics as well as by Protestants and essayed by Philip Sidney and his sister;[34] and a few religious verses had appeared in popular anthologies, notably by another Catholic, Jasper Heywood, in *The Paradise of Dainty Devices* (1576–1606).[35] Robert Holland's *Holie Historie of Our Lord and Saviour Jesus Christs Nativitie, Life, Actes ... Gathered into English Meeter, and Published to Withdraw Vaine Wits from all Unsaverie and Wicked Rimes and Fables* (1594) was written expressly to be sung to psalm-tunes.[36] At the cheap end of the print-market, penny godlies and godly broadside ballads were a large part of the stock-in-trade of the ballad salesman.[37] The distinction between religious and merely moral is not always easy to draw, and this alone suggests that one should not underestimate the amount of versified spiritual nourishment in circulation in the late sixteenth century. As previously observed, Southwell's popularity must have been helped by the fact that he often writes in sententious *catenae* directly in the English tradition of popular wisdom literature.

But elite circles, where the Protestant repudiation had had most effect, spent a long time coming round to the idea that imaginative religious poetry was a genre in which the educated Protestant could write; theorists tended to support the idea that they could, but poets themselves were slow to take up the cue. Puttenham's *Arte of English Poesie*, written mid-century and first published in 1589, identified poetry itself as having religious origins.[38] Sidney's *Defence of Poetry*, written between 1581 and 1583, defensively makes the claim that poetry can still be used for sacred purposes, in its discussion of pagan prophecy and the psalms of David. 'But truly now having named [David], I fear me I seem to profane that holy name, applying it to poetry, which is among us thrown down to so ridiculous an estimation. But they that with quiet judgements will look a little deeper into it, shall find the end and working of it such as, being rightly applied, deserveth not to be scourged out of the Church of God.' Matthew Parker and others prefigured Southwell, at least, in advocating poetry based on the Bible as an alternative to secular verse.[39]

Critiques of an exclusively pagan and secular poetry had also begun to be mounted by European Protestants, most notably Guillaume Salluste du Bartas.[40] His pioneering *La Muse Chrétienne*, including his defence of divine poetry in the form of an invocation to the muse Urania, was first published in his native France in 1574. Its ideas would have been accessible thereafter to Englishmen who could read French; in addition a parallel French and Latin edition of *L'Uranie* was published by the ubiquitous John Wolfe in 1589, and a Latin translation of du Bartas's epic *Divine Weeks and Works* appeared in 1591, also in London. Previously in 1584, the fashion for du Bartas at the Scottish court had borne fruit in some translations: Thomas Hudson's *The Historie of Judith*, and a rendition of *L'Uranie* and portions of the *Divine Weeks* by James VI, both published in Edinburgh by T. Vautrollier.[41] *The Triumph of Faith*, Josuah Silvester's translation of another poem of du Bartas's, was published in 1592[42] in a volume including extracts from the *Seconde Semaine*; and John Eliot included portions of *Divine Weeks* in *The Survay of France* (1592) and *Ortho-Epia Gallica* (1593). But compared with du Bartas's massive popularity in later years, this is only slender evidence of interest from the London book trade. English translators at this period may have been dissuaded by the fact that Sidney was said to be undertaking a translation of *La Semaine* in the mid-1580s, a work which does not survive.[43]

Cumulatively this is evidence of interest in du Bartas's *oeuvre*, suggesting that he was seen to be an important figure. But it is strongly biased towards the educated reader, and until the mid-1590s had a dispersed and piecemeal quality outside the Scottish court, not capitalising on the work's potential popular appeal. The first substantial London publication of du Bartas, from two different publishers, comprised two translations from his Biblical epic *Divine Weeks and Works*: *The First Day of the Worlds Creation*,[44] and *Babilon, a Part of the Seconde Weeke*. The year that it occurred was also the year of *Saint Peters Complaint*, 1595; and the chronological proximity becomes more startling on observing that the date on which the first was entered was some years before, 14 August 1591. It is as if the presence of Southwell in the market-place helped the value of all religious verse, and made it a more urgent matter to print.[45]

The works of each poet must undoubtedly have helped the reception of the other; but although du Bartas went on to be a bestseller comparable to Southwell, his sales were not kick-started by martyrdom, and if one can gauge the initial popular reception of a writer by the number of editions called for within the first few years of publication, Southwell is the clear winner. Despite the religious differences of the two poets, du Bartas's arguments and Southwell's certainly have points of similarity; more than fortuitously, since Southwell may well have encountered du Bartas's writings on the Continent.[46] If so, translations of du Bartas were given their first major launch on the London market almost simultaneously with the original verse of a first-generation disciple of du Bartas's, and perhaps because of the interest that the disciple had provoked. To stress Southwell's importance is not to deny du Bartas's, nor the added stimulus to debates on religious poetry in 1595 which would have been provided by the first appearance in print of Sidney's *Defence of Poetry*.[47] One need not look to any *one* writer to provide a total explanation of the change in attitude to imaginative religious poetry in the mid-1590s; but among the writers that contributed to that change, literary criticism has been slow to recognise how powerfully Southwell acted as a stimulus.[48]

But though du Bartas may have provided Southwell – and more importantly Southwell's Protestant readers – with a rationale for sacred verse, he was not a model whom Southwell followed closely. Most obviously, du Bartas's religious verse, unlike Southwell's, takes Genesis and religious allegory as its two chief subjects; and du Bartas did not write much lyric verse. Southwell hardly alludes, either, to du Bartas's most distinctive trope, the heavenly muse Urania who inspired poets to treat of heavenly matters. It has been an orthodoxy that the heavenly muse was evoked along a strong Protestant line of descent – Sidney, Spenser and the Spenserians – and as far as that goes, it is true. Southwell's use of muses is very sparing – two lines in his total poetic output[49] – and related to an overt wariness about the place of woman in verse. His audaciousness is, in fact, largely a question of doing away with neo-platonic machinery and other transitional figures between human and divine; his poetry seeks an apprehension of God with which even a heavenly muse would interfere.

This is only one way in which Southwell made a distinctive contribution to poetical theory and practice. The common perception of Southwell is of a missionary poet, writing for the spiritual solace of his recusant patrons, and with little awareness of current literary debates: a myth which owes something to the historiographical perception of late Elizabethan Catholicism as a beleaguered minority group confined to a few aristocratic houses. But read without preconception, Southwell's dedication to his cousin seems written primarily for the attention of other poets and only secondarily for a general audience, Catholic or non-Catholic. As such, it hits hard.

Poets by abusing their talent, and making the follies and fayninges of love, the customary subject of their base endevours, have so discredited this faculty, that a Poet, a Lover, and a Liar, are by many reckoned but three wordes of one signification. But the vanity of men, cannot counterpoyse the authority of God, who delivering many partes of Scripture in verse, and by his Apostle willing us to exercise our devotion in Himnes and Spirituall Sonnets, warranteth the Arte to bee good, and the use allowable. And therefore not onely among the Heathens, whose Gods were chiefely canonized by their Poets, and their Painim Divinitie Oracled in verse: But even in the Old and New Testament it hath bene used by men of greatest Pietie, in matters of most devotion ... But the Divell as he affecteth Deitie, and seeketh to have all the complements of Divine honor applied to his service, so hath he among the rest possessed also most Poets with his idle fansies. (p. [1])

There are some points of similarity to Sidney's *Defence of Poetry*, and it is quite possible that Southwell had seen a manuscript copy of the work.[50] But it goes a long way beyond Sidney, in areas of different emphasis or simply of contention. Sidney pleads for poetry to be recognised as a suitable vehicle for religious endeavour; citing many of the same biblical precedents, Southwell assumes that the onus of proof is all the other way, and proceeds to condemn non-Christian subject-matter as a dangerous waste of time for poets. 'For in lieu of solemne and devout matter, to which in duety they owe their abilities, they now busy themselves in expressing such passions, as onely serve for testimonies to how unwoorthy affections they have wedded their wils.' If directed at the admirers of the author of *Astrophil and Stella*, the sonnet-sequence alluding overtly to Sidney's adulterous love for Penelope Rich, this would have been particularly painful. But the preface carefully avoids naming names, and so is not intended to be read primarily as a critique of Sidney, or of any poet in particular. This only enlarges Southwell's target-area; he is, in fact, accusing most mainstream poets of profanity, in an all-embracing condemnation of the effects of the Protestant poetic.

Southwell continues: 'And because the best course to let them see the errour of their workes, is to weave a new webbe in their owne loome; I have heere layd a few course threds together, to invite some skillfuller wits to goe forward in the same, or to begin some finer peece, wherein it may be seene, how well verse and vertue sute together' (p. 1). His preface to *Saint Peters Complaint*, 'The Author to the Reader', sets out a double programme for correct reader-response. Peter's contrition and that of all saints is to be taken as an exemplar, 'Learne by their faultes, what in thine owne to mend' (l. 6), and used as a touchstone to discern good and evil in art.

> This makes my mourning muse resolve in teares,
> This Theames my heavy penne to plaine in prose.
> Christes Thorne is sharpe, no head his Garland weares:
> Still finest wits are stilling Venus Rose.
> In Paynim toyes the sweetest vaines are spent:
> To Christian workes, few have their tallents lent.   (ll. 13–18)

So central is this concern to Southwell's programme that it even appears within the body of the poem, voiced by St Peter himself. This is not a violation of history, as might appear; the whole poem is a meditation on the Gospel narrative of St Peter's denial rather than a retelling of it, and Peter, as protagonist, directs the meditational experience of the reader. In this context, the writer forces the reader to see poetry less as one imaginative genre among many, than as a revelation of his true priorities. Profane and lying poetry becomes a microcosm of all sin, and the virtuous poetic text its only counter.

> Ambitious heades dreame you of fortunes pride:
> Fill volumes with your forged Goddesse praise.

> You fancies drudges, plungd in follies tide:
> Devote your fabling wits to lovers layes:
> Be you O sharpest greeves, that ever wrung,
> Texte to my thoughts, Theame to my playning tung.   (ll. 31–6)

Southwell's call is to writers even more than to readers: a call not simply to contrition, but to the creativity of contrition. Referring to the genre of complaint in which he is writing, he makes a further point which has considerable relevance to the Catholic-Protestant debate on the legitimacy of addition to the Scriptures: how the subject-matter of personal sin exceeds even the lamentations of Jeremiah. This helps to disarm criticism, given the widely recognised piety of prolonged contrition.

> Sad subject of my sinne hath stoard my mind
> With everlasting matter of complaint:
> My threnes an endlesse Alphabet do find,
> Beyond the panges which Jeremy doth paint.   (ll. 37–40)

It would be exceedingly helpful to know what poems apart from *Saint Peters Complaint* were included in Southwell's original selection, but a number of Southwell's short lyrics continue the programme set out above. 'Lewd Love is Losse', has a similarly reproving first verse:

> Misdeeming eye that stoupest to the lure
> Of mortall worthes not worth so worthy love:
> All beauties base, all graces are impure:
> That do thy erring thoughtes from God remove.
> Sparkes to the fire, the beames yeelde to the sunne,
> All grace to God from whom all graces runne.   (ll. 1–6)

Where 'Lewd Love is Losse' is directed both at reader and author, a lyric like 'Davids Peccavi' returns to interrogating poetical practice via the poet. David, the Psalmist, stands for poets in general, and particularly for those who essay religious topics.[51] David accuses himself not simply of being attracted by 'wiles of wit' and 'subtle traines', but of actually constructing them; if he had been merely a reader, he could deny positive ill-doing, but as an author, his authorial skill has led him into greater sin.

> If wiles of wit had over-wrought my will,
> Or subtle traines misled my steppes awrie,
> My foile had found excuse in want of skill,
> Ill deede I might, though not ill doome denie:
> But wit and will must now confesse with shame,
> Both deede and doome, to have deserved blame.

> I Fansie deem'd fit guide to leade my way,
> And as I deem'd, I did pursue her track;
> Wit lost his ayme, and will was Fancies pray,
> The Rebell wan, the Ruler went to wrack:
> But now sith fansie did with folly end,
> Wit bought with losse, will taught by wit, will mend. (l. 19–30)

As with St Peter, the poem has as much contemporary relevance as historical, and may even contain a specific allusion. Part of the historical background for David's contrition is his illicit love for Bathsheba, who hovers on the poem's margins in the same position as the profane muse whom so many of Southwell's other poems condemn, and is equated with errant 'Fancie'. If the audience is intended to think beyond the generalised notion of a poet to specific contemporary examples of poets, this contrition may, too, be a pointer to further concealed polemic. Even after his death – in fact, particularly after his death – Sidney had an exemplary status as a writer, and it is highly possible that Southwell, and Southwell's initial audience, knew of Sidney's attempts to versify the Psalms: a project which would have eased any identification with David.[52] As already suggested, Southwell was constructing a model of poetic virtue alternative to that imputed to Sidney; and, like any thoroughly Christianised one, it was a model which forbade poets to indulge in physical or mental adultery. There is no need to argue for a one-to-one equation of Sidney to David, or, for that matter, Bathsheba to Penelope Rich; but given the range of poetic exemplars available to the contemporary reader, the text leaves open the possibility, and it would have aided Southwell's condemnation of secular poetry and poets.

'Loves servile lot' concludes with the brisk admonition, 'Seeke other mistres for your minds, / Loves service is in vaine' (ll. 75–6). But Southwell's conception of female inspiration was not uniformly misogynistic. As commented earlier, he does not entirely eschew the heavenly muse as a trope, even though his use of her is sparing. His poems on Mary Magdalen make a common baroque demand which was later taken up by Crashaw and others, for attention to be paid to the exemplary contrition of a female subject. His epitaph on Lady Margaret Sackville celebrates her as an example of religious womanhood, while 'At Home in Heaven' puts forward Esther and Judith as female exemplars, combining beauty and virtue (ll. 37–8). More significantly, the latter poem feminizes the soul in describing the only acceptable human response to the Divine. Audaciously equating Christ with Samson in his moment of amatory weakness, it adopts, and deliberately reverses, the medieval and Petrarchan convention of abject lover and wayward mistress for the relationship between Christ and the soul. The title of the poem, 'At Home in Heaven', implies that if the soul looks away from Christ it is to be construed as adultery.

> This lull'd our heavenly Sampson fast asleepe,
> And laid him in our feeble natures lapp.
> This made him under mortall load to creepe:
> And in our flesh his god head to enwrap.
> This made him sojourne with us in exile:
> And not disdayne our tytles in his style. . . .
>
> O soule do not thy noble thoughts abase
> To lose thy loves in any mortall wight:
> Content thy eye at home with native grace,
> Sith God him selfe is ravisht with thy sight.
> If on thy beautie God enamored bee:
> —Base is thy love of any lesse than hee.   (l. 13–18, 25–30)

It is possible to fix a terminal date to Southwell's poetic theories, since Southwell's editors conclude that his poems must all have been written before June 1592: the date when he was arrested, imprisoned and forbidden access to writing materials. Previously, he seems to have compiled for his cousin a collection of short lyrics prefaced with a dedicatory letter; but although he seems to have expected it to be circulated in manuscript, no copy of this collection survives. One cannot now tell what was in it, but given the tenor of his dedication, it probably included a number of the poems critical of current poetic practice, and may have been tailored to a wide audience outside his immediate Catholic contacts – whether or not that audience was actually exploited at the time. After Southwell's arrest an unknown editor prepared a collection of fifty-two lyrics, excluding *Saint Peters Complaint* but incorporating other items from the previous collection, and retaining the prose dedication and introductory poem; copied by scribes, this forms the basis of many Southwell manuscripts that remain to us.[53] But to publicise Southwell's ideas, printing proved more important than manuscript circulation. Southwell's theories altered directions of composition when his writings became fully public: both because he was copied, and because he was reacted to.

Lines of Southwell's such as 'Give not assent to muddy minded skill, / That deemes the feature of a pleasing face / To be the sweetest baite to lure the will' ('At Home in Heaven', ll. 31–3) seem designed to annoy poets who wrote on both amatory and religious topics. The most prominent of these in the mid-1590s, and inheritor of Sidney's mantle of Protestant exemplarity, was Edmund Spenser. As far as I know, no critic has considered Southwell as a possible influence on Spenser, and it is true that their verse has few superficies in common; but I want to suggest that Southwell's verse elicited an agonistic reaction from Spenser.[54] Though there is no positive evidence that Spenser knew Southwell's poetry, it is hard to imagine that he did not, given its enormous and immediate publishing success. A poet committed to maintaining the moral high ground for Protestantism, as Spenser was, might well have found it very unpleasant reading, and he might have borrowed its best ideas for the Protestant cause; the two reactions need not have been exclusive of one another.

A small battalion of recent critics has reminded us that Spenser was committed to using verse for religious concerns.[55] By 1595, the year of the publication of *Saint Peters Complaint*, he had condemned popery in *The Shepherd's Calendar*, celebrated Protestantised virtue in *The Faerie Queene*, and gestured, at least, towards a religious poetry more positive than polemic and more overt than allegory. *The Shepherd's Calendar* had declared that poetry should 'fly back to heaven apace' (October, l. 84), while the *Tears of the Muses* had displayed du Bartas's muse Urania weeping through neglect.[56]

> Such happines have they, that doo embrace
> The precepts of my heavenlie discipline;
> But shame and sorrow and accursed case
> Have they, that scorne the schoole of arts divine,
> And banish me, which do professe the skill
> To make men heavenly wise, through humbled will.   (ll. 517–22)

But in some ways, Urania might legitimately have accused Spenser of not having the courage of his convictions. Anti-Catholic verse was hardly a controversial medium during Elizabeth's reign; allegory is a generic way of distancing oneself from criticism; and complaint that something is not done is not the same as doing it. With Spenser, as with other elite Protestant writers in the period before 1595, there is a crucial hesitancy surrounding religious poetry: a widespread willingness to admit that poetry was an acceptable means of celebrating divine subject-matter, but in practice, a reluctance to break out in

Catholic poetics and the Protestant canon

any direction that might lead to accusations of idolatry. There were other alternatives: polemic, moralistic allegory, or paraphrase of Biblical matter, sometimes accompanying du Bartas-led invocations of the divine muse. Southwell's verse pointed out and condemned another alternative, which the Protestant poetic in most manifestations did not forbid: to use the language of religious poetry for amorous verse. Given the fact that Southwell had defined the terms of the polemic, it was a hard accusation to answer.

One aspect of Spenser's timing was particularly unfortunate. *Amoretti and Epithalamion*, published in 1595 – and so chronologically close to *Saint Peters Complaint* – falls into the exact category which Southwell was condemning.[57] Read now, Sonnet 72 seems nothing more than a jocular confession of masculine helplessness in the face of beauty; but looked at with a critical sensibility newly informed by Southwell's strictures, it would have dug its own grave deeper the further one read.

> Oft when my spirit doth spread her bolder wings,
> In mind to mount up to the purest sky,
> It down is weighed with thought of earthly things
> And clogged with burden of mortality,
> Where, when that sovereign beauty it doth spy
> (Resembling heaven's glory in her light),
> Drawn with sweet Pleasure's bait it back doth fly
> And unto heaven forgets her former flight.
> There my frail fancy, fed with full delight,
> Doth bathe in bliss and mantleth most at ease,
> Ne thinks of other heaven but how it might
> Her heart's desire with most contentment please:
> Heart need not wish none other happiness
> But here on earth to have such heaven's bliss.

Southwell's indictments would, too, have affected the reading of lines such as those in Sonnet 88, ostensibly inspired by Spenser's wife, 'Of which beholding the Idea plain, /Through contemplation of my purest part, / With light thereof I do myself sustain / And thereon feed my love-affamished heart' (ll. 9–12). The neo-Platonist could have claimed that these lines were consistent with Christianity, offering glimpses of the Divine through the human;[58] but Southwell, or an admirer of Southwell's, could have retorted that, in that case, there was no need of the human. In 'Lewd Love is Losse' Southwell takes pains to make this point.

> If picture move, more should the paterne please,
> No shaddow can with shaddowed thing compare,
> And fayrest shapes whereon our loves do seaze:
> But seely signes of Gods high beauties are.
> Go sterving sense, feede thou on earthly mast,[59]
> True love in Heav'n, seeke thou thy sweet repast. (ll. 7–12)

Though it is a polemical point that Southwell does not exploit, his response to the prevailing Protestant poetic exactly inverts arguments between Catholic and Protestant theologians about the efficacy of praying to saints before images.

Spenser's next separate work, *Four Hymns*, was written between 1595 and 1596, and published in 1596 with a dedication dated 1 September.[60] It has long been recognised as a significant and influential statement of his beliefs; in his study of Spenser's literary career, Patrick Cheney has even seen it as announcing a new vocation in religious verse.[61] Certainly, there is a new confidence in Spenser's direct address of a divine theme. But the timing, together with the subject-matter, strongly indicate that Spenser was inspired by an external factor: the necessity to formulate a coherent critique of Southwell, and retain Christian virtue within Protestant poetry. Southwell is not mentioned in the dedicatory epistle: it would be very surprising if he were. But when considered in this light, certain aspects of the packaging of the *Four Hymns* make better sense than hitherto: in particular the dedicatory epistle, addressed to Margaret, Countess of Cumberland, and Anne, Countess of Warwick.

> Having, in the greener times of my youth, composed these former two Hymns in the praise of Love and Beauty, and finding that the same too much pleased those of like age and disposition (which, being too vehemently carried with that kind of affection, do rather suck out poison to their strong passion than honey to their honest delight), I was moved by the one of you two most excellent Ladies to call in the same. But, being unable so to do by reason that many copies thereof were formerly scattered abroad, I resolved at least to amend and, by way of retractation, to reform them, making instead of those two Hymns of earthly (or natural) Love and Beauty, two others of heavenly and celestial... (p. 324)

Together with the hymns themselves, the dedication reads as a defiant, anti-Southwellian reassertion of how earthly love may point towards true religion. If the discussion with his dedicatee is not a fiction, it might well have been inspired by her reaction to Southwell's critical statements; yet, conveniently, the fact that she is actually cited as the generator of the idea has two effects. Firstly, it renders Southwell invisible; secondly, the reader is invited to interpret Spenser's partial *volte-face* as inspired by gallantry, rather than a dead rival's challenge.

How to read Spenser's retractation has long been a matter for critical debate. Most critics now agree in discounting Spenser's claim that the sacred poems post-date the profane, and assert that the hymns were all written at the same time.[62] If the profane poems were written before the sacred, and Spenser was indeed unable to call them in, then his new-found embarrassment is significant in itself; but if they were all written simultaneously, Spenser's story dramatises a poetic reconsideration which is no less suggestive for being exemplary and not literally true.[63] It may, perhaps, be intended as an oblique apology for his former poetic excesses; yet where the dedication retracts, it does so in a strikingly unapologetic manner, only admitting that amorous poetry may prove unwholesome if read in the wrong spirit. His idea of emending and reforming does not involve suppression, but, at most, a natural supplanting of profane by sacred; and, despite his claim that the two sacred hymns are 'instead' of the two profane ones, all four appear in the published work and are clearly intended to be taken together.

Famously, Southwell wrote a sacred parody of a love-song by Sir Edward Dyer.[64] The information which Spenser's dedication gives us, together with the whole structure of *Four Hymns*, borrows from the idea of sacred parody as advanced by Southwell in this poem and in others: earthly love is redeemed by its heavenly component, earthly beauty points towards the divine ideal.[65] Yet the two approaches are not the same. Even while recognising the sensuous appeal of earthly beauty, sacred parody sets out to transmute base material, and ultimately to invalidate its original by comparison to the beauties of the Divine. Spenser, on the other hand, uses his fourfold structure to argue for completeness. As in the Proem to Book IV of *The Faerie Queene*, 'looser rimes' (st.1) may be criticised, but love itself is seen as a potential source of religious ennoblement. In his edition of the *Shorter Poems*, Douglas Brooks-Davies has said, '[The universe] may contain opposites, but those opposites are *linked* to each other. For Spenser, illumination is obtained through a careful process of understanding, not by cavalier and arrogant rejection' (p. 321). Yet before one uses arrogant rejection as a flail for Southwell, it is as well to reflect on the different conditions in which the two poets were writing: conditions which would have determined the formal devices they employed. To Southwell, writing primarily to fulfil missionary goals, soteriological urgency and clarity of meaning had to take precedence over Spenser's leisurely marriage of opposites.[66]

If Southwell did stimulate Spenser into a reassessment of his ideas on religious verse, then it was a remarkably successful interpolation into one of the most carefully planned literary careers of the Renaissance: a career which aimed to Protestantise previous Virgilian and other models of the poet's mission.[67] The reasons for Spenser's turn from courtly to contemplative poetry have, over the years, called forth much scholarly debate.[68] Renaissance literary theorists agreed that the hymn was a major genre, and it is, of course, highly possible that it did fit in with Spenser's career plans; in a Renaissance poet's reflective maturity, love-lyrics transmuted naturally into hymns. But in the literary context of the time he was writing, Spenser must also have been concerned to define Protestant poetic virtue against such public Catholic condemnations as Southwell's. Even while they complete the publications list on Spenser's *curriculum vitae*, the *Four Hymns* have a reactive quality. But perhaps Spenser need not have feared the competition, since, for at least one contemporary poet, Spenser's name was so strongly associated with religious poetry that his poetic persona was appropriated to validate even a genre in which he had not written, and which Southwell had pioneered. The anonymous author of *Marie Magdalens Lamentations, For the Losse of Her Master Jesus* (1601) writes in the preface:

> If you will deigne with favour to peruse
> Maries memoriall of her sad lament,
> Exciting Collin in his graver Muse,
> To tell the manner of her hearts repent:
> My gaine is great, my guerdon granted is,
> Let Maries plaints plead pardon for amisse.   (f.A4b)

One needs to pause on the pastoral name 'Collin', which in poetry of this date usually refers to Spenser's *alter ego* Colin Clout.[69] In lamentation, conclusions are often voiced by a commentator on the main text, allowing the weeping figure to weep on, and thus enhancing its exemplary value.[70] Here, Mary Magdalen's voice is claimed for the lamentations which comprise the main body of the text, and Colin's for the summary and exhortation at the end: a position where the poetic persona traditionally intrudes, since it implies authorship. As in the present case, it can have a disingenuous effect: this poem is not a long-undiscovered work of Spenser's. But it claims the best-respected English writer of religious verse as a character within the fiction, using the privileges of the pastoral academy; and in so doing, it erases another pastor, the poet who was primarily responsible for bringing religious lamentation back into fashion.

THE CALL TO REPENTANCE

Southwell's writing drove at least one other author to rethink his professional career. But in contradistinction to Spenser, Thomas Lodge was moved to a *via negativa* similar to Southwell's own. Lodge was a Catholic convert, whose conversion seems to have been secret and prolonged; but on a public level, it culminated in 1596 with his publication of the religious meditation *Prosopopeia*, and a renunciation of his previous writing. Ostensibly inspired by Southwell's *Mary Magdalens Funeral Tears*, first printed in 1591, it may have been inspired by *Saint Peters Complaint* as well, and certainly alludes to 'Peter his apostasie, Marie her losse & misse of Christ'.[71] In the preface, Lodge anticipates a number of objections which are relevant to meditations in both prose and verse, and makes a public recantation of secular writing:

Some there be that will accuse the stile, as to stirring, some the passion, as too vehement. To the first I will be thankfull, if they amend mine errour: to the next I wish more judgment, to examine circumstances. Some (and they too captious) will avowe that Scriptures are misapplied, fathers mistaken, sentences dismembred. Whome I admonish (and that earnestlie) to beware of detraction, for it either sheweth meere ignorance, or mightie envie, for the detracter first of all sheweth himselfe to be void of charitie, and next of all extinguisheth charitie in others ... Briefly, our Lord send a plentifull harvest of teares by this meditation, that the devout heereby may wax more confident, the incredulous beleeving: ... that now at last ... I maye bee ... cleansed from the leprosie of my lewd lines, & beeing washed in the Jordan of grace, imploy my labour to the comfort of the faithfull. (pp. 11–13)

Lodge supplies a case-study of one whose public conversion to Catholicism resulted in a complete change of subject-matter, but his urge to imitate Southwell was not unique. For poets of the generation after Southwell's, *Saint Peters Complaint* must have been a collection which both invited imitation and demanded critical engagement. The fact that George Herbert was influenced by Southwell is, as already mentioned, something of a critical commonplace; influence can imply reworking, but also derivativeness. Herbert's editor F. E. Hutchinson seems to have been the first to point out that two of Herbert's juvenilia, written at the age of sixteen and preserved in Isaac Walton's *Lives of the Poets*, show strong resemblances to Southwell's prefatory lines to *Saint Peters Complaint*. Where Southwell, for instance, writes 'Christes Thorne is sharpe, no head his Garland weares: / Still finest wits are stilling Venus Rose' (*SPC*, Author to Reader, ll. 15–16), and 'Ambitious heades dream you of fortunes pride: / Fill volumes with your forged Goddesse praise. / You fancies drudges, plungd in follies tide: / Devote your fabling wits to lovers layes: ...' (*SPC*, l. 31–4), Herbert begins his first sonnet in very similar vein, perhaps alluding to the martyr's death of his predecessor.

> My God, where is that ancient heat towards thee,
> Wherewith whole showls of Martyrs once did burn,
> Besides their other flames? Doth Poetry
> Wear Venus Livery? only serve her turn?
> Why are not Sonnets made of thee? and layes
> Upon thine Altar burnt? Cannot thy love
> Heighten a spirit to sound out thy praise
> As well as any she? ... (ll. 1–8)

Again, one need not assert that Southwell was the *only* writer who might have influenced the young Herbert to combine verse and virtue; other models could have included not only Spenser and du Bartas, but satirists such as Hall. Yet the dissociation from feminised inspiration militates against the programmes of both Protestant poets, and while it borrows from the tropes of misogynist satire, its linkage with evangelical fervour is extremely Southwellian. A passage such as the sestet of the second sonnet prefigures Herbert's later inventive way with tradition, combining Southwellian renunciation of the muse with a satirical anatomy of woman:

> Why should I Womens eyes for Chrystal take?
> Such poor invention burns in their low mind
> Whose fire is wild, and doth not upward go
> To praise, and on thee, Lord, some Ink bestow.
> Open the bones, and you shall nothing find
> In the best face but filth, when, Lord, in thee
> The beauty lies in the discovery. (ll. 8–14)[72]

As so often with early works – Middleton's *The Wisdom of Solomon Paraphrased* being an example from the last chapter – these sonnets are consciously programmatic: a paradigm of the moral aims appropriate for a poet, which acts also as a career-plan. Southwell, then, can be seen not merely as lending Herbert stylistic models, but as helping to influence Herbert's entire poetic career from its undergraduate beginnings; as far as we know, Herbert hardly wrote any secular verse, Latin or English.

Most Southwell-influenced poets, though, did not get beyond derivative imitations. In the late 1590s and for some time thereafter, a large number of imitations of *Saint Peters Complaint* appeared; and given the fact that Southwell still tends to be seen primarily as a poet for the recusant minority, the character and origin of these deserve consideration. Southwell's own poems continued to be printed in clandestine Catholic editions even after his verse had entered the publishing mainstream, and he was imitated by other Catholic poets who had their texts circulated in manuscript and published by secret presses; but, more conspicuously, he was copied by the authors of long poems written for direct or almost direct publication by the London book trade.[73]

Two have been attributed to Gervase Markham: *The Teares of the Beloved: Or, the Lamentation of Saint John* in 1600, and *Marie Magdalens Lamentations* in 1601.[74] Others may be added, among them W. Broxup's *St Peters Path to the Joys of Heaven* (1598), and Nicholas Breton's two works *Marie Magdalens Love* (1595),[75] and *The Ravisht Soule, and the Blessed Weeper* (1601). The manuscript poem *Davids Harp Tuned Unto Teares*, in thirteen sections with titles like 'Urias complaint', 'Amons passions' and 'Absaloms rebellion', indicates its moralistic versatility, as well as its overlap with genres such as the secular complaint.[76] Samuel Rowland's *The Betraying of Christ* (1598) contains no fewer than three imitations: the title-poem, 'Judas in despaire', and 'Peters Teares at the Cockes crowing'.[77] G. Ellis's *The Lamentation of the Lost Sheepe* (1605) dramatises in Southwellian vein the repentance of an unnamed protagonist who compares himself to Judas and Mary Magdalen. And, though most of these were both written and published within the Protestant mainstream, Richard Verstegan published 'Saint Peeters Comfort' in his *Odes* (1601), and a similar poem occurs in a miscellany published openly but almost certainly taken from a Catholic manuscript, *The Song of Mary the Mother of Christ and the Tears of Christ in the Garden* (1601).[78] Like its poetic progenitor, they demonstrate how lamentation could be a genre equally acceptable to Catholic and to Protestant.

A number of these writers – notably Nicholas Breton and Gervase Markham (if the identification is correct) – have in common a prolific, heterogeneous output and a professional willingness to write to order; and this suggests that publishers were ready to back the trend by commissioning works. The anonymous *Saint Peters Ten Teares* of 1597 is one of the imitations most obviously written to benefit from the fashion.[79] Its frequent false quantities and rhymes may indicate haste; and, though it was not published until two years after *Saint Peters Complaint*, it was first registered at Stationers' Hall in April 1595, only a few weeks after the first edition of Southwell's book. The subsequent delay in getting printed may well have been because it was felt to impinge too much on the earlier poem.[80]

Southwellian pieces tend to be characterised by a combination of two factors: the internalised lament and call to repentance of a figure from the Gospels – St Peter, St Mary Magdalen, St John – together with prefatory material which repeats Southwell's criticism of secular verse and calls for poets instead to write about sacred things. They both reinforce and challenge the common equation of Protestantism with experiential inwardness: reinforce because of their popularity in Protestant England, challenge because the inspiration is Catholic. The answer to this paradox is perhaps to be found in the suggestion that 'the account of Christ's inner struggle given in the Calvinist passions, having detached itself ... from its biblical locus, becomes the exemplary subtext for Calvinist representations of Christian selfhood'.[81] Accounts of the struggle of Peter or Mary Magdalen could also be used for exemplary purposes both by Protestant and by Catholic: even more efficaciously than Christ's temptation in some ways, since they begin from a presumption that the protagonist is sinful.

Catholics could employ these texts for devotional purposes against the background of a late-medieval heritage of affective meditation, supplemented by a Counter-Reformation spirituality imported from the Continent: and in time nearer home, since the Capuchin monks within Henrietta Maria's entourage – five of them English – influenced courtly spirituality in the 1630s among Catholics and others, and had a tradition of writings emphasizing the gift of tears.[82] But Protestants could utilise the genre only if these twin backgrounds were downplayed, and this downplaying was made possible by the amount of time which had elapsed between the break with Rome and the 1590s. In that time there had arisen a distinctive Protestant internality which, though its rationale for the call to repentance would have been different, nevertheless had many similarities to that of the Catholic. Continental meditative treatises, both Catholic and Protestant, were used by English Protestants,[83] and Protestant dissociation from Catholic devotional traditions was at most times more rhetorical than actual. There was little in medieval spirituality comparable to the Stabat Mater and the Sorrowful Mysteries of the rosary, but describing the sufferings of Peter, John or Mary Magdalen by the Cross; so to that extent prayers by these figures would not have been suggestive of prayers to them. In the agonised narratives that Southwell gives Peter and Mary Magdalen, their sainthood is implied only by the fullness of their surrender or the context of future biblical events which the reader supplies: nothing that a Protestant could not have accepted. But it was the consciousness of sin that, above all, made Peter and Mary Magdalen acceptable to Protestants as well as Catholics, where Mary would not have been.[84]

Peter's betrayal of Christ, in Southwell's models such as Luigi Tansillo's *Lagrime di San Pietro*, has been seen as a typological acknowledgement by Catholic writers of pre-Counter-Reformation papal corruption. Though this is almost certainly one of the readings that Southwell intends, it is quite possible to read *Saint Peters Complaint* without realizing its presence.[85] For the Protestant, the generalised message of man's betrayal of Christ through sin would have been the dominant one. The case of Mary Magdalen has been complicated – at least for the twentieth century – by the highly eroticised longing for Christ which so often accompanies her imagined presence, and upon which critics have so obsessively commented.[86] Yet this is to some extent an imaginary problem: in the literary context of the soul's experience of grace, Mary Magdalen's Christ-centred swoons and ardours were directed towards the highest possible object, and so employed the language of love more legitimately than the same emotions directed towards another human creature. This is not incompatible with Protestantism, and the later inter-denominational popularity of emblem books like *Pia Desideria* shows how amorous commonplaces could be actively exploited. But even while it stimulated the genre of lamentation, Protestant piety in England had not tended to encourage it: personal complaints for sin like Catherine Parr's *The Lamentacion of a Sinner* (1547), voiced not by a biblical or allegorical figure but by the poet as repentant exemplar, are more characteristic of the genre in England before the mid-1590s. Here, as elsewhere, a preference for secular verse over questionable kinds of religious verse was an unintended consequence of anti-Catholic polemic.

These are the gaps that Southwellian prefaces challenge with their pleas for poets to address religious themes, whether those prefaces are Southwell's own or written by imitators. Sometimes separate from the main body of the poem and sometimes comprising the poem's first few stanzas, they can be astonishingly schematic – even in metrical terms, there seems to be little deviation from the Southwellian six-line stanza[87] – and it would be merely iterative to quote them all. But a late example now attributed to John Ford, *Christes Bloodie Sweat* (1613), is a good – if shameless – illustration of this type of copying. Summoned to 'the Arke, and mercie-seat of merrit' (l. 27), the poet is ordered to mend his ways:

> Thou (quoth it) that hast spent thy best of dayes,
> In [thriftlesse] rimes (sweete baytes to poyson Youth)
> Led with the wanton hopes of laude and praise,
> Vaine shadowes of delight, seales of untruth,
> Now I impose new taskes uppon thy Pen,
> To shew my sorrowes to the eyes of Men.   (ll. 31–6)

Christ then speaks, in terms which rewrite the governing metaphor, conclusion and rhetorical patterning of the first stanza of *Saint Peters Complaint*:

> Here then unclaspe the burthen of my woes,
> My woes, distil'd into a streame of teares,
> My teares, begetting sighes, which sighes disclose
> A rocke of torment, which affliction beares:
> My griefes, teares, sighes, the rocke, seas, windes unfain'd
> Whence shipwrackt soules, the Land of safety gayn'd.   (ll. 43–8)[88]

Comments made in a recent edition of the poem illustrate, only too well, how Southwell's influence tends to be underplayed and distorted. The editors point out that Southwell wrote a poem with the title 'Christs bloody sweat', but the copying from *Saint Peters Complaint* is not mentioned at all.[89]

But it would be wrong to portray these poems as an entirely derivative body of work. Genuine debates can be entered into, even while Southwell's main conclusions are being echoed, and his stanzaic form copied. In an imitation of Southwell published by a Catholic secret press, *Saint Marie Magdalens Conversion* [1603–4], the anonymous author 'I.C.' shifts the focus of Southwell's moral theory. The theme becomes not the renunciation of love-poetry, but the internalisation of epic and tragedy. The subject becomes, precisely, the subject: and a female subject, as if to stress still further the division between public and private emotion, or external and internal. The muse, renounced by Southwell, comes back into play as one of Mary Magdalen's other roles.

> Of Helens rape, and Troyes beseiged Towne,
> Of Troylus faith, and Cressids falsitie,
> Of Rychards stratagems for the english crowne,
> Of Tarquins lust, and lucrece chastitie,
> Of these, of none of these my muse nowe treates,
> Of greater conquests, warres, and loves she speakes,
> A womans conquest of her one affects,
> A womans warre with her selfe-appetite,
> A womans love, breeding such effects,
> As th'age before nor since nere brought to light... (f.A3a)[90]

Changing its metre, the topos made its way into Catholic ballads. That on the martyrdom of Nicholas Garlick, Robert Ludlam and Richard Sympson begins:

> May *Corridon* discourse of Kings,
> may peevish *Pan* be bolde
> To pen and painte, in paper things,
> that should be graven in golde.
> No, no, yet we, sometimes do see,
> for want of better muse;
> *Silvanus* may admitted be,
> *Apollos* place to use.
> Then though that I a sinner am,
> by me it may be pen'd.
> Of GARLIKS gaine, of LUDLAMS fame,
> and SIMPSONS happie end.[91]

What is initially a surprising beginning to a martyr-ballad turns out to be a deft overturning of convention. Even while distancing itself from the tradition of using shepherds to voice political criticism, it exploits that tradition to declare two things: the nobility of the subject, and the rusticity of the narrator when such high themes are being considered. It is an apology, in both senses, for writing in the low genre of ballad. If the writer was a priest – as is certainly probable – the pastoral narrator refers to *pastor*, with the kind of exemplary force that Spenser gave the pun for Protestants in *The Shepherd's Calendar*.

Imitations of Southwell's prose also occurred. Thomas Nashe's *Christs Teares Over Jerusalem* (1593) and Thomas Lodge's *Prosopopeia, Containing the Tears of the Holy Marie* (1596) and Nicholas Breton's *Mary Magdalens Love* (1595) have long been recognised as deriving directly or obliquely from *Marie Magdalens Funeral Teares* (1st edn. 1591).[92] In *A New Letter of Notable Contents* (1593), which Gabriel Harvey wrote to his publisher John Wolfe, this is even used as a reproach of Nashe:

> Now he hath a little mused upon the Funerall Teares of Mary Magdalen; and is egged-on to try the supplenesse of his Patheticall veine, in weeping the compassionatest and divinest Teares, that ever heavenly Eye rained upon Earth; Jesu, what a new worke of Supererogation have they atcheived? (f.B3a)[93]

Nashe and Harvey were long-standing antagonists, and the occasion of Harvey's letter was Nashe's preface to *Christs Teares Over Jerusalem*, in which he had expressed contrition for his treatment of Harvey. The letter compares genuine values with sham, and links the poetry of tears with crocodile insincerity.[94]

Though overt reference to Southwell often entered literary discourse through exploitation of the negative connotations of his writing, another literary quarrel shows that Southwell was not without his Protestant defenders. Among much else, Joseph Hall's *Virgidemiarum* satirises the poetry of tears. Borrowing the Sybil's admonition from Book VI of the Aeneid, *Procul, o procul este, profani* (l. 258), he begins one poem with a parody of the familiar Southwellian division between sacred and secular.

> Hence ye profane: mell not with holy things
> That Sion muse from Palestina brings.
> Parnassus is transform'd to Sion hill,
> And Iu'ry-palmes[95] her steep ascents done fill.
> Now good Saint Peter weeps pure Helicon,
> And both the Maries make a Musick mone ...
> Ye Sion Muses shall by my deare will,
> For this your zeale, and far-admired skill,
> Be straight transported from Jerusalem,
> Unto the holy house of Betleem.   (I viii, ll. 1–6, 13–16)

Hall's heavily ironic praise ends in an anti-Catholic sneer. Southwell and his imitators are flown to the Virgin's house at Loreto, notorious for its own ability to fly through the air.[96] Hall's governing idea that satire is the only moral kind of poetry is both a deliberate paradox and a declaration of world-weariness, but it may include the implication that overtly religious verse is tainted by popery: a deliberately selective criticism, since Hall writes of Spenser earlier in the poem 'But let no rebell Satyre dare traduce / Th'eternall Legends of Thy Faery Muse' (1 iv, ll. 21–2).[97] This was certainly the impression that John Marston had. His collection *Certaine Satyres* (1598) includes a 'Reactio' which systematically refutes Hall's poem, and presents an apologia for a wide range of religious verse. Inviting 'Granta's white Nymphs' to come and watch Hall railing 'Gainst Peters teares, and Maries moving moane', he urges Hall in turn to extend his condemnation further still.[98]

> At Bartas sweet Semaines, raile impudent
> At Hopkins, Sternhold, and the Scottish King,
> At all Translators that doe strive to bring
> That stranger language to our vulgar tongue,
> Spett in thy poyson theyr faire acts among.
> Ding them all downe from faire Jerusalem,
> And mew them up in thy deserved Bedlem.   (ll. 40–6)

Marston goes on to put words into Hall's mouth:

> Shall Painims honor, their vile falsed gods
> With sprightly wits? and shall not we by ods
> Farre, farre, more strive with wits best quintessence
> To adore that sacred ever-living Essence? ...
> *No, Poesie not fit for such an action,*
> *It is defild with superstition*:
> *It honord* Baule, *therefore polute, polute,*
> *Unfit for such a sacred institute.*
> So have I heard an Heritick maintaine
> The Church unholy, where Jehovas Name
> Is now ador'd: because he surely knowes
> Some-times it was defil'd with Popish showes. (ll. 47–50, 59–66)

Marston's simile of the heretic refusing to worship in a church once used by Catholics is ostensibly an illustration, in reality the nub of the argument. As his editor points out, Hall nowhere actually says that poetry is polluted because it was used to celebrate pagan gods; but Baal-worship could denote both pagan and Christian idolatry, and these lines pick up on Hall's implication that overtly religious poetry is written by English papists. While not advocating Catholic practices himself, Marston widens the debate to point out that poetry also forms a part of pagan and infidel worship, and that it is the duty of true believers not to shun the medium but to utilise it for the best ends. Directing attention away from the Catholic provenance of the religious poetry in question, he provides a rationale for exploiting it.

But among those conscious of Catholic connotations, Hall's attitude was perhaps more usual. One set of manuscript verses from the early seventeenth century shows another Protestant poet linking the poetry of tears with Catholic devotional practice for purposes of condemnation. The title of 'ye Second pt of ye Ladies lamentation for ye death of her beloved Lord' seems designed both to evoke and to rebuff a Catholic interpretation. The suggestions of the Stabat Mater are obvious, even though the dead man wept over by the lady seems to be a lover and not a son; but they are explicitly disavowed.[99] The speaker in the first half declares 'Yet for his death I shed such store / That now mine eyes can weepe no more', but she is reproved in Part 2 of the poem:

> Have you never [th]e Scripture reade
> That countermaundes to morne for deade
> Did Marie for her dearest sonne
> With yell controule what God hath done
> No no she knew(?) to gods decree
> Both men & all thinges subject bee.

The woman continues to lament 'As though to god or saintes she cryed', but this does not hinder the moralistic conclusion:

> For by [th]e waie you must learne this
> The spirite of comforte quenched is
> As soone by carnall sorrowinge
> As lust, selfe love, or other sinne
> Therfore looke up & cheere thy harte
> & w[i]t[h] this sinne have thou no p[ar]te.

John Davies of Hereford's *The Holy Roode* (1609) is patently an imitation of *Saint Peters Complaint*, but it too embodies a critique of tears-poetry: differently slanted from that above, and less easy to categorise religiously. As so often, external evidence of Davies's religious sympathies may be an insufficient guide; though he was described as a Catholic around 1611, and taxed as one in 1615, this does not necessarily help to interpret a poem published earlier.[100] Passages in it, aided by a shift from Southwell's first-person narration to an omniscient, admonitory poetic voice, seem positively designed to suggest comparisons between Gospel and Renaissance betrayals of Christ: consistent with a Protestant stance, but not necessarily incompatible with Catholicism, since *Saint Peters Complaint* has sometimes been read – like its Continental models – as a regretful Catholic admission of papal corruption.[101]

> Soule-wracking Rocke, (Faiths Rocke of ruine) Peter,
> Art thou for Christ his Church a fit foundation,
> That in Faith, from Faith, sans Faith art a fleeter?
> Tends thy faiths fleeting to Faiths confirmation?
> If that stand fast, that hath so false a Ground,
> It most miraculous must needs be found! (f.B4a)

Davies implies that Peter, so far from being an automatic model for all Christian repentance, could hardly do less than bewail his uniquely terrible sin: 'Weepe Peter weepe, for fowle is thine offence, / Wash it with Teares springing from Penitence' (f.B4b). But in the end, Peter only weeps when Christ's eyes are turned on him: an imaginative variation to the Southwellian prototype, downplaying the human role in repentance and foregrounding that of the divine in a manner perfectly consistent with orthodox Reformed theology.

These two examples underline the paradoxical position of the poetry of tears. Pious and popular genres, Catholic and mainstream, had used tears as part of their affective repertoire before Southwell, and continued to do so independently of him. The penitential psalms were rendered into metre by both Protestant and Catholic,[102] and the efficacy of tears was also stressed in the type of moralistic verse which overlapped with popular devotional matter, written by Thomas Churchyard and others. Going even beyond conventional exhortations to repentance in fast-day sermons and those for other penitential occasions, tears could be deliberately elicited by preachers; yet the association of tearful devotion with popery sometimes meant that when mainstream preachers were reclaiming it for Protestants, they needed to spell out the fact. Writing in 1631, John Lesly lamented 'the Raritie or rather Nullitie of Orthodoxe Tractats in this Argument', citing as predecessors 'Two onely Popish Discourses, the one of Bellarmine, the other of Bessaeus'.[103] On the secular side, madrigalists and metaphysical poets incorporated tears into their love-lyrics, and the genre of complaint would have been unthinkable without literary lamentation. But the cult of the penitent was an important part of the Counter-Reformation aesthetic, and tears-literature was sufficiently associated with popery to make anti-Catholic criticism stick.

REPENTANCE, CONVERSION AND AUTOBIOGRAPHY

Tears-literature called to repentance, repentance was the necessary prelude to conversion, and though conversion was potentially a part of spiritual life for any Christian, it often necessitated changing doctrinal allegiance. Ecstatic repentant weeping was frequently experienced by converts, including those changing from Protestantism to Catholicism; on reading Robert Persons's *Christian Directory*, Thomas Poulton claimed that 'a marvellous light broke in upon me. I shed floods of tears for many days.'[104] The rest of this chapter argues that Southwell's most important heirs were two poetic converts to Catholicism, William Alabaster and Richard Crashaw. Both, I believe, utilised the tropes of tears-literature in full awareness of this implication; and for both, it therefore makes sense to read their tears-poetry as – to some extent – spiritual autobiography.

As already commented, it is difficult to establish other than by internal evidence how much Southwell was read among poets. One poet, William Alabaster, comes from the very classes where proof is lacking. Though he converted to Catholicism in 1597, his subsequent apostasy might seem to necessitate stretching the boundaries of how religious allegiance is defined; but the poetry that survives is only from the time of his conversion. Unusually, we have first-hand evidence of how it was composed. Alabaster's extraordinary manuscript autobiography, preserved at the English College in Rome and hardly noticed by literary historians, yields evidence of how the poems were written at various periods during his conversion.[105]

As early as Michaelmas 1596, Alabaster delivered an exhortation 'with much more fervour and feeling of Devotion, and with a greater tendernes of harte towardes Christes Crosse and Passion, then it seemed to the hearers that the protestantes were wont to feele or utter'.[106] He compares his state after his conversion to that of the spiritual drunkenness of the Apostles: 'for so woulde any man have judged also of me, if he had seene and heard me riding alone [to Cambridge] with such variety of countenance and action, as now weeping, now singing, now speaking to God, now to myself' (p. 120).

And by his own testimony, it was in this state that he wrote his verses:

And when the floodes of teares came downe uppon me, I could do no lesse but open the gates to let them pass: I was wont often to walke into the feildes alone, and being then summer ther I wold sett me downe in certaine corne feldes, where I could not be seene nor heard of others and here passe the tyme in conferences between almightie God and my soule, sometimes with internall meditation uniting my will to god, somtimes [forming] and contryving the same meditations into verses of love and affection, as it were hidinge of the fyer under ashes, with the reding wherof I might afterwardes kyndle my devotion at new tyme againe. And I did sett some tymes a certayne strife and wager between my present affections and future, my present persuadinge to devise sonnets now and so full of fyerie love and flaminge ardour towardes Christ, that then it sholde serve for a patterne and sample for the tyme to come, to shew upp and conserve my hart in devotion, but on the contrarie parte my future devotions made offer so to maintaine <and> increase the heate and vigour of love and affection in me, that when I should come afterwardes to reed over my former sonnets I might wonder rather at the coaldnes of them then gather heate by them; And thes verses and sonnetes I made not only for my owne solace, and conforte, but to stir up others also that shold reed them to soew estimation of that which I felt in my self... (pp. 122–3)

When imprisoned by the Cambridge authorities, he delivered to his friends – either orally or on paper – 'certaine sonnets of devotion' which he had made in prison (p. 133). At other times, he spent a considerable period studying controversial theology in preparation for public disputes – which, in fact, were never allowed to take place – and probably beginning to write his sonnets. Unsurprisingly, therefore, many of these combine explicitly controversial points with meditational fervour.

The appearance of *Saint Peters Complaint* would have been timely for Alabaster. In the absence of positive evidence, all one can say is that it would have been surprising if he had not known Southwell's writings. 'Upon Christ's Saying to Mary "Why Weepest Thou?"', Sonnet 21 in the collected edition of Alabaster's works, has a Southwellian basis in the Gospels and certainly seems designed as an endorsement of Southwell's weeping protagonists. But it principally reads as an apologia directed towards those whose devotional practices are different, demanding of its readers why their devotion is not as all-consuming as Mary Magdalen's and how they can justify *not* weeping.

> I weep two deaths with one tears to lament:
> Christ, my soul's life, out of my heart is fled,
> My soul, my heart's life, from me vanished,
> With Christ my soul, and with my soul, life went.
> I weep, yet weeping brings mere discontent,
> For as Christ's presence my tears seasoned,
> When through my tears his love I clearer read,
> So now his loss through them doth more augment.

It is not Christ, but an unseen interlocutor of Protestant tendencies that prompts the indignant response in the opening of the unfinished Sonnet 18:

> My tears are of no vulgar kind I know,
> For elemental water strives with fire,
> But my tears do with flame of love conspire...
> Therefore I rather think that they do flow
> From those spiritual springs that are entire
> Unto the lamps of heaven...

In a sonnet such as number seventy-one, 'The difference 'twixt compunction and cold devotion in beholding the passion of our Saviour', the subject is actually the inferiority of Protestant devotional techniques:

> When without tears I look on Christ, I see
> Only a story of some passion,
> Which any common eye may wonder on;
> But if I look through tears Christ smiles on me.
> Yea, there I see myself, and from that tree
> He bendeth down to my devotion,
> And from his side the blood doth spin,[107] whereon
> My heart, my mouth, mine eyes still sucking be;
> Like as in optick works, one thing appears
> In open gaze, in closer otherwise.

In context, the phrase 'optick works' appears to be referring to the magnifying quality of tears; their lens-like roundness and transparency, convex against the eye, has this effect in reality but even more so in metaphor.[108] Details of crucial soteriological importance become visible, 'Christ smiles on me'; and the liquid instability of tears makes possible the narrative of a moving picture, 'He bendeth down to my devotion'. Alabaster's concluding quatrain makes even more explicit the superior perception that tears bring; they are spectacles, without which mortals cannot see.

> Then since tears see the best, I ask in tears,
> Lord, either thaw mine eyes to tears, or freeze
> My tears to eyes, or let my heart tears bleed,
> Or bring where eyes, nor tears, nor blood shall need.

In Sonnet 15, the vapours drawn from the earth towards the sun become 'purest argument' condensing into clouds of devotional weeping: 'And these conceits, digest by thoughts' retire, /Are turned into april showers of tears.' Sonnet 70, 'A morning meditation (2)', goes even further in identifying tears with thought.

> The sun begins upon my heart to shine,
> Now let a cloud of thoughts in order train
> As dewy spangles wont, and entertain
> In many drops his Passion divine,
> That on them, as a rainbow, may recline
> The white of innocence, the black of pain,
> The blue of stripes, the yellow of disdain,
> And purple which his blood doth well resign;
> And let these thousand thoughts pour on mine eyes
> A thousand tears as glasses to behold him,
> And thousand tears, thousand sweet words devise
> Upon my lips as pictures to unfold him:
> So shall reflect three rainbows from one sun,
> Thoughts, tears, and words, yet acting all in one.[109]

As the Passion necessarily inspires both ineffable joy and ineffable sorrow, so the happy intuition of God's presence in the sun, or Son, prompts the poet consciously to summon a 'cloud of thoughts' that will stimulate weeping. The prismatic prettiness of 'dewy spangles' is subverted by Alabaster's interpretation of what the colours mean – innocence, pain, disdain and stripes, and the sanguinary purple of dishonoured kingship – but the reader is still invited to luxuriate in the visual glory; indeed, it is by this means that the glory is vindicated. The sestet explains how these thoughts are identifiable both with tears and with words, since all are means to increase devotion. But between thoughts and words, there comes the necessary mediation of tears; and tears, like Christ, are placed second in the Trinity of the last couplet.

The sonnet relies on visual allure and on allusion to the visual, but both are made instructional. The function of tears is to act as spectacles to behold Christ, and that of words to refer back to pictures in which Christ may be expounded. A controversial point is being made: secondary to Alabaster's devotional purpose, but nonetheless important. The Church of England included a number of theologians who manifested extreme unease with the visual element of worship, extending the notion of idolatry even to the imaging power of the mind.[110] The effect of Alabaster's conclusion is to deny any inherent difference between word and picture as an appropriate medium for understanding: a more holistic statement than any English Protestant poet could have made in the 1590s.

Tears are prescribed as a devotional necessity, but also as a sign of personal repentance. This is explored in Alabaster's sequence of penitential poems;[111] indeed, number sixteen makes the distinction between their various functions, then draws them together.

> Three sorts of tears do from mine eyes distrain:
> The first are bitter, of compunction,
> The second brinish, of compassion,
> The third are sweet, which from devoutness rain ...
> Never did contraries so well agree,
> For the one without the other will not be.

Sonnet 12 sets the tone of the sequence as Alabaster demands that his tears become autonomous agents, running to Christ again and again to ask His forgiveness: 'One after other run for my soul's sake, / And strive you one the other to overtake, / Until you come before his heavenly throne.' His eyes partake in the same rhetoric of detachment in Sonnet 13: 'Then you two characters, drawn from my head, / Pour out a shower of tears upon my bed ...' Tears are ontologically versatile, dissolving and blending in a flow of illustration the devotional intercourse between man and God: they are messengers, rain, fountains, pearls, the sea, and (in Sonnet 17) amber-drops making a treasure out of something loathsome:

> In tears draw forth thyself until there be
> Sufficient for thee to be enrolled;
> For as the scorned fly which is surprised
> Within the drops of amber that doth fall,
> By this his tomb beginneth to be prized ...

Lastly, in a commonplace to which these associations add force, tears are the means by which Alabaster writes. In Sonnet 24, 'The Sponge', he declares: 'My tongue shall be my pen, mine eyes shall rain / Tears for my ink, the place where I was cured / Shall be my book'.

CRASHAW AND THE ENGLISH CATHOLIC BAROQUE

As Alabaster's autobiography shows, it is not simply a conceit to refer to tears as an authorial medium where both poetry and tears are elicited from the poet by a conversion-experience.[112] Both tears and poetry are *symptoms* of conversion, and notions of authorial creativity become secondary to those of religious fulfilment and evangelism. Southwell uses the poetry of tears as part of his ministry, writing speeches for biblical figures to achieve an outwardly-directed means of exhortation; but Alabaster, the convert, positions the anonymous repentant self inside the text rather than beyond it. These two ways of exploiting the genre, both essentially didactic, are both present in the work of the last poet to be considered in this chapter, Richard Crashaw: like Alabaster, a convert-poet whose conversion pervades much of his verse.

It has been usual, and rightly so, for recent critics to point out that most of Crashaw's religious poetry was written while he was still a conforming member of the Church of England; but, as will be argued below, conversion-experiences could take many forms, and take up periods of time both inordinately long and remarkably short. Alabaster's was sudden, Crashaw's less so, Lodge's – to recapitulate a previous example – may have taken over a decade; and since one tends only to know about the doctrinal explorations of those who finally became Catholic, it may have been an imaginative impetus to other writers in a manner that is now irrecoverable. Even when a conversion took place near-instantaneously, the convert was assenting to a previously learnt body of theological discourse; and where a conversion was more considered, it involved processes of deliberate exploration, such as reading, praying, dispute, discussion, and – inevitably – a certain degree of imaginative role-playing which could be vented in poetry. There is no contradiction in recognising that Crashaw could assume a Catholic mentality while still a conformist, and it is helpful to approach his poetry in this light.

Precedents from Southwell and Alabaster may both be invoked in a poem considered to be one of Crashaw's most characteristic, 'The Weeper'. It describes the exemplary ecstatic penitence of Mary Magdalen, the type of the ideal convert – in itself a Southwellian link, since Southwell wrote two poems about her. One passage begins with a banishment of the profane echoing the opening line to

Southwell's 'Loves garden grief', 'Vaine loves avaunt, infamous is your pleasure, / Your joy deceit' (ll. 1–2):

> Vain loves avant! bold hands forbear!
> The lamb hath dipp't his white foot here.
> And now where're he strayes,
> Among the Galilean mountaines,
> Or more unwellcome wayes,
> He's follow'd by two faithfull fountaines;
> Two walking baths; two weeping motions;
> Portable, & compendious oceans. (st. XVIII, XIX)[113]

Crashaw's emphasis, and Alabaster's, is primarily on tears as a signifier of devotion and charitable love, defined against the perceived Protestant rigidity of justification by faith alone; but while Alabaster's use of the trope is consciously transgressive, Crashaw could employ it in the context of the Laudian pieties of his time. 'On a Treatise of Charity', written by another Cambridge man, Richard Crashaw, for Robert Shelford's *Five Pious and Learned Discourses* (1635), is a Laudian advocacy of charity as a neglected virtue.[114]

> No more the hypocrite shall th'upright be
> Because he's stiffe, and will confesse no knee: ...
> Nor on Gods Altar cast two scorching eyes
> Bak't in hot scorn, for a burnt sacrifice:
> But (for a Lambe) thy tame and tender heart
> New struck by love, still trembling on his dart;
> Or (for two Turtle doves) it shall suffice
> To bring a paire of meek and humble eyes.
> This shall from hence-forth be the masculine theme
> Pulpits and pennes shall sweat in; to redeem
> Vertue to action ... (ll. 39–40, 43–51)

The Laudian agenda is obvious in the definition of charity as a necessary addition to faith rather than an inevitable consequence of it, and the poem's polemical slant is enhanced by a conclusion that argues it is uncharitable to call the Pope Antichrist: 'In summe, no longer shall our people hope, / To be a true Protestant, 's but to hate the Pope' (l. 68).[115] Two connected equations will occur again often in Crashaw's writing: of tears with genuine religious fervour, and of piety with pliability.

Like Alabaster's, Crashaw's religious poems explore ecstatic and tearful surrender, and, as with Alabaster, this is almost certainly connected to the process of conversion. For many years it has been taboo for academic historians to speak of Anglo-Catholicism before the nineteenth century, and the epithet is certainly anachronistic. In re-adopting ceremonial Laudians perceived the Church of England as a rival to Rome, and were quite capable of utilising fierce anti-Catholic polemic where tactically appropriate. Nevertheless, it is hard to observe those who – like Crashaw – started off Laudians and ended up Catholics, and not conclude that Laudianism contained within itself the potential for experimentation with Rome. Within theological writing daringly Catholic doctrines might be promulgated, but always within the disciplinary confines of the Church of England; within poetry, however, experimentation was more generically permissible and less likely to be censured. It may be noted that Crashaw wrote no theological works during his time at Cambridge.

But the sense of edging up to Rome seems authentically present in the Latin poem that Crashaw wrote to solicit money for the rebuilding of Peterhouse chapel; it includes a dangerous joke, written in full awareness of how charged the name of St Peter was.

> Scis Ipse volucres
> Quae Rota volvat opes; has ergò hîc fige perennis
> Fundamenta Domus Petrensi in Rupe; suámque
> Fortunae sic deme Rotam.[116]

If this seems daring, it was not the most overt pro-papal statement made within Laudian religious verse at this period. The poetic miscellany of the Laudian cleric Alexander Huish also demonstrates that the papacy could be referred to positively by members of the Church of England. Huish's translation of the Latin hymn 'Petrus beatus' includes the lines 'Sure keeper of the fold, Church teacher doctrine sound', and is completely without disavowal.[117] Yet Huish was acknowledged by other high-churchmen as an orthodox member of the English church. His parishioners at Beckington in Somerset petitioned Parliament on account of his liturgical innovations, and he was among the clerics sequestered by Parliament; yet such dignitaries as the Dean of the Chapel Royal, the Dean of Chichester and the Bishop of Bath and Wells were prepared to sign a testimonial in his favour.[118] But it could be a hard equilibrium to maintain. Though Huish himself seems to have stayed a loyal Anglican, his friend and co-translator John Lewgar converted to Rome not long after the two collaborated.[119] Like the wise man who built his house upon the rock, Crashaw's play on the name of his college conflates architectural sturdiness with theological certainty; movement is the implied opposite, yet movement is necessary if one is to attain a position of steadfastness. It is against this background that one is to see the liquidity of Crashaw's religious verse: tears signify conversion and repentance, their flow enacting the ontology of change.

Even in a non-religious poem, 'Upon the Death of a Gentleman', Crashaw conceptualises weeping as poetic fluency.

> Nothing speakes our Griefe so well
> As to speake Nothing, Come then tell
> Thy mind in Teares who e're Thou be,
> That ow'st a Name to misery.
> Eyes are vocall, Teares have Tongues,
> And there be words not made with lungs;
> Sententious showers, ô let them fall,
> Their cadence is Rhetoricall.   (ll. 23–30)

If it had not been for the necessity to prepare for the process of conversion, the rhetorical showers of Crashaw's religious verse might never have broken. Crashaw's translation of Psalm 137 renders verse 6, 'If I do not remember [Jerusalem], let my tongue cleave to the roof of my mouth', as an image of poetic *accidia*; and the whole psalm – a favourite among recusants for its narrative of dispossession, and famously set to music by Byrd – equates weeping with singing and dryness with dumbness.

> Which when I lose, ô may at once my Tongue
> Lose this same busie speaking art
> Unpearcht, her vocall Arteries unstrung,
> No more acquainted with my Heart,
> On my dry pallats roofe to rest
> A wither'd Leafe, an idle Guest.   (v. 4)

This was how Crashaw chose to describe his conversion after it had happened. 'To the noblest and best of Ladyes, the Countess of Denbigh', begins by identifying the liminal position of the near-convert: 'What heav'n-intreated Heart is This? / Stands trembling at the gate of blisse' (ll. 1–2), and enlarges upon it in a prolonged simile. The paradox here is that irresolution is static, conversion fluent.[120]

> What fatall, yet fantastick, bands
> Keep The free Heart from it's own hands!
> So when the year takes cold, we see

> Poor waters their owne prisoners be.
> Fetter'd, & lockt up fast they ly
> In a sad selfe-captivity.
> The' astonisht nymphs their flood's strange fate deplore,
> To see themselves their own severer shore. (ll. 19–26)

CRASHAW CRITICISED

This chapter has aimed to argue that there was a fluent indigenous tradition of tears-literature within England after the Reformation, mainly fostered by Catholic and pro-Catholic writers but with substantial outward seepage; and so it is time to return to the questions with which this chapter began. The invisibility of Southwell and the deracination of Crashaw within English literary history are not separate phenomena, but symbiotic; where one is underemphasized, the other looks alien. Tracing the post-Reformation English tradition of tears-literature is not simply an academic exercise; as long as Crashaw's supposed foreignness continues to render him invisible, it has large canonical implications. Some recent critics have been aware of the falsity of this foreignness. Thomas Healy's biography of Crashaw – with justifiable weariness that it should still be necessary – emphasized the fact that Crashaw composed most of his poems within the Anglican church; a recent bibliography of Crashaw criticism and a volume of essays – both, suggestively, compiled by the same scholar – have attempted a boldly revisionist approach to Crashaw's work.[121]

Yet, so far, they seem to have had less effect on received wisdom than those belonging to an earlier school – though not necessarily writing at an earlier date. In her massive and influential study *Protestant Poetics and the 17th-Century Religious Lyric* (1979) – the very title of which is telling – Barbara Lewalski deliberately left him alone on account of his un-Englishness: 'Crashaw writes out of a very different aesthetics emanating from Trent and the Continental Counter-Reformation, which stresses sensory stimulation and Church ritual (rather than Scripture) as a means to devotion and to mystical transcendence' (p. 12). In this, she concurs with Crashaw's most recent editor, George Walton Williams: 'Richard Crashaw may be considered the most un-English of all the English poets ... he is the leading representative of [the baroque], a style which is fundamentally foreign to the spirit of English poetry.'[122]

It has been the aim of this chapter to demonstrate the exact opposite; and, to do so, it has traced the widespread mainstream acceptance of one Counter-Reformation trope. But among English Catholic poets as well, Crashaw was anything but isolated. Counter-Reformation practitioners of the poetry of tears, Tansillo and Marino, were translated and imitated by them well into the seventeenth century: sometimes in imitation of Crashaw, sometimes independently. Sir Edward Sherburne wrote:

> Fond Muse in vaine thou seekst a mourning dresse:
> Art hath no passion can our greifs expresse ...
> What sing in neat composures, 'whilst I see
> My sacred Lord hang on a cursed Tree?
> Ah better I (as greife my Soule doth fill)
> Into a flood of endlesse Tears distill ...[123]

Catholics perceived it as a devotional lack. In a miscellany belonging to the Collingwood family, a poem on the efficacy of weeping points to its rarity in contemporary England:

> A heart contrite black swanne in these last yeares
> With magdalen are almost none or few
> Who doe with teares our Saviours feet bedew
> Paule may with teares admonishing be founde
> Not sighes but scoffes mongst hearers now doe sownd ...[124]

The longevity of the tradition is illustrated by the work of the mid-seventeenth-century poet Eldred Revett, who may well be punning on the name of a poetic predecessor in 'Marie her ointment':

> Anointed God who was before,
> Mary anoints her Saviour;
> Her Alabaster-box doth shed
> The liquid Narde on's sacred head ...
> What fall's [sic] on his Necks whiter skin
> Is Alabaster'd up again ...
> She then at's feet her-self doth throw
> Descending yet to Heav'n, so;
> When from her eyes she scatters streams
> To pay the custome of those gems ...[125]

Again on the topic of Mary Magdalen, Edward Thimelby equates blood and tears in an entirely Crashavian manner.

> Did my eyes wash thy feet t'intice
> Thy bleeding feet to wash my blood-shott eyes?
> Oh take thy blood and pardon back:

> Restore the teares and sinnes I lost:
> To me hell's dearer for thy sake,
> Then heaven at so deare a cost:
> Though my sight ran astray, is't meet
> My wandring eyes should draw thy weepeing feet?
> And have thees springs forgot to keepe
> Their floodgates ope? What mountain stopps
> Their currents, that they dare not weepe
> With thee? Without thos corrall dropps,
> Thees christall waves can be no sea;
> Without thees perles, that blood no *Erithre*[126] ...
>
> Speke to this hart, my soules Phisician,
> And it will yeeld us waters of Contrition.[127]

Thimelby certainly knew Crashaw, and was to some extent an admirer of his; they were both in the retinue of Cardinal Giovanni Battista Pallotta, and Thimelby wrote a verse-letter praising his colleague.[128] But in the verse-letter which follows this, Thimelby deftly uses this admiration to express his dissociation from the other poet.

> I'm yet a libertin in verse, and write
> Both what the spirit and the flesh indite,
> Nor can be yet our Crashaws convertite.
> Methinkes your misticall poetik straine,
> Does not so sanctify a poet's veine,
> As make divinity itself prophaine.   (p. 40)

Thimelby allows Crashaw to be exempted from his strictures, if not by name – 'Yet still except we prophets, saints, and kings; / Who hears a heaven's voice, of heaven sings' (p. 41) – but his impatience with Crashavian poetic convention is plain. Clearly, Crashaw was enough of an influence both to be copied, and to infuriate some of his copyists to subsequent agonistic dissociation. A few couplets later, Thimelby writes, 'You know temtation once brought me too in, / To faigne a teare or two of Magdalen, / But she, a sinner once, forgave the sin.' Later still, Thimelby uses libertine terms to formulate a critique of another aspect of the English Catholic poetic tradition, turning round Southwell's call to sacred parody by implying that all religious language has been invalidated by double-entendre.

> A rapture, alter, sacrifice, a vowe,
> A relique, extacye, words baudy now,
> Our fathers could for harmeles termes alow.

> But now the very spring of poesy
> Is poysond quite, and who would draigne it dry,
> Must be a better Hollander then I ...
> Had one no poet, but a painter bene
> Of naked truth, weir't not a lesser sinne
> To call it Venus, then a Catherin?
>
> (p. 42)

Thimelby has a small place in literary history as the first of Crashaw's hostile critics, and he anticipates a very usual twentieth-century objection to Crashaw's work. Crashaw, like many other mystics, designedly uses the linguistic commonplaces surrounding sexual surrender as metaphors for religious ecstasy. But students both of sexuality and of religion at this period have been less broad-minded than Crashaw himself: perhaps because, until very recently, interest in one has commonly accompanied a distaste for talking about the other. This has led to a reductionist approach within Crashavian criticism, where his religious ecstasy has been assumed to be totally sexual in origin, albeit veiled with the lies of repression. Inevitably, it has been linked to Crashaw's supposed foreignness. It is hard to know how serious Frank J. Warnke was being when he declared in 1970 that Crashaw was 'a kind of sport in English literary history, an exotic Italian import like pasta or castrati',[129] but those who have been alerted to the phenomenon of othering will not be surprised at the apparently arbitrary introduction of eunuchs here.

Crashaw has been laid on the psychiatrist's couch more than once. Robert Ellrodt's essay in the *Sphere History of Literature* – a volume last revised in 1986 – declared easily that 'Crashaw's ecstatic piety aims at self-annihilation ... an insight into the human heart can hardly be expected from such a poet, but he himself is a case for the psychologist.' The recent bibliography of Crashavian criticism makes it clear how often Crashaw's sexuality has attracted concerned or dismissive comment.[130] Psychoanalytical explanations assume, as so many conventional literary-critical discussions do, the *uniqueness* of Crashaw; this has the effect either of vastly overemphasizing his originality, or of abnormalizing much of medieval spirituality – together with whole tracts of mainstream Counter-Reformation devotional culture across southern Europe and Mexico.[131] Paradoxically, it has been admiration for Donne and Herbert which has contributed to uncertainty about Crashaw's status. Much attention has recently been paid to ways in which literary texts have been used to construct ideals of Britishness, and perhaps the critical gaze should now turn to the ideologies fostered by Anglicanism; certainly, the Church of England's supposed *via media* has been used normatively to damn Crashaw. In 1968, George Williamson called Crashaw's 'excesses in the expression of devotional love' 'offensive to modern taste', and went on with a passage which, though it is largely commenting on Herbert, is still worth quoting in full.

Herbert expresssed this aim of the Laudian church in these words: 'And all this he doth, not as out of necessity, or as putting a holiness in the things, but as desiring to keep the middle way between superstition, and slovenliness, and as following the apostle's two great and admirable rules in things of this nature: the first whereof is, *Let all things be done decently and in order*: the second, *Let all things be done to edification*, I Cor. xiv.' These two rules comprise our duty to God and man: 'the first being for the honour of God, the second for the benefit of our neighbour.' Crashaw was more concerned with the first object, and Herbert with the second.[132]

In the pro-Anglican, anti-Catholic context set out by his earlier comments on Crashaw, Williamson's other dichotomies fall smoothly into place. Herbert distinguishes between seemliness and edification, and God and one's neighbour, but Williamson forces the reader to prioritise one at the expense of the other. Since Crashaw's ritualism has been impugned, this invites the reader to side with Herbert; and in an emphasis that the historical Herbert would not have cared for, Herbert becomes more concerned with edification than seemliness, and more anxious to edify his neighbour than please God.

Despite his pro-Anglican preconceptions, George Williamson puts no confessional cards on the table here. But the early modern English religious lyric had, in the mid-twentieth century, some influential Anglican apologists – one thinks of T. S. Eliot and Helen Gardner – who, because of their Anglicanism, were conscious of standing out against the tide. But while arguing that Christianity was still a valid intellectual position for the literary critic, the terms of their riposte were still essentially humanist: that the intellect and poetical ability of Donne and Herbert helped to validate Anglicanism. Paradoxically, therefore, they came to share with agnostic critical discourse a high regard for the interrogatory subject within religious poetry, or a notion that the fight was the thing. Critics arrived at a consensus that the best poems were those which displayed confrontational demonstrations of the passionate intellect versus the divine, despite the fact that the orthodox Christian resolution was welcomed by some and deprecated by others. The unintended consequence of this was the formation of a kind of Anti-Soppists' Club: the preconception that a dry-eyed spirituality is better, and that the best religious lyrics of the period must display not a childlike sensuousness and vulnerability, but a questing adult intellect grappling with God. This was a terminology that had been around since before the war. Joan Bennett, in 1934, said of Donne's religious poetry that 'profound emotion works upon Donne's intellect not as a narcotic but as a stimulant', and, in the background, one can feel Crashaw evoked as a silent point of comparison. Speaking of Herbert, she privileges his confrontational poems. '[Herbert's] poetry is not the record of quiet saintliness, but of continued wrestling and continued submission; the collar is not easily worn.'[133]

This is, as she suggests, the Herbert of 'The Collar', and the Donne of 'Batter my heart, three person'd God'. In these two frequently anthologised poems, and others read as especially fine and especially typical of the writers, the end comes at exactly the moment of submission to the Divine. Sometimes, as with Herbert's 'So I did sit and eat', the last line is lavishly suggestive of spiritual delights following upon submission: but it is still the end. The selection of these poems privileges a twentieth-century English spirituality of the unsaid, and Crashaw, with cardinal bad taste, begins where Donne and Herbert leave off. But if Crashaw is usually criticised as too extreme for greatness, at other times – astoundingly – his subject-matter is made the sole criterion by which to judge him a minor poet. To quote Crashaw's most recent editor again: 'Crashaw is not a major poet. He shows himself deficient in many respects, but he was a master of the voice which he chose for his own. It is a small voice, and among discriminating critics, few are sympathetic to it. It is the voice of the ecstatic vision, the sensuous transcended and made sublime, the suavity of pain, the long-sought joy of mystical death. It is a voice of confident and unquestioning faith. This voice is a small voice, yet no other English poet has ever sung so well with it.'[134] Out of context, ecstatic visions and the rest seem topics large enough to please, and one would be less surprised if it were judged that Crashaw was not equal to the challenge; yet this is not the criticism. Perhaps these notions of unimportance are responding, most of all, to general critical priorities within English departments of the late 1960s.

Catholic poetics and the Protestant canon

Though most critics within the last few decades would be horrified at the idea, critical discourse on seventeenth-century religious poetry is still highly prone to denominationalist judgements: a variety of feelings, articulated or not, that there are right ways and wrong ways to write devotional poetry within the Christian tradition. The critical history of Crashaw in the twentieth century also reveals, in exaggerated form, a number of culture-bound assumptions about how devotional verse should be read. Both the writing and reading of religious poetry at this date are tricky problems for those from non-Christian religions, for atheists, or for the agnostic majority; but they are no less so for practising Christians, few of whom would translate comfortably into the devotional culture of three or four centuries earlier. The answer, perhaps, is to leave aside aesthetic judgement for the time being and interrogate our literary preferences for what they reveal about denominationalist conditioning, overt or covert. It may be that the radical discomfort that baroque verse produces in a twentieth-century reader is a measure of its success; it pursues the kind of limits-exploration that Foucault has taught us to value, if inspired by ethical reasons opposite to his. But neither selective blindness nor the Protestantised aesthetic will be solved until Crashaw and his predecessors are read, on a far larger scale than hitherto; and until the English Baroque, with all its attendant Catholic implications, becomes as unproblematic a term for literary critics as it is for architectural historians.

But, at the last, a personal note may not be out of keeping for a chapter which has dealt with canon-formation and the Protestantised assumptions of the English common reader. When this chapter was almost written, I read a pair of essays by the clerical scholar Herbert Thurston, published in the Jesuit periodical *The Month* in 1895 – exactly three hundred years after Southwell's execution. The manner of their citation by Southwell's editors, and by the few other bibliographers by whom they had been noticed, had not led me to expect much – at most, a few analogues with contemporary poets.[135] But in their scholarly defence of Southwell's importance, popularity and influence, they are pieces of a scope which, given adequate exposure, might have helped to influence a different canon-formation at a time when English was becoming a university subject. Reading them, I was struck by their anticipation of a number of points which, a century later, I had arrived at independently: and, inevitably, was annoyed that I had wasted so much time re-traversing the same ground. But my own researches had been directed by a consciousness of a gap in critical discourse, and the near-invisibility of Thurston's two pieces is, in itself, part of the shadowed history of post-Reformation Catholic writing in this country. In a mainstream journal they might have helped to dictate orthodoxy; but since they were concealed in a Catholic periodical, literary scholarship has hardly been affected. Perhaps this essay, less innovative but published in the scholarly mainstream, may have slightly better luck.

PART II
Loyalism and exclusion

CHAPTER 3

Catholic loyalism: I. Elizabethan writers

In most parts of Elizabethan and Stuart England, being a Catholic necessitated membership of an alternative community: a recusant nucleus, with a penumbra of those whose allegiances were less sure or less exclusive. But there were exceptions to the rule, and of these, three are especially recurrent as stimuli to the Catholic imaginative writer. First, there was the court. At certain times during the period covered by this study, conspicuously during the queenship of Henrietta Maria, royal households could provide a highly privileged environment for some English Catholics; and even at the height of persecution, Catholic ambassadors had to be catered for. But to set against this comparative visibility, the court displayed a Protestant monarch's personal example to a uniquely intense degree. All England was, in theory, a virtual community of courtiers; and so it is not surprising that to many Catholics outside the court, the monarchical person served as a focus for overt and passionate protestations of loyalty, of a kind that would have been less necessary towards a king or queen of their own faith. But among Catholic courtiers, or courtiers who became Catholics, there could be vehement differences from this model.

Some Catholic converts at court were treated in such a way as to make their personal betrayal of the monarch clear. Toby Mathew, for instance, was urged by the king himself to take the Oath of Allegiance; and as in his case, this could be the prelude to exile, involuntary or self-imposed.[1] Earlier an Elizabethan courtier-poet and convert, Henry Constable, had explored the condition of alienation from Elizabeth in many of his sonnets. His shift from secular to sacred verse – as in so many cases – is concurrent with his conversion, which happened around 1589; and Constable's editor Joan Grundy believes that one of the most important contemporary manuscript-sources for his verse, known as the Todd MS, may have been made by Constable himself to mark a terminus to his period in England. His collection, *Diana*, was published in 1592 after his exile, with the Epistle to the Reader describing the sonnets as having been 'by misfortune left as Orphans': exile, it is suggested, forces not only a physical departure, but a negation of authorship which has to be alleviated by pity and patronage. The conceit was picked up by the bookseller Richard Smyth in an edition of two years later, within a dedicatory sonnet which asks 'her maiesties sacred honorable Maydes', the twofold Charities, to look mercifully upon 'these Orphan Poems'. To introduce them in the Todd MS, another sonneteer lamented Constable's exile in terms of seasonal migration:

> Englands sweete nightingale what frights thee so
> As over sea to make thee take thy flight?[2]
> And there to live with native countryes foe
> And there him with thy heavenly songs delight?
> What did thy sister swallowe thee excite
> With her for wintres dread to flye away?
> Whoe is it then hath wrought this other spite
> That when as she returneth thou shouldst stay?
> As soone as spring begins she cometh ay,
> Returne with her and thow like tidings bring,
> When once men see thee come what will they say?
> Loe now of English poesie comes the spring.

This comprises a series of disingenuous questions. Constable had possible imprisonment to fear, as the last couplet admits: 'Come feare thou not the cage, but loyall be, / And ten to one thy Soveraigne pardons thee.' Constable, the nightingale, is adjured not to fear imprisonment, then metamorphosed back into a man capable of feeling guilt at disloyalty: a metrical answer to Constable's metrical exploration of loyalist preoccupations, which this chapter discusses. For clarity's sake, the titles of the four chapters within this section separate the themes of loyalism and exile; but this sonnet shows how closely the two are linked.

Indispensable as the title of John Bossy's *English Catholic Community* has been to the formulations of historians working on the topic, to think in terms of several English Catholic communities is perhaps most helpful of all. Two types of English Catholic community were to be found overseas: the groups of lay or clerical expatriates which gathered in certain towns or cities on the Continent, sometimes attached to the entourage of an aristocrat; and the monasteries, convents, seminaries and schools which were founded or re-founded on the Continent, not only by the English, but by the Scots and the Irish. This study can address only a small fraction of their richly multilingual literary cultures, but it is one highly relevant to the theme of imaginative polemic. The circumstance of exile had one consummate advantage over living in England, the freedom to be outspoken. This manifested itself less in what was said, than in a greater access to print, and – as in the lengthy texts and elaborate staging of Jesuit drama – greater opportunity for the leisurely elaboration of polemical messages.

Historians have become familiar with the idea that, in late sixteenth-century and early seventeenth-century England, Catholicism was the enemy against which an emergent Protestant nationalism defined itself, and which shaped English allegiances within Europe. Literary critics, too, have studied how this topic made its way into imaginative writing.[3] But absent from these discussions has been a consideration, or even a consciousness, of the other side: how English Catholics' experience of diaspora, combined with the necessity to re-evangelise a nation from overseas, shaped their ideas on nationhood. It is a surprising omission, since the war between Jesuits and Appellants, the group of clerics who wished to appeal to Rome against Jesuitical encroachments of the late 1590s, has long been visible to historians. Running from the end of the sixteenth century and for much of the seventeenth, it split the English clerisy on issues of ecclesiastical government that had an enormous relevance to perceptions of the state and the nation, as well as of the Church. *Inter alia*, this section gestures towards a topic that awaits its real chronicler; and in the meantime, it acts as an anthology of Catholic homesickness and politicised nostalgia. The chapters on exile are thematically organised, but the preceding chapters address reactions to historical events, and so are chronologically arranged; even so, the subject-matter gives it an episodic character which is unavoidable. Scholarly and pamphlet-debates are accretive, their assertions, answers and disagreements dictating the trajectory of a topic in a way that imaginative material cannot match.[4] But though imaginative genres were not the main media in which controversies were conducted, they can be an unmatched guide to response; and, crucially, they remind us that responses to anti-Catholic accusation were often not fierce, but conciliatory.

CATHOLIC LOYALTY: DEFINITIONS AND DISAGREEMENTS

For the greater part of the period covered by this study, disloyalty towards the sovereign was to the Protestant statesman what idolatry was to the Protestant theologian. Both identified papalism as a prime Catholic ill, and more generally, both were comprehensive accusations levelled against Catholics, acting as unifying theories to explain all manifestations of popish perversity and misbehaviour. Both, too, are misrepresentations inspired by the warped generalities of anti-Catholic polemic. Catholics defined idolatry differently from Protestants, but condemned it as heartily; and, because it was extraordinarily difficult to evade the personal obligation of loyalty altogether at this period, not even the Gunpowder Plotters would have considered themselves disloyal. The execution of Mary Stuart provoked some Catholic writers to speak of Elizabeth as if she had forfeited all claim to loyalty, and others argued that the commonwealth had the right to depose a heretical monarch; though taking its bearings from Continental resistance theorists on both sides of the religious divide, this was a position almost solely associated with popery in England up to the eve of the Civil Wars.[5] Both attitudes could arise from a sense that the temporal repercussions of the Catholic faith demanded greater obedience towards ecclesiastical leaders than crowned heads, yet this is an emphasis more characteristic of the clerisy than the laity, and not uniformly the case even among clerics. More strikingly, both betoken a high regard for the *abstract* virtue of loyalty to monarchs, and a conscientious wish to be able to obey them in all things.

Even in highly controversial Catholic texts like *A Conference About the Next Succession* [1595], this rule holds good. Numbering Robert Persons among its authors, this explored justifications for deposing an heretical monarch and – while asserting that the matter could not be determined during the Queen's life – suggested a Spanish successor to Elizabeth, the Infanta Isabella. Loyalty is differently defined and differently directed, but the necessity for it is not questioned.[6] This is not to deny that Catholics sometimes relaxed into subversive talk – Anthony Munday's complaint about anti-monarchical gossip among the seminarists at the English College in Rome was probably better-founded than many of his assertions[7] – nor that English Catholics could engage in actions that went well beyond anything they committed to theory. Persons was not above official conspiracy, and throughout Elizabeth's reign, unofficial groups of Catholic extremists aimed to depose or assassinate her. But, again, their shared aim was to bring about a situation where Catholics could unreservedly be loyal to the monarch, and opposing biblical injunctions could be resolved. The instruction in 1 Peter 2.13–14, 'Submit yourselves to every ordinance of man for the Lord's sake: whether it be to the king, as supreme; or unto governors', could be countered by Acts 5.29, 'We ought to obey God rather than men': yet this was not a mitigation, but a double duty. English Catholic apologia throughout the Tudor and Stuart period is full of a desire to ascertain the occasions on which civic disobedience was necessary, a preoccupation which suggests their enormous conscientious engagement with the problem. Nothing was a more effective determinant of the public behaviour of priests or lay recusants, and, for this reason, it does most of them a disservice to equate Catholicism with subversion: to adapt another frequently-cited text, it was their aim to re-integrate tributes to Caesar with those to God, and most would have hoped that this could be accomplished by the conversion of the reigning monarch. More silently, the pragmatic accommodations of church-papists – hardly acknowledged in Catholic pamphlets except as a prelude to condemnation – might often have included the desire to be seen to be loyal.

This study includes two chapters on Catholic loyalism: the first deals with Elizabeth's reign, the second with the reigns of James I and Charles I, and the difficulties faced by Catholic loyalists during the Civil Wars and Interregnum. Understandably, many previous historical accounts of the Elizabethan Catholics have circled around this question of allegiance.[8] Though there is plenty of work to be done on the later periods, this concentration on Elizabeth's reign is not surprising. The parameters of the debate were set up twelve years into the reign, with Pius V's excommunication of Elizabeth in the papal bull *Regnans in Excelsis* (1570). As Thomas Clancy has pointed out, it was the arrival of the seminary priests a decade later that prompted the need for the bull's practical implications to be seriously explored: most notoriously in the 'Bloody Questions' contrived for Edmund Campion's trial, where the prisoners were compelled to state whether they would support the Crown or the Pope in a variety of hypothetical circumstances, all interpreted to confirm the assumption that the desires of pope and monarch were fundamentally opposed.[9] From Campion's execution onwards, while

Catholics maintained that priests were only suffering for their religion, government officials countered that they were paying the penalty for treason. It was a distinction which had, to the non-sceptical, a dual advantage. While proclaiming the superiority of Elizabeth's disciplinary procedures to Mary I's burnings for heresy, it attempted to justify those procedures to the sizeable number of influential Englishmen who still adhered to the old faith, and the great Catholic powers in Europe.

Catholic priests, therefore, had a need publicly to separate politics and religion where their accusers had conflated them. Many martyr-narratives, so many that it became a self-perpetuating hagiographical trope, recorded how the last words of the condemned included protestations of loyalty to the queen, and some make it clear how this was part of a staged dialectic. At his execution on 2 November 1583, the gentleman John Bodye

> appealed upo[n] his faith w[hi]ch he said was the cawse of his death: But S[i]r Will[ia]m Kingsmell told him he died for high treaso[n] against her Ma[jes]tie wherof he had ben sufficiently convicted in dede (quoth he) I have be[en] sufficiently convicted for I have been condemned trator(?) and yo[u] may make the hearinge of a blessed masse treaso[n] or the sayinge of an Ave Maria, treason But I have comitted no treason although in deed I suffer the punishment dew to treaso[n] ...[10]

The sheriff interjected to point out that the pope had excommunicated Elizabeth, 'and yo[u] foresake her and cleave to him', to which Bodye replied that he acknowledged her his lawful sovereign 'in all temporall cawses and none other':

> yo[u] shall do well the[n] said S[i]r Will[ia]m Kingsmell to satisfie the people in the cawse of your death because otherwise they may be deluded by your faire speeches yo[u] shall understand (quoth he) good people all that I suffer death for not grantinge ... her Ma[jes]tie to be supreme heade in christes church in England w[hi]ch I may not nor will not graunt well the[n] quoth Mr Shriefe aske her Ma[jes]tie forgivenes and the[n] desyre the people to pray for yo[u] In troth (quoth he) I must needs aske her Ma[jes]tie forgivenes for I have offended her many wayes as in usinge unlawfull games ... but in this matter yo[u] shall pardon mee And for the people because they and I ar different in religeon I will not have them pray for me. But I pray god longe to preserve her ... Even queene Elizabeth your queene and mine and I desyre yo[u] to obay none other ...

Alastair Macintyre has observed that when rival conclusions are argued back to rival premises, 'the invocation of one premise against another becomes a matter of pure assertion and counter-assertion', and that the ensuing debates are 'necessarily interminable'.[11] But the Elizabethan authorities could risk Catholic counter-assertion on the scaffold, because the noose put an end to it.

Though the Bloody Questions and the execution of Catholics were uniquely crude attempts to articulate the difference, loyalty is not the same as loyalism. In this period, the Catholic loyalist is traditionally defined as one who sought to reconcile obedience to the reigning monarch with the practice of Catholicism, a balance which tended to necessitate de-emphasizing the power of the papacy. The nature of the claims monarchy could make for itself, and the degree of obedience one could accord to a monarch who was not a co-religionist, were topics which created many-branched rifts in the ranks of English Catholics; and though these rifts were internally generated, governments could and did exploit the stress-points. Michael Questier has recently argued that the wording of the 1606 Oath of Allegiance, which all English Catholics were theoretically obliged to take after the discovery of the Gunpowder Plot, was designed to lay itself open to many different interpretations, and thus encourage internecine conflict.[12] Though this oath affected lay Catholics most directly – most priests did not wish to draw attention to their presence in the kingdom – and despite the fact that it described the papal claim to a deposing power as 'impious and heretical', some priests took it. But well before the Oath of Allegiance, it had become clear that conflicts between monarchical and papal interest had a particular relevance to English Jesuits, unique among the Catholic clerisy in having made vows of obedience to the pope; and both lay and ordained Catholics could find this a good reason to distrust the Jesuit. There is an anti-Jesuit theme to many of the clerical quarrels which arose in the 1580s and 1590s, the most notorious arising in 1598 when the appointment of the archpriest George Blackwell to oversee England's secular clergy gave rise to suspicions that he was a tool of the Jesuits, more open to pro-papal and pro-Spanish policies than ones designed to placate the English monarchy.

Though this chapter is not primarily concerned with tracing the involutions of these quarrels, they occasionally obtruded into Catholic imaginative writing;[13] and they are one reason why, from this period onwards, imaginative protestations of loyalty to the monarch are not all directed wholly towards the Protestant reader. In one text discussed below, Anthony Copley's *A Fig For Fortune*, they are a reproach to Jesuits; but even in non-polemical texts primarily intended for a Catholic audience, certain pre-emptive strategies are visible. In a manuscript at Lille from the archives of the English Benedictine nuns, there survives a fervent but anonymous and undateable piece of rhythmical prose, roughly divided into verses but drawing on the conventions of prayer; written in the persona of a martyr, it disavows suspicions of disloyalty as early as the first verse.[14]

> It is told me I must Dye
> Ignominiously by the hand
> of the Executioner. -
> O Happy News.
> I see myselfe honoured with
> the Livery of Jesus.
> I receive the Judgment of Death
> as an Enemy to Caesar,
> As Designing the Death of my King
> And the depriving him of
> his crowne, his government.
> Whilst in the meantyme
> my Jesus knowes;
> my conscience rejoycing testifies
> that I never yet harboured
> In my heart at any tyme
> so much as one Disloyal thought
> Against my king as sovereign,
> And the conscience
> of my accusers must testifie
> At the last dreadful Judgment,
> to the glory of my God
> and the Justification of truth,
> that I am perfectly Innocent
> of all and every one of the crimes
> Of which they swore me guilty.

But all Catholic and pro-Catholic writers had more need than most to prove their loyalty, and so may have been more inclined to address questions of loyalism than they would have been otherwise. Certainly they figured among the English monarchy's most vehement defenders. Henry Howard, Earl of Northampton, was known to be pro-Catholic all his life and is said to have died a Catholic; yet his *True and Perfect Relation of the Whole Proceedings Against ... Garnet, a Jesuite, and His Confederats* (1606), written to justify the Crown's trial of the Gunpowder Plotters, upheld the freedom and authority of the sovereign, and attacked the papal usurpation of temporal power and the defenders of Catholic resistance. The Venetian ambassador observed that because Howard was considered a Catholic, it gave his writing greater authority.[15] If Howard was indeed a Catholic, he was not alone among his co-religionists in having no difficulty with the idea of separating temporal and spiritual power; later, John Barclay's romance *Argenis* was promoted by the Stuart monarchy to enhance their absolutist claims. Yet when they wrote, such Catholics were well aware of the preconceptions which they were defying. This could result in protestations of loyalty and devotion to the monarch which – until one considers the weight of prejudice they were counteracting – seem hyperbolic even by the standards of the time. Many such texts are dedicated to the monarch, with these protestations most thickly present in the dedicatory apparatus. Often there was little chance that the royal addressee would have seen the text, yet this, in one respect, was not the point – the dedication was an earnest of good faith and a declaration that the author's loyal sentiments could bear scrutiny.[16] They are, too, an affirmation of hierarchy rather than a negation of it. In their articulation of the distance between addresser and addressee, they make few overt claims to greater wisdom than the monarch, yet they exploit to the full the counsellor's privilege of sugared persuasion.

In the two following chapters, which are chronologically arranged, some emphases may seem unfamiliar. This is partly because any map of Catholic writing on loyalism must have different contours from one which plots Protestant loyalism – or what is often the same thing, Protestant writings about Catholic disloyalty. Occasionally – as with the execution of Mary Stuart – Catholic denigrators of Elizabeth, Catholic loyalists and Protestant polemicists were all imaginatively captivated by the same incident, if to different effect. But viewed from the Catholic perspective, the defeat of the Armada in 1588, or the discovery of the Gunpowder Plot in 1605, cease to be landmarks and become embarrassments: sometimes written about from motives of dissociation, mostly ignored. Because loyalists were concerned to stress ecumenical possibilities and reasons for Catholic toleration, the monsters on the map are fewer, yet still oddly recognisable; in the only extended study of Catholic loyalism to date, Arnold Pritchard rightly emphasizes how the myth of the evil Jesuit was as much a Catholic Appellant creation as a Protestant.[17]

A complete map would have to concentrate on non-imaginative genres, because major intellectual contributions to political theory are not, on the whole, couched in the form of poetry, drama or sustained allegory. But the subject-matter of this chapter is something that, by the nature of things, occurs more spasmodically: the use of imaginative genres to advertise the writer's loyalism, or explore conscientious issues pertaining to the topic. Tests of loyalism often depended on the efficacy of detecting potential disloyalty by means of hypothetical cases. As with other controversial questions, answers could be pre-prepared in a manner that would have been particularly useful in oral debate. Catholic notebooks and archives commonly have sheets of questions and answers which could have been used for memorisation as well as reference, and whenever a hypothetical question demanded an answer which was not among those commonly anticipated, educated Catholics would have had access to a number of casuistical authorities from which to synthesize a reply. But they would also have had to undertake acts of imaginative projection, which have obvious implications for fictionality.

MARY STUART: SAINT AND PROVOCATION

Hope stimulated imaginative projection; and for Elizabethan England, no monarch focused Catholic hope more effectively than Mary Stuart. Of the seventeen-year period between her deposition from the Scottish throne and her execution, when she was held captive in England, Michael Lynch has said that she 'became a virtual Catholic icon to the exiled Catholic communities abroad, both Scottish and English'. Long before she became a Catholic martyr, her confessional captivity was held to be exemplary, and pictures of her were commissioned.[18] Most Catholics probably accepted that she was heir to the English throne, though it was crucially important not to articulate the implications of this; prominent loyalist though he was, Thomas Tresham supported the claim in his private writings. Sir Arthur Champernoun, a correspondent of Robert Cecil's, reported meeting a group of gentlemen in the provinces who protested their loyalty to Elizabeth, but were banded together to take action to secure a Catholic successor in the event of her death.[19] It was an equilibrium shared by many. Most Catholics would have had no conscientious difficulty with practical anticipation of Elizabeth's death, many made no secret of hoping for it, and both Allen and Persons supported anti-English initiatives in Europe – but only extremists took independent action against the Queen with the intention of deposing or assassinating her, and placing Mary on the throne.

Some of these conspiracies are well-known – the rising of the Northern Earls in 1569, the Ridolfi Plot of 1571 and the Babington Conspiracy that provoked Elizabeth to order Mary's execution – and in some, Mary was undoubtedly implicated. Yet there were others at which she expressed a grieved surprise that was probably genuine.[20] Among these was the plot concocted by William Parry, which came to light in late 1584.[21] A distinctive feature of this plot was Parry's claim that he had papal approval to assassinate Elizabeth, and Thomas Tresham may have been behind a petition drawn up shortly afterwards which repudiated Parry and all his accomplices, professing fervent loyalty to Elizabeth and denying that the pope or a cardinal could authorise anyone to commit regicide.[22] Another Catholic or pro-Catholic loyalist went further, and expressed his dismay in versified narrative. In the Bodleian there survives a poem in poulter's measure, apparently written shortly after Parry's execution on 2 March 1585, and entitled 'The Seventeenth of November'.[23] The title gives the date of Elizabeth's accession: traditionally a time for anti-Catholic activity,[24] which makes its appropriation by a Catholic author all the more striking. Only Book 2 survives, which begins by an entirely apocryphal episode in Parry's story: perhaps suggested by rumour, but more probably invented to satirise pro-Spanish sympathies among English Jesuits. Lamenting Rome's defeat at the hands of Elizabeth and his own loss of temporal power, the pope conceives the idea of subduing England with the financial backing of Spain;[25] and on a trip to the Spanish court, he points out to Philip II that in the days of Mary I, the Spanish monarchy used to rule Britain.

> They make their moane to you most able for your might
> most readdy for the loue you beare unto the redcrosse knight.
> In their late mistris dayes they held you for their kinge.
> Your absence of your owne accord the chang of rule did bring.
> It was agaynst their vowes a successour to beare
> when you so kynd so catholique in full possession were.
> O take them into grace and winne them for your owne
> that vowe themselues and all is theirs to you their Lord alone.   (f.3b)

Striking a Habsburg pose, his 'chin thrust out w[i]th hanging lipp and look raysd up on hye' (f.3b), Philip confesses some responsibility for England's state, resolves to do what he can and cultivates a few Jesuits. Up to this point, there is hardly anything in the poem which could not have been written by an anti-Catholic author.

But though the writer is so critical of the papacy's claim to temporal power, his pro-Catholic loyalist sympathies become clearer in succeeding passages. He is emphatically anti-Jesuit, describing them as 'fretting wormes of Christendome' (f.10a) who only infuriate a government which has tried to deal kindly with recusants.

> They may not lewdly doe and say they suffer wronge
> Who treason plott must feele ye paines yt therunto belonge.
> Nor will their orders chardge ought lessen their offence.
> w[i]th subjects duty to ye Prince noe Canon may dispence.
> It is no cruelty to use the former lawes
> longe falne asleepe or make moe new on new arysing cause. (f.10a)

Jesuits forsook their country, yet are now trying to stage an aggressive return, with double filial disloyalty to the State: they 'hold it nowe nor sinne nor shame yer Countrys wombe to perce', yet she 'remaynes a mother still most easy, kynd and myld' (f.10a). Finally Jesuit activities overcome her extreme reluctance to take action, and the writer reflects on the dashed hopes of Catholic eirenicists with bitter irony.

> But nowe the State perceaves what she was loth to caste,
> to give such crimes abortive birth she is compelde at laste.
> Yet never man diseasd w[i]th putrifying sore
> that hastened to corrupt the rest of members sound before
> more hardly could be drawne to sawe the rotten part
> then she was brought to prune the boughes yt hazarded the hart ...
> Let others holde their waye to winne and reconcile
> and w[i]th their praiers assist those heads that labour it the while,
> The Pylots of the Churche that knowe what Rocks to shunn,
> and howe to shape the safest course have happely begunn. (ff.11a, 12a)

Parry is selected as the tool of the conspirators, and having insinuated himself into the court,[26] he plots the assassination of Elizabeth. This gives the poet an opportunity to display his ideological dissociation from both Spanish and papal forces.

> He [Parry] reades and reades agayne the Cardinall Comoes letter[27]
> Wherin for this most holy deed the Pope becomes his debter.
> Call you it holynesse by treason to procure

> the fate untymely of a Queene, yt else might longe indure?
> Or were your skarlett hatts not redd enough and deepe
> but in the warme blood of a Prince you let them lye in steepe? (f.15a)

On two occasions Parry fails to nerve himself up to the deed, and so tries a different set of tactics; he seeks out the impecunious noble Edmund Nevell, and persuades him into discontent and revengeful feelings. Nevertheless, Nevell demurs when Parry sets out the plan.

> [Parry] reades him Allens booke[28] wherin to myndes preparde
> ech sentence for a warrant serves & yet ye gallant sparde
> to showe howe weake himself found all those meanes to be.
> He names of all sortes of Divynes yt in this poynt agree:
> then how dispenced from Rome; by whom perswaded to it,
> then after he were knowne in Court how easely thei may doe it.
> But Nevell drives him of as not resolved yet
> W[hi]ch castes poore Parry into rage & many a fearefull fitt. (f.18a)

'Myndes preparde' is a direct quotation from the official account of Parry's trial, and is noticed by the anonymous author of the moral reflections at the end of this tract.

> *D Allens booke redoubled his former conceites, every word was a warrant to a prepared mind.* See how the smoothe words of that Catholique booke are enterpreted and conceived. One spirite occupieth the Catholique reader with the Catholique writer, and therefore can best expound the writers sence in his readers mouth, even to bee a booke fraughte with emphaticall speaches of energeticall perswasion to kill and depose her Majestie, and yet doeth the hypocrite writer, that traitor Catholique, dissemble and protest otherwise. (p. 50)

The alarmed Nevell betrays Parry and Parry is questioned, denying everything even when Nevell says it to his face; but he subsequently confesses in the Tower, pleads guilty and is executed.

> And as he vaynly lived so in a vayne he dyes
> confesseth all the proofes for true but purpose he denyes ...
> The praise be sent to him [i.e. God] w[i]th her the safety rest;
> the comfort dwell amonge us longe, the greife possesse their brest
> that sett his handes on woorke and make it all their joye
> to haste that lamentable day yt bringeth our annoye. (ff.19b, 20a)

Prepared minds, alert to subversive meanings half-concealed by the smooth words of loyalist discourse, would not have belonged only to Catholics at the time of Mary Stuart's own execution in 1587. The horror of many English and Scottish Catholics was echoed by those English Protestants who deplored Mary's religious beliefs, but were alarmed at the precedent for executing a prince that had now been set. Sir John Harington's famous epigram on the topic would have appealed to both persuasions, and its commonness in manuscript probably testifies to a widespread, religiously diverse sympathy for Mary Stuart: appropriately enough, for the work of an author who favoured religious toleration and liked to keep his own confessional allegiance ambiguous.[29]

> When doome of Peeres & Judges fore-appointed,
> By racking lawes beyond all reach of reason,
> Had unto death condemn'd a Queene anointed,
> And found, (oh strange!) without allegeance, treason,
> The Axe that should have done that execution,
> Shunn'd to cut off a head that had been crowned,
> Our hangman lost his wonted resolution,
> To quell a Queene of nobles so renowned.
> Ah, is remorse in hangmen and in steele,
> When Peeres and Judges no remorse can feele?
> Grant Lord, that in this noble Ile, a Queene
> Without a head, may never more be seene.[30]

This is a piece that achieves its effect not by forswearing loyalist tropes, but by exaggerating them. As often with writing that strains at the boundaries of loyalism, great emphasis is placed on the respect due to monarchy itself, and thus to *other* monarchs; the reader is reminded of Mary Stuart's status as an anointed queen, who, arguably, is unable to commit treason against another monarch. Harington calls the judges' decision 'strange', and implies that it was mistaken; without saying that the law was broken, he asserts that it was tortured. The convention of blaming a monarch's subordinates for misgovernment is negated by the very perfunctoriness of its application; as he points out in the first line, the judges at the trial were 'fore-appointed' by the Queen.[31] Though Harington refrains from voicing the conclusion that Elizabeth was wrong to issue the warrant for Mary's execution, he compels the reader to observe his reluctant act of refraining. And, as in the next chapter, admissions of allegiance due to a prince are qualified by the assumptions of gender-hierarchy; the end of the poem can be taken either as a simple plea that the situation should never occur again, or a neatly contemptuous prayer that all female monarchs may henceforward be subdued by a husband.

Harington uses a miraculous formula from martyr-narrative, the axe's supposed reluctance to sever Mary Stuart's neck,[32] to refine his condemnation of the trial itself; but many Catholic writers reversed his priorities, reporting the dubieties of the trial in order to claim Mary as an instant martyr for the faith. Her fall was pamphleted, versified and dramatised across mainland Europe by Frenchmen and other Continental writers, and by exiled Englishmen and Scotsmen, in all major European languages.[33] But though the majority of these writings are hagiographical, many are not. Two Scots authors, Adam Blackwood and George Buchanan, demonstrate that nationality is less of an ideological predictor than the geographical location of a writer. The expatriate Blackwood, based in France, is best-remembered for dubbing Elizabeth a heretical she-wolf in *De Jezebelis Angliae Parricido*, a much-anthologised Latin poem written in the hopes of arousing European indignation and stimulating Henri III to revenge; but Buchanan's writings on the topic, especially *Ane Detectioun of the Duinges of Marie Quene of Scottes* [1571], commissioned by the Scottish government, conclude a process of dissociation that had begun in Scotland when Mary was deposed.[34]

Blackwood's position has analogues in the bitterest of English Catholic accounts of the Reformation, Nicholas Sander's *De Origine ac Progressu Schismatis Anglicani*, and in the more populist polemic of Richard Verstegan; but they should not be taken as speaking for all Catholics. Many Catholics acknowledged Mary as martyr, yet intended no politicised reproach; Robert Southwell was a Jesuit, yet his poem on the execution of Mary, 'Dum morior orior', hardly bears out the association that both Catholics and Protestants often made between Jesuitism and professed disloyalty. The famous line 'Once Mary called, my name now Martyr is', clearly rendered the poem subversive enough for Mary's name to be suppressed in some manuscripts, such as that in Lambeth Palace Library.[35] But this may have been due merely to its subject, not the treatment of the subject. The poem's emphases are heavenly, spiralling around the martyrological paradox that Mary's triumph lies in her death. Mary herself is the speaker, but from a position of immortal objectivity; and this fixed gaze on eternal good has the effect of minimising, even trivialising, the temporal inexpediency of her death to Catholics.

> Alive a Queene, now dead I am a Sainte,
> Once N: calld, my name nowe Martyr is,
> From earthly raigne debarred by restraint,
> In liew whereof I raigne in heavenly blisse. . . .

> A prince by birth, a prisoner by mishappe,
> From Crowne to crosse, from throne to thrall I fell,
> My right my ruthe, my titles wrought my trapp,
> My weale my woe, my worldly heaven my hell.
>
> By death from prisoner to a prince enhaunc'd,
> From Crosse to Crowne, from thrall to throne againe,
> My ruth my right, my trapp my stile advaunc'd,
> From woe to weale, from hell to heavenly raigne. (ll. 13–16, 29–36)

Nor was Mary even necessarily a Catholic heroine. Writing in the 1620s, the anonymous Catholic author of a life of Mary Stuart uses his introduction to deplore what his co-religionists have said. 'I beseech my Reader to beleive that never History was more falsyfied by partial Hereticks ... to decry a poor Princess. it [sic] passed so far; that some Catholicks, either ignorant, or negligent, taking not the pains to read, and examine reasons, have resigned themselves over to an indifferent belief of all the defamatory Libells of the Enemies of our Religion, as if one should creditt the history of Jesus Christ compiled from the relations of the Scribes and Pharisees.'[36]

IN PRAISE OF ELIZABETH: SONNETS, *IMPRESE* AND CATHOLIC MODERATION

One verse-miscellany, compiled by a Catholic, nevertheless includes a complaint voiced by a spectral Mary Stuart, acknowledging her own faults and extolling Elizabeth I's magnanimity.[37] It illustrates a common bias of the historical complaint: though giving a voice to the defeated, it tends to reinforce the status quo by articulating the repentance of erstwhile conspirators. As a natural consequence, the genre overlaps with royal panegyric. The next two writers to be discussed, Henry Constable and Thomas Wright, were Catholics who wrote in genres even more directly assimilable to the praise of Elizabeth: the Petrarchan sonnet, and the versified devices of the Accession Day tilt.

Something of Constable's activity has already been described, and from that, it will be clear that his use of genre needs – against the grain of much current criticism – to be interpreted in autobiographical or, at the very least, autodidactic terms. His editor has said of him: 'His life itself reproduces some of the symmetrical patterns he loved to employ in his verse; in this respect, as in his idealism and his obedience to his two ruling passions, patriotism and religion, it could truly be described as his "best piece of poetrie"'.[38] The Italian sonnet-form which Constable used for all his poems was traditionally employed to marry emotional contradictions: beauty and cruelty, love and death, freezing and burning, reward and punishment. Where the female addressee was Elizabeth, or, later, the Queen of Heaven, Constable used its conventions to express how his loyalties were divided between the Catholic religion and the demands of the Crown.

As a Catholic convert, and a lifelong ecumenist on both sides of the religious divide, Constable had ample opportunity to internalise the techniques and contradictions of mediation. During his early career, he acted as spokesman in Paris for the Protestant cause, and wrote a controversial pamphlet, circulated in manuscript, answering the argument that Elizabeth's Catholic subjects owed her no allegiance since her excommunication.[39] His best-known pamphlet is a plea for toleration of the Huguenots, *Examen Pacifique de la Doctrine des Huguenots*, published anonymously in Paris in 1589 and later translated into English as *The Catholike Moderator*.[40] Constable also converted in 1589, though he only fully admitted it in 1591. After his conversion Constable was involved in attempts to convert James I to Catholicism, supporting his claims to the succession in a pamphlet attacking Robert Persons, but the surviving verse only yields evidence on two fronts: Constable's perception of how a poet should conduct himself towards princes in general, and poetic emotion directed towards the person of Elizabeth. Constable's most sustained period of acting as courtier seems to have been during the period 1588–9, directly – and perhaps not coincidentally – before his conversion. His degree of real intimacy with Elizabeth must remain speculative, though he is referred to as 'Favorito de la Regina' in a contemporary account of his conversion; it is not in doubt that he used his favourite genre, the sonnet, to express and encode the dubieties of Catholic loyalism in love-poetry.

Though Constable's sonnets to Elizabeth and the Virgin Mary have attracted most critical attention in a loyalist context, they are not the only instances of his blending of the two, judicious both in conflation and in separation. Another example, more enigmatic than any of these, is his sonnet to Mary Talbot, Countess of Shrewsbury.

> Playnlie I write because I will write true
> If ever Marie but the Virgin were
> Meete in the realme of heaven a crowne to beare
> I as my creed believe that it is yow.
> And soe the world this Ile and age shall rue
> The bloud and fire was shed and kindled heere
> When woemen of youre name the croune did beare
> And youre high worth not crownd with honour due (ll. 1–8)

This is, perhaps, one of the most disingenuous beginnings ever given to a sonnet. Constable might have been writing as truthfully as he claims, and his homage to the Countess of Shrewsbury is unambiguous, just as a compliment needs to be; yet the scrupulous double-entendre invites the reader to speculate on Constable's own confessional sympathies, without ultimately making it clear what they are. The line 'I as my creed believe that it is yow' authenticates his admiration for the Countess; but, gratuitously raising the question of Constable's creed, it redirects the reader to the unresolved theological crux in the previous lines. The doctrine of the Assumption and Coronation of the Virgin was traditional rather than biblical, and though most Protestants would have agreed with Catholics that the Virgin Mary was 'meete' to wear a crown in heaven, most too – especially pre-Laud – would have denied that she did so already.[41] The Countess was herself a Catholic, and part of the compliment is that the poem can be read in a pro-Catholic light; yet Constable himself may not have been writing as a Catholic, and may have deliberately directed the poem towards an audience larger than merely his addressee.[42]

The lines praise Mary Talbot and leave open the possibility of many different levels of admiration for the Virgin; but the two are, audaciously, pitted against two earthly monarchs. In lines 5–8, Constable regrets the upsurges of militant Protestantism during the reigns of Mary I in England and Mary Stuart in Scotland; and the reference to fire goes further, strongly suggesting that he believes the Marian martyrdoms should never have happened. Mary Talbot, he suggests, deserves a crown more than the two queens in whose reign the atrocities were committed, who have brought the sacred name of Mary into disrepute. Both queens, for different reasons, could certainly have been disapproved of by Elizabethan Catholic loyalists – Mary Stuart had allowed herself to be associated with plots against Elizabeth, while Mary I had married Philip of Spain[43] – but all the same, these very critical references deflect the reader's attention away from the suspicions of pro-Catholicism aroused by the first quatrain. The ending of the sonnet does not resolve matters: with the term 'sacred' it elaborates the initial comparison between Mary Talbot and the Virgin, and it opposes Mary Talbot's incandescent gaze to the cruel burnings inflicted by Mary I, but as far as his own religious sympathies go, Constable becomes no more explicit. One is meant to take more seriously than usual the religious language so ubiquitous in sonnets, but the reader is left to determine who God's foes are, and who are to be identified as His own people.

> But god which meant for rebell fayth and sin
> His foes to punish and his owne to trye
> Would not youre sacred name imploy therein
> For good and bad he would should yow adore
> Which never any burnt but with youre eye
> And maketh them yow punish love yow more (ll. 9–14)

This merging of earthly and heavenly queens continues in the Constable's sonnets on the Virgin Mary; but many of those in the group of four sonnets headed 'To our blessed Lady' are not intended to suggest hyperdulia so much as admonition to monarchs. As Constable commented on his exile – again to the Countess, in a letter written around the end of 1591 – he would 'live contented w[i]th how little soever I shall have' if he could never get permission to return to England, 'serving no other mistress but god Allmighty, who I know will love me if I love him, & in whose company I can be when I will';[44] a conventional shift from love to religion which contains a wholly autobiographical bitterness. In his holy sonnets, the perfection of the Virgin is used as a reproach: not to mankind, nor to women in general, but specifically to queens. In one sonnet, he issues the general injunction 'Cease then, O Queenes who earthly crownes do weare / to glory in the pompe of worldly thynges' (p. 185, ll. 9–10). Elsewhere, he uses Mary's queenship to accuse himself of an overweening love for earthly monarchs; as Grundy points out, this could also refer to Constable's lack of preferment by James VI of Scotland and Henri IV of France, but Elizabeth remains the monarch primarily suggested.[45]

> Sovereigne of Queenes: If vayne Ambition move
> my hart to seeke an earthly prynces grace:
> shewe me thy sonne in his imperiall place,
> whose servants reigne, our kynges & queenes above. (ll. 1–4)

The brief shift into the conventions of love-poetry in the next quatrain, and the equally sudden repudiation of them, demand to be read as a formal means of expressing first Constable's welcome into the circle of Elizabeth's admirers, then his banishment from it on becoming a Catholic; Constable was effectively exiled from England until Elizabeth's death, one of the reasons why he was anxious to conciliate James. The love-language which Elizabeth encouraged from her admirers is transferred to another object, the Virgin Mary; and the fact of its being a transference rather than a conflation is the most definitively Catholic note of the poem, since Catholics must have disliked the vocabulary of hyperdulia when employed for Elizabeth.[46]

> And if alluryng passions I doe prove,
> by pleasyng sighes: shewe me thy lovely face:
> whose beames the Angells beuty do deface:
> and even inflame the Seraphins with love.   (ll. 5–8)

Constable concludes by a repeated affirmation of his loyalty to God and the Virgin, which overrules the disloyalty to the Crown assumed by Protestants to be implicit in Catholicism – and, within the poem, in the Catholic practice of referring to the two in nearly-equal terms. The tact of the sestet is in portraying earthly ambition, and earthly love, as training for that to be found in the heavenly court. Without that justification, it would be vain; with it, and only because of it, the English court is acceptable.

> So by Ambition I shall humble bee:
> when in the presence of the highest kynge
> I serve all his, that he may honour mee.
> And love, my hart to chaste desyres shall brynge,
> when fayrest Queene lookes on me from her throne
> and jealous byddes me love but her alone.   (ll. 9–14)

The end of this sonnet is picked up in the beginning of the next, where Mary's perfections diminish all other aspirants to her crown.

> Why should I any love O queene but thee?
> if favour past a thankfull love should breede?
> thy wombe dyd beare, thy brest my saviour feede;
> and thow dyddest never cease to succour me.   (ll. 1–4)

Constable is unusual among Catholic loyalists in barbing his praise of Elizabeth. At the other, pietistic extreme stands an individual whom Constable may well have known: Thomas Wright, a secular priest who was part of the Earl of Essex's entourage in the mid-1590s, and in 1595 also emblematist to him for the Accession Day Tilt.[47] Much has already been written about these occasions, held on 17 November during Elizabeth's reign, during which courtiers jousted for the Queen's favour. The allegorical playlets which accompanied entries into the ring, and the emblematic *imprese* born by the knights, both invite decoding; and new historicists have found them a perfect means of illustrating how the Elizabethan court manipulated emblematics and mythological allusion for political ends. They were often used to allegorise internecine rivalry at court, yet, because of the nature of the Accession Day, these quarrels were subsumed into an expression of unity. To quote Roy Strong, they were part of 'a great national festival ... a day on which the imperial cause triumphed over the papal'.[48] Of all occasions, they seem the least likely to have been open to Catholic contribution; but in the year 1595, this nearly happened. Among the papers of the Earl of Essex's friend Anthony Bacon are a number of copies of designs for *imprese*, dated that year and endorsed as originating from Wright.[49]

Wright was, admittedly, already conspicuous for his loyalism.[50] Through the early 1590s he had consistently disagreed with the pro-Spanish policies of the Society of Jesus, and had written a tract insisting that English Catholics should pursue a constant policy of submission to the Crown and opposition to all forms of outside domination, papal or not. Just before his trip to England in June 1595 he broke with the Society and entered the country as a secular priest under the guardianship of the Earl of Essex. It was a very public, totally unprecedented way of joining the English mission, and it indicates how the missioners' usual means of entering England had acquired connotations of disloyalty to the Crown. Essex would have been an obvious protector, since he was known to favour toleration towards Catholic loyalists and had previously supported a number of individual Catholics. His political sympathy for them found a response in a number of cultural pointers:[51] it has been argued, for instance, that there is an association between the madrigal, practised by a number of Catholic composers, and the rises and falls of Essex's reputation.[52]

Paul Hammer has commented that Essex's secretaries 'employed not only their scribal skills, but also their erudition and their literary talents ... to advance Essex's interests', and this can be extended to the Earl's clients; there were several reasons why Essex's protection of Catholics like Wright was not entirely disinterested. During his period in Essex's entourage, Wright is known to have supplied his protector with anti-Spanish intelligence; and Essex's exploitation of Wright's emblematic gifts argues, at least, the projected idea of a mutually beneficial relationship. Essex gained a new iconography of royal servitude, while Wright was seen to be engaged upon a task that spoke well for the pro-monarchical fidelity of English Catholics; and given the capacity of the *impresa* to conceal a double meaning, Essex's trust argues that he believed Wright would incorporate no elements of subversive papalism into his designs.

As scholars have increasingly come to recognise, Essex's jousting was no frivolity but a crucial part of his political career;[53] and Wright's designs seem to have been attended to in Essex's circle generally. The *imprese* survive in multiple copies of three texts, two of which seem to have been written before the Accession Day Tilt, and the other afterwards as a commentary on it.[54] Of these texts, the first has Essex as addressee. A picture of the world is used to praise his person, wisdom and 'martiall facts' in France, Flanders and Lisbon; and another of an eagle suggests his ability to soar above the 'Dartes & boultes' shot by those envious of his glorious fortune. Other devices suggest courses of future action: for instance, a rainbow's connotations of peace are employed to suggest that Essex might usefully act as peacemaker for both England and Europe. The verse refers to Britain's old enemy Spain, but also gives a snapshot of the Wars of Religion as they were in late 1595, when France's declaration of war against Spain had been published and Spain was considering an invasion of northern France.

> Iberus[55] force w[i]th Albio[n] doth contend:
> Religions haughtie ensignes are displaide
> The furious frenche will scarce to peace descend
> when shall a fatall league w[i]th all be maid?[56]
> Ah peace, & truce unfained we shall see
> yf they would know thy noble curtesye.[57]

The second set of Wright's *imprese* are headed as addressed to Elizabeth, and they may be simply a set of commendatory emblems addressed directly to her by Wright. But given the date of their endorsement they seem much more likely to be a form of indirect address to the Queen: in other words, Wright's suggestions for *imprese* to be borne by Essex at the Accession Day tilts. They consist of directions for a picture with a motto and a verse of explanation, both of which are in Latin, and there are eleven in all:[58] (1) a lioness with one of her paws lifted above her head, with an eagle flying nearby, captioned *Accedit no[n] laedit (*He approaches and does not harm); (2) sunbeams passing through a hollow glass directed towards England, captioned *Feci faciam* (I have done, I may do); (3) a dolphin in a golden bridle and crowned with a rose-garland, captioned *Dominaris utrique* (You may rule by both means); (4) the Zodiac-signs Leo and Virgo accompanied by fruitful vines, olive trees and a sheaf of corn, captioned with astrological signs and *Elizabeth Deus saturitatis* (Elizabeth, god of plenty);[59] (5) a loadstone being hammered on an anvil, captioned *Ut fortior appareat* (Thus it may show itself stronger); (6) a broken hourglass, and a scythe almost broken, with a glory above, captioned *Frangendo fabricas* (In breaking you make); (7) sunbeams passing through a glass and beating on a lily, captioned *Candor illaesus* (Unharmed purity); (8) a sundial with sunbeams beating on it, captioned *Mutatur mane[n]s* (It changes, staying the same); (9) a lion[60] tearing apart a masked wolf with one paw and cradling a baby in the other, captioned *Uterq[ue] utriq[ue]* (Either to either); (10) a chariot containing three crowns and three sceptres, drawn by a lion, a mermaid, a hart and a unicorn, and captioned *Quis cursus securior?* (What journey is more secure?); and (11), a buffalo frightened by a red rose and an elephant frightened by a lily, captioned *Omnia virtus* or *Utrinq[ue] pavor* (Virtue is everything; fear in both cases).

These *imprese* may have been undertaken at Essex's suggestion, or they may have been unsolicited, simply a means of winning favour with his protector. But the fact of their quasi-official preservation in the Bacon papers, and the number of copies that survive, suggest that they were read and seriously considered for the day. Though Essex could have born only one *impresa*,[61] eleven alternative *imprese* equalled eleven possible political identities for the following year. The act of choice was replete with significance, since it announced Essex's priorities to the public audience at the tilts; but these multiple copies suggest that even those *imprese* that were eventually discarded were first shown round Essex's coterie and copied; and this in turn may indicate that some kind of communal decision was sought on Essex's strategies of self-presentation. The running-order of the *imprese* may have been significant, but easier to quantify are the significance of individual images and the cumulative effect of iterated ones. Several images recur – the royal lion, and the sunbeams of Divine regard. Several concepts, notably purity, are given a number of different iconographical realizations: the burning-glass, the Virgin of the zodiac. Some of these convey general moral messages, the tone of which is usually evident from the mottoes quoted above; others, like the chariot able to travel by land, by sea and through poison and traps, represent Elizabeth's imperial omnipotence.[62] But some are more particularised. It was a period when Essex was out of favour, and it is not surprising that some images, like the shattered hourglass and the loadstone on the anvil, seem intended to convey his ability to serve Elizabeth despite past trials.

Yet others have a topical flavour. The hovering eagle in the first device is intended to designate the Habsburg threat of England's continued skirmishes with Spain, specifically the eviction of Spanish troops from their last foothold on the shores opposite England at the start of 1595;[63] it is warded off by England's majestic lioness, and the explanation reads *Hesperiae moles accedit*[64] *ad Albion oras / Tangere vix poterit, laedere qui poterit?*[65] (The trouble of Spain approaches the shores of Albion; he was hardly able to touch them, so who could harm them?) Other comments on foreign policy are included, of a kind which seem to go beyond simple flattery and verge on the programmatic. The bridled dolphin crowned with roses implies that England is heir to territory within France, and the explanation reads

> The dolphin is lord of the sea,[66]
> no other is faster than him.
> Rosy garlands discipline the land.
> England is the power; under obligation to her
> are the French kingdoms, the island of Ireland, the vast ocean.[67]

In the context of the time, this appears to be a large concession on Essex's part; the various attempts in the autumn of 1595 to make Elizabeth resume military support for the French were frustrated by Elizabeth's determination to reclaim Calais for England in return, a project which Essex himself tried and failed to alter. This verse emphasizes Elizabeth's *responsibility* towards France; but if it represents Essex's own thoughts rather than Wright's, it is certainly a change of direction. Perhaps the implications of heirship in the figure of the dolphin are a suggestion that though England is owed Calais, there need be no hurry in pressing the claim; or perhaps, in the context of an extravagant poetic assertion that the surrounding lands and wide seas should all pay homage to Elizabeth, England's particular claims on Calais are intended to seem as grandly fictional as the rest.[68]

The inspiration of all these ideas must remain speculative. Perhaps they originated with hopeful suggestions of Wright's, or perhaps they were arrived at after discussion with Essex or his advisors, revealing more about their current priorities than Wright's own. But either way, Wright would have had a personal interest in their conception and circulation. First and most obviously, these *imprese* are extravagantly patriotic and pro-monarchical; though the sentiments are ostensibly Essex's, the cause of Catholic loyalism would have benefited from Wright's being recognised as the author. There is no need to go beyond this and try to extract subversive Catholic meanings from the texts; the whole intention of Wright's career was to demonstrate that Catholicism did not necessarily accompany subversion.

But a large puzzle remains: a considerable amount is known about Essex's eventual presentation at the 1595 Accession Day tilts, and none of it suggests that Wright's *imprese* were used. Essex appeared as a knight poised between Love and Self-Love, with the ambassadors of Self-Love – a hermit, a soldier and a secretary – trying unsuccessfully to woo him. Essex's squire spurns them, and dedicates his master to a life of service to the Queen. Like some of Wright's *imprese*, this allegorises Essex's absence from royal favour; a marginal note to the speeches, directed to Essex, stressed how it was 'the Queen's unkind dealing which may persuade you to self love'. But though each of the three characters embodied qualities associated with the earl, the unsympathetic character of the secretary was designed to suggest Essex's supreme rival, Robert Cecil; unlike Wright's *imprese*, the emphasis of the piece is internal, domestic and factional.[69] It is hard to see how the two could have been combined; and, indeed, they probably were not. A large quantity of evidence, far more than usual for such events, has enabled scholars to reconstruct the running-order of the presentation; and no *imprese* are so much as mentioned.

Possibly Essex regarded his return to favour as so important that wider concerns had to yield to it; possibly some of Essex's advisors distrusted Wright and sponsored this allegory in order to supplant Wright's own.[70] But another explanation seems more powerful than either of these. The third of November had seen Essex's acute temporary embarrassment at being the dedicatee of a book printed abroad on the subject of the succession: the notorious *Conference About the Next Succession to the Crown of England*, already referred to in this chapter.[71] Elizabeth forgave Essex almost instantly, but the sheer length and insistence of this theatrical vow to the Queen suggests his continued nervousness. This may explain why Wright's emblems were not included; the *Conference* could only have exacerbated gossip about Essex's crypto-popery, and this might have made him reluctant to endorse even a Catholic loyalist in a public manner.[72] But this does not diminish the interest of Wright's accomplishment; and, of course, he may also have been involved in the presentation that finally took place.[73]

Either way, Elizabeth was extremely unimpressed by the eventual production. Rowland White records how at the end she swept off to bed, saying 'that if she had thought their had bene so moch said of her, she wold not have bene their that Night'.[74] This must have delighted Cecil's faction;[75] and it may have been soon after the event, as a riposte to them, that Wright wrote a third, parodic set of *imprese*, conceived as a pasquinade and aimed at Robert Cecil. They comprise two texts, the *imprese* themselves and the separate, versified explanations. Cecil is portrayed as an indolent ass, a bloodthirsty owl and a poisonous scorpion embracing Essex's bee, all with connotations of misgovernment: the ass, for instance, eats up a rope of straw as fast as a maiden – Elizabeth – weaves it, with the rhyme

> The careful wenche bothe night and day
> Dothe labour to conserve
> Hir Kingedom, but this lazie Asse
> Dothe make it all to sterve.[76]

The identification is clinched by the ending: 'And so pasquin who had raved all this in a trans awoke & wished he could change his heles fearing they would not serve to ru[n]ne away not daring tary for ye pretending upright Secretary his pas[s]port for post horses.'[77] This alludes to the point in Essex's entertainment where a postboy rode in on a worn-out horse with a packet of letters, which he passed to the Secretary and the Secretary to Essex; the message is that no minion of Essex's can hope for aid from Cecil.[78] Wright himself had no cause to be friendly to Cecil, since earlier in the year Cecil had challenged Wright's intelligence on Spanish activities; but more generally, the pasquinade's concern for the safety of the kingdom would have had the effect of stressing Wright's own unimpeachable loyalism. If Cecil himself knew about it, this would certainly help to explain his later imprisonment of Wright after Essex's final fall from favour.[79] This is the last evidence of Wright's emblematic activity that survives, and may denote the period of Wright's greatest ascendancy in Essex's favour. His fortunes ebbed as Essex's did, and Essex became less and less able to help him. But, even when thrown into jail at Cecil's behest in the late 1590s, Wright continued to furnish Essex with foreign intelligence; perhaps, too, he may have supplied him with more *imprese*.

ALLEGORY AND PETITION: LOYALIST WRITING, 1595–1603

For reasons other than the Tilt, 1595 was a significant year in the chronicles of Catholic loyalism. Wisbech Castle, which had been used as a prison for prominent Catholics since 1579, has given its name to a series of skirmishes known as the Wisbech Stirs. Firstly in 1587, and most divisively in 1594–5, the Stirs anticipated a feud between regular and secular clergy which was to continue, in various metamorphoses, well into the seventeenth century. The matters of immediate controversy were various. In 1598, the appointment of George Blackwell as archpriest to oversee the secular priests in England offended those priests, since he was felt to be too pro-Jesuit; while the controversy over Richard Smith, who took up the succeeding office of Vicar Apostolic in 1625, stemmed largely from the unwillingness of the regular clergy to be funded *via* the archdeaconry he had appointed, rather than by direct patron-client arrangements. But the common factor to all these quarrels – apart from loquacious pamphlet-feuding – is the fear that administrative power would become the monopoly of one side or the other, through the mis-apportionment of ecclesiastical authority. Nearly as common – among the secular clergy, at least – was hostile myth-making about Jesuits. Sometimes fairly and sometimes not, Jesuits tended to be identified with Spanish interests, and with a concern to uphold the Pope's temporal power. As the natural counter-balance to this polemical identification, Catholic authors of anti-Jesuit propaganda made a point of stressing their own loyalty to the Crown.

Among lay supporters of the Appellants, few were more outspoken than Anthony Copley.[80] Like both Constable and Wright, Copley expresses his Catholic loyalism by praising Elizabeth, but he goes further than they do in hinting at the claims and possible consequences of loyalty. His versified allegory *A Fig For Fortune* (1596) is a barely concealed plea for Catholic toleration, couched in terms of hyperbolic praise, with an argument at once elaborate and transparent. An 'Elizian out-cast' (f.A4a) ranges through the desert of affliction on his jade Melancholy and encounters a number of characters. First comes Cato's ghost, the spirit of despair, who nearly persuades him to suicide; then the spirit of Revenge exhorts him towards treason; but finally he is mounted on the steed of Good Desire and brought to Mount Sion. He is catechised by the hermit Catechrysius and enters the Temple of Peace; but while the Sionites are all worshipping, Doblessa – or Fortune – tries unsuccessfully to besiege them.

Running through the piece is the common pun on 'Elizabeth' and 'Elysium', which Jeffrey Kemp has described as expressing 'England's surprising potentiality'.[81] Here, its use is almost literalistic: not quite a paradise for pagans, but certainly one for those not of the true faith. Its delights and its limitations are both made clear, as the Elizian finds when he tries to penetrate Mount Sion: 'The Temple gates were fower and this was it / Which none but Europe-spirits might admit'. The porter has orders 't'admit in no Elizian' (p. 64) until Catechrysius argues the case. But if admission is temporary deracination, the Elizian is full of pious hopes for a remedy. During the general thanksgiving for deliverance, the Grace of God hovers over the congregation like a virgin, showering down roses, and the Elizian thinks that this must be Elizabeth herself.

> And still I call'd upon Elizas name
> Thinking those Roses hers, that figure hers,
> Untill such time as Catechrysius came
> And pointing me unto his faithfull teares
> (Teares of the zeale he bare t'Elizas name)
> He told me No; she was an Esterne Dame.

The poem ends with the Elizian making his way back 'Sollicited with an especiall importune / Of home-ward zeale, and of Elizas name, / Wherto I bend, and say; God blesse the same' (p. 74, *vere* 84).

Near the beginning, Cato's despairing ghost confides to the protagonist:

> Whilom I was a man of Romes rejoyce
> Whiles happy Fortune my estate uppropped:
> But once when Caesar over-topped all,
> Then (loe) this mid-night shape did me befall. (p. 2)

The midnight shape is to be read as any English Catholic who places papal claims before monarchical. Given that Copley was fervently anti-Jesuit, the portrait may be intended to cast a particular slur on them; but it could be applied to any exile or hard-line recusant with no respect for the Crown. The association of Cato with stoicism is particularly pointed, and indicates how Copley pulled no punches when dealing with his fellow-Catholics; like other persecuted groups, English Catholics derived comfort from the stoic ideal of personal integrity preserved in the midst of trouble.[82] The fact that the character is a personification of despair points to Copley's belief that all attempts to restore Catholicism by defying the monarchy are futile; using an argument akin to Donne's in *Pseudo-Martyr* (1610), Copley is implying that a martyr who dies in defiance of the monarchy is nothing more than a suicide. The ghost's patriotism is admitted, but vividly shown to be mistaken.

> Yet for my Countrey is a part of me,
> And it is all subjected to disgrace,
> Loe, that's my serpentine obscuritie
> For which I spight, and spit on Caesar's face ... (p. 3)

Later in the poem, Catechrysius equates disloyalty and suicide by referring to Cato's action as 'Treason to God' (p. 29). Revenge, the next evil spirit, is an outward-looking intensification of similar traits, and Copley's borrowings from anti-Jesuit rhetoric become correspondingly clearer; Jesuits were frequently accused of being masters of equivocation and disguise, and the protagonist is advised to imitate the chameleon in 'polliticke dissimulation / Of contrarie language' (p. 16). But as if to compensate, Copley's vision of glory includes a number of points characteristic of anti-Protestant polemic. It emphasizes the spiritual power of the papacy – the temple of Sion is placed on a 'Rock in shining glorie' (p. 21) – and Catechrysius is seized by a mystical rapture while praying before a crucifix, which he addresses as 'the image of our Lord' and 'The true Character of his sufferance' (p. 50).

A Fig For Fortune was published in 1596, the same year as the second edition of the first three books of Spenser's *Faerie Queene*, and the first edition of Books IV–VI. The central idea of the knightly quest, and the knight's several detentions by representatives of spiritual darkness, was a medieval allegorical topos which Spenser had resurrected for Book I of his epic, and Copley's poem engages, in turn, in a topical Catholic reworking of Spenser's last four cantos: by specific allusion, and to a greater extent by narrative reminiscence. Just as the Red Cross Knight falls into the company of Despair in Canto 9, Copley's protagonist encounters Cato's ghost and the spirit of revenge. Moving to Spenser's Canto 10, Copley adopts his original's progression from the topics of repentance and contemplation to a description of the heavenly Jerusalem; but though Copley's Mount Sion begs comparison with Spenser's Cleopolis, or London, it is – as pointed out above – clearly not situated in England. Copley's use of Spenser's Cantos 11 and 12, which tell of the fight with the beast and the victory celebrations, gives the best clue to his anti-conformist polemical intentions. The beast's allegorical name Doblessa points the reader towards Duessa, the personification of popish falsity in *The Faerie Queene*, and lifted from earlier cantos in Book I. This begs the question of whom a Duessa-figure might represent in a Catholic poem. Described as having 'no Altar, nor no Sacrament / No Ceremonie, nor Oblation' (p. 70), she is clearly Protestant; but, further, she is to be identified with the Church of England, whose fortune is in the ascendant as the established religion in Elizium. This is especially clear in passages like the following, where Copley satirises the Church of England's partial and inane retention of vestments and ceremonial. During the Zionites' Christmas worship, Doblessa comes bearing an olive-branch,

> Pretending mutuall honor of that feast:
> And all her rabble-rout she did command
> As much in outward fayning to protest,
> But underneath their plausible attire
> They all bare balles of venym and wild-fire. (p. 70)

Before the fight between the two sides, Catechrysius exclaims 'Oh, that Eliza were / A Sionite to day to see this geere' (p. 72); immediately, Doblessa sees that 'all her guile' is 'Detected and Alarum'd over all' (p. 73), and begins to scale the city walls, reviling the name of Sion. Eliza, it seems, has believed herself to be a Sionite all along, misled by Doblessa's deceptive use of ceremony. If Copley's reworking of Spenser is mainly an appropriation of Spenser's loyalist mythography to give allegorical flesh to disagreements with members of his own church, it is also a riposte to Spenser's anti-Catholic offensive.

Copley incurred the common fate of moderates, obloquy from both sides. According to his own statement four years later in his controversial pamphlet *Another Letter of Mr A.C. to His Dis-Jesuited Kinsman*, *A Fig For Fortune* 'was ... called in by the Protestant for the Catholicke matter thereof',[83] but was also disapproved of by Robert Persons. The poem, Copley asserted, was written 'in attestation to the world of my Catholike soul to God and his Church, and of my resolution against ... Jesuitical obloquie ... I give in that Poeme her Majestie some praise and honour as for temporall state, which a Jesuit cannot endure in the behalf of the house of Austrich. ... *Basto non placuit Jesuitis* nor Puritanes; which (me thinkes) were those fathers not religious so much, as but reasonable good Catholikes it might [please them] in regard of the matter though not of the methode' (pp. 57–8).[84]

Despite his plaintive tone, Copley was not alone at this date in allegorising optimistic Catholic projections of a future under Elizabeth. R.C.'s *Palestina* (1600),[85] an allegorical romance printed surreptitiously in England and taking the reconversion of England as its subject, is dedicated both to Elizabeth I and the Virgin Mary. As in Constable's sonnets, the similarities between the two queens are stressed. But while Constable is anxious to avoid conflation, the reader of the dedication to *Palestina* is positively encouraged towards it: not because the author accords Elizabeth semi-divine status, but because he can thereby pay tribute to Mary while sincerely exploiting the conventions of monarchical panegyric. Neither name is actually mentioned. The dedicatee's dowry is 'little England', 'the largest heavens her fayrest inheritance' (f.¶3a), and the author apostrophises her in terms that do for either Mary or Elizabeth, but evade final identification: 'so worthie of the highest renowne, as no one is worthie to pronounce thy name'. The next sentence to this, 'By whom next unto God wee not onely live, but labour with joy', exploits the ambiguity: 'next unto God' could refer either to Mary's position as Mother of God, or to Elizabeth's as God's vicegerent. But the dedication continues in a more daring manner with the next few sentences, as Mary moves into the referential foreground to a degree that risks alienating the other dedicatee. The author describes his offering as 'but a harsh discourse of a sometime happie countrey, yet it is with a heartie wish it were not so greatly weaned from thee'. The sentiment can also be read as applicable to Elizabeth, but, either way, the Catholicism of the author becomes apparent at this point; insofar as the Queen is being addressed, the country weaned from her is not a geographical unit, but the aggregate of Englishmen exiled for their faith.

Framed in an allegory of an evil Enchanter, a frail Lady and a Prince who comes to rescue her, the plot is largely that of the Fall of Man and the Gospels, but based around the polarisation of two episodes: Eve's sin in Genesis, and Mary's encounter with her kinswoman Elizabeth, when Elizabeth is pregnant with John the Baptist. The theme is how, by God's intervention, even aged women can bear children. Given the Queen's advanced age and unmarried state, the forced parallel between the two Elizabeths absolutely precludes a literal application of the passage, in favour of an allegorical. A real heir is not intended, but instead, Elizabeth is being urged towards incubation of the recovered Catholic faith. As so often, a difficulty arises. Everything about the text implies that it was designed primarily for the eyes of Elizabeth, but there is no way of ascertaining if it was sent to her, or whether it reached her. A specially bound copy or presentation manuscript might indeed have been dispatched to her, but as with more straightforward petitions, it was most likely to have got no further than a government official. The multiplication of copies in print is important in this context: not only as an additional way of giving the text publicity and bringing it to the attention of its primary addressee, but to disseminate the dream among sympathisers, and make of it an object of prayer. This double-pronged use of an open letter was not especially novel, nor restricted to Elizabeth's countrymen. Thirty-five years before *Palestina*, Richard Shacklock had translated the Portuguese bishop Jeronimo Osorio da Fonseca's *Epistola ad Elizabetham Angliae Reginam de Religione* (1st edn. 1562), and urged Catholics in his own preface to pray for the queen, that her counsellors might persuade her 'to come oute of the cockring bote of scismaticall noysomnes, in to the stedfast arcke of Noy, that is of holsome and catholyke unitie' (f.A3a).

R.C.'s concluding sentiment in the dedication sums up the mission of the loyalist allegorist: 'I cease & admire thee, with those who never cease to admire thee, and wish unto thee what thou hast not'. The reader is invited to fill in the lacuna – Mary does not possess England, nor Elizabeth the Catholic faith – and it stands for the ideological gap between Queen and author. However genuine the loyal feelings of the writer, there would be no need for allegory without theological difference. Though allegory is usually thought of as the prime genre of concealment, and new historicism has tended to concentrate on its usefulness for imaginative politicised subversion, this is only half the story; the strong link at this period between loyalist writers and allegorical narrative points to the need for a more flexible model. The codes of allegory also demonstrate a placatory quality, the courteous desire to please those of similar opinions while not antagonising other readers. There is, too, an impatience with the heavy veils of real deception, and a preference for disguises which are sometimes as light as a changed name. This romantic fictive nomenclature, barely sweetening the author's advice, allowed real situations to be fictionally extended and resolved. By means of the onomastics of decency, the future could be postulated without offence; and for Catholic loyalists, who had everything to gain from a change of state religion, allegories were attractive as the genre of futurity. With transparent relevance to the state of English Catholicism, *Palestina* ends by retelling how the Jews became subjugated to the Romans and the high priest's ornaments were annexed by Herod, then by the Romans themselves. The beginning of Christ's ministry, and of the world's salvation, is left to the last sentence and a sequel by another author,

which whosoever shall prosecute, and shew in what sort hee uncharmed the Lady, which was enchaunted by eating of the fruite of a tree, by choaking the inchaunter with no other thing, then what also a tree did beare, shall both finde a most pleasant entrance, and when hee hath entred, an endlesse entising paradise. (p. 200)

Maureen Quilligan has commented that traditional definitions of allegory rely too heavily on metaphors of layered concealment, failing to take into account the genre's horizontal narrative quest for meaning.[86] Like his model Spenser, Copley uses the plot-device of a quest to reveal theological error through action, while the author of *Palestina* utilises the fall and rise of Christian soteriology to explain and predict the fortunes of English Catholicism. Most strikingly, both extend their lessons past the final page, leaving the onus on the reader to bear the salvific process onward and complete the narrative. Since Elizabeth was the primary addressee, her salvation would have been the most intended by this, if she ever saw either text; but this type of open petition to the monarch is intended to be read, absorbed and acted upon by all its readers, in case God's plan is for indirect influence. What may seem *naïveté* to the twentieth-century reader is, in fact, a highly literal, strikingly activist conception of prayer.

CHAPTER 4

Catholic loyalism: II. Stuart writers

The writers recorded in the previous chapter would have welcomed as a long-postponed answer to prayer the reports that Elizabeth died a Catholic;[1] and this devoted optimism continues in Catholic responses to James I, at the time of his accession and well beyond. But this chapter, continuing directly from the last, and also encompassing loyalist writing from the reign of Charles I, the Civil Wars and the Interregnum, demonstrates changed emphasis as well as simple continuity. One such shift is especially noticeable. Catholic writers under Elizabeth caught the habit of addressing her as *personally* beloved, able to exact loyal behaviour from her subjects for this reason; but Catholic loyalists under the first two Stuart monarchs, in the great age of English absolutism, figure among those inspired by a more public royal myth, the imaginative imperatives of abstract obedience. By their nature, these ran downwards from the monarch into every household in the kingdom, with wide personal resonances which are perhaps most poignantly illustrated in the work of women authors. As has already been commented, there was no greater determinant of Catholic loyalist behaviour throughout this period than the need to reconcile the double biblical duties of obeying God and submitting to the ordinances of men; and for married women, owing direct fealty to their husbands, Paul's injunction in 1 Peter 3.1, 'Likewise, ye wives, be in subjection to your own husbands' seemed to bear a similar relation to Matthew 19.29: 'And every one that hath forsaken houses, or brethren, or sisters, or father, or mother, or wife, or children, or lands, for my name's sake, shall receive an hundredfold, and shall inherit everlasting life.' Dual submission to religious and secular authority had many practical complexities for both sexes, and some of these are explored in pamphlet literature;[2] yet it is no coincidence that so many of the most powerful imaginative articulations of its difficulties were conceived by married women, or – which is not always the same thing – voiced in the persona of a married woman.

'GREAT AUSTIN': JAMES I AND THE LOYALIST IMAGINATION

Even while king of Scotland, James had allowed both English and European Catholics to think that he was in favour of toleration, and their jubilance at his accession was increased by one of the first acts of his reign, the release of the priest William Weston from prison.[3] Even the outspoken poet Ralph Buckland included a prayer in *Seaven Sparkes*, published just after James's accession in 1604 or 1605: 'By the hand of thy great servant JAMES, shake off our yoake: that we may finde him an honourable comforter... Deserve he the resemblance of thy owne Title: *Prince of peace*' (p. 12). Possibly for this reason, the Gunpowder Plot of 1605, so destructive to the hopes of Catholic loyalists, is more of a landmark in mainstream writing than in Catholic: not only because of the part which popular literature had to play in its mythification, but because of the thematic bearing it gave to more complex works. Critics have long been aware of the jesuitical equivocation practised by the witches in *Macbeth*, and B. N. de Luna has argued that *Catiline* was inspired by Jonson's need to dissociate himself personally from the Plot, since he was known to have consorted with some of the conspirators; at the very least, the play capitalises on a topical preoccupation with treachery.[4] Where Catholic writers refer to the topic, on the other hand, it tends to be with epideictic dissociation. 'What good is it to conceal so many particles of secret flame?' exploded John Barclay in the Latin poem appended to his pamphlet *Series Patefacti Nuper Parricidii* (1605): 'Ah, miserable ones, give over your threats. The thunderbolt knew its gods, and does not know how to sin against the mighty Thunderer.'[5]

But long past the time when the Gunpowder Plot had given a new focus to Protestant distrust of Catholics, and the Oath of Allegiance had increased the difficulties of Catholics themselves, Catholic allegorists continued to nurse hopes of James's conversion.[6] Nowhere are these hopes made more explicit than in John Abbot's *Jesus Praefigured*, published in Antwerp in 1623.[7] Its theme is the true church and Abbot's hopes for rebuilding it in England, and the poem's governing conceit is architectural; Charles, for instance, is urged to become a pillar alongside the Apostles (pp. 41–2). Another historical parallel between present monarch and past saint is that of

James I with St Augustine of Hippo, where Abbot expresses the delicate hope that James will appear among the doctors of the Church.

> If to thy Harpe weare added one more string,
> Then thou, no Swan could more divinely sing.
> But wee have hope all numbers now shall meet
> To make thy Musique absolutely sweet ...
> Our Churches Pearle, bred in thy mothers eyes,
> Againe begotten by a sea of cries.
> Great AUSTEN, shall I with more wondring eye,
> Behold thee when thy Muse doth mount on high,
> Or love thee more when thou dost creepe so lowe,
> As doe thy humble Retractations shew?
> To thinke amisse is fraile-Mans common case,
> To change for better, is a speciall grace. (p. 18)

Mary Stuart, who has appeared in a throng of martyrs earlier in the poem (pp. 15–17), now evokes a comparison with St Monica, Augustine's mother, who won over her heretic son by weeping and prayer.[8] Abbot's ostensible addressees are managed with remarkable tact: the direct compliment to James modulates into an apostrophe to Augustine, and a round generalisation in the concluding couplet. James is presented with an acceptable model for conversion, and reminded that Augustine's glory is actually enhanced by his former heresy. The crowning flattery occurs in Abbot's disparagement of the Spanish Netherlands, where heresy has begotten treason: 'Ill-nurturde swaines, not taught what is a King, / A God on earth, a Consecrated thing' (p. 39). Abbot exploits the contrast to portray Catholicism as a doctrine highly favourable to absolutist principle: an emphasis which will recur.

The publication date of 1623 suggests Abbot's awareness of the trip which Prince Charles and the Duke of Buckingham took in that year to pay court to the Infanta Maria of Spain, and the volume does indeed have a double dedication to the Prince and the Infanta, exhorting them to act as father and nurse to the new church in England.[9] This trip may account for the truncated form in which *Jesus Praefigured* was printed. Though originally intended as five books it comprises only two, and publishing it before completion may have been an opportunistic attempt to press into service a half-completed text: whether at Abbot's instigation, or from a manuscript that he had supervised at some stage. The few explicit references to the match give the impression of being grafted on, as do the passages where Abbot is writing for the eyes of a royal audience.[10] This, and the whole timing of the volume, suggests that its instigators believed allegorical projections of England's future were being overtaken by events. Abbot's obvious anxiety to intervene in the process can be accounted for by recapitulating a suggestion made earlier in this study: that in lending themselves so well to fictional extrapolation, allegories could be both a form of prayer and a call to it. Another Catholic poet poignantly expresses how, because a successful outcome of the journey to Spain would be an answer to prayer, news of the journey itself requires a sustained faith in divine providence: understandably enough in an age where communications were uncertain, and more particularly since the government had imposed a news blackout on the affair.[11]

> The Prince is gone for Spaigne: Ceasse heavens to frown
> And w[i]th a blest event his wishes crowne ...
> But staye; heer's one affermes hee is not gone,
> And that my wishes to the winds are throwne.
> Not soe: wher e're hee is my prayers still
> Shall all attend t'advance his princly will.
> Yet most beleeve w[ith] me, & constant are
> That longe e're this hee breathes the Spanish ayre.
> And puritans, how s'ever they dissemble,
> As their gran-masters doe, beleeve & tremble.[12]

Middleton's powerfully anti-Catholic *A Game At Chess* may be the best-known and most popular piece of imaginative writing inspired by the Spanish marriage, but it is more typical of retrospective reaction to it than of what was written at the time when events were unfolding. Catholics were not alone in welcoming the Spanish initiative, and some conformists used the occasion to versify appeals for ecumenical understanding;[13] yet both groups became quieter when Charles returned unmarried, and overt anti-Catholicism began to dominate imaginative conception of the event. *A Game At Chess* is an allegorical drama in which white and black chess-pieces stand for good Protestants and evil Catholics, and it was performed in August 1624, when the marriage negotiations were over but still topical. In terms of this section, its existence illustrates one difference that was bound to arise between Catholic and Protestant uses of allegory, when each explored a political event that would have benefited the cause of Catholicism. The Catholic allegories discussed above aim to sway future events by a combination of fictive persuasion and directed exhortation to prayer; but so far from being a projection of futurity, Middleton's play celebrates God's completed providence in delivering the land from popery.[14]

English Catholics could write allegories on recent history as well. But John Barclay's *Argenis*, first published abroad in 1621 and being read in England soon afterwards, is as much about live political issues as historical event; in fictionalizing European history of the late sixteenth century as Heliodoran romance, it touched on topics that were still controversial at the time of writing. One such was the Catholic/Protestant divide in France; the name of the sage Iburranes anagrammatises that of Pope Urban VIII, and a chapter of the book is devoted to satirising his enemies, the Hyperephanians or Huguenots, led by Usinulca or Calvinus. This display of hostility to Protestants does not appear to have made the book any less attractive to either James or Charles, and again, this may partly be to do with the politeness of allegory; under romantic names – even where those names are explained in a key[15] – potentially offensive characters are at least one remove from recognisability, and while readers can object to them if they wish, they are relieved of the necessity to do so. But another point is also relevant. Though Huguenots professed Protestantism, they went against monarchical dictates; the religious convictions of both Stuart monarchs may have been a less significant factor in their enjoyment of Barclay than a shared belief in absolutism.[16]

In this context, the emphases of Barclay's anti-Huguenot passages are significant. The doctrine of predestination is ridiculed, in terms that would not have amused some Jacobean churchmen: 'So, from the same puddle of wickednesse, shall some goe out cleane, others polluted. As if you thrust a Goose or Swan into the water, you may take them out perfectly drie; where other Birds, in the same waters, and often with lesse stay there, hurt the order and use of their wings' (p. 135). But just as in Barclay's earlier romance *Euphormio*, more satirical attention is given to the subversiveness of religious groups than to their actual religion. *Euphormio* includes abuse both of Jesuits and Puritans for presuming to oppose their ideologies to the monarch's; the puritan Catharinus is even seen smoking at the end of a banquet, demonstrating his defiance of all James I's literary edicts. Similarly in *Argenis*, Barclay's main criticism is not of the Huguenots' religion, but of their ungovernability. By a combination of disrespect, loose personal morality and beliefs tending towards atheism, they have become 'another Countrey, and another people', and a natural magnet for the seditious:

> In mindes so affected, what free command, thinke you, can Kings have over them? They have possessed themselves of Cities, Souldiers, and almost whole Provinces; out of which, with a prowd scorne, they debate, how farre it is fit the King should be aided, or neglected: To whom ... if they promise any aide, they brag of their fidelitie, ... forgetting, that good subjects should not exact such securitie; ... So they make themselves Judges of the gods, and of their Princes; and measure what dutie they owe to either, not by Religion, but according to their owne dispositions. (p. 136)

ABSOLUTISM, MARITAL OBEDIENCE AND STRATAGEMS OF PERSUASION

Barclay's imaginative efforts must certainly have helped to prepare the way for the growing friendliness towards Rome which has been recognised as characterising the Stuart court in the 1630s;[17] at any rate, *Argenis* pleased the Stuart monarchy so much that it was translated into English three times in eight years. James I commissioned a translation of the Latin original from Ben Jonson in 1623, and Charles I another from Robert Le Grys in 1628. Lois Potter suggests that another translation of Barclay's *Argenis* by Kingsmill Long, in 1625, was to celebrate Charles I's marriage to Henrietta Maria, since at one point in the story a son of Hyanisbe (Queen Elizabeth I) marries the daughter of the French king.[18] If so, it was an appropriate wedding-present for a queen whose imaginative contribution to the cause of Catholic loyalism was, perhaps, greater than any other individual's discussed in this study.

Critics have always recognised that Henrietta Maria's Catholicism and her dramatic ingenuity were inseparable: and sometimes, like William Prynne, they have commented on this with hostile intent. Henrietta Maria astonished the English by performing as an actress, commissioned literary texts for theatrical presentations from writers like Walter Montague and Sir William Davenant, and exploited the technical and iconographical skills of Inigo Jones. Though she and her ladies sometimes performed in dramas which had not been specially commissioned,[19] it is her patronage of new material which has attracted most attention. In this role, her most original contributions to the theatrical life of the Caroline court were a pastoral drama, Walter Montague's *The Shepherd's Paradise* (1633), and a number of masques.[20] Masques have been the subject of much illuminating recent criticism,[21] and because of this, a detailed assessment of all the dramatic productions undertaken by Henrietta Maria is unnecessary here; this chapter aims to identify the imaginative similarity which Catholic loyalism brought to genres superficially very dissimilar, and masques need not only be discussed in conjunction with other masques. The following account will concentrate on a single production, *The Temple of Love*, Henrietta Maria's Shrovetide masque of 1635, and the way in which its commendations of Catholicism are simultaneously definite, courteous, loyal and submissive.[22]

In the fullest account to date of Henrietta Maria's masques, Erica Veevers's *Images of Love and Religion: Queen Henrietta Maria and Court Entertainments* (1989), *The Temple of Love* is treated as important testimony of how the queen used plays and masques at court to promote ecumenism and enhance the image of Catholicism.[23] It was the first official court function after the arrival in England of the papal envoy Gregorio Panzani, who may be represented within the action in the character of Orpheus.[24] The Temple itself, at first glimpsed through mists but then revealed in its full splendour, is the central image of the masque both literally and symbolically; as Veevers points out, it would have evoked comparisons with the Queen's chapel, also being built by Inigo Jones, and hence with the Catholic church in England. It shares these visual allusions with a later masque, *Luminalia*, and both masques have a heavily sacerdotal cast-list: flamens and arch-flamens in *Luminalia*, and in *The Temple of Love*, Brahmani, Magi and priests of the Temple itself.[25]

The masque begins with a view of Parnassus, 'the place where the souls of the ancient poets are fained to reside', which is succeeded by a vision who, like Aurora, appears from 'a great cloud of a rosy colour': 'a beautiful woman; her garment was sky-colour set all with stars of gold, veil hanging down behind, and her hair in artificial curls graciously dressed, representing Divine Poesy, and by her a milk-white swan'. To unpack the full implications of the figure of Divine Poesy, one must refer back to du Bartas's use of the Muse of Astronomy, Urania, and so to the arguments advanced in chapter three of this study. The opposition postulated earlier between Southwell's virtual repudiation of muses and du Bartas-inspired Protestant invocations of the divine muse would be inappropriate as a means of interpreting this particular recurrence of the iconography, over thirty years on; but Divine Poesy represents a Catholic appropriation of sacred verse very similar to Southwell's. Rounding up the spirits of pagan poets, she extorts contrition from them: 'Vex not our sad remembrance with our shame! / We have been punished with ill-gotten fame, /For each loose verse, tormented with a flame' (ll. 110–12). It is probably to Davenant the librettist, who was himself to convert to Catholicism later, that one can ascribe this resurrection of a former generation's Catholic poetics.[26] But the re-feminisation of Catholic divine poetry was very appropriate to the Queen's agenda, and can be seen in the context of two earlier masques, *Chloridia* and *Tempe Restored*, which present a feminised, highly Marian iconography of virtue.[27]

Henrietta Maria is famous for having introduced a fashion for neo-Platonism to the English court, and *The Temple of Love* exploits it.[28] Here again, the relationship between Catholic loyalism and allegory manifests itself. Neo-platonism, which seeks to discern eternal truths behind the veils of mortal perception, has an inbuilt tendency towards allegory and can itself be a useful allegorical device. Though there is no reason to suppose that Henrietta Maria promoted neo-Platonism as a philosophical fashion merely for ulterior motives, it forms a continuum with her religion; given that neo-Platonism is often couched in religious language, it was easy to conflate the two; and since – even in the Caroline court – there was more reason to be publicly circumspect about Catholic sympathies than neo-Platonist, a Catholic message may often lie veiled behind professions of neo-Platonic ideals of love.[29] As with any allegorical identification, this can easily be over-exploited, and Catholicism need not always lie beneath neo-Platonism. Nevertheless, the opening of Somerset House Chapel and Panzani's arrival to British shores are good external reasons why *The Temple of Love* might preserve a mood of topical excitement among Catholics, and it seems fair to acknowledge that the initiate might have read a dual meaning into such lines as 'And now th'enchanted mists shall clear, / And Love's true temple straight appear, / Long hid from men by sacred power' (ll. 403–5).

Even within the text there are clues pointing towards a sectarian interpretation, though all the overt religious reference in *The Temple of Love* is satirical, and includes nothing that would not have pleased Charles. Puritans have a prominent part to play, as modern devils. A magician describes them as 'fine precise fiends, that hear the devout close / At every virtue but their own, that claim / Chambers and tenements in heaven as they / Had purchased there, and all the angels were /Their harbingers' (ll. 274–8).[30] This sets the scene for the marriage at the end of the masque between Sunesis, or Understanding, 'a man of a noble aspect' crowned with a flaming garland, and Thelema, or Free Will, a young woman 'in a robe of changeable silk'.[31] Figuring the theological implications of alternative both in her dress and her name, Thelema stands as a reproach to predestinarians, as well as an iconographical realization of the beauty of changing one's mind. Her marriage to Sunesis epitomises how the understanding should ally itself to human free will – in effect, to a notion of the theology of grace which is interpretable in a Laudian manner, but also in a Catholic. The fine-tuning of the masque's controversial element is apparent in the fortuitous survival of the costume-design for Thelema, the caption of which reveals that the character was originally called *Gnome*, or Divine Will; and it gives added edge to the sung dialogue between the two.

> SUNESIS Come melt thy soul in mine, that when unite,
> We may become one virtuous appetite.
> THELEMA First breathe thine into me, thine is the part
> More heavenly, and doth more adorn the heart.
> BOTH Thus mixed, our love will ever be discreet,
> And all our thoughts and actions pure;
> When perfect will and strengthened reason meet,
> Then love's created to endure. (ll. 478–85)

Descending from heaven, Chaste Love showers down blessings and points to how the newly married couple mirror the royal pair: 'And now you may in yonder throne / The pattern of your union see' (ll. 501–2). Given this, it is worth looking more closely at the dialogue above. Thelema counters Sunesis's request 'Melt thy soul in mine' with 'First breathe thine into me', and, since they then sing a duet of joyful union, one is led to assume that Sunesis has done just that. But Thelema adds a crucial, very feminine qualification: 'Thine is the part / More heavenly, and doth more adorn the heart.' Because masculine understanding is stronger than feminine affectivity, the heart has a stronger need of the head than the head of the heart. But, chivalrically, Understanding yields to the heart, literally breathing his soul into a personification of free will, a surrender which invites a soteriological interpretation. The masque presents a possible model of how Charles might succumb to the wishes of his wife, one which is entirely compatible with the harmonious ecumenism which informs the masques of both. With all Catholics, loyalism accompanied a perpetual, hopeful commendation of their own religious beliefs; and ecumenism can often be a polite evangelism. Henrietta Maria's ecumenical programme co-existed with a sturdy maintenance of the Catholic faith, and would not have eschewed this type of light-handed encouragement towards Catholicism. Like Henry Constable, Henrietta Maria would have seen herself as a Catholic moderator; and like him – though more affirmatively – she employs poetic models of power and abjection to this end.[32]

Ecumenism is unnecessary without prior difference. The enactments of religious, political and marital harmony which take place in the masques of Charles and Henrietta Maria were intended to reassure, but could not entirely disguise the fact that the interests of king and queen were not identical. Veevers has suggested that the pro-Catholicism of *The Temple of Love* and *Luminalia* shows Henrietta Maria responding to pressure from papal agents and French ambassadors to promote Catholicism more actively; but because she was an English queen as well as a French princess, Catholic proselytism had to stay as an undercurrent to public statement. Without enormous public tact, Henrietta Maria's duty of testifying to her religion would have cut across the duty she owed to the English crown; and the fact that her political interests were frequently different from Charles's made a public show of solidarity all the more important.[33] But marriage to a husband of different confessional sympathies had difficulties which common wives shared. As queen, she represented the country of her birth as well as that of her adoption, and had incomparably more religious autonomy than a private citizen; but as wife she was bound to defer to Charles, and Charles's absolutist beliefs made him patriarchal in the extreme.[34] Scholars have recently been careful to modify the comparison between king and husband or father, commonplace at this date, by commenting that some theorists argued for a direct relationship between the two, and others only for an analogical one.[35] But the choice would have been no help to a Stuart queen. She could be commanded by the authorities of her native country and her religion; but, uniquely in every generation, she could know no difference between husband and king.

Veevers's emphasis is on the political specificities surrounding and informing each masque, and on how religious neo-Platonism and Catholic veneration of Mary could be co-opted to affirm female power; but these masques also externalise Henrietta Maria's particular loyalist obligations, as stratagems of deference towards a husband who was also the monarch. Within the canon of Stuart masques, those commissioned by both Charles and Henrietta Maria are distinctive in their glorification of married bliss. Laudatory references to the ideal happiness of Charles and Henrietta Maria are commonplace,[36] and in their jointly mounted masque *Salmacida Spolia*, they are praised as 'tuning [their] thoughts to either's will' (l. 470). Yet even in an ideal marriage – perhaps especially in an ideal marriage – and even in a union of two royal individuals, the exemplarity of traditional gender roles still prevailed. Henrietta Maria's use of the language of beauty is ultimately deferential, an acknowledgement that this was all the sovereignty women had. Yet, by the chivalric consensus on which the masque depended, female beauty had absolutist claims to rival any made by a Stuart monarch; and the theme of *The Temple of Love* is, precisely, the guidance of the masculine principle by the feminine in love. More generally, a masque's visual amazements can represent a privileging of beauty, and lend themselves to neoplatonic equations of beauty and truth: as it says in *Luminalia* when the Queen appears: 'Look there, correct your judgements by your sight!' (l. 342). Both conventions can be co-opted in attempts to reverse the structures of sovereignty by pleasing, but, by the same token, both spring from the fact that those structures exist. Like some texts discussed above, Henrietta Maria's masques had a primary addressee in the monarch, even though their presentation was a public affair,[37] and the pro-Catholic messages discussed above were directed above all at Charles. They are couched in a way that positively draw attention to the obligations of marital obedience; because of the exactions permitted of beauty, these can be extracted as much from the husband as the wife at a fictive level.

This balance did not emerge easily, and Henrietta Maria's progress from zealous bride to emollient consort was, to some extent, the taming of a Catholic shrew. From the time of her marriage and arrival in England, the queen had had to juggle several different and conflicting loyalties: to her husband, to France and to Catholicism. Before her marriage she had written promises to

Louis XIII, her brother, and to Pope Urban VIII, that she would pursue the cause of the English Catholics.[38] By Urban VIII, in a letter accompanying the papal dispensation for her marriage, she was asked to be the 'Esther of her oppressed people' and reminded of Clotilde, the virtuous queen of France who converted her husband to Christianity, and of Queen Aldiberga, whose marriage brought religion to Britain.[39] Pious Catholic queens could also be found nearer home, and a manuscript history of Mary Stuart preserved in the Beinecke Library indicates in its conclusion that it was written in celebration of Charles I's marriage; it addresses Charles himself, and its use of the Queen of Scots as an exemplar is unabashed. Charles's blood-relationship to Mary is seen as the single most important endorsement of his monarchy, and the situations of Mary and Henrietta Maria are reconceived as type and antetype, with the new queen able to repair the wrong that was done the old:

> The Queen of Scotland your Grandmother was given to France, and France hath rendered you a Princesse according to the heart of God and yours; a Bloom of our Lillies, a Daughter of a King, a Sister of a King, a Wife of a King... Great Majesties of Britain... as you make but one heart, so make but one Religion... (pp. 178–9)

The two exhortations, one from the Supreme Pontiff and one anonymous, are nevertheless very similar: a fact which testifies both to the widespread optimism with which the marriage of Charles and Henrietta Maria had been greeted across Catholic Europe, but also to the way in which those expectations were governed by acceptable notions of feminine behaviour.

Henrietta Maria's early behaviour as queen took its bearings from the orthodox piety of the female exemplars commended to her, but she differed dangerously from them in being apologist, assertive and unwelcome. The optimism at her marriage with Charles seemed to be vindicated by the concessions that the English monarchy was prepared to make, since the marriage treaty contained a secret clause in which James I promised to permit Catholics to practise their faith privately so long as they obeyed the laws of the realm; James I gave public demonstrations of his good faith by ordering the release of imprisoned recusants, a return of recent recusancy fines and a full suspension of the penal code, while Henrietta Maria was promised royal chapels with her own priests.[40] Henrietta Maria could, perhaps, have been forgiven for thinking that inflexible religious practice on her part would bring further results. From the early years of the marriage, there survive numerous anecdotes of the queen's intolerance of Protestant worship. In the summer of 1625, a time when Charles had been pressured by Parliament into more stringent controls on Catholic activity, she and a group of French friends – laughing, talking and accompanied by equally vocal small dogs – paraded several times through a hall in which a Protestant service was being held.[41] In June 1626 she visited Tyburn and prayed for the souls of the Catholics who had perished there, a story which soon became inflated into the rumour of a full-scale barefoot pilgrimage to honour Catholic traitors: an indication of what the court, and the country, was prepared to believe.

Henrietta Maria extended this inflexibility even to her public duties as queen. She refused to attend her own coronation in February 1626, on the grounds that she would be being anointed by a Protestant archbishop – and the fact that she subsequently stayed away from the opening of Parliament may have been an act of dissociation from the proceedings of a Protestant nation, rather than the fit of adolescent pique as which it has usually been seen. Commenting on this occasion, the Duke of Buckingham said to Charles that a king who could not command his wife would make a poor impression on Parliament, and Charles in turn made a habit of complaining to Buckingham about the Queen's disobedience.[42] Anxious to justify his severity to the Queen's mother Marie de Medici, Charles received considerable support from her, and she wrote to her daughter that she should obey her husband in all things except religion.[43] A crisis came in the summer of 1626, when Charles, in a fit of domestic absolutism, sent away most of the French members of the Queen's household: a move which angered the French court and led to the dispatch of an Ambassador-Extraordinary to England, the Marshal de Bassompierre, who spent the next few months effecting a resolution and reminding Charles of obligations in the marriage-treaty which the bad behaviour of the French had given him an excuse to neglect. The treaty was never strictly enforced, but English Catholics were to feel more at ease in the succeeding years; and after Bassompierre's departure, no more is heard of the Queen's disobedience.

Bassompierre's role as mediator had earlier been undertaken by Sieur de Blainville, and the fact of ambassadors being sent to intervenc in the marital differences of the king and queen is suggestive, in itself, of the international implications of their marital disharmony: implications which led to widespread anecdotalising scrutiny of the royal couple's relationship at the time when it was most under strain.[44] One quarrel, precipitated when Henrietta Maria refused to attend the opening of Parliament in February 1626, ended in a well-known exchange between the two. Charles had wished the queen to watch the ceremonies from the Countess of Buckingham's house, but she refused to go across the courtyard, saying that it was raining, even though Charles and Buckingham believed it was not. Her behaviour may partly have been prompted by a warning from Blainville that she should not associate with the Countess. Buckingham asked the Queen to apologize and she refused; in the end, Blainville himself persuaded her to go, which Charles felt to be so presumptuous that he ordered Blainville out of London. The quarrel lasted until Henrietta Maria gave in, saying that if Charles believed that being mistaken about the weather was an offence, she would too.[45] Even more than most English queens, Henrietta Maria has suffered from the Jean Plaidyesque school of biography; this episode has usually been written up in a manner which elicits from the reader one of the special pleasures of historical voyeurism, the sense that the curtains of the state bed have been twitched aside. But quite apart from anything else, this interpretation depends on a notion of privacy which even the preservation of the anecdote argues against.

The story itself has an almost parodic similarity to homelier narratives of wife-taming. In Act 4 of *The Taming of the Shrew*, when Petruchio and Katherine are about to set off for a journey, Petruchio tests her by making her say that the moon is shining when the sun is out, then that it is the sun after all. The wearily submissive Katherine replies:

> But sun it is not when you swear it is not,
> And the moon changes even as your mind.
> What you will have it named, even that it is,
> And so it shall be still for Katherine.   (scene 5, ll. 20–3)

If reported accurately, the above anecdote illustrates that Henrietta Maria, at one point in her marriage, was appropriating the predetermined echoes and silences of a tamed wife: a role which did not prevent her lapsing into further quarrels with Charles, but which need not, at the time, have been other than a genuine attempt to do what was fitting. But her duties as representative of her country and her faith would have made it impossible to sustain a perfect submissiveness of this kind, and it is in this light that one must view manifestations of her intellectual independence from Charles. The historian sensitive to conscience ought never to assume that any individual in early modern Europe endorsed philosophical and theological systems for entirely self-interested reasons, yet one should not be blind to the incidental benefits of those systems in individual cases. Henrietta Maria introduced a fashion for neoplatonism to the English court, and the elevated discourses of neoplatonism, with their high conception of marriage, had the very practical effect of enhancing the position of a wife; she made a prominent and distinctive contribution to the masque culture of the Stuart court, and masques lent themselves to such quasi-diplomatic techniques as tactful commendation in perfomance and concession without disgrace for the primary addressee. As glorified realizations of exemplary behaviour, they were an attempt to exact complementary obligations from Charles. Henrietta Maria's disobedience contained within itself a performative externalisation of religious dissent; the elaborate obeisances of her masques did the same, but they were a means of sweetening necessary religious difference.

Martin Butler has said of masques: 'The humanist tradition of *laudando praecipere* licensed panegyric as an arena in which counsel might be offered, in which discreet criticism could be advanced, or in which analogy and oblique allusion could be employed to insinuate a commentary on topical events. And yet the risks were considerable and the advice was unlikely ever to be unconstrained by the limits of tact.'[46] As Veevers has shown, masques could be used to commend Catholicism both visually and doctrinally. But flattery within a masque is an articulation of distance, and an admission that only indirect admonishment is permissible: a dialectic evolved to express the hierarchy of monarch and subject, which could also make masques an extremely suitable genre for a wife to write in. We are not accustomed to think of masques, or any sort of drama, as a form of chaste conversation coupled with fear;[47] and previous feminist criticism of Henrietta Maria's masques has tended to see her acting and patronage more straightforwardly, as a means of female empowerment.[48] But a ubiquitous message of Henrietta Maria's dramatic presentations, the all-conquering power of a feminised religious love, is consistent with St Paul's injunction that wives professing the true faith and married to unbelieving husbands should use indirect means to convert them. To call this feminist is misleading; but, paradoxically, it counts among the incentives that prompted early modern women towards finding a voice.

This is realized in at least one other text by a woman writer from this period. *The Tragedy of Mariam, Fair Queen of Jewry* by Elizabeth Cary, Lady Falkland, has a plot which turns on a question of female loyalty. Mariam, the protagonist, is executed by her husband Herod after she accuses him of assassinating her relatives in order to gain the throne. Herod is portrayed as a tyrant, while Mariam's conscientious crises are lengthily explored; and as most critics of the play have pointed out, the play articulates the question of whether marital disobedience can be justified in extreme cases, while supplying no obvious answer. Cary criticism – as so often with the imaginative creations of early modern women writers – has also tended to centre around the question of whether the dilemmas of the protagonist can be seen as reflecting those in Cary's own life. Cary professed a high doctrine of marital submission, yet the publicising of her conversion to Catholicism in late 1626 led to her permanent separation from her Protestant husband. Her daughter's biography records that even after the separation, Cary would refrain from 'things most ordinarily done by all, and which she did much delight in, for hearing from some other that he seemed to dislike it'.[49] The disobedience of both Mariam and Cary is cut down to an irreducible minimum, but in both cases, it brings about marital rupture.

There are other similarities. Mariam's rebellion is prompted by loyalty towards her family and its priestly line, and so, like Cary's, it can be read as stemming from religious imperatives. The two loyalties are linked by the wiping out of the rightful line of succession, heavily stressed in the play's argument. As Mariam's mother Alexandra says of Herod to her, 'this his hate to thee may justly prove, / That sure he hates Hircanus's family' (Act 1, l. 126). Mariam's grandfather Hircanus and brother Aristobolos have been murdered by Herod to gain the throne, his best title to which is in Mariam's name. As with Antigone, the honour of the family has devolved on Mariam; and if Mariam dies, the last rightful heir to the Jewish throne dies – in the play, no other is nominated.[50] Since this is the Jewish monarchy, this means the simultaneous eradication of the kingly and the priestly line; however perfect her subservience, this is why Mariam is obliged to object. As a woman, she is unable to be either priest or king herself, the 'double honour, shining doubly bright' (Act 1, l. 117); but her conscientious claims rest on the fact that she is the repository of legitimacy.

In my view, it is mistaken both to read *Mariam* as straightforwardly autobiographical, and to deny any connection between Mariam's preoccupations and Cary's.[51] The source for the play, Thomas Lodge's edition of Josephus, has an introduction commending the value of historical exemplars for interrogation of oneself and instruction of others; and I intend to argue elsewhere, at greater length, that it is possible to read *Mariam* as an autodidactic play, if not an autobiographical one.[52] Plenty of writers discussed in this study demonstrate how imaginative writing could be a form of experimentation with Catholicism, and I believe that Cary can be classed with these: indeed, that her religious quest was the cause of her autodidactic programme. It is a commonplace of criticism dealing with early modern drama that historical selection, seemingly without overt comment, can invite some very unidirectional conclusions when put in context. The parallel between English Catholics and the conquered Jews under Herod is hard to ignore in the light of Cary's religious history; the Catholic text *Palestina*, discussed earlier, makes considerable capital out of it.

Cary was dramatising a genuine contemporary ambiguity in Mariam's dilemma, since Catholic women married to unsympathetic Protestant husbands faced a clash between the two submissions demanded of them.[53] There was general agreement that mixed marriages were undesirable – a consensus which, in at least two cases, was censored during marriage negotiations for Charles during the 1620s[54] – and husbands were exhorted to use their authority to convert heretical wives.[55] But there was no clear agreement among moralists as to the right course of behaviour for orthodox wives married to unbelieving husbands[56] – though homilists writing from outside the status quo, first Protestants and then Catholics, tend to be happier with the idea of marital separation in the case of religious difference.[57] As so often with gender-issues, it was an area where moral discourse was full of half-articulated contradictions; and by giving dramatic flesh to those contradictions, Cary passes the final responsibility over to the reader.

Just as Henrietta Maria's masques had a primary addressee in the king, Cary's drama may principally have been intended for her husband. In the biography it is said that Falkland read Cary's writings, and it would certainly have been very difficult for a piece to achieve any sort of manuscript circulation without his seeing it. The Herod-figure, sometimes conflating enormities committed by more than one historical Herod, was often used within drama as a means to explore issues such as tyranny, monarchy, authority and the subject's obedience to the king;[58] but despite this, I believe that Herod may have been a thickly veiled historical exemplar for Falkland, intended to prompt change by dissociation. If this is the case, the allegorical stratagems used by Henrietta Maria, and the historical parallelism of Cary, may have been employed to very similar ends. In their persuasions of a monarch towards a course of action or away from it, masques can be masterpieces of tactfulness, and the personal nature of their address makes them analogous to closet-dramas written for a coterie audience. In Cary's biography, written by her daughter, Lord Falkland is described as 'very absolute' (p. 194). Could the persuasive tactics of a masque also have been used within the patriarchal rule of the home, tactics intended to prompt not an association of a ruler with particular virtues, but a husband's dissociation from a figure of notorious wickedness and marital tyranny, and hence an acknowledgement of his wife's conscientious rights?

If so, the parameters of the request are clearly defined. Like some masques the play is full of critique, but is clearly also a celebration of existing power-structures. This would explain the extravagant claims of subservience the play contains, as a counterbalance to criticism. To make the plot of *Mariam* work, we have to assume that Mariam has performed breathtaking feats of marital submission up to Act 4 Scene 3, never complaining to Herod at her family being eradicated. Herod's order to have her killed precipitates her outburst, but is not referred to within it. Her upbraidings have nothing to do with the fact that he planned for her to be put to death, only with his murdering her relations:

> Your offers to my heart no ease could grant,
> Except they could my brother's life restore.
> No, had you wish'd the wretched Mariam glad,
> Or had your love to her been truly tied:
> Nay, had you not desir'd to make her sad,
> My brother nor my grandsire had not died. (ll. 111–16)

In its oddly timed motivation, derived straight from Josephus, the whole scene reveals Mariam's scrupulous avoidance of even the most legitimate self-interested claims. Neither Herod's tyranny towards her two relations, nor even his death-threats towards herself, is enough on its own; it is the cumulative effect of the two tyrannies that prompts her to resistance. Renaissance overdetermination of the female helps her to personify both functions: she *is* the monarchy and she *is* the church. Where silence was part of female exemplarity, to state 'I am the church' was a paradox almost along the lines of the Cretan who said that all Cretans were liars; and yet the seventeenth century contains a further paradox, the small army of women for whom the divinely inspired dictates of conscience were an imperative to publish. Within the play there is enormous emphasis on Mariam's princely and priestly blood; this is an externalisation of the claims of conscience, the kind of externalisation which allowed a female author to stress their overarching importance, while still appearing personally disinterested.

One must return, then, to the idea of chaste conversation coupled with fear: which is certainly a form of passive resistance. In contemporary translations of the Bible the word 'conversation' means 'behaviour', but even in early modern vocabulary it also had the meaning of interpersonal discourse. Either way, it implies suggestion rather than assertion, and the kind of problem-play that *Mariam* is would have lent itself supremely well to this kind of indirect admonition. In such a case, Cary would necessarily have had to achieve the impartiality for which the play is so remarkable: only a genuine balance would further her case, only a genuine question not arouse suspicions that she was the instructor rather than the suppliant. Contemporary moralists recommended similar strategies as a means of allowing wives a way to query their husbands' behaviour, while still respecting domestic order. In a sermon, Thomas Gataker asked how far a wife might admonish her husband, and answered his own question by saying that she should have 'due respect and regard of the husbands person and place'. She should therefore 'move the matter ... by way of question, or as craving advice, as Rebecka seemeth to move the matter a farre off unto Isaack, submit her advice and opinion to his judgement and discretion, as Ester to Assuerus his'.[59]

The Book of Esther in the Old Testament, like the story of Herod and Mariam in Josephus, deals with a Jewish queen married to a king both pagan and tyrannical. When the Persian king Ahasuerus's councillor Haman puts out a decree that all the Jews should be massacred, his wife Esther visits the king to plea for her people; her request is answered, and Haman is hanged. What makes this particular story so conducive to a dual moral of religious loyalty and marital obedience is the circumstances of her plea. It is an unbreakable Persian law that if anyone visits the king without being summoned, they will be executed unless the king holds out his sceptre as a sign of mercy. Even though she is the queen, this applies to Esther; and so she risks martyrdom when she makes her request, until Ahasuerus is moved by her beauty and pardons her. If *Mariam* leaves itself open to equations between English Catholics and the conquered Jews, the Book of Esther in the context of Caroline England was a story that positively invited them. Its potential appropriateness to a Catholic queen married to a Protestant monarch of absolutist opinions was recognised by Urban VIII, even before Charles and Henrietta Maria were married; his marriage-letter to the queen, cited above, includes an injunction that she should be the Esther of her oppressed people.[60]

Francis Lenton, who was given the title of Queen's Poet by Henrietta Maria, may have known this when he wrote 'Queen Esters Haliluiahs and Hamans Madrigals', a manuscript poem dated 1637.[61] But in the context of the Caroline court, it was a piece of historical parallelism that was obvious enough. As with *Mariam*, one should not expect a one-to-one correspondence between past and present actors; described as a 'greedy king' (f.27b), tyrannical and avid for concubines, Ahasuerus is portrayed with a distinct lack of sympathy, and a parallel at all points between him and Charles would have been both mischievous and inept. As with the characterisation of Herod in *Mariam*, it may actually have been intended to encourage dissociation in Charles if he figured among the projected readership. But the descriptions of the Persian law, so unbreakable that one decree can be countermanded only by another decree, and the fact that the monarch is responsible for that law, lend themselves to parallels with Charles's personal rule during the 1630s. Henrietta Maria's early disobedience in refusing to come to Parliament is probably alluded to in the poem's account of Ahasuerus's first wife, Vashti, refusing to attend her husband's summons.[62] The counsellor Memucan gives his opinion on this, enlarging upon the radical effect of marital disloyalty on the common weal.

> He stronglie Argues by Induction,
> That Vasthi had not to the king alone,
> Done wrong by her miscarried Libertie,
> But also unto all the Princes nie,
> And all the people that shall heare of this,
> Shall judg Queene Vasthi, to have done amisse:
> And backs his Judgment with a Reason too,
> what it may cause all other women doe,
> For when the deed of this disloyall Queene,
> shall spread abroad, and through the land be seene;
> And knowne to other women, in their eyes
> They shall their lawfull husbands then despise,
> And, by this badd example, they shall stand
> In open warr against their heades Command:
> And shall defend it with this warranty,
> Vasthi our Queene did so, and so will I.   (ff.20b–21a)[63]

The Bible story with its neat reversal, Vashti's undesired absence counterparted by Esther's unsummoned attendance, had been appropriated before to provide good and bad exemplars for the Catholic wife. Sir John Harington's epigram, 'To his Wife against women recusants', adjures his 'deerest Mall' to 'Ensew not Vasties sample but detest her, / And rather follow her successor Esther.'[64]

In preparation for the mission to save her people, Esther adorns herself 'as once faire Judith did' (f.45b); Catholics were sometimes suspected of using the Apocryphal story of Judith slaying Holofernes as a justification of tyrannicide,[65] but here it seems intended only to demonstrate that there are precedents for a virtuous woman to dress herself seductively in order to promote her faith. Lenton adds considerably to the vague Biblical descriptions of Esther's attire, in which she is described only as being 'in her royal robes', and 'gloriously adorned' (ch. 5.1, and Apocrypha, ch. 15.2):

> her golden locks so crisp'd, and aptly twin'de,
> whose every haire a kingly soule might bind ...
> A Carbuncle on her Christall brow she pight,
> whose lustrous beames expelld the shady night,
> Upon her head a silver Tince[66] she pin'd,
> Loose waveings [sic] on her shoulders with the wind,
> Gold on her golden haire, whose Ivory neck
> the rubies rich, and saphiers blew, did deck:
> And at her eares two pretious pearles, more rare,

> then the Shebean Queene did ever weare,
> Throughe Indian Lawne, appear'd her snowy breasts,
> Like Laeda's swans within their downy neasts ...
> The musk and Civett Amber, as she past,
> Long after her, a sweet perfume did cast;
> Adorn'd with Ceres guifts, and Ophir gold,
> how glorious was this goddes to behold! (ff.45b–46a)

It is probably no coincidence that a number of these imagined details, from the tinsel headdress to the barely-veiled bosom, sound like those from a masque-costume.[67] If this effect was intended by Lenton, it gives further imaginative specificity to Henrietta Maria's project to commend her faith through masquing realizations of beauty.

That faith may have been shared by Lenton himself, or he may have been responding to the Queen's in a manner that is pro-Catholic, but nothing more. Much of Lenton's other work, especially his printed collection of anagrams upon the names of the female masquers in *Luminalia, Great Britains Beauties, or the Female Glory* (1638), suggests a coterie poet attentive to the exemplars chosen by the Queen, whose works would have found a keen audience in the Queen's court even without his official title.[68] In the Huntington Library copy, 'Queene Esters Haliluiahs' is followed by a translation of Psalm 83 'wherein David curseth the Enimyes of the True Church', but – perhaps deliberately – it is not made plain who is to be identified as the true church, and who as the enemies. *Great Britains Beauties* is a little more suggestive. Its subtitle echoes Anthony Stafford's controversial work of a few years before, *The Female Glory* (1635), which attempted a synthesis of Marian devotion with Anglicanism; and the verses on the Queen insistently allude to Marian imagery. Anagrammatising MARIA STVART to I AM A TRU STAR, Lenton writes that Henrietta Maria is

> A Morning Star, whose Rose at blush and smile,
> Shewes the dayes solace, and the nights exile;
> A radiant Star, whose lustre, more Divine,
> By Charles (our Sun) doth gloriously shine:
> No wandring Planet, that moves circular,
> But a tru, constant, loyall, fixed Star:
> A Star whose influence, and sacred light,
> Doth beautifie the day, and blesse the night;
> Which shining brightly in the highest Sphaere,
> Adornes those smaller Stars, which now appeare

> Before her presence; by whose gracious sight,
> Their numerous feet now pace with rich delight:
> O happy they approach unto that Throne,
> Where vertues are the constellation.
> And let it be proclaimed nigh, and far,
> That our Illustrious Queene, Is a tru Star. (p. 2)

Alluding to the Marian titles *Rosa Mystica* and *Stella Matutina*,[69] the verse emphasizes both Henrietta Maria's royalty and her subservience; to be chief petitioner to the monarch is her utmost dignity. Though her 'tru, constant, loyall, fixed' qualities are celebrated, the language of astrology is co-opted to express the 'influence' that a star may have: certainly on lesser stars, perhaps on the sun. The couplet 'O happy they approach unto that Throne, / Where vertues are the constellation' can be taken both as continuing the litanic sequence, casting Henrietta Maria as a recipient of her subjects' prayer, and as referring, Esther-like, to the Queen's own role as petitioner. More daringly, and perhaps giving a clue to Lenton's own beliefs, the equation of Henrietta Maria with the Blessed Virgin silently endorses the practice of petitioning the latter.

This Marian imagery has come a long way from Constable's. When applied to Elizabeth, it emphasizes Mary's virginity to a quasi-autonomous degree; when describing Henrietta Maria, it has the effect of foregrounding Mary's roles as type of Christ's bride, the Church, and chief petitioner of God. These are theological concepts which are characteristically Catholic, and carry connotations of subservience: for both these reasons, they were an imaginatively potent means by which Catholics could flatter and exhort a Catholic queen, while sustaining the imperative of marital obedience. Christianity's insistent feminisation of the Church, which tends at most periods to be more affirmatively exploited by Catholics than by Protestants, had exceptional power throughout the seventeenth century in England, when applied to the Stuart succession with its repeated history of Protestant kings and Catholic consorts.[70] It could bring political and imaginative hope to recusants – and, as Prynne showed, it could scare puritans.

But to personify the Catholic church as an obedient wife could also, later on, be a justification of quietism. 'A Lamentation by the Church in England for her Present Misery', a Catholic ballad preserved in a manuscript dating from the 1640s,[71] has the refrain

'At our house at home, at our house at home / I am good wife and beares noe rule / till my good man comes home':

> This house is Englands Ile
> of late renown'd by fame
> but now by errors guile
> is fallen out of frame
> and I the Church the goodwife am
> w[hi]ch makes this wofull mone
> and Jesus Christ is my goodman
> w[hi]ch now is gone from home
> But some parhaps will say
> why is your goodman gone
> then answer them I may
> because true faith is flowne
> And unitie In veritie
> hath left her house alone
> for error lewde hath truth exclude
> w[hi]ch makes him be from home

The second part of the ballad is voiced by the 'goodman', Christ, from his lodgings in 'portingale and france'. Even the distribution of polemical commonplaces is governed by the assumption that the natural flow of instruction is from husband to wife: the wife complains of the late dearth of hospitality and the growth of lust, covetousness and avarice, and the husband, in impeccable Pauline manner, teaches her that it is all due to the heresies of 'frier Luther'. Yet the ballad ends uncertainly. Part 1 concludes with the church looking forward to the time when she 'shall beare rule / When my good man comes home', but Part 2 portrays the husband as sharing Christ's human powerlessness and unable to sway events by any means other than prayer.

> Good god cut short their hornes
> which rulest the harts of kings
> and Evermore Doth scorne
> the author of novell things
> wherfore good wife be thow content
> my presence though thou misse
> for I partake thy sad lament
> And wander for thy blisse
> from our house at home, from our house at home,
> I am good man, and heare complaints
> from my good wife at home[.]

CONCLUSION

If this poem is contemporaneous with the manuscript, it may be an imaginative response to the Civil War phenomenon of Catholic neutralism. A greater tolerance of Catholics at court had not resulted in a reduction of recusancy fines, and as Keith Lindley has pointed out, 'the Catholics had little cause to hope for toleration from the regime of Charles I, Laud and Strafford';[72] it was the first instinct of many to stay inconspicuous, and some never emerged. But despite the importance of this as a factor in determining Catholic behaviour during the Civil Wars, there were other ways in which the legacy of Catholic loyalism had never been clearer. This is partly by contrast with the other side; it is one of the enormous ironies of English intellectual history that just as English Catholics had largely disowned resistance theory, English Puritans appropriated it.[73] But one need not be taken in by Parliamentarian propaganda about Charles's popish army, or even Christopher Hill's comment that Catholics were 'solidly royalist', to acknowledge the large contribution made by Catholics to the King's cause.[74] For many, it was the natural one to join: not only because of Henrietta Maria, but because they would have found it impossible to align themselves with the religious sympathies of the Parliamentarians. An anonymous commentator wrote in 1642 that 'the Catholiques in this Kingdome give all lost, if ... this Parliament be not subdued'.[75] Regional studies of allegiance have suggested, especially for Lancashire, that there could be a disproportionately strong Catholic presence among Royalist field officers.[76]

Anti-popery has long been recognised as a significant factor in promoting distrust between court and Parliament; and given the current historiographical emphasis on the Civil Wars as England's 'wars of religion', one looks forward to a full-scale reconsideration of the Catholic role in them.[77] But of a period where Catholics seem so inconspicuous and so many other unofficial religious groups thrived, some counter-factual speculations are irresistible. The religious ferment of the period might have thrown up a covert radical Catholicism, eager to exploit what freedom of worship the period had to offer, or a Jesuit-led revival which used the discontinuities of state religion as an opportunity to promote appeals back to Rome; and yet, neither appears to have happened. Historians have traditionally – perhaps correctly – seen the period as one dominated by the 'Cabal' of Thomas White *alias* Blacklo, which aimed to establish an episcopal regime under the direction of the chapter of secular clergy which had taken over the administration of English Catholicism when Richard Smith, their bishop, fled overseas in 1631. In both his administrative leadership and his writings, White privileged secular authority over papal, and his treatise *The Grounds of Obedience and Government* (1655) urged recognition of the *de facto* regime. His attempt to persuade the Independents to extend principles of toleration to Catholics, though dustily answered by its addressees and held against him at the Restoration, was the most inventive Catholic response to the peculiar opportunities of the period; and even this was mesmerised by the principle of official toleration in an age where, to many other groups, this mattered less than ever before.[78] The omnipresence of loyalist protestations in imaginative writing must certainly have helped to create a mid-century climate in which toleration dominated Catholic concerns, perhaps even stunting them; but the present writer knows of no imaginative response, internecine or other, to Blackloist conceptions of loyalty.[79]

Loyalists of the 1620s and 1630s often became the Royalists of the 1640s, and here it is possible to follow the careers of a few writers mentioned earlier. John Abbot reappears with the poem *The Sad Condition of a Distracted Kingdome. Expressed, in a Fable of Philo the Jew* (1645), which retells a legend that God had asked the angels for their opinions after creating the universe. The story's topical application to the King and Parliament is obvious, and its contrast with Abbot's other allegory, *Jesus Praefigured*, could not be more striking: the one is replete with courteous proselytism, the other fulsome with identity of interest.

> Who sayes who's faulty? He or they?[80] The King
> A God on Earth, a consecrated thing
> Cannot transgresse, and being the only source
> Whence Justice, and our Laws derive their force
> Must needs be pure.   (f.B4b)[81]

Abbot's case illustrates a more general rule. Plenty of imaginative royalist writing survives from Catholic pens, and plenty is fervently loyalist, but its content tends not to be identifiably Catholic; the need to support the king must have suppressed the articulation of difference from him.[82] One exception, also anticipating *Paradise Lost* in dealing with the fall of the angels, occurs in a manuscript volume in the National Library of Wales, attributed to Charles Arundell, which chillingly argues that a Catholic state governed solely by the monarch, but answerable to the Inquisition, is better than the ills of Parliament.[83]

> Were I a prince all Courts and prisons too
> should bee put downe, I would reserve but two
> such choice of courts, such multidude [sic] of lawes
> make us forgett, (if not forgoe) Gods cause.
> wee find the heathenish blasphemous event
> of curst Com[m]ittees since this Parliament,
> In any Christian state there's use of none
> But Bedlam and the Inquisition. (p. 12)

The poem from which these lines come, 'The Creation', illustrates the author's preoccupation with parallels between Parliament's insubordination and the entry of sin into the newly created world. 'The first Parliament', another poem from this manuscript, explores the parallel in most detail. God surveys everything and sees that it is good, then calls his angels and declares his intention of making them rulers of man and beast, the sea and the land: 'and to avoid all possible dispute / Thus signed what he had said Le Roy le veult'. But, in a deliberate equation of the fall of the angels with the fall of man, God's one proviso is made to be that they should not eat of the tree of knowledge; the apple becomes an emblem of *arcana imperii*.

> Give names, make Lawes dispose as yow thinke best
> yours is the tree of Life and all the rest
> Save onely one, Bee not inquisitive
> to try that tree tis my prerogative
> hee that presumes to touch or tast that tree
> shall dy with all his curst posterity... (pp. 16–17)

The Parliament begins to overreach itself, and on a day when all the Lords are sitting 'a member of the Lower howse / and with a countenance audatious' tells them that his fellows plan to rebel and eat the fruit.

> They say they will noe longer Subject bee
> to Church or King they'le have a parity
> they say there is in nature noe such thing
> as pope or prelate, Emperor or King
> they will not still be fooles, still bee soe stanch
> downe with that favorite tree both roote and branch ...

> Shortly my Lords bee wise and looke about yow
> Let it bee donne or else they'le do't without yow... (pp. 17–18)

The weaker part of the House is convinced, while the wiser go along with the rebels 'for want of hart'. They realise their error as soon as they have eaten, and as they descend into pandemonium, the poem ends. The topical root-and-branch allusion, stemming originally from the standard visualisation of hierarchy as a tree, is here grafted on to the Tree of Life. A Catholic dendrology is given as the ideal, with the pope at the top of the tree, and prelates having precedence over emperors and kings; yet the hierarchies of church and state join in one line, where an appositional structure reflects how both may serve as a bulwark against the terrors of popular rule. In wartime, the conflict between papal and Stuart claims could be de-emphasized, and the theoretical similarities between the two would have served to reassure. If the poet's yoking of Royalism and Catholicism seems to anticipate Jacobite loyalties, this is no coincidence. As the discussion of Thomas Howell in the next chapter will demonstrate, Anglicans began to appropriate Catholic tropes during the Civil Wars to express their loyalty to a church *in absentia*; but in some future study, it may be possible to date the inner rings of the Jacobite oak back to the Catholic loyalists of the Elizabethan Settlement.

CHAPTER 5

The subject of exile: I

The Civil Wars, which forced Anglicans into the subterfuge and exile that Catholics had long known, prompted them to appropriate Catholic lamentation and protestation, but also to dissociate themselves from Catholic writers. As a counterpart to the quotation with which chapter three began, where Constable is implored to return from exile, there follows a passage from Cowley's 'Elegy on the death of Mr. Crashaw', referring to how Crashaw became a canon at the shrine of Loreto after his conversion and departure from England, and just before his death.

> How well (blest Swan) did fate contrive thy death,
> And made thee render up thy tunefull breath
> In thy great Mistresse Armes? Thow most divine
> And richest Offering of Lorettoes Shrine! ...
> Angels (they say) brought the fame'd Chapell there;
> And bore their sacred load in triumph through the aire.
> Tis' surer much they brought thee there; and They,
> And Thow (their charge) went singing all the way.
> Pardon, my Mother Church, if I consent
> That Angels lead him when from thee hee went.
> For ev'en in Errour sure no danger is,
> When joynd w[i]th soe much Piety as His.

Sincerely laudatory of Crashaw's poetic achievements, solicitous to minimise the wrongness of theological error, and ending gracefully 'And I myselfe a Catholique will bee / Soe farre at least, great Saint, to Pray to Thee', the passage nevertheless stresses the *appropriateness* of Crashaw's foreign end. So far from lamenting England's loss, as Constable's supporter does, Cowley celebrates Loreto as the most seemly haven that Crashaw could possibly have found; and one must look back to another passage quoted earlier in chapter two, Hall's suggestion in *Virgidemiarum* that Southwell ought to be transported to

Loreto, to appreciate the double-edgedness of this. Catholics have, literally, to move their home as the Blessed Virgin was supposed to have done. Though Hall's use of the trope is satiric and Cowley's encomiastic, both defend the deracination of Catholic poets; and since Cowley was living away from England at the probable time of writing, within the exiled Stuart household at the Louvre, his elegy betrays the necessity to distinguish himself politely from Catholic exiles in an environment where Catholic and Anglican were on unusually intimate terms.[1]

This tonal dissociation is all the more apparent when one compares Cowley's elegy with a second counterpart to the poem on Constable, another sonnet to an absent male friend. Sometimes – as with Nicholas Oldisworth, a conformist who wrote verses to and about his Catholic friend George Bacon – the sonnet can be used to yoke homosocial protestations of friendship with articulations of ideological and religious distance;[2] but in a group of sonnets in a manuscript of early seventeenth-century verse in the Huntington Library, convincingly attributed by Anthony G. Petti to Toby Mathew the younger, the sonnet, 'Upon the Sight of Dover Cliffs from Callis', equates the griefs of exile with those of separation.[3]

> Better it were for me to have binn blinde
> then with sadd eyes to gaze upon the shore
> of my deare countrey, but now mine no more
> w[hi]ch thrust[e]s me thus, both [out] of sight and minde,
>
> Better for me to have in cradle pined
> then live thus longe to choake upon the coare
> of his sadd absence, whom I still adore
> w[i]th present hart, for harts are not confind
>
> Poore hart, that dost in so high tempest saile
> against both winde and Tide, of thie friends will
> what remedie remaines, that cann availe
> but that thou doe w[i]th sighes, the sailes fullfill
> untill they splitt, and if the body die
> T'is well ymploy'd, the soule shall live thereby

One must beware of always identifying poet with poetic persona, especially in the deceptively frank medium of the sonnet. But in view of the overtly Catholic nature of the group of sonnets, combined with numerous invitations to the reader to interpret the poems personally, the topic of exile may be an autodidactic projection of a possible fate, or, more soberly, it may be autobiographical fact. Mathew – if the poems are indeed his – converted to Catholicism in 1607 and was exiled three times during his life, around 1608 and 1618, then permanently in 1640.[4] The sestet evokes emblem-literature with its picture of a sailing heart to signify exile, but exploits verbal ambiguities that would be outside the reach of an emblem. These are the most difficult feature of the poem, pivoting on the phrase 'of thie freinds will'. The heart may be sailing away against wind and tide as a means of suggesting that the poet's friend does not want him to go, or – as the placement of the comma may help to suggest – because it is his friend's will that the poet should go. Not only ambiguous in itself, it necessitates a re-reading and reassessment of the earlier half of the poem. The reader's first inclination is to understand the second quatrain as reinforcing the first, yet, depending on the identification of the friend, the one may qualify the other instead: the poet's mortal friend is absent on the Continent, yet, if the poet stays in England, his heavenly friend Christ is absent.

This sonnet, taken in conjunction with Mathew's life, displays the double legacy of exile from England: continental travel might be deeply undesired, yet it could have positive results. Mathew and his friend George Gage, to whom the above sonnet is probably addressed,[5] acted as agents to acquire works of art for pre-Civil War English collectors, some of whom – like the Earl of Arundel – had crypto-Catholic sympathies themselves;[6] other Catholic priests like Richard Lassels, whose use of the term 'Grand Tour' is the first recorded in the Oxford English Dictionary, were to become travelling tutors, and were able to facilitate the progress of Royalist exiles about the Continent during the Civil Wars and Interregnum. The role of these priest-virtuosi within Catholic literary culture, and more generally in English cultural history, has been the subject of an important – though still little-known – study by Edward Chaney.[7] Though their travel-writing and guidebooks cannot be addressed at length here, these were as important as their collecting in formulating the ideal of continental travel as an essential component of the élite Englishman's education. As Chaney points out, a serious awareness of the Catholic contribution to this chapter of English art-history argues for the backdating of a cultural fashion which is usually thought of as eighteenth-century, or Interregnum at the very least. As so often, one must be wary of supposing that a movement cannot have been important when it was primarily associated with Catholics – or later, Jacobites.[8]

English Protestants were not necessarily more insular than English Catholics. All scholarly debate was conducted in an European arena; and though the Reformation discouraged foreign travel among English Protestants wishing to avoid popery and political unrest, such travel was never quite curtailed – Milton and other Protestants even stayed at the English College in Rome.[9] But English Catholics were necessarily more disposed than English Protestants to look predominantly abroad for intellectual intercourse, and a forced familiarity with the Continent could mean – most strikingly, perhaps, in the early seventeenth century – that exiled Catholics were more responsive than most Englishmen to the vanguard of European taste. But as a class, virtuosi have been neglected by Catholic historians – perhaps out of a feeling that they cannot be said to have suffered. Richard Lassels might have agreed, to judge from an uneasy passing comment of his: 'God ... gave me both leisure and meanes to studdy and live hansomely abroad, whiles bettre men than I were forced to studdy how to live at home.'[10] But the tempestuous heart emblematised in Matthew's sonnet suggests that even the cultured continental existence of a priest-virtuoso might not have been without exilic sorrow.

Whatever the local and temporal variations in enforcing penal laws, the great majority of English Catholics had every reason to feel alienated from the country they lived in; and from the beginning of Elizabeth's reign to beyond the period covered by this study, motivations to leave it would have been various. Children were sent abroad for a Catholic education,[11] young men would have made the journey to train as a secular priest or Jesuit, and men and women to embark upon the religious life in the other Orders. Scholars, especially in the years immediately after the Elizabethan Settlement, left to continue their study at foreign universities, and contribute to the flow of controversial prose from foreign presses; other scholars, aristocrats or musicians found posts in ducal households or in cardinals' entourages, or received pensions from the Spanish Crown; the failure of the Northern Rising in 1569 sent many political refugees overseas; and some laymen and laywomen would simply have assented to the lines given to Thomas Hoghton in the prosopopoeic Catholic ballad 'The Blessèd Conscience', 'Like frighted bird, I left my nest, / To keep my consciènce'.[12] Some exiles found it hard to survive, and others, it seems, came over only to die: an inscription in S. Gregorio, Rome, reads in English 'Here lies

Robert Peckham, English and Catholic, who, after England's break with the Church, left England because he could not live in his country without the Faith and, having come to Rome, died there because he could not live apart from his country.'[13]

Forbidding travel abroad, and withholding permission to return, could both be used as punitive measures. Some individuals were exiled, others were refused government licences when they asked to leave the country for the sake of their consciences. At the beginning of Elizabeth's reign, several priests were arrested when they tried to travel to the continent illegally; but the statute of 1585 'against Jesuits, seminary priests and such other like disobedient persons' declared that any priest who had been ordained by papal authority was guilty of treason once he came to England. Permitted travel abroad for Englishmen was circumscribed, almost less by popery itself than by the foreign localities of English popery: travel-licences issued by the Privy Council often stipulated that the traveller must not visit the towns in which English Catholic exiles were concentrated, St Omer, Rheims, Douai and Rome.[14] For the Protestant, travel to Rome was tainted by the remembrance of pilgrimage, and present fears of the Inquisition; as R. S. Pine-Coffin has pointed out in his bibliography of travel-literature, from the 1540s it seemed almost impossible for any Protestant to compile a travel-guide without reflecting on the sinfulness of the Roman clergy.[15] Yet Catholic emphasis on Protestant usurpation of England and the spiritual efficacy of journeying can be seen as a double retaliation, accusing the non-traveller of sin.

Some of the texts discussed in these two chapters, like 'Walsingham', and 'Jerusalem, my happy home', are well-known from anthologies. Some, like the English Jesuit dramas, are frankly obscure – and so, a few introductory remarks on the latter may be useful.[16] The Jesuits pioneered theatre as an educational tool, and the term 'Jesuit drama' is generally used for the school and college dramas of the English Catholics, but it is not unproblematic: a college was not necessarily under Jesuit control at the time any one play was put on, nor were all authors who wrote Catholic school drama themselves Jesuits.[17] The centres of this drama were the English colleges at St Omer, Douai, Rome, Valladolid and Seville, and the plays tended to be written by masters at the colleges and performed by the schoolboys or seminarians on public occasions: prize-days, or the visit of some ecclesiastical or secular dignitary.

They could be performed in the refectory, or another great hall, or even outdoors on occasion. Though they were usually in Latin, plot-synopses known as *argumenta* or *periochen* were distributed to the audience. These were long plays, and most characteristically tragedies, but the main action could be punctuated by interludes, which sometimes commented on it and sometimes were simply intended as a divertissement. The topics and historical periods which dominate English Jesuit drama hardly figure, often for obvious reasons, in English mainland drama: stories from the persecuted early Church, from Byzantium during the period of the Iconoclast controversy and from Christianity's embattled beginnings in pagan Britain. Many foreground the martyr. But other genres than tragedy could be appropriate vehicles for didactic and controversial messages, and other historical periods were tackled. In particular, the dramatists' location away from the English mainland meant they could be more outspoken than any other Englishmen; and those who were unequivocally opposed to Tudor or Stuart regimes took advantage of this, resulting in some of the most powerfully subversive texts ever to come from English pens.

Writing on exile in the Italian Renaissance, Randolph Starn has recently said, 'However the borderlands and otherwheres of exile may be perceived or plotted on a map, it is clear that they occupy cognitive as well as physical space. They ... constitute moral and political ground.'[18] To this, one can add religious – and further comment that more than any other theme in English Catholic discourse, exile prompted a self-conscious addressing of the authorial role. One need not necessarily agree with the sentimental idea that all major artists are inner exiles in their own culture to admit that the link between exile and literary creation is hard to ignore; and the classical precedent of Ovid, the Renaissance testimonies of Dante and Petrarch, and the Judaic experience at all times, remind one that English Catholics were not alone in defining the poetic consciousness as exilic. A. Bartlett Giamatti has described Renaissance culture as having to assert exile from secular antiquity, or scriptural paradise, 'in order to refashion, or revive, or give rebirth to, or regain, what had once been purer, holier, or simply more whole ... [E]xile is the precondition to identity.' Petrarch believed that one should never borrow or lift the words of predecessors, but ingest them and make them one's own by digestive transformation; and it has recently been argued that his theory may have been inspired by a need to transmute into literary form the crises of geographical exile and his own temporal distance from classical antiquity.[19] Certainly, both in exile abroad and in yearning after the old religion at home, the English Catholics undertook many textual refashionings, digestions of history and transformations of genre to express the peculiarity of their plight.

WEEPING ENGLAND

Weeping *for* England is something that all early modern England was urged to do, at the death of some great figure or in response to some tragedy. Weeping *England*, more specifically, is the topos of the mourning woman who mourns in some way for England or the English nation. Sometimes the woman herself *is* England, mourning; sometimes she mourns England as an other; sometimes she is the soul of England's body. In the sixteenth and seventeenth centuries she was ubiquitous: in lamentation, especially in the many translations and paraphrases of the Book of Lamentations;[20] in satire; in funeral elegies for public figures; and in the royalist tracts of the Civil Wars. The sorrows of English Catholics sometimes vented themselves in elegy and its various sub-genres such as lamentation and complaint, sometimes in texts of other kinds that modulate into the elegiac. Weeping England figures prominently among their elegiac personnel, and their use of her is distinctive: she is an exhortatory instrument, giving voice to lament, and deliberately deferring the consolations of elegy in order to stimulate the reader to action.[21]

One such text begins:

> Descend from heaven, O muse Melpomene,
> Thou mournful goddess with thy sisters all.
> Pass in your plaints the woeful Niobe;
> Turn music to moan with tears eternal.
> Black be your habits, dim and funeral ...

The tragic muse and the tearful Niobe are in a public role here; as chief mourners for the nation, they represent weeping England. A funeral elegy on Mary I, the poem belongs to a sizeable category of texts – with hindsight, also a sad one – written during and just after Mary's reign by Catholic writers, congratulating her on the fact that the Reformation had now been quashed. George Cavendish, the writer, was better known as the author of a Life of Wolsey which had an extensive circulation in manuscript, and the elegy comes from a poetic sequence called 'Metrical Visions', appended to the Life in some manuscripts.[22] The sequence combines funeral elegies, on Henry VIII and Edward VI as well as on Mary, with complaints voiced by those who have lived during these monarchs' reigns and come to bad ends. An early Catholic loyalist, Cavendish praises Mary for her orthodoxy but criticises neither Henry nor Edward for their religion. The pope, cardinals and all Catholics are asked to pray for her 'Which late restored the right religion' (l. 71), and Cavendish, praising Elizabeth, urges her to follow in Mary's footsteps.

Grief, then, is succeeded by consolation: so far, so decorous. But the manuscript is curiously arranged. The elegy on Mary comes *after* the author's farewell to the reader, which is dated 24 June 1558, before Mary's death; and written as an afterthought, placed at the bottom of the page after the author's farewell, is an epitaph of a very different sort, an epigrammatic Latin rhyme: *Novus Rex, nova lex. Nova sola Regina, probet pene ruina* (New king, new law. A new queen ruling on her own may prove almost a disaster). In Cavendish's hand like the rest of the manuscript, it seems likely to have been written after both the main body of the work and the elegy on Mary, some time into Elizabeth's reign when Cavendish had reason to revise his opinion of her. As an *envoi* to the *envoi*, it completely devastates the comfortable conclusion. If one reads the manuscript in the obvious order, the rhyme stands as a warning before the elegy on Mary, qualifying the whole by the voice of disillusion; yet Cavendish does not cancel his praise of Elizabeth. The piece becomes forcibly multivocal, not because it preserves two different political opinions, but because it allows two temporally separate reactions to Elizabeth's government.

The poem illustrates a trend which one can discern even in unified elegiac compositions by Catholics at this date. These lament in highly public, yet highly personal terms the passing of Catholic orthodoxy and the advent of heresy, characteristically described in funereal tropes. The tendency is nearly always towards personification of this orthodoxy, in keeping with the emphasis Catholics placed on the visible church – a feminised church, just as personifications are most commonly female – and sometimes the speeches of these personifications are called complaints. Critical discussions of the female complaint are still often based on a restrictive conception of complainants; not all have been beheaded or recently deflowered, nor are they even necessarily an exemplar of Christian contrition.[23] Most Catholic examples are lofty matrons, often mothers weeping for their children.[24] Their lament is dissociated from personal sin, yet inspired by familial sin; it is a maternal rebuke of the kind which, proverbially, one had to be an adamantine sinner to refuse. They take their bearings from the prophetic threnes of Jeremiah and Lamentations, but their utterance has more to do with the bearded prophet than with the main female personification in those texts, erring Jerusalem.

This has implications for how elegy currently tends to be defined. Lamentation was central to a number of Renaissance definitions of the elegy, and Sidney asked rhetorically what moralists could find to complain of in 'the lamenting Elegiac; which in a kind heart would move rather pity than blame; who bewails with the great philosopher Heraclitus, the weakness of mankind and the wretchedness of the world'.[25] But in current criticism, the link between elegy and lamentation has been weakened: not because lamentation is a dead form – war-poetry proves the contrary – but because commentators have played up the sceptical elements in elegy, and vastly underestimated its didacticism. Abbie Potts has said, for instance, that 'elegy is the poetry of sceptical and revelatory vision for its own sake, satisfying the hunger of man to see, to know, to understand';[26] and in an article published in 1994, W. David Shaw tells us that 'the most important aesthetic decision an elegist can make is to identify, not with the conventional consolations available to the mourner, but with the uncertainties of a puzzled and questioning reader looking perhaps for the first time into the eyes of death or grappling with other limitations'.[27] Though this barely concealed agnostic agenda may find wide acceptance now, it cannot be read back retrospectively. In what may be a natural accompaniment to a genre's perceived agnostic tendencies, recent critics have also tended to privilege the poet's subjectivity, and this too has sidelined the lamentation. Lamentations are exhortatory; they purport to be the voice of objective woe interrogating the reader, subjectivity beginning with that reader's response.

In *Ars Poetica*, Horace gave an account of the beginnings of elegy: 'Verses yoked unequally first embraced lamentation, later also the sentiment of granted prayer.'[28] This was a massively authoritative definition to the Renaissance, one which would have continued to influence generic thinking long after elegy moved into metres other than the elegiac; and two of its implications are particularly relevant to Catholic poetry.[29] First, though Horace is talking about the etiology of elegy, his description of how the genre fuses a two-stage process, lamentation and granted prayer, reflects the classic internal progress of a funeral elegy. The two, however, could be separated: Barbara Lewalski notes that Elizabethan and Jacobean critics distinguished between mourning elegies and anniversaries, which omitted the lamentation of funeral elegies,[30] and conversely, lamentations have various ways of implying consolation, yet subtracting it from their overt subject-range. Secondly, the 'sentiment of granted prayer', which is the Loeb translation of Horace's *voti sententia compos*, is not the only possible one: *sententia* is an ambiguous word. Horace was probably referring to inscriptions associated with votive offerings, which were commonly couched in elegiac couplets; but one can also take the phrase as referring to something in the future, 'the idea of granted prayer', 'the determination' or 'the purpose of granted prayer'. This suggests the trajectory, observable in many Catholic poems, towards an idea of consolation in the future to be supplied by the reader, rather than something contained in the present body of the poem. Within these poems, the common elegiac pairing of lamentation and consolation tends to be subverted or fended off, sometimes quite elaborately. There *can* be no good side to heresy; and among users of the weeping-England topos during the sixteenth and seventeenth centuries, Catholics are unusual in mainly using her to signify lamentation for heresy. Heresy is a totalising explanation for sin; identification of it may incorporate satirical or moralistic rebuke, but goes beyond both; and this suggests the necessity to look carefully at the work of Catholics or suspected Catholics in moralising or satirical vein, in case they hint at this explanation for wrongdoing.

Another opening stanza musters a crowd of female personifications, though this time England is the mourned rather than the female mourner.

> My mournfull Muse Melpomine drawe neere,
> Thou saddest Ladie of the sisters three,
> And let her plaints in paper now appeere:
> Whose teares lyke Occean billowes seeme to bee:
> And should I note the plaintiffes name to thee?
> Men call her Truth, once had in great request,
> But banisht now of late for crafts behest.[31]

This is the beginning to Thomas Lodge's 'Truth's Complaint Over

England', a poem appended to his tract *An Alarum Against Usurers* (1584). Lodge was a Catholic convert,[32] whose official conversion happened some time after 1584, but there is reasonable evidence for his recusancy dating from 1580; his public repentance was probably the culmination of a protracted conversion-experience, and his poems from the early 1580s need to be read with this in mind.[33] 'Truth's Complaint', conventionally enough, uses the myth of the Golden Age as a foil for present ills.[34] The speaker, Truth, is thereby cast as Astraea, the nymph who left the earth at the end of the Golden Age; and though Astraea was one of Elizabeth's poetic titles, Elizabeth is certainly not intended. The Catholic sympathies of the poem are at their most overt at the end, albeit half-concealed by a pun. Truth complains: 'such colours now are made, / That those would mend the misse, doo daunce in shade' (f.40a). The reader is alerted by the slightly clumsy construction; 'miss' clearly means 'what's missing', but also puns on the Latin 'missa', or Mass. In a neat double-entendre, those who claim to mend the Mass by reformation dance in the shade of spiritual darkness, while those Catholics who aim to mend the Mass by restoring it are forced to perform their rituals in obscurity. At the end of the poem Truth withdraws herself, forced away by the English. 'You Ilanders adieu, / You banish me, before I fled from you' (f.40a). Complaining of England's ills, she also laments England's spiritual death; in reminiscing about England's happier days, she has been commemorating something which she is then obliged to put to sleep. There is closure about Truth's decision: but with it, very little visible consolation.[35]

Yet there is an implied one: truth lives on, though in exile. If one takes Lodge's poem in a vacuum, it suggests no overt possibility of return; truth is dead to England, England is spiritually dead, and Truth is the agent of death, in that she accedes to the islanders' suicidal banishment of her. But one also has to consider its effect on the reader. Truth deliberately excepts some Englishmen from her strictures, those who 'beare a part and helpe to waile [her] mone', but they 'daunce in shade'. Because they are too small and marginalised a community, her continued residence is, literally, unviable. But Lodge is addressing Englishmen: and specifically the Catholic caucus in his circle of readers, who would have recognised the signal. If what Truth says were meant to be taken as literally true, there would *be* no audience, certainly no effective one. By assertion of the ill, the poem exhorts. The Envoy, 'Beleeve me Countrimen this thing is true' (f.40a) is not simply a reinforcement of what has gone before: coming emphatically outside the rhyme-scheme, and outside Truth's own speech, it demands – implicitly, if not overtly – an active moral response from the audience. Death has been dealt, and a funeral hymn sung, but the audience are being invited to contradict the genre – to resurrect England, and to prove Truth wrong. Exile is a reversible death, because however real and imminent spiritual dangers are, abstractions like Truth do not really die like kings. But the fact of Truth being an abstraction hardly absolves the audience from personal response.

Truth departs because England can boast only scattered Catholics, not a coherent church. With overdetermined versatility, she herself stands for that church: one reason why Catholic writers were able to make a freer use of weeping England than those from other religious persuasions. She was particularly appropriate to what they wanted to express, as demonstrating the visibility of their Church. It was an easy extension from that to the Blessed Virgin, and the many faces of Mary which weeping England could also connote: mourner at the Cross, especial patron of England, and mother-figure personally beloved of Catholics.[36] Mary was the special patron of many shrines in England, and shrines, regions and towns could all lament, both on their own behalf and as a synecdoche of the nation. One of the most famous post-Reformation Catholic poems begins:

> In the wracks of Walsingham
> Whom should I choose,
> But the Queen of Walsingham
> To be guide to my muse?
>
> Then thou, Prince of Walsingham,
> Grant me to frame
> Bitter plaints to rue thy wrong,
> Bitter woe for thy name.   (ll. 1–8)[37]

Either Christ or Henry VIII could be meant by the title 'Prince of Walsingham', and the ambiguity is probably intentional. Syntactically speaking, the 'wrong' could be a wrong done to the Prince, or by him; and either way, it would result in 'bitter woe' for him. If Henry VIII is meant, the poet's 'Grant me' is nothing more than a sardonic courtesy; if the Virgin Mary, Queen of Walsingham, is legitimising the poet's muse, Henry is hardly in a position to forbid criticism of himself. This poem illustrates particularly well how the

Virgin Mary, as queen of all female personifications, links the transcendent and the topologically immanent: the abstraction of *the* Church with the local specificity of *a* church. The long-standing association of Gothic ruins with elegiac musing in English poetry has Reformation antecedents; outrage at the physical effects of the dissolution of the monasteries was felt by many Protestants as well as by Catholics, and from an early stage, lamentation comes from all sides.[38] Where a conformist is writing, partial consolation always lurks in the background: the despoilations were terrible, and English hospitality is impoverished for lack of monasteries, but at least popish abuses have now been done away with. For Catholics, this was not a possible reaction. Though the protracted affirmative reappraisal of Gothic in England was certainly interconnected with softening attitudes towards Catholicism, the pleasure of ruins as a later elegiac topos was despite a Catholic aesthetic, as well as because of it.[39]

The place, or more specifically the medieval architectural complex, is personified – 'Such were the works of Walsingham / While *she* did stand' (ll. 21–2). Despite the ease of conflating female personifications within a poem, one still has to be alert to the fact that within the same poem they may be forcibly dissociated: which is what happens in the two last verses. Mary has been not merely banished, but supplanted; she departs, like Lodge's Truth, and leaves the personified shrine Walsingham to mourn.

> Weep, weep, O Walsingham,
> Whose days are nights,
> Blessings turned to blasphemies,
> Holy deeds to despites.
>
> Sin is where Our Lady sat,
> Heaven turned is to hell.
> Satan sits where Our Lord did sway:[40]
> Walsingham, O, farewell.   (l. 37–44)

Jesuit dramas could also hark back to a medieval golden age. William Drury's *Aluredus sive Alfredus* is one example: a drama about Alfred the Great performed at the English College, Douai, in 1619, and translated during the Interregnum by Robert Knightley.[41] Like many English Jesuit dramas, the play contains embedded lamentations, serving as prologue, chorus or, as in this case, the epilogue spoken by St Cuthbert.

> O wretched England! Would thou still did'st know
> that ancient happy state; thou wouldst not now
> As from ye world thou seperated art,
> So from ye worlds true faith be kept apart:
> Thou wouldst not then be cald an Isle ingrate
> ffrom Heav'n rebelliously degenerate;
> Nor wouldst thou consecrated Temples spoile,
> Nor them with sacrilegious Hands defyle;
> Nor let unparent=like thy Children bee
> Shipwrackt upon ye Rockes of Herisy.
> But England's now a Stepmother, alas,
> which once of Saints a fertile Parent was.

Implicit in the motherhood of weeping England is a generational judgement, since Catholic laments present change and heresy as something which has happened recently. Retelling the defection of the younger generation and the orthodox lamentations of the older, they oppose themselves to the Protestant vision of long-standing corruption in the pre-Reformation Church. Knightley's translation, quoted above, actually alters Drury's original by ending on this melancholy note; Drury's text concludes with a loud appeal to the Douai boys to fight and suffer for the reclamation of England, a startling demand which, of necessity, was common in English Jesuit drama. Consolation is denied within the text; but the text has the task of stimulating the reader, or the audience, to provide extra-textual hope and the possibility of consolation in time. In this context, the potential affective value of weeping England was clearly so great that the usual rule against female parts in Jesuit drama could be relaxed to allow for personification. A play by an author who was neither Jesuit nor English, but which may very well have been inspired by English Jesuit drama, makes analogous use of its choruses. In Nicolas Vernulaeus's *Henricus Octavus* (1624), written for Porc College in Louvain, a number of choirs – vicious and virtuous personifications, English virgins and English exiles – lament the schism.[42] The song of the virgins has the refrain *Crudelis Amor* and evokes weeping England, prefixing the first scene of Act II in which Catherine of Aragon laments her fate; the Virtues, in between Acts III and IV, interject dire predictions into the perverted epithalamium chanted by the Vices; and immediately before the last act, the English refugees hymn their own departure. The parallels between Catherine's lot and theirs are quite intentional, stressing how exile too is a divorce.

> Our churches lie gutted and burned to the ground,
> Blessed ashes are whirled on high by the winds,
> Ungodly flames our altars destroy,
> While Christ is driven from his sacred shrines.
> Gold in the churches is greatly desired,
> So shrines are plundered for the riches they yield.
> The plunderer revels in riches around him ...
> Some will dwell on Belgian soil,
> Some inhabit fields of Italy
> And others will touch on western Spain.
> Nameless, wretched exiles we will be,
> Scattered in a trice all over the world.[43]   (ll. 1,690–6, 1,724–8)

Prologues, epilogues and choruses are usually the most directive portions of Jesuit drama, but in *Brevis Dialogismus* (1599), one of the earliest surviving plays from St Omer, exhortation forms the plot of the play. Weeping Anglia figures prominently in that plot, her tears and proprietorial, motherly role towards the schoolboys designed to encourage filial and chivalric impulses as well as religious ones. The text summarises the plot thus:

At the beginning, ANGLIA presents herself with a tearful complaint, now destitute, bereft even of her own protectors. A youth ... cheers her with soothing speech. Then ASTUS, deceitful and crafty, and INDIGNATIO ... mark down every Christian for death by his English name, but the English battle-lines, though scattered across the globe, are glowing in opposition, and the followers of Thomas seek to emulate his deeds and for the praise of the faith prepare to risk death. Sad Anglia adds further motivation with her grief, and arouses their manly spirits to re-enact Thomas' virtue.[44]

This is an extreme example of the kind of exhortation with which lamentations, and Catholic lamentations in particular, commonly end; and in their deferrals of consolation and closure, Catholic martyr-poems can be very similar. Like funeral sermons, Renaissance funeral elegies classically offset mourning with the epideictic formulas of consolation: among these, Alastair Fowler lists the ages of life, the gifts of the Spirit, regeneracy, sainthood and relation to Christ. The dead person is a pattern, and their salvation is assured. This is also the message of martyr-poems, but in these, the fact of consolation is suborned to outrage. Some consolations are simply not appropriate: executions upset the natural cycle of youth, maturity, age and death. Others reproach by their very appropriateness: if the dead man was so saintly, what does that say about the regime that put him to death? These disruptions formally reflect the effects of the political oppression of Catholics, stretching to their limit the antithetical relations which exist within any genre.[45] The famous poem written on the death of Edmund Campion in 1581 exemplifies these disruptions, its very opening undermining the whole convention of literary commemoration.

> Why do I use my paper, ink, and pen,
> And call my wits to counsel what to say?
> Such memories were made for mortal men.
> I speak of saints whose names shall not decay. (ll. 1–4)[46]

So far is the poem from expressing resignation at Campion's death, particularly towards the judicial mechanisms that enabled it to happen, that the poet even appeals to the highest legal authority to recognise injustice.

> My sovereign liege, behold your subjects' end:
> Your secret foes do misinform your grace;
> Who for your cause their holy lives would spend,
> As traitors die – a rare and monstrous case.
> The bloody wolf condemns the harmless sheep
> Before the dog, the while the shepherds sleep. (ll. 67–72)

This is an unimpeachably loyalist protestation; to exonerate the Queen herself, blame – as usual – is thrown on her advisers. But the next verse is less correct.

> England look up: thy soil is stained with blood.
> Thou hast made martyrs many of thine own.
> If thou have grace, their death will do thee good;
> The seed will take that in such blood is sown ... (ll. 73–6)

The association of the Queen with England is implicit, but – if one exploits the opportunity for iconic elision opened up by the text – only too easy to make; Elizabeth's femaleness made her identifiable with her country in a sense that a male monarch was not. England is the main personification here, as she is not in Lodge: more actively evil than in Lodge, she sacrifices martyrs. She is much more analogous to the wanton Jerusalem of Lamentations; as if by Jeremiah, England – and implicitly Elizabeth – is being urged to repentance and urged to weep. The above quotation alludes to the saying 'The blood of the martyrs is the Church's seed', and, indeed, the end of the poem exhorts sympathetic auditors to imitate Campion's calvary. Ordinary consolation is rendered qualitatively different; the dead person's exemplarity becomes not merely programmatic, but urgently so. Even more than Lodge, this demands an extra-textual sequel: the listeners are to produce a flourishing church, watered by Campion's blood.

> We cannot fear a mortal torment, we:
> This martyr's blood hath moistened all our hearts;
> Whose parted quarters when we chance to see
> We learn to play the constant Christian's parts.
> His head doth speak, and heavenly precepts give
> How that we look, should frame ourselves to live. (ll. 157–62)

It would be wrong to give the impression that non-Catholic texts cannot challenge the auditor in an analogous manner. Weeping England, or weeping for England, can spur towards action in these, albeit a different kind of action. Distinctively Protestant messages were put across by a reassortment of personifications: a 1542 pamphlet, *The Lamentation of a Christian Against the City of London*, has a Christian speaker, ungendered but probably male, railing against London as the Whore of Babylon, rife with Mariolatry: it would have been more difficult to use an identifiably female speaker here. A mainstream publication responding to a plague outbreak, Thomas Brewer's lamentation *The Weeping Lady: Or London Like Ninivie in Sack-Cloth* (1625), has striking structural similarities to the deferred consolations already discussed. It is a compound of prose and verse, a lamentation framed by an Epistle to the Reader and a Conclusion. The Epistle looks forward to a time beyond the plague: 'My intent in erecting this poore Monument of Misery, was, to make this Ladies Teares out-live Her Teares: That, when (by the infinite Mercies of God[)] they shall bee wip'd off ... We may, in the view of this, and other ... Remembrances of Her, re-view them; in them, those infinite Mercies; and in both, be made mindfull of them, and eternally thankfull for them' (f.A3a). In the body of the lamentation London laments the loss of her sons and daughters, and concludes with an exhortation to stave off the plague by fearing God and honouring the king: 'Levell your words, and Actions to the will / Of Him, has power to pardon, or to spill, / And I shall soone be well' (f.c3b). The title to the Conclusion suggests the optimistic ending: 'The Authors comfortable Conclusion[,] and thankfull Remembrance of Gods great mercies, in the happy surcease of this dangerous Contagion' (f.c4a). Consolation is voiced by the author in his authorial persona; London is not made to dry her eyes and mitigate the effect of her reproach. The conclusion provides an end to what the epistle has inaugurated, even though both were written and published at the same time. The consolation is detached, not deferred; the plague was over and could be used as a completed exemplum, whereas the plight of Catholics had to remain in the present tense.

Though this link between the personification of weeping England and the separation of consolation from lament is characteristically Catholic, texts like *The Weeping Lady* show that neither factor was unique to Catholic texts. It was more natural for Catholics to make the connection with Mary; individual conformists could hold Mary in high regard, but nevertheless, veneration of her was one of the doctrinal demarcations separating Catholic from Protestant, and controversial impedimenta were inseparable from the way she was invoked in a text. There was nothing particularly Catholic about the formal demands of deferred consolation; but in practice, for most of the period covered by this study, Catholics had more reason than most to avail themselves of it. This, though, was to shift in the Civil War and Interregnum;[47] as so often, late sixteenth- and early seventeenth-century English Catholic writing can seem proleptic of Royalist lamentation. Among English Protestants, if they also happened to be Royalists, the Civil Wars were the first sustained period that one would have felt called to use weeping England as a condemnation of heresy, rather than merely a reproach of moral turpitude or an icon of misfortune: weeping England became weeping Anglicanism. Jeremy Taylor wrote in *The Great Exemplar* (1649) that 'the voice of the Church is sad in those accents, which express her own condition ... her song is most of it Elegy' (Part 1, p. 140).

Were Anglicans inspired by the use that Catholics had previously made of the trope, or did they derive it independently from the same biblical and literary sources? The former must have played some part, especially given the use that Lodge, and other Catholics, made of it for covert complaint within mainstream publication. With some occurrences of the topos, it is hard to believe that the author was not referring as well to a more overt Catholic usage. James Howell's *England's Teares*, appended to his allegory *Dendrologia* and published in 1644, is a speech of England's which uses some highly Marian vocabulary.[48] England laments 'I that have been alwayes accounted the Queene of Isles ... I that have been stil'd by the Character of the first Daughter of the Church' (p. 158), and says of the personification Religion, 'I heare that Reverend Lady (that

Queene of soules, and key of Heaven) make her moane ... that that Seamelesse garment of Unity and Love, which our Saviour left her for a legacie, should be torne and rent into so many Scissures and Sects' (p. 165), and then, almost echoing the *Salve Regina*, 'O consider my case, most blisfull Queene, descend, descend againe in thy Ivory Chariot; resume thy Throne' (p. 169). A few pages earlier, Howell has taken pains to point out that he is not a papist: which is what liberates him to write in this manner. But his inspiration is plain, licensed by the requirement to assert the unified body of Anglicanism. As with Howell's Catholic analogues, the ending of the piece is an appeal rather than a resolution. Like most prayers, it interrogates futurity from a position of passive moral confidence: the ungodly triumph, but thy will be done. And like any public supplication, it tries to shame the auditor into action. As with Howell's Catholic analogues, this is not a consolatory text; and because of its overriding anxiety to stimulate the reader into action, it throws very little light on the personal sensibilities of the author. But though these are not qualities which one associates with current definitions of elegy, they extrapolate on the lamentation that has been central to elegy from the start.

JESUIT TRAGICOMEDY AND THE LESSONS OF EXILE

Elegy was not the only genre that was consciously individualised to express affection for England and the plight of the Catholic exile. Some incursions of the elegiac mode into Jesuit drama have already been quoted, and two allegorical tragicomedies, both dateable to the early seventeenth century, demonstrate how even the overall structure of a play could be conceived in response to polemical and exhortatory stresses. The genre is unusual, since most surviving English Jesuit plays are historical tragedies, and most lost plays are identifiable as such. Historical tragedy was in itself a conscious attempt to make plays relevant to the performers, since – as described in the introduction to this chapter – the selected narratives tend to be those which invite parallels with contemporary religious events; and since so many end with a martyr's triumph, they belong to a christianised tradition of tragedy which evades rigorous Aristotelean definition. But in *Captiva Religio* and *Psyche et Filii Eius*, the two plays discussed below, tragicomedy is used to model the Catholic future in a very different manner from the elegiac. While lamentation exhorts its hearers to dry England's tears, tragicomedy heartens them by optimistic imaginative projection.

As Dante pointed out, exile is a figure for allegory;[49] and the allegorical component of these dramas is as crucial as the tragicomic. Allegory and polemic are natural companions, and in the Jesuit drama of the English, one can even argue that tendencies towards allegory are strongest when polemic is at its most overt. This happens not through any intent to disguise – in preaching to the converted there is no need for that – but through an impulse towards imaginative transmutation, universalising the plight of the English by vesting that plight with abstractions. This may sometimes have been the role of the allegorical interludes between acts, using music and dance to lighten the tragic atmosphere, that played so large a part in the total experience of Jesuit drama, but of which few well-documented instances remain; certainly, the Jesuit educationalist Joseph Jouvancy was later to argue that both tragedy and ballet could be used to depict the victory of religion over idolatry.[50] But something of the possible didactic role of allegorical figures can be seen in the dialogue between Comoedia and Tragoedia, in the prologue of the allegorical tragicomedy *Captiva Religio*, performed at the English College, Rome in 1614.[51]

COMEDY Not with the flapping of wings.
TRAGEDY Nor with winged shoes on the feet.
C Not with the feathers of sails.
T Nor in the triumphs of war-chariots were they carried.
C You have brought them to London.
BOTH Most excellent men.
C Here the port is a sure anchorage for beaked prows.
T Here, the sweet Thames laps at pleasant banks.
C See, a glittering bridge of martyrs with sacred foliage [i.e. palms].
T Here prison oppresses the pupils of the Roman faith with hardships.
C Here religion is captive.
T It is weighed down by bitter ills.[52]

Water is often invoked to describe the English Jesuit condition: it symbolises tears, the English channel which separates the exiles from their mother-country, and rivers as a synecdoche of cities. The generic personifications begin by setting the scene, and supernaturally transporting the actors over the English Channel to London; water is both a division between Rome and London, to be overcome by travel, and a means of access to the heart of England's capital city. Then in a startling and apocalyptic vision, combining the trajectory of the actors' travel with the probable outcome of their mission, a bridge is thrown to the subject of the play, captive religion. England's attractiveness is not diminished, but the audience is warned that it is a country where Catholics may languish in jail while the sweet Thames runs softly. The second part of the prologue shows Comedy and Tragedy abandoning their scenic function and acting in character, as they squabble about whether tragedy or comedy is more appropriate to a play set in mourning England, and come up with the English compromise of tragicomedy.

COMEDY Now the rest is for your ears.
TRAGEDY And your eyes – if you please –
C To be taken in. We are leaving.
T We who have come to you as Prologue, in preparation.
C We have taken a unique indulgence, in respect to you.
T Tragi-
C Comedy advances on to the stage.
T I don't care for laughter, I prefer sighs.
C I prefer laughter, I don't care for sighs.
T Sad tears are appropriate for mourning England.
C It's appropriate to console mourning England by means of sport.
T Alas!
C Ha, ha!
T Alas for me!
C O festival day!
T Tears . . .
C Come, jokes.
T Weep.
C Laugh.
T It's resolved, English-style.
BOTH Audience, may you give up your time with well-disposed minds.[53]

The element of apology in the final resolution of Comedy and Tragedy is understandable, given the usual bias towards the tragic in Jesuit drama; but there is also a recognition that tragicomedy is uniquely appropriate for the plight of the English Jesuits. The ambiguity of being English and Catholic, natives of England who faced imprisonment and death whenever they returned from exile, is translated into genre. What seems stranger in the twentieth century is the proposition with which Comoedia begins, that it is possible to become accustomed to the situation in England by giving it comic treatment. But this is to be seen neither as hysteria nor entirely in terms of trench humour, though there is certainly an element of the second: a transcendental importance is invited for comedy, in recognition of the fact that though the present state of English Catholics is pitiable, an ending of unspeakable happiness is reserved for them.

Captiva Religio was performed three times in January and February 1614, and a contemporary account of the production survives.[54] Written by Federico Gotardi, a Venetian spy in Rome, it complains that the play took five hours to describe the wretched state of the Catholic church in England. The scene was London; at the back of the stage there were prisons and dungeons filled with Catholics, and above the facade, in letters of gold on a red background, were the words CAPTIVA. The plot – punctuated by comic scenes ridiculing Calvinist ministers and parish priests – concerned one Finson, an English gentleman who had come to Rome in the days when England was still Catholic. On his return to England he finds that those adhering to the true religion are being oppressed, and to help them, he takes a position as jester to the Minister for Justice, or Chancellor. While failing to gain their freedom, he prevents them being further persecuted. He then tries to make his way back to Rome, leaving a note revealing his true identity, but before leaving the country he is apprehended by order of his master, who receives him back with great celebrations. Gotardi reports that one of the students acting the play had been a comedian for James I, and was famous for the strength and beauty of his leaps.[55] Assuming that this student played the jester, the plot was clearly designed to showcase his physical talents; Gotardi thought the play foolish, but had to concede that it was very well-acted. More than that, it projects a possible collective future from this student's particular past. Richard Helgerson has commented on the 'enabling pose' of the court jester, privileged to voice uncomfortable things to the monarch;[56] while the jocose quality of this play may certainly have been intended to console mourning Englishmen, it also recognises the potential power that jokes had to sway the decisions of authority. But the English College in Rome staged a number of anti-Henrician dramas at around this date,[57] and in this context, one may also be intended to remember a less eirenical Catholic jester: William Somers, court fool to Henry VIII, who was said to have called Anne Boleyn a whore and Elizabeth a bastard.[58]

Exile inspired at least one other Jesuit drama with a tragicomic plot, and the trope of water recurs. An anonymous, titleless Latin play in the Bodleian, which has been given the title *Psyche et Filii Eius*,[59] claims in the chorus to Act III that the waters of the rivers near Jesuit colleges have the power to extinguish heresy, while stressing that since rivers run into the sea, they are a signifier of return as well as of separation.

As Hope escaped the hands of bloody Hate, so have those few escaped the rage of heresy who now drink the waters of Baetis, Tiber or Pisuerga. May heaven grant them an easy return to England. (f.81b, ll. 1523–6)[60]

The play is an allegory of England's troubles. The sons of Psyche, who represents the English church, are led astray by an irresponsible tutor, Thelima or Free Will. Psyche's response is to order in her sleep a rose, representing Faith and Wisdom, to be gathered from Paestum, the city of Lucania celebrated for its twice-blowing roses,[61] here signifying a revival of the Catholic faith. Of her sons, Eros – the Catholics – accepts the challenge. Mysus – Heresy – complains bitterly that this task has been given to Eros, and stirs up some of his brothers – Orge, the populace, and Thrasus, audacity – against Eros; but he fails to influence the others, among them Elpis, representing the English exiles. Mysus sets a trap for Eros and his companions, which Elpis betrays to Psyche. Psyche then hands over her sons to the tutor Philosophus – the pope, or church authority – who forms their minds to better ends. The theme of tutelage is instantly recognisable as belonging to Jesuit drama; but despite that, *Psyche* would be even more inscrutable than most allegories without the prologue, epilogue and choruses. As the chorus to Act I reveals, these contain the characters' identifications and transform the play into polemic. The enigma of the first act is both something to decode, and something that proclaims the truth to a dangerous extent only possible under expatriate conditions.

The riddle is solved, for we have applied this to our misfortune: it is not lawful to speak of true matters unless under an enigma. England, under the name of Psyche, longs for the rose, the flower of ancestral faith, which once in its wanderings poured its happy odours into kingdoms, with many a shoot. Ah! it is shameful to tell what the stench is like now, where once the fragrances were so sweet. England knows this, she mourns, she groans, she laments . . . All Catholics lie hid under the form of Eros. Mysus oppresses them, Mysus whom I call heresy, Heresy, more mutable than Proteus, assuming all shapes, she does not think it disgraceful to speak from the jaws of a monster, provided that she can pronounce the sentence of death against the Catholic. (f.80, ll. 1,452–9, 1,463–7.)[62]

Though the allegory ostensibly hides, it is more accurate to call it revelatory. Catholics are understood by the *schema* of Eros, named after the god of love whom Psyche loved and lost in the classical legend, while the term *figura*, used as an alternative to *schema* in describing the personification of heresy, often describes ghosts and so suggests the phantasmic quality of false faith. Significantly, too, it is given in the plural. The many throats of heresy are intended to evoke the Lernaean Hydra which Hercules vanquished, a very common figure used both by Catholics against Protestants and, in England, by Anglicans against Dissenters: in both cases, it is a nightmare vision of the excesses of individual judgement. Here it is arrived at by combining Mysus with Orge, heresy with the populace, as the chorus to Act II makes more explicit: 'Oh, if only some Hercules would crush the sprouting heads of the hydra with the club of faith, and liberate England' (f.81a, ll. 1,504–5).[63]

Imagery is allegory on a verbal level, expounded as soon as created. On other levels – the stage-property of the rose, and the allegorical functions of the characters, probably enhanced by costume – it has the chance to sink in visually before being explained. Both also serve as *ornatus*, a rhetorical and aesthetic quality much valued by the Jesuits. Nigel Griffin, distinguishing between *ornatus* in word and in spectacle, says: 'They were images, moving images, themselves a significant part of the whole imagery that would run through the entertainment, reflected in costume, decor, language and text.'[64] In Psyche's case, this results in considerable iconographical complexity. First, she is a gracious, vulnerable and grief-stricken woman:

You have seen the tears of Psyche! They have a mystery: a mystery that may be better taught by means of tears than by tongue. Psyche (now you know that she conveys the changing fortunes of England) is rocked on the surge of a sea of cares, fearing shipwreck; nor is this an empty terror, since heresy presides over the rudder. Oh, England, England . . . (Chorus to Act II: f.80b, ll. 1,476–81)[65]

The first Bodleian cataloguer of this play defined it by Psyche's attribute of tears, *de lugentis Angliae facie*. Called forth because her sons are divided against each other, and her soul is alienated from the body, her weeping makes a double affective point.[66] It has all the moral reproach of Southwell's weepers, and, as with a Mary Magdalen or a St Peter, the reader is intended to interpret the weeping by supplying the narrative background. Here, the story of the play represents an invented sequel to the classical legend of Psyche. She is obviously more mature than when she wandered the earth in search of another Eros, yet she still represents exile and dispossession: the soul alienated from its heavenly abode and, on a more temporal level, the Catholic faith driven out of its homeland and embodied in the English colleges in mainland Europe.

CHAPTER 6

The subject of exile: II

Plays like *Psyche et Filii Eius* demonstrate one of the main topics discussed within this succeeding chapter: how, to quote Randolph Starn again, 'name-calling was one of the few obvious pleasures of exile'.[1] A list of some of the other subjects tackled within Jesuit drama – the break with Rome, and the martyrdoms of Sts Thomas a Becket, Thomas More and John Fisher – give a stronger impression still of how this exiled theatre was drawn towards material that was highly problematic on the legitimate English stage, treating it with a Catholic fury which would have been, quite simply, unstageable there. But if the incidental advantages of exile affected subject-matter within Jesuit drama and elsewhere, they did not themselves intrude as a subject; in expressed opinion, they hardly weighed against its defining sorrows. These were not simply a matter of being removed from home, family and possessions. In his massive *Anatomy of Exile*, Paul Tabori has distinguished between the *destierro*, the man deprived of land, and the *destiempo*, the man unable to pass time within his own country, and has described the exile as living in the present and the past simultaneously.[2] These chapters prove, if nothing else, the imaginative potency of nostalgia to the English Catholics.

Yet one should be wary of letting that become a dismissive value-judgement. As research on post-Reformation religious communities abroad gathers pace, it will become clearer how medieval patterns of life were sustained on the Continent by English, Scots, Irish and Welsh men, women and children, long after the Reformation – in some cases to this day – and how there was a constant interchange of individuals between the mainland and these religious colonies: a phenomenon which indicates great practical resilience within the Catholic communities of the British Isles, rather than the reverse. Nostalgia could itself be exploited for utilitarian reasons, as within the seminaries that trained priests to return to England: the cult of the Madonna Vulnerata at the English College in Valladolid demonstrates how yearning for England could be projected onto the Virgin Mary, piously supposed to have England as her dowry. But within England as well, Catholics perceived themselves as historical exiles from the time when England belonged to the true faith, and – in a unique intensification of the Christian commonplace – as spiritual exiles from heaven.

'AT HOME IN HEAVEN': HYMNS AND THE SOUL'S EXILE

As the last chapter demonstrated, the dispossession of *Psyche et Filii Eius* ends optimistically; and this is echoed in another genre, the Catholic hymn. If Rome equalled Babylon for the militant Protestant, and Protestant nationhood defined itself by excluding Catholics, the Catholic ideal of the heavenly city drew on the Book of Revelation to imagine bejewelled fortifications which Protestants might besiege in vain. 'Thy wales are made of precious stones; / thy bulwarkes, diamondes square', sang the anonymous priest-author of one of the most famous mainland Catholic texts of the period, 'Jerusalem, my happy home'; and Anthony Copley's *A Fig for Fortune*, discussed in chapter three, visualises the Church of England scaling the walls of Mount Sion, only to be beaten back by the orthodox. Just as Jerusalem is both the despoiled city of Lamentations and the heavenly destination of the soul, the present griefs of exile are counterbalanced by the future consolations of heavenly citizenship, in an intensification of the Christian view that all mortality is exile;[3] a lyric of Southwell's is entitled 'At home in heaven'. It is in this light that one must read 'Jerusalem, my happy home'.[4]

> Hierusalem, my happie home,
> when shall I come to thee?
> When shall my sorrowes have an end?
> thy joyes when shall I see? ...
>
> Wee that are heere in banishment
> continuallie doe mourne;
> We sighe and sobbe, we weepe and weale,
> perpetually we groane.
>
> Our sweete is mixt with bitter gaule,
> our pleasure is but paine,
> Our joyes scarce last the lookeing on,
> our sorrowes still remaine;

> But there they live in such delight,
> such pleasure, and such play,
> As that to them a thousand yeares
> doth seeme as yeaster-day. (st. 1 & 13–15)

After listing a number of saints singing hymns in heaven – Mary and other virgins, Ambrose, Augustine – in the company of Simeon and Zachary from the New Testament, the ballad culminates in 'There Magdalene hath left her mone, / and cheerefullie doth singe, / With blessèd saintes whose harmonie / in everie streete doth ringe' (st. 25): after which, there is only a reprise or variation of the first verse.[5] The selection of Mary Magdalen is not an arbitrary end to the catalogue; as the poets discussed in chapter two suggest, she stands above all for the Catholic weeper, and her change from sorrow to joy is to be read as the climax of the hymn's promises.[6]

One of the most important surviving Catholic manuscript-miscellanies, BL Add.MS. 15,225, preserves a text of the hymn, and with it, another ballad-evocation of the heavenly Jerusalem. This is a translation of a text that was Englished at least twice by contemporary Catholics, St Peter Damian's *Ad Perennem Vitae Fontem*, which begins by expounding the linked *contemptus mundi* commonplaces that lie behind all the conceptions of exile described above: banishment is a prison, prison a banishment, and the soul is alienated from heaven as long as it remains in the body.

> My thirstie soule desyres her drought
> at heavenlie fountains to refresh;
> My prisoned mynd would faine be out
> of chaines and fetters of the flesh.
> She looketh up unto her state
> from whence she downe by sinne did slyde,
> She mournes the more the good she lost,
> for present ill she doeth abyde.
> She longes, from roughe and dangerous seas,
> to harbour in the haven of blisse,
> Where safelie ancoreth at her ease
> and shore of sweete contentment is.
> from bannishment she more and more
> desyres to see her countrie deare;
> She sittes and sendes her sighes before;
> her joyes and treasures all be there. (st. 1–2)[7]

This does not render the whole of St Peter Damian's hymn: starting off in a reasonably accurate manner, it speedily modulates into imitation alone. In the imaginative exercise of translation, texts undergo revivification when, for whatever reason, they can be read as having topical relevance; and the same text translated by two religiously similar individuals at similar dates can still throw up striking differences in the imaginative emphases of different authors. In particular, the two final verses of the Latin are missing in 'Jerusalem, thy joys divine' which ends on an ecstatic vision of heaven; but they are translated in another version, that appended to *The Meditations, Soliloquia, and Manuall of the Glorious Doctour S. Augustine* (1631);[8] to a degree which may argue for clerical authorship, this translation accentuates the relevance of the lines to those risking their lives on the mission-field. But its didactic efficacy would have been wider. Like a pilgrim, the soldier is a Christian exemplar partly because of his lack of worldly ties, being dependent on what he can carry. The conception of exile as dispossession would have had particular relevance not only to clerics studying abroad, but to those Catholics who, without being exiled from their country, suffered civic privations and financial penalties in the hopes of being rewarded by a heavenly pension.

> Christ, thou Crowne of Souldiers,
> Grant me this possession,
> When I shall have leave to quitt,
> This dangerous profession;[9]
> And vouchsave to lett me have,
> Amongst thy Saints, my session.
>
> Give me strenght [*sic*], who labour in
> This battayle, yet depending,
> That when I have fought my best,
> Some peace may by attending.
> And I may obteyne thy self,
> As my reward not ending, Amen.   (p. 98)[10]

Speratory verse,[11] as this kind of text can be termed, stands in an antigeneric relation to elegy. Both lament, but whereas elegy aims only to console or exhort towards consolation, speratory verse emphasizes the objects of hope. It is partly a question of the relative space apportioned to the polarities of grief and joy, partly the relative specificity with which the latter is imagined. As the hymn 'Amount, my soul, from earth awhile' shows, the negative delights of heaven are almost as potent as the positive ones; there are 'noe rude nor raillinge heretikes / that new religions make' (st. 46), 'noe persecutinge potentate ... workmaister or pursivant' (st. 47), and 'There tiburne nothinge hath to doe, / noe rope nor racke is knowne' (st. 48). But all these texts have also in common a detailed, evocative and sensuous description of heaven which takes its bearings from the description of the new Jerusalem in the Book of Revelations: 'Amount, my soul' describes how 'the gates with precious pearles are framed, / there rubies do abound' (st. 10).[12] But they also go well beyond. The appeal to the senses of smell and taste in 'Jerusalem, my happy home' may be Ignatian in inspiration; it can be justified both in Ignatian terms and, more generally, because most Catholics felt that the senses could legitimately be stimulated to aid devotion. The difference between the ecstatic language of English Catholics and English Protestants may not be great, and as the transmission history of this text shows, Protestants could respond to almost all of this Catholic vision of heaven.[13] But one difference between the churches was in the degree of their willingness to evoke a synaesthetic heaven as part of religious worship; and given the difficulties surrounding the celebration of High Mass with its customary accompaniment of incense, passages such as the following might well have had a particularly potent effect in stimulating Catholic longing for heaven.

> There is nector and Ambrosia made,
> there is muske and Civette sweete;
> There manie a faire and daintie drugge
> are troden under feete.
>
> There Cinomon, there sugar, gro[w]es;
> there narde and balm abound.
> What tounge can tell or hart conceive
> the joyes that there are found? (st. 18–19)

There is nothing arbitrary about this list of delights. First – deliberately as a point of departure rather than a signifier of ultimate bliss – it christianises pagan gods' fare, nectar and ambrosia; then, with very similar effect, it refers to the courtly perfumes of musk and civet; then herbs are scattered on the ground, a festival activity that was particularly associated with saints' days in the medieval church. The implied synasthaesia of the action – herbs smell sweetly when trampled, but are also a 'drugge' when eaten – is continued in the pairing of cinnamon and sugar, two luxurious foodstuffs which are fragrant when growing. Because they smell most powerfully when damaged, crushed herbs and spices were a martyrological commonplace: Southwell's Mary Stuart begins her prosopopoeic verses, 'The pounded spice both taste and sent doth please'.[14] The medicinal references culminate in nard and balm, scenting the air and providing ointment for the wounded soul; and it is because of this reassurance that they come last in the catalogue, summarising and distilling the benefits of the rest.

But despite this level of detail, the verses foreground the paradox of all religious language: the impossibility of describing transcendence.[15] It is the burden, described as the 'under-song' in one manuscript, to 'My thirstie soule desyres her drought':

> Iherusalem, thy joyes devine –
> noe joyes may be compar'd to them;
> Noe people blessèd soe as thine,
> noe Cittie like hierusalem.

The phrase 'under-song' had a double meaning in contemporary usage: a subordinate song or strain, especially one acting as an accompaniment or burden to another; and, figuratively, an underlying meaning or undertone.[16] Here, both literal and figurative meanings have relevance to the ballad's structure. The beginning of the ballad creates a gap between the sorrows of the verse and the aspirations of the chorus, with sorrow predominating; but as it progresses, the chorus gains in incremental effect, and the subject-matter of the verse comes increasingly to match that of the chorus – perhaps the reason why the translation veers away so pronouncedly from St Peter Damian's original.[17] By the end, verse and burden are a continuum: the last stanza shows how, as with the dialogue of Tragedy and Comedy in *Captiva Religio*, generic conventions have been used first to divide grief from joy, then to unite them again. 'Jerusalem' is both the first and last word in the chorus, and the same word ends the last stanza, knitting up verse and burden and conceptualizing hope as a city.

> We can imagine but a shade, –
> it never entred into thought
> What joy he is enjoyn'd that made
> all joy, and them that joy, of nought.
> My soule cannot the joyes contayne, –
> let her, lord, enter into them,
> For ever with thee to remayne,
> within thy towne hierusalem.   (st. 27)

MARY IN EXILE: THE MADONNA VULNERATA

Because heaven is an aspiration shared by any Christian, and all Christians are obliged to think of themselves as exiles on earth, any of these ballads were potentially able to seep into the mainstream with very little alteration – but not with none. Stanza twenty-three of 'Jerusalem, my happy home', describing how 'Our ladie sings magnificat / with tune surpassinge sweete' was omitted in the printed version, even though the other verses describing saints were left in: a cursory piece of censorship, which nevertheless calls attention to the peculiarly sensitive manner in which passages describing Mary were observed or read by Protestants.[18] As suggested above, this argues a difference between Catholic and Protestant modes of reading: though individual Catholics and individual Protestants show wide differences in their devotion to Mary, Catholics were, in general, free from the governing Protestant anxiety about over-veneration. This stimulated an applicability of Mary to all types of exemplary womanhood. As the stanza above illustrates, the soul is commonly described as female; the interlocking complementarities of Christ and Mary, Christ and His Church, and Christ and the soul could all be co-opted into amatory discourse, and thence – as very differently with Oldisworth and Mathew – the condition of English Catholicism could be used as an analogy to the exilic gap between parted friends or lovers.

The equation of Mary with English Catholicism was, in any case, appropriate for a number of reasons. Medieval England was thought of as Mary's dowry, and because of the *Salve Regina*, all Catholic Christendom perceived her as the help of exiles. 'Hail, holy Queen, mother of mercy ... To thee do we cry, poor banished children of Eve; to thee do we send up our sighs, mourning and weeping in this valley of tears ... After this our exile, reveal to us the blessed fruit of thy womb, Jesus.'[19] Another reason may be hinted at in *Psyche et Filii Eius*. Though this play's primary purpose was probably not evangelistic, it externalises guilt and calls for repentance. The pivotal scene comes in Act IV iv, where each of Psyche's sons comes in to beg forgiveness. Elpis – the English exiles – comes first, acting as a conscience, and soon Mysus, Orge and even the tutor Thelima repent. The playwright – possibly another argument supporting a Valladolid provenance – may have been alluding to the expiation which the English College at Valladolid regularly made on behalf of their countrymen to the last of Psyche's guises: the Madonna Vulnerata.

The Madonna Vulnerata is a statue of the Virgin and Child. It was removed from one of the city churches in Cadiz in 1596, when English troops under the Earl of Essex destroyed the new Armada that was assembling there, and sacked the city. In the market square it was desecrated: the Child Jesus was cut away almost entirely, both the Madonna's arms were cut off, and her face was slashed removing part of her mouth and nose. The Count and Countess of Santa Gadea rescued it to put in their private chapel in Madrid, and eventually agreed to give it to the students and professors of Valladolid so that they should make reparation for the insults offered it by their countrymen. Untill very recently a mass and litanies of reparation were regularly offered at the College, with the Sunday within the octave of the Feast of the Immaculate Conception being celebrated as the Feast of the Vulnerata, and it is traditional for seminarians to kneel before the statue, like Psyche's sons before their mother, and vow to return as priests to England.[20]

The Madonna Vulnerata became to expatriate Catholics an emblem of English Catholicism. Though the iconoclasts intended to cancel the intention of the original sculptor to create a figure worthy of veneration, Catholics reinterpreted the remains as a unique combination of statue and relic.[21] Iconoclasts characteristically remove or disfigure the face, arms and attributes of an image to suggest mutilation and shame – the Lady Chapel at Ely is a *locus classicus* of this – but to a Catholic seminarian viewing the image, these marks of bitter experience would externalise the wounds inflicted by England's heresy and his own exile.[22] It was a visual reminder of the power of the heretics, increasing militancy and zeal. And it is, perhaps, Valladolid's supreme example of the spirit of Counter-Reformation Europe. Stephen Greenblatt has said that 'wounded artifacts may be compelling not only as witnesses to the violence of history but as signs of use, marks of the human touch, and hence links with the openness to touch that was the condition of their creation'.[23] This openness to touch is a sign of the Vulnerata's violated condition, but at the same time it marks her receptivity to the prayers of the scarred seminarians.

In a manuscript account of the solemnity at the installation of the Madonna Vulnerata, the didactic importance of having the statue in the College chapel is compared to 'the example of that Romane

The Madonna Vulnerata. By kind permission of the Collegio Inglese, Valladolid

Empresse which kept the garments of her husband imbewed(?) with his blood and mangled with the swordes of his enimies, and shewed them everie day to his childeren, that with this ruefull spectakle, she might refresh dayly the memorie of there fathers death' (f.54a).[24] This installation was no less of a theatrical presentation than a Jesuit drama, and had no less of a polemical point to make. Though Kevin Sharpe has called for closer attention to be paid to religious practices by historians of 'accredited rituals and ceremonies',[25] a common evidential difficulty is that individual orders of service – as opposed to royal occasions combining religious and secular elements, or collective religious practices which achieved liturgical permanence – are rarely well-documented; but for the installation of the Madonna Vulnerata, accounts survive which give a valuable summary of the ecclesiological details.[26] On the eve of the festival, 7 September 1600, the statue was borne veiled and in secret to the nearby Carmelite church at dawn. Friars exposed it in veneration in the principal chapel, which was adorned with tapestry. At vespers, it was taken in a solemn procession to the cathedral accompanied by twenty of the English students and Jesuit fathers bearing tapers, and followed by the laity. At the entrance to the cathedral the procession was re-formed and the Madonna borne to the English College, with Philip III's consort Margaret meeting it at the College gates. The bishop then placed the statue above the high altar of the College chapel and conferred the title of Vulnerata upon it. There was an all-night vigil and, after High Mass the next day, the Feast of the Virgin's nativity, another procession of the confraternities, the religious orders, the clergy and people took part. A large crowd waited outside the College while the Queen became the first to pay veneration to it, and after hymns in Latin and English, the College dined at the Queen's expense.

The account refers to the encounter in the chapel between the Vulnerata and Queen Margaret as between the 'only Queene of heaven' and 'the only Catholicke Queene of the earth' (f.56b). But the ceremony was also designed with another queen in mind, since much of it was performed not on the Virgin's nativity, but on Queen Elizabeth's. As Helen Hackett has recently pointed out, the undeniable popularity of Marian vocabulary in Elizabethan panegyric seldom indicates a simple equation of the two, even in the latter years of Elizabeth's reign;[27] but many Catholic commentators were not inclined to be aware of nuances. Still more, they noticed and resented England's deletion of saints' days and introduction of royal festivals in the Book of Common Prayer, which was read as an impious substitution. As the account makes clear, the coincidence of birthdays was noted, and used to make the festival a restitution for English impiety. It was felt to be a suitable day

> not only to repayre and recompence the injuries committed by those faythlesse hereticks against this farest image in Cades, but also to blott out the impietie of other there fellows in England who with notable follie and flatery (& no doubt w[i]thout consent or knowledge of her Ma[jes]tie) have <razed out in> ther Kalenders the name (& obscured) and memorie of this most happie feast, and in stead thereof ridiculously placed in redd letters (her) nativitie <of Queene Elizabeth> canonizing her alive which the Catholicke church doth not use nor permitt with any saincte how holy so ever he be, preferringe in this manner, as it seemeth her byrthday <wherewith have entred so many dolefull calamities to that unfortunate realme of England>, before the byrth of the most blessed mother of God . . . (f.53a)[28]

As the erasures and additions in the two different hands make graphically clear, opinions of Elizabeth were mixed among the expatriate Catholic community. As it stands, this document epitomises the topical Catholic conflict between loyalism and dissociation from the English Crown,[29] and it goes on to compare Elizabeth unfavourably with the pious Queen Margaret; but both these queens are further set against the focus of the whole solemnity, the Queen of Heaven. Mary is adjured to soften the resolve of her earthly English counterpart, and effect the reconversion of England.

> I will not omitt to make mention in this place of the great hope conceived by divers principall persons of much pietie and discretion, that the sacred Queene of heaven mother of mercie may with this occasion and notable example of the catholicke Queene of Spayne mollefie the hart of the Queene of England, and open her eyes to looke to her salvation whilst shee hath tyme: and nowe at least in her declining age to seeke for pardon at Gods hands amending the errors of her life past which, as it were much to be wished, so may it be hoped for, if that be true which I have hard credibly reported, that not many yeares agoe shee was accoustomed and parhaps still continueth, to recuere (i.e. recur?) in her fitts of melancholy and affliction to the glorious virgen . . . (f.61a)

Like some of the texts discussed in chapters three and four, this is diplomacy by remote control: a manifestation of the politics of prayer. Though accounts of the solemnity may well have reached English ambassadors abroad, there seems to be no record of them being invited to it – the continuance of the Spanish war with England would have made it unlikely – and the probability is strong that Elizabeth never heard of the ceremonies conducted for her conversion. As with some of the authors discussed in chapter three, the strong and literal faith of the religious professionals who organised the event would not have recognised a great need for publicity, even while making of the solemnity an important civic event which must have had a considerable ideological effect upon the citizens of Valladolid.

There was a tradition at other Jesuit colleges, possibly inspired by Valladolid, of conducting Marian veneration in a manner which referred to the state of England. At the opening of the St Omer church, the Abbot of St Bertains carried a statue of the Virgin in procession, the Litany of Loreto was sung, and in the middle of the College's central court a temporary chapel was erected to receive the statue. It was placed on an altar decorated with gilt vessels, and the thrones for the celebrants were given titles from the Litany that could apply equally to the Virgin or to a seat, *Sedes Sapientiae* and *Thronus Solomonis*; then poems and prayers were recited in honour of the Virgin, imploring her help. The Annual Letters, from which the account is taken, continue: 'Then they placed our afflicted and prostrate England, so wickedly ruled, under the trust and patronage of the Most Clement Mother. They reiterated in loud voices prayers to the Holy Virgin for the conversion of England. I cannot easily describe the religious fervour and emotions of soul produced on this occasion.'[30] In the longer history of devotion to Mary in Catholic countries, this political specificity can be paralleled many times; she was thought to have a special potency in putting down heretics,[31] and the radical words of the Magnificat on power, its promises to put down the mighty from their seat and exalt the humble and meek, may also explain why Mary has been so often venerated by protest-groups of various political affiliations.[32]

Catholics, then as now, believed Mary to be an uniquely powerful intercessor with God; if she was not divine, like Christ, the Immaculate Conception and Assumption set her apart from other saints, and she was accorded a veneration that in folk piety often approximated to divine worship.[33] For the English Jesuits, trained to obedience, celibacy and combativeness, the associations and didactic messages evoked by the image would have been very different from those experienced by the lay person. Mary's submissiveness to her divine call would have inspired emulation of her example by missionaries, and – as can be seen from the manuscript account of the Valladolid ceremony – English Jesuits would have been more aware than a Valladolid layman of the extent of iconoclasm in England, and would have interpreted the Vulnerata differently. The solemnity, instituted by Englishmen, defies English orthodoxy by adhering to Spanish; and the centrality of Mary, a character so inconspicuous in the New Testament and consequently so susceptible to the erasure of the Reformers, became a symbol of doctrinal defiance.[34] The pious Catholic conception of England as Mary's dowry had especial resonance at Valladolid. In *The Running Register*, Lewis Owen reports on a picture at the College: Mary spreading out her mantle, with her hands over kneeling Jesuits who are presenting her a scroll, upon which is written *Sub umbra alarum tuarum manebimus, donec transeat iniquitas* (We will remain under the shade of your wings till the wickedness passes). The superscription was *Anglia dos Mariae* (England, Mary's dowry: p. 54).[35]

The solemnity was made important by being spectacular. Drapery, as often in Spanish religious festivals, played an important role in this. It was a tangible show of patronage: Philip III and Margaret sent hangings of cloth of gold for the College chapel and porch, and some time after the Madonna's installation a guild of pious women, *Las Camareras de la Vulnerata*, was formed to arrange the mantles with which the statue's mutilations were concealed. Patronage and piety are impossible to separate; the rich draperies of the solemnity displayed firstly a decorous public benevolence, and secondly a reparation and glory foreshadowing that of heaven. The Madonna herself was clad in a 'rich mantle or cloake of sylver curiously wrought with flowers of gould, an with it a crowne of pure beaten gould, richly inameled and guarneshed with pretious stones' (f.53b). As well as the hangings sent by Philip III and Margaret, 'the forefront and walles of the Colledge were also covered with other hangings of silke' (f.56a).[36] Pinned on them were 'divers poems, epigrammes, and hieroglyphickes in prayse of our blessed Ladyes Nativitie, and of the solemnitie and receiving of this her image' (f.56a). This again was a custom which, although originating in France, had currency among the Jesuits in Spain and Portugal; it was even raised to the status of a precept in rulings on the *ludus*, or Jesuit literary festival. Nigel Griffin says of them: 'These small works of art, each operating in more than one direction and at more than one level of perception, might be directly functional in that they encapsulated flattery of important guests attending the *ludus* . . . but, more usually, they simply reflected the general theme and general tenor of the items, both verbal and pictorial, that were on display and contributed to the spectacle as a whole.'[37]

Flattery is here extended to include hyperdulia, for all the hieroglyphics preserved at the end of the manuscript account at Rome are in honour of the Virgin, juxtaposed with a few congratulatory *carmina* to her. They expound emblematic images of her as protectress against all evils, and particularly those of heresy.

There was paynctcd a plane tree most beautifull and florishing, under whose pleasant shade, were men taking their rest, and serpentes flying yt, as from their contrarie.
The shade of the plane-tree cherishes the bodies of those dried up from too much heat: and this tree puts crafty snakes to flight by its leaves. You, pious Virgin, are the plane-tree, driving away heat and the Syrian: lying in this shade, one remains safe from the enemy. Therefore, rest under the health-giving shade of Mary; you who flee harmful flames and heretics.[38]

The other hieroglyphics are, in succession: a palm-tree weighed down heavily, upon which nevertheless the boughs are growing strongly;[39] priests carrying the Ark of the Covenant through the River Jordan dry-shod, and the people following them; the Virgin as guardian of a vineyard; a woman treading on a dragon; an eagle-winged woman fleeing from a dragon who casts a river between them, which the earth drinks up; a rose from which bees suck honey and whose fragrance kills dung-beetles;[40] a ship guided by a star and lighthouse.[41] As is the characteristic of emblems, these hieroglyphics are complex. But certain themes recur: exile, represented by rivers; oppression from heavy weights; spiritual guidance, refreshment and guardianship represented by the star, the lighthouse, the plane-tree and images of the Virgin; and the loathsomeness of heresy in dragons, dung-beetles and serpents. These hieroglyphics, like *Psyche et Filii Eius*, demonstrate the highly visual, highly ornamental and highly schematic manner in which the English Jesuits often preferred to represent themselves, their enemies and the Marian protection of their nation.

EXILE AND ITS POLEMICAL ADVANTAGES

The Madonna Vulnerata may be referred to in at least one Jesuit drama other than *Psyche et Filii Eius*.[42] *Leo Armenus*, a tragedy written by Joseph Simons and set in Byzantium in the midst of the controversy between iconodules and iconoclasts, has a scene in which a statue of Mary is mutilated.[43] Theophilus, the young son of the iconodule hero Michael Balbus, is eavesdropped upon at his devotions before the statue by Sabatius, the son of the iconoclast emperor Leo Armenus, who soliloquises 'What a disgusting sight! Are you so foolish as to venerate the images of heavenly beings? Caesar, he is trampling on your commands.'[44] The unwitting dialogue continues.

THEOPHILUS O Mother! Light of the world! World's Salvation! Through how much danger, and fear of the destroyers, has your child continuously preserved you safely! Allow me to express a few thoughts from my careworn heart.*
SABATIUS Foolish little boy, are you offering words to an image?*[45]

This establishes the mutual incomprehension of the iconodule and the iconoclast; and since a pro-iconoclast reading would deplore the almost complete omission of the Godhead in this scene as an object of praise and prayer, one must remember that the Counter-Reformation continued the medieval tradition of intense Marian veneration, and that in dramatic terms, Marian veneration is a convenient shorthand way of identifying a Catholic. Whereas for Theophilus the statue of Mary is holy, both in itself and as a reminder of Mary's position as chief intercessor to God, Sabatius sees the action as vain: at first because it is pointless, and then, after Theophilus delivers a long pictorial litany of the Virgin's beauties, because it demonstrates a blasphemous reverence for empty ornamentation: *Pictam profana mente veneratur Deam* (He venerates a painted goddess with blasphemous thoughts).[46] The word 'goddess' betrays the theological question genuinely at issue in this scene: not whether the veneration of images is justifiable, the question on which the Iconoclast controversies hung, but whether hyperdulia is no more than Mariolatry. Somewhat anachronistic in a Byzantine context, this had a direct and painful relevance for the post-Reformation Catholic, since Mary – unlike Christ – was effectively exiled from English worship on a public level. Theophilus's perception of Mary's intercessory power is enhanced by the consciousness that she too has experienced alienation from her country: another pointer to the fact that this scene is meant to be read primarily as a topical commentary, since up to this point in the play the iconodules are persecuted, rather than forced into exile.[47] The scene continues with Theophilus pouring out his grief to Mary, in a manner which finally stings Sabatius into confrontation:

THEOPHILUS Tell me, Mother, what is the cause of all the heresy that tears apart the Eastern world? Rare is the faith that holds to the eternal course. Piety withers, and evil flowers bloom.
SABATIUS That piety withers and evil flowers bloom is your father's doing, and yours.
THEOPHILUS Indeed, even the flock of your faithful ones is dwindling: victims of the sword, victims of grief, victims of banishment. Of those who honour you, their Mother, with frankincense – O Mother, how immeasurably much you merit such honour – few are left in the world.
SABATIUS Yes, there are a few. But once I gain control of things I shall see that those impious ones die.[48]

On Theophilus's final request, *O flecte Regem virgo, ne quis te mihi / Disjungat unquam Regis irati furor* (O Virgin, turn the emperor from his ways so that no rage of his may ever take you away from me), Sabatius bursts out of his hiding-place in a fury and strikes the image with his hand. Theophilus defiantly declares that it is unharmed, *Sic flos inventae vernet illaesus tuae* (Then let this flower you have found keep on growing undisturbed*), and pleads that Mary may stretch out a hand to help her image and her worshipper. Sabatius wounds the face of the image with his dagger, since he is unable to smash it by force, and exits.[49] In a long lamentation with the refrain *O vulnus! acre vulnus! immanis manus!* (The scar, the savage scar! The ruthless hand!), an abbreviated version of which is given below, Theophilus laments the defacement of the image.

Do I see this? Why do my eyes not turn in their sockets and refuse to see the atrocity? Grief of mine, give vent to your sobbing and fill my eyes with a flood of tears . . . Your radiant face, your serenely majestic brow, your solemn and lovely eyes – all disfigured? . . . Stars, hide your radiance, for a villain has deprived the Virgin of hers. Sun, hide your glorious face, for one more glorious than yours has been disfigured. Flowers, do not bloom, for the Queen of the flowers is injured. Roses, wither and fade, for the Mystical Rose has been seared. Black pitch disfigures the head white with lilies, see, Mary's lily-crowned head has been damaged by a thorn.* . . . Heavenly Advocate, Father of the glorious Virgin, and, of course, you her Son – I do not ask that you hurl an angry thunderbolt from heaven to avenge the outrage done to your Mother. Beyond any doubt, the guilty one will be punished. Anyone who mistreats your Mother will receive his just deserts. But do help me to be eternally faithful in my reverence for Mary, and for every saint whose picture Leo has done violence to. Grant that I may carry her image forever in my heart. This is my fondest desire. Mother, help your suppliant.[50]

Theophilus appeals to God to renew His call for Marian veneration, and for external and internal iconodulia: 'Help me to be eternally faithful in my reverence for Mary ... Grant that I may carry her image forever in my heart'. But his distress is indicative if not of doubt, at least of an appalled recognition that worship has lost its innocence. In a play written over a hundred years after the activities of the first English iconoclasts, the shock of image-breaking to a Catholic is nowhere given more eloquent or suggestive expression. The lover's rhetorical device of *enumeratio*, so often used in medieval hymns to the Virgin, is twisted to record the devastations that Sabatius's weapon has wrought on each feature of her face; and Theophilus himself addresses the *mater dolorosa*. Roses and lilies, attributes of Mary and the martyrs, are subjected to acts of violence and ritual despite: plucked so that they fade, smothered with black pitch and stabbed with thorns. Reformation is seen as the rape of the Church.

A number of other Jesuit plays – some surviving, some not – were more explicit still. Of those that do not survive, the plays performed at the English College, Seville in the late 1590s, *Anglia Lapsa Resurgens* (1595), devised by Robert Persons, and *Cicilus Atheos, Non Anglicanus*[51] (1598) suggest a sturdy polemic in their titles. *Henrico VIII*, a lost play by William Drury, was performed at Douai in 1623, and its content and tone may have had an analogy in the cluster of historical dramas performed at the English College, Rome in the early seventeenth century, dramatising the lives of Sts Thomas Becket, Thomas More and John Fisher. Other tragedies performed at St Omer make the same parallel as *Leo Armenus* between English Catholics and the oppressed iconodules of iconoclast Byzantium; *Captiva Religio* and *Psyche et Filii Eius*, both discussed above, use allegory to enhance their anti-Protestant explicitness. In their efflorescent, protracted and unequivocal condemnations of the effect of Protestantism in England, these plays rank among the most subversive texts ever written by Tudor and Stuart Englishmen. They could never have been performed publicly on the English stage, nor issued by a mainstream publisher in England; and through their very outspokenness, they testify to the practical advantages and incidental consolations of exile.

Though the plays dealing with the Henrician Reformation would have been the most shocking of all to a Protestant Englishman, much of English history before the Tudors was interdicted in England as well. *Brevis Dialoguismus*, the dramatic dialogue on St Thomas Becket quoted earlier, can be seen as the marginalia to a later play, *St. Thomas Cantuar*. This is a five-act dramatisation of the saint's life, first performed in 1613 at the English College, Rome, and revived in 1617.[52] If not quite a chronicle, it is structurally more straightforward than the former play; but the supernatural framing of the play dictates the audience's response. St Joseph of Arimathaea speaks the prologue and validates what is to come. Legend cast St Joseph, the disciple who begged Pilate to be allowed to bury Jesus's body in his own tomb, as one of the first missionaries to Britain and the founder of Glastonbury. His remarks are directed to those who follow his example, but achieve the martyr's glory that he himself was denied.

Saviour, I have submitted to the lot you have imposed, I have given your faith to the Britons . . . it was not permitted to moisten it with the dew of our blood; the glory of the martyr, a reward of sweetness, was not yet given to Britain; thereafter it shall be given, and blood poured out will open heaven for Britons. And often an Englishman made glorious with blood will penetrate beyond the stars: Alban saw those covered entrances, and others deserved to have their laurels touched with their blood. And now a famous head aspires to the purple – Thomas. He may be observed overthrowing the impious commands of powerful kings for your sake. He will prove this, that there is an easy road from earth to heaven for the brave: Thomas points the way.[53]

After only two years as Archbishop of Canterbury, and after a Royal Council at Northampton during which Becket and Henry II had come into conflict over whether the State should have jurisdiction over clergymen convicted of crimes, Becket was obliged to flee secretly to France, where he remained for six years.[54] In Act I ii of the play he is seen arriving back in England, underscoring the relevance to seminarians of a story where a return from Continental exile leads to martyrdom. Act II chronicles the rekindling of the quarrel, on account of certain bishops who had infringed the prerogatives of Becket's see at the King's instigation; a subsidiary character, Peter Beleius, mediates anxiously between the opposites of ecclesiastical and royal supremacy. The denouement is set in motion in Act III, when the four knights Brito (Richard de Breton), Thracius

(William de Tracy), Ursius (Reginald Fitzurse) and Moravilla (Hugh de Morville) are sent on their way by Henry to murder Becket, and it is dramatised with a sophisticated degree of irony. The knights' manhunt is counterpointed with a hunt in which the king is taking part; during it, he receives a supernatural warning of the fatal effect of his words by an angel disguised as an eremite, and he hurries to Canterbury, only to arrive too late. But this fatalism is set in the optimistic context of martyrdom, by an angel who gives Thomas a similar warning of impending slaughter. The assassination takes place at the end of Act IV, and it is in Act V that the didactic import of the tragedy becomes most striking. Henry and the knights repent, again assisted by the angel-eremite; one may be intended retrospectively to equate the knights with four souls returned from purgatory, who accompany St Joseph of Arimathaea in the prologue.

Thomas and Henry personify Church and State, and where Thomas is reasoned and adamantine, Henry is immature, grandiloquent and wilful. Though the king develops throughout *S. Thomas Cantuar*, his development – for good didactic reasons – is not towards an autonomous maturity, but a recognition of his own immaturity. He is first seen in royal panoply, giving vent to a Marlovian speech which nevertheless betrays a need to convince himself that his power is real: 'We do not bear imagined sceptres, I do not occupy a theatre for short dramas as a timid pretend-tyrant up to the applause' (I iv).[55] This emphasis on Henry's youth gives psychological consistency to the blend of bluster and wish-fulfilment that prompt his fateful words to the knights. Kingly entertainment – a festival in II i and the hunt in III ii – turns sour as the distinction between reality and fantasy becomes forced on Henry, and the words of the Earl of Leicester, quoted below, become ironic as Henry ends the play in subservience and shame, having unwittingly awarded Thomas the prize of martyrdom.

> The theatre will give the occasion importance and glory, the king himself sustains the leading [places] among the first men . . . Let everybody note, according to your law, who of the chorus abides by the rules unusually well, so that everyone may carry off the appropriate palm that each has deserved. (II i)[56]

This scene is replete with a double meaning that only becomes evident when Leicester's addressees are considered. They are described as *feciales*, or representatives from the Roman college of priests who performed various ambassadorial functions; and from Leicester's speech it becomes clear that they are superintending the games, making the rules and leaving the king as a figurehead. The word *praesul* means both public dancer and bishop, and *motus* both dancing and rebellion; and so the exemplary chorus-member seems intended as a type of Becket, even before the passage mentions the palm that rewards both winner and martyr.

State power in *S. Thomas Cantuar* is portrayed as something not inherently bad, but ideally to be subjected to Church control for fear of the havoc that kings – left to themselves – will cause and later regret.[57] In this respect, the play is suggestively similar to Edmund Campion's *Ambrosia*, probably the first Jesuit drama written by an Englishman. Put on when Campion was teaching at the Jesuit College, Prague in 1578, *Ambrosia* deals in part with St Ambrose's reproof of the emperor Theodosius for ordering a massacre, and ends with Theodosius being brought to admit Ambrose's maxim that 'The emperor is within the church; he is not above it.'[58] As I have argued elsewhere, Campion may have written this play as an autodidactic means of fitting himself for a career in European courtly circles, for which he seemed to be destined at the time he wrote the play.[59] Most English Jesuit dramas, though, are preoccupied with exploring the didactic import of history, with particular emphasis on its applicability to the future lives of the playwrights, actors and audience; and the personal implications of historical typology, or truth as re-enactment, also run powerfully through *S. Thomas Cantuar*. The story of Becket and Henry II is an historical one; victory at the festival prefigures the triumph of Becket's martyrdom; and the boys acting the parts, together with the boys and masters in the audience, were being exhorted to act out Becket's example in their own lives.

Recent history was also incorporated into the scheme. For the early seventeenth century, Becket occupied a chronologically central and pivotal place in the roll-call of English martyrs, between the early Christians and those who suffered at the Reformation. The angel that warns him of his martyrdom in Act IV ii emphasises the inspiration he will be to post-Reformation Catholics: not only to individuals like Persons, Campion, Southwell, Walpole and Garnet, whom some of the older members of the audience at the English College would probably have known, but to an earlier generation who stood out against the Henrician regime.[60] The most prominent of the Henrician martyrs were St Thomas More and St John Fisher, heroes of the two other surviving historical plays from Rome, *S. Thomas Morus* and *Roffensis*.[61] It is More's story in particular for which Becket's becomes the type. Both martyrs are called Thomas and both monarchs Henry; both Thomases move in courtly circles, and are personal friends of the monarch until the two quarrel over Church discipline; and Henry VIII, because of these very analogies, had a personal animus against the cult of Becket.[62] There are two dramatic versions of the story that survive from English Jesuit colleges, Rome's *S. Thomas Morus* and *Morus*, a play from St Omer.[63] The first play is an extravaganza and the second a chamber treatment of the story – *S. Thomas Morus* is five acts long, with an intermedium between each act, as opposed to *Morus*'s six scenes – and these differing lengths make for different emphases. But more important is what they have in common: a willingness to set the story in a supernatural context, and a selectivity of biographical detail that downplays More as layman.[64]

More's life was suited to dramatisation for a number of reasons, not least because his name lent itself so well to typological reflection. Thomas Stapleton's biographical *Tres Thomae* (1588, repr. 1612) places More alongside biographies of the apostle Thomas and – again – Thomas Becket.[65] A series of essays on More's personal qualities rather than a conventional life, Stapleton's biography becomes of most obvious use to the two dramatists towards the end, where the events surrounding More's trial and execution are outlined. *Morus* concentrates on these events, with a large cast but few characters that are other than one-dimensional. The most distinctive scene, which can only be described as a dream-sequence, is at the end. Henry VIII is grieving for More, having just heard of his execution, when an angel appears and identifies himself as England's Genius. He introduces a series of visionary tableaux composed in a baroque idiom, the first of which is described as follows: *Deducuntur vela et apparet in caelo Christus. Hinc Morus, illinc Roffensis; tum alii duo Martyres, Angelis supra capita eorum palmas et coronas trementibus* (The curtains are pulled away and Christ appears in heaven, More on one side and Fisher on the other; then two other martyrs, with angels waving palms and crowns above their heads: scene 6). The angels sing a panegyric studded with allusions to Virgil's messianic fourth Eclogue, and then a further scene is discovered with statue-like representations (*instar statuarum*) of Edward VI, Mary and Elizabeth.

The subject of exile: II

England's genius reminds Henry that this is no mere pageant, but a theatre of death (*funesto hoc theatro*) and goes on to describe Edward and Elizabeth in terms of explicit invective.

You will acknowledge the same [i.e. your fate] as this, your son. Through truly appalling offences, and through cruelty poured out in every intemperance, you lust for him so much; but a son of such a kind who, dug out from the bowels of his mother with a sharp sword, first drained life from a parent in being born, and deprived her from use of the light whom he himself should have looked to as a light; a son who will never be his own master in the future,[66] but shall be destroyed by a premature death pledged for him in a cup poisoned by those very vipers which you now fondle in your breast – the last offspring, either male or female, to be begotten from your pestiferous seed . . . The child in the third place after her tyrant father will occupy the rear place in your evil lineage – she is out of that abominable-souled she-wolf, that shall be begotten because of your incestuous loves;[67] a daughter who puts on in one form all her father's and all her mother's [iniquities] . . . And here let there be an end of your abominable stock![68]

Rome's *S. Thomas Morus* also demonstrates the interpenetration of the political and the supernatural. In Act I ii, even before the character of More has been introduced, the malign influence that precipitates the plot and the Reformation is brought on stage in the form of a 'Cacodaemon': a spirit with a name that bespeaks blindness both physical and moral, who tempts Henry towards tyranny.[69] Before the Cacodaemon arrives, Henry is musing on the fact that More and Fisher are going to be the prime obstacles to his divorce from Catherine, which he hopes will secure stability for the kingdom; and before the spirit goes, it convinces Henry that he is unassailable.

Henry is shattered after the first visitation, *Quam callet omne mentis arcanum meae!* (How it understands every secret of my mind! I ii, p. [4]); and he calls Cromwell, Audley and Cranmer, who comment on the signs of his perturbation but are sceptical about the idea of a ghost. The Cacodaemon then re-enters and speaks prophetically to the company, renewing the suggestion that the king ought to be all-powerful. Cromwell is told that he will be led into the way of corruption with an iron rod, Cranmer that he will be guided by avarice and a mitre; and both men complain of a sense of burning, proleptic of hell, after they have received these orders. Audley is the last to succumb, at the promise of military glory. The Cacodaemon departs after threatening that they will be unable to enjoy the object of their temptation, and foretelling how spiritual illumination will depart from England, with a few glorious exceptions: 'Thus, and thus, must it happen; may blood poured out by an enemy extinguish the lights of the lamps; may that precious blood be poured out, even though it is More's.'[70] The Cacodaemon magically ensures that Henry, Cromwell and Audley retain no memory of his orders, but they unconsciously act upon them: the plot of *S. Thomas Morus* after the Cacodaemon's departure is of escalating court chicanery. The emphasis is less on More's character than on princes persecuting him without a valid cause, and the inspiration, consequently, less Stapleton than Sander. The vivid character-portrayal of More in *Tres Thomae* has been smoothed out, and the idealised features of a martyr superimposed. More and Fisher even engage in dialogue with the Chorus (II i), which in this play has a supernatural function, combining the normative voice with the divine. Being supererogatory to the propagandist requirements for celibates, More's family hardly figure.[71]

Rome's *Roffensis* [1610–20] is a companion piece to *S. Thomas Morus*. Dealing with the trial, condemnation and execution of St John Fisher, which occurred directly before More's, it may have drawn not only on the sources already enumerated but on Richard Hall's life of Fisher, which enjoyed a wide manuscript circulation.[72] Many of the scenes in the two plays – which may have been written by the same author – are almost interchangeable.[73] This reflects the inseparability of More and Fisher: not only chronologically as victims of the same purge, but as men whose perceived integrity was difficult even for ideological opponents to undermine, and whose posthumous glory embarrassed the Tudors. The differences in the two characterisations are minor – mostly referring to Fisher's age and infirmity – which again reflects the de-individuating, hagiographical effect of martyrdom on character. It is not to denigrate Fisher's considerable achievements to say that, to the lay person then and now, More's was by far the more charismatic personality.[74] But in order to present the clerical and lay experience of martyrdom as equally glorious, individual character and achievement could be subsumed to didactic efficacy.[75] Since Fisher and More were of equal martyrological stature, Fisher's story is not a predella to that of More's; instead, the two make up a diptych.

Roffensis differs from *S. Thomas Morus* most in its feminisation of the story of the schism. Anne Boleyn is provided with a kinsman,

Bolenus, who acts as spokesman for her,[76] and the ills of Catherine of Aragon are lamented in the choruses spoken by four personifications of countries, Roma, Anglia, Germania and Hispania, who in themselves demonstrate how a slight to a princess could iconographically be seen as one to her native country. The usual polarisations of womanhood are imposed on Catherine and Anne Boleyn, making the one a saint and the other a whore, with the added force of the fact that one represents Catholicism and the other Protestantism. In the first chorus, the echo of Revelations in the Vulgate, *Cecidit, cecidit Babylon* (Babylon the great is fallen, is fallen: Revelation 14.8, 18.2), has a miserable irony.

ROME   The queen has fallen, fallen from her throne, and, her marriage-bed deserted, she laments the preferred embraces of a seductress. What does violent love not dare, and lust when joined with power? . . .

SPAIN   See, a new seductress enters the marriage-bed of our prince. What does holy piety gain by him? What does the glory of great fathers gain? Alas, she is despised, she is despised, her great virtue is made inglorious, and a famous descendant of kings is being driven far away from the court of the king.[77]

These English plays' overt condemnation of the religious settlement in England becomes even more striking when compared with dramatic treatments of Henry's reign and the Reformation on the mainland. Mainland playwrights had three main options: to write with a strong pro-Protestant bias, like Samuel Rowley in *When You See Me, You Know Me* (1605); to rewrite contemporary events in such a way as to leave religion out altogether; or to attempt to leave gaps which would both satisfy the censor and elicit internalised glosses from the audience.[78] For polemical reasons, Henry's divorce from Catherine of Aragon and marriage to Anne Boleyn is consistently identified with the advent of heresy in Catholic accounts of the Reformation; and for reasons merely chronological, the two are hard to separate in narrative. In *Henry VIII*, Shakespeare and his probable co-author Fletcher bypass the problem, rewriting the episode as to be almost entirely secular in its implications. Where religious matters intrude, they are so contextualised as to be without threat: Wolsey calls Anne a 'spleeny Lutheran' (III ii, l. 100), but, at this point in the drama, Wolsey is about to fall.[79] Catherine's integrity is made clear in the trial-scene and her ill-luck lamented, while her death becomes a transmogrification; but despite Anne Boleyn's detractors within the play, she too is portrayed sympathetically. As Cranmer points towards England's coming golden age in the play's last scene, the audience is encouraged towards a joyous teleological endorsement of Henry's remarriage: and perhaps, or perhaps not, towards reading the infant Elizabeth as a Protestantised Truth, the daughter of Time.[80]

This was only one solution to the internal and external censorships imposed on those mainland playwrights who touched on the subject of England's break with Rome. But *Sir Thomas More*, co-authored by Anthony Munday and others, illustrates a similar solution to a similar difficulty.[81] Both plays emphasise the humaneness of the central Catholic characters – Catherine of Aragon in *Henry VIII*, More in *Sir Thomas More* – but sidestep the difficulty of explaining without offence the religio-political reasons why More's execution might have been expedient, or Henry's divorce from Catherine necessary.[82] Of the two, the former was the more difficult; Henry's motivation towards the royal divorce is still a contentious matter among historians, but there was no doubt about the fact that More and Fisher were executed because they refused to accept the royal supremacy in matters of religion. The playwrights' inevitable difficulty is well illustrated in Act IV i from *Sir Thomas More*, where More and Fisher first refuse to subscribe to the Oath of Succession.

Enter Sir Thomas Palmer.
PALMER My lords, his majesty hath sent by me
    These articles enclosed, first to be viewed
    And then to be subscribed to. I tender them
    In that due reverence which befits this place.
With great reverence.
MORE Subscribe these articles? Stay, let us pause:
    Our conscience first shall parley with our laws.
    My lord of Rochester, view you the paper.
ROCH. Subscribe to these? Now good Sir Thomas Palmer,
    Beseech the king that he will pardon me.
    My heart will check my hand whilst I do write:
    Subscribing so, I were an hypocrite.
PAL. Do you refuse it then, my lord?
ROCH. I do, Sir Thomas.
PAL. Then here I summon you forthwith t'appear
    Before his majesty, to answer there
    This capital contempt.
ROCH. I rise and part,
    In lieu of this, to tender him my heart.

He riseth.
PAL. Will't please your honour to subscribe, my lord?
MORE   Sir, tell his highness I entreat
   Some time for to bethink me of this task.
   In the meanwhile I do resign mine office
   Into my sovereign's hands.
PAL. Then, my lord,
   Hear the preparèd order from the king:
   On your refusal, you shall straight depart
   Unto your house at Chelsea, till you know
   Our sovereign's further pleasure.   (ll. 69–93)

Sir Edmund Tilney, Master of the Revels, marked for deletion the parts of the scene concerned with Fisher's impeachment and More's resignation, noting in the margin that the whole scene had to be altered.[83] Tilney was as literalistic as most censors, and does not seem to have queried the play's most explicit reference to religion, which comes during Margaret Roper's prophetic dream in Act IV ii: she sees More 'in Chelsea church, / Standing upon the rood loft, now defaced, / And whilst he kneeled and prayed before the image, / It fell with him into the upper choir, / Where my poor father lay all stained in blood' (ll. 37–41). But his objection must have been to the Oath being addressed at all, as much as to the manner of treatment. The latter is intensely economical and tactful: economical because it compresses the process of decision-making into less than a page, reducing to a minimum the possibility of misreading, and tactful because it presents the king's messenger as prescient and the king's unnamed oath as indisputable, while emphasising the element of conscientious private judgement involved both in subscribing and refusing to subscribe. Fisher's point is not that only hypocrites subscribe to the Oath of Succession, but that he would be a hypocrite if he did so reluctantly.

As a whole, the scene makes considerable demands on an audience: they are expected both to supply the historical data that makes the action explicable, and to decide where they stand when they have done so. But their judgement is not entirely undirected. After subscribing, Surrey says to Shrewsbury: "'Tis strange that my lord chancellor should refuse / The duty that the law of God bequeaths / Unto the king', and Shrewsbury replies: 'No doubt / His mind will alter, and the bishop's too. / Error in learned heads hath much to do' (ll. 106–110). This is not a remark that the audience is invited to condemn; and here, the role of poets in the play is suggestive. The character Surrey in the above quotation is identified by the playwrights with the poet Henry Howard, Earl of Surrey.[84] In Act III i, a debate between the two poets on the comparative merits of statesmanship and verse displays More as an apologist for poetry and Surrey for politics, since 'poets were ever thought unfit for state' (l. 195). To Surrey's claim that the art is at a low ebb, More retaliates by declaring that 'This is no age for poets: they should sing / To the loud cannon *heroica facta*' (ll. 203–4).[85] Throughout the rest of the play, an opposite point is driven home: just because these are interesting times, this is no age for poets. This is done by identifying the poetic temperament with the conscience; More reflects of himself in the Tower:

> That part of poet that was given me
> Made me a very unthrift.[86]
> For this is the disease attends us all:
> Poets were never thrifty, never shall. (v iii, ll. 61–4)

Poetry is seen as the reason for More's decline and death, when he is transplanted to an alien ideology; it is identifiable in the play's terms as a kind of quixotry, that of championing an unnamed lost cause. Even Surrey, the poet who disavows poetry, does not escape; in the last speech in the play, the playwrights were almost certainly counting on the audience's awareness that ten years after More, Surrey – a fellow-Catholic – shared More's fate of decapitation on a charge of high treason.

> A very learned worthy gentleman
> Seals error with his blood. Come, we'll to court.
> Let's sadly hence to perfect unknown fates,
> Whilst he tends progress to the state of states. (v iv, ll. 119–22)

Despite Surrey's earlier minimisation of the importance of poetry, the clear message to the audience is that the poetic temperament, when faced with the exigencies of statesmanship, invariably comes to grief. In terms of More, this links poesy with popery as his capital crime; poeticisation becomes fantasy, and fantasy becomes error.

Were it for no other reason than this, the play would demand to be read as a critique of Catholic heroism. But the writer whose contribution to the text was greatest, Anthony Munday, notoriously had connections with the English College in Rome and with counter-Catholic espionage.[87] In his *English Romayne Lyfe* (1582) he describes his time in Rome from February to May 1579, ostensibly as a student at the English College, which he later represented as a mission to gather information about the English Catholics. On his return to England, he informed against the College member Ralph Sherwin at the trial which led to Sherwin's, Edmund Campion's and Alexander Briant's martyrdom in December 1581.[88] From 1582 he was pursuivant to Richard Topcliffe, the Elizabethan priest-catcher, and was active in searching out Catholic books; this may have been how he obtained a manuscript copy of one of the play's major sources, Harpsfield's *Life of More*.[89] Being a co-authored play associated with Shakespeare, *Sir Thomas More* has often been scrutinised to establish the authorship of different portions. Even so, no-one has answered the question of how one of its co-authors could be a man so rabidly anti-Catholic; and the mystery seems destined to remain insoluble. But Munday's pamphlet *A Discoverie of Edmund Campion, and His Confederates* (1582), though largely devoted to denunciation of Catholic treachery, includes a description of the martyrs' exemplary behaviour on the scaffold which can be seen as prefiguring his characterisation of More; and, by the time Munday participated in the writing of *Sir Thomas More* in the early 1590s, it is possible that through an obligation to understand his quarries, he may have developed a certain degree of sympathy for them.[90] More's integrity and loyalty to the King are never questioned, and the lack of specificity about the articles that More refuses to sign has almost the effect of transforming the action into an allegorical battle of duty versus individual conscience: a battle that those of puritan inclination would have been able to sympathise with, even while deploring More's views. But the difficulty about mentioning either Catholic or Protestant tenets leaves a void at the centre of *Sir Thomas More*. As performed before a contemporary audience, a play of this kind could certainly have had its danger-points led up to, and exploited, with breathtaking dramatic effect; but if this particular play does not quite come off for a twentieth-century reader, it is because of the anxious eye kept on Sir Edmund Tilney.

The fate of this scene demonstrates how, even when using extreme brevity and circumspection, the theatre in England found it difficult to dramatise the break with Rome without running into objections from the censor. But censorship on this matter – admittedly of an opposite kind – also operated in a Catholic country like Spain. In Calderón's *La Cisma de Inglaterra*, which dramatises Henry's infatuation with Anne and its repercussions, the playwright was not allowed to say that Henry thought himself head of the church, or to have Anne or any other villain expounding Lutheranism, since informing the populace about the details of heresy was considered to be dangerous.[91] Calderón resorts to the technique of *decir sin decir* (saying without speaking out) that was often employed by Golden Age playwrights; by a simple statement made of Anne, *y aunque en público la ves / católica, pienso que es / en secreto luterana* (And though she seems a Catholic in public, / I have a strong suspicion that in private / She is a Lutheran: Act i, ll. 454–6) the Spanish audience was prompted to attach to her figure all the vivid images of Protestant wickedness that the term would have implied.[92]

Like *S. Thomas Morus*, *La Cisma de Inglaterra* uses the device of prophetic dream. The play begins with Henry waking up from a vision of Anne that prefigures his passion for her, giving a tragic inevitability to all his subsequent actions, and leading to a second, more blatant omen:

> Were it lawful to interpret dreams
> You might suppose these letters were the subject
> I've just been dreaming of. With my right hand
> I wrote at first, and this could only mean
> I jealously defended the true doctrine,
> As represented by Pope Leo's letter.
> And that I wanted to dim and quench its light
> With my sinister hand well indicates
> How I confused the night and day, the poison
> And the antidote. To let my greatness say
> Which has the victory, let Luther sink
> Down to my feet, and Leo rise to my head.
> *He makes to throw down Luther's letter at his feet, and to put
>   that of the Pope on his head, but [he confuses them and]
>   does the opposite.*[93]

Anne, it seems, has literally bewitched Henry. Carlos, her ex-suitor, describes her as *de los hombres bellísima sirena, / pues aduerme a su encanto los sentidos, / ciega los ojos y abre los oídos* (That siren who enchants men's quietened senses, / Blinding their eyes and opening their ears: Act i, l. 346–8), as *en fuego . . . veneno* (poison wrapped in fire: l. 338) and as a *movíl de cristal y plata / en su curso los cielos arrebata* (moving body of crystal and of silver, / That in its course wrenches the very heavens / From their fixed place: ll. 339–40), all epithets that emphasise the power of her sexuality to enchant, confuse and confound. The further image of Anne as a magnet (ll. 365–72) makes explicit her role as conductor for half-understood but devastating elemental forces. The effect is heightened, if anything, because Anne is never heard expounding heretical issues; through the techniques of hint and suggestion that Calderón employed to circumvent the censor, she is seen as Antichrist's passive agent. As with Vittoria in *The White Devil*, of whom the crystalline metaphors are reminiscent, the religious context encourages the identification of female religious deviance with hieratic evil;[94] and, harking back to the polemical metaphor with which this study began, Anne may be seen as the Catholic analogue to Vittoria. Neither the livid flash nor the glistening religious whore were confined to Protestantism.

In their various treatments of the English break with Rome, Shakespeare, Munday and Calderón all show how a playwright's referential field and treatment of historical event had to be circumscribed, if he was an obedient citizen of either a Catholic or a Protestant country. The complex disobedience of the clerics at the English College in Rome – travelling to the Protestants' Babylon, being ordained by papal authority and intending, in many cases, to commit high treason by returning to England – is compounded still further by the plays that they wrote and performed; against the loyalist ingenuities of former chapters, these texts have a stunning outspokenness. Catholic exiles might lament their geographical removedness from England; but it meant that of all Englishmen, they were the most freed from censorship.

Conclusion

How should one measure Catholic failure, or Catholic success? The Protestant succession is a fact, and plots against it, some sponsored by leading Catholic figures in conjunction with Spain, had a habit of failing. But in recent historical debate, this judgement has been tempered by pointing to the visibility and freedom of Catholics within the Caroline court; though this never translated into toleration country-wide, it provided opportunities for aristocratic evangelism which were to continue in the courts of Charles II and James II, with such success that the causes of English Catholicism and Jacobitism became intertwined after 1688.[1] Even without counterfactual speculation, even if it is legitimate to regard the re-introduction of the Catholic succession as a doomed cause, it was also one which took over two centuries to die. But Catholicism itself continued alive in England, in the rest of Britain and in British outposts on the Continent. Paradoxically, it was through asserting membership of the universal Church that they became – as John Bossy has demonstrated – members of a sect: and a sect they were to remain, sometimes almost invisible, sometimes unassimilable and reproachful, and often routinely disadvantaged, until the emancipations and second springs of the nineteenth century. Recent historians have united in describing the Reformation as a success, and England was a Protestant nation throughout this time; yet because one should not overlook the Catholic element within that Protestant nation, the terminology of success and failure has limits. Protestantism did not win everyone over, Catholicism did not die out; while a cause still has adherents, one cannot say that it has completely failed.[2]

Is it best, though, to measure that adherence quantitatively or qualitatively? As commented in the introduction, historians have been very concerned with assessing the regional distribution of Catholics, on the assumption that statistical prominence is a measure of relative success.³ Perhaps their concern – though necessary – has been too narrow, since this line of enquiry is limited by its own methodology: to be a Catholic sympathizer was to acknowledge interest but defer commitment, while the whole aim of the church-papist was to evade visibility. If these historians do not take the recusant as the ideal in quite the same sense that the missioners did, recusancy is certainly seen as a benchmark. Yet as historians have usually concluded, 'good' Catholics were only part of England's Catholic population – how large a part, we shall probably never know. The ideological dilutedness of the church-papist is something which missioners would, officially, have regarded as relative failure; yet in specific cases, especially with aristocratic potential converts, Catholic proselytisers – sometimes for years on end – regarded a combination of conformity and sympathies towards Rome as a highly promising seedbed. Definitions of success and failure, as here, can sometimes collide. In the current fluctuating state of early modern historiography, what is more urgently needed than such definitions is a constant and serious acknowledgement of two things: the Catholic presence in England, and the English Catholic presence outside.

But whatever methods future researchers develop to extend the Catholic headcount beyond recusancy-rolls, their approach would still be largely quantitative if it stopped there. Such lines of enquiry give little help to those concerned with assessing the *distinctiveness* of early modern English Catholicism, and, in particular, the nature of its grip on some English mentalities, imaginations and souls. Many of the imaginative reactions to Catholicism discussed above are highly personal, others pronounce for a group more than for an individual, and yet others subordinate the personal to the discursive: but all, in some degree, testify to the lively importance of Catholicism in the biography of an individual. Hagiography is more help here than some mainstream historians might care to admit, for it has always recognised the necessity for qualitative history, of a kind which assesses the nature and degree of the zeal with which a given individual promotes a given discourse. Zeal, which can be eirenical as well as polemical, is a constant element in English Catholic literary culture: not simply because it forms a large part of the subject-matter of Catholic books, but because of the difficulties and dangers that Catholics so often surmounted in producing and distributing their texts. No-one can deny the bibliographical evidence for a vigorous underground Catholic literature, and this book has, in addition, been particularly concerned to emphasize how much Catholics contributed to and influenced mainstream imaginative discourse: sometimes visibly, more often not, and sometimes – as with the imaginative spectres of anti-Catholicism – just because they were there. Zeal can manifest itself not only in clandestine, separatist literary activity, but in the infiltration of Protestant discourse; and it could stimulate a countering fervour in imaginative Protestant responses to the idea of popery. To trace all these emanations of zeal, the historian, the literary critic and the bibliographer need to join forces.

Finally, a book built around the idea of the controversial imagination would be incomplete without a recognition of its most powerful practical effect. The imaginative use of Catholic-Protestant controversy ideally stimulated a mental impregnability which, when tested at the scaffold or in jail, could be seen to be spectacularly successful.[4] This is a topic which literary scholars are particularly well-equipped to explore, since Catholic leaders and writers encouraged a systematic fomentation of imaginative empathy with historical martyrs, not only by literary exhortation and prayer, but by ballad, drama and picture.[5] From the 1580s onwards[6] the evidence of Jesuit drama, and of other literary and artistic data, demonstrates that the martyrological ideal was persistently instilled by imaginative means into boys and young men at the English Catholic colleges and seminaries on the Continent: a conditioning which has its most visible effect in priestly lives and deaths, but which must have had a corresponding – if less quantifiable – effect on the male Catholic laity who also received their education at the Colleges, and the men, women and children among whom the priests had their ministry. Something of this has been discussed in chapter six, but in a follow-up study to this, I hope to examine at length a phenomenon which, in this study, I have called 'autodidacticism':[7] how, encouraged by their teachers' imaginative acculturation, Catholic youths colluded with them in a self-propelled internalisation of the martyrological ideal. Drama, in particular, was used for this end, foregrounding a recognition that, through the role-playing of imaginative projection and trial, one might become better-equipped to achieve real-life heroism.[8]

English Catholics were not braver than English Protestants, and in the Reformation period, as Foxe and others bear witness, it was

Protestants who first wrote in many of the potentially controversial, potentially autodidactic genres which Catholics were later to adopt: the complaint, the exemplary prison-verse, the epistle to family members. But Catholics had to be brave for longer, and their imaginative techniques for stimulating bravery are consequently more sophisticated than anything that English Protestantism can show. Their consistency in behaving like the saints they venerated, at trial, in prison and on the scaffold, was perhaps the supreme achievement of the controversial imagination, turning worldly defeat into spiritual success; and however incredible the idea of suffering and dying for one's faith has become to the late-twentieth-century European academic, to acknowledge Catholic success in these theatres is the least that an un-zealous posterity can do.

Notes

INTRODUCTION

1 Guiney's papers for volume II are held at the Holy Cross College, Worcester, Massachusetts.
2 There has, too, recently been some interest in the relationship between Catholic casuistical techniques and fictionality: see Steven Mullaney, 'Lying Like Truth: Riddle, Representation and Treason in Renaissance England', *ELH*, 47 (1980), pp. 32–47; Ronald J. Corthell, '"The Secrecy of Man": Recusant Discourse and the Elizabethan Subject', *ELR*, 19 (1989), pp. 272–90.
3 E.g. in Stephen Radtke, *James Shirley, his Catholic Philosophy of Life* (Washington: Catholic University Press, 1929); Dennis Flynn, *John Donne and the Ancient Catholic Nobility* (Bloomington: Indiana University Press, 1995); B. N. da Luna, *Jonson's Romish Plot* (Oxford University Press, 1967); Lisa Hopkins, *John Ford's Political Theatre* (Manchester University Press, 1994). Two recent accounts of the literature addressing the controversy over Shakespeare's Catholicism can be found in Richard Wilson, 'Shakespeare and the Jesuits' (*TLS*, 19 December 1997, pp. 11–13) and Peter Milward's letter responding to the article (*TLS*, 2 January 1998).
4 'Some Aspects of Yorkshire Catholic Recusant History, 1558–1791', in G. J. Cuming (ed.), *Studies in Church History*, IV (Leiden: E. G. Brill, 1967), pp. 98–121 (esp. p. 101).
5 The most recent list of local societies is to be found, with much else, in J. Anthony Williams, 'Sources in Recusant History (1559–1791) in English Official Archives', *RH*, 66:4 (1983), pp. 331–442. See also the Catholic Archives Society's *Directory of Catholic Archives in the UK and Eire* (1984).
6 Ceri Sullivan, *Dismembered Rhetoric* (London: Associated University Presses, 1995) is a more recent study of English Catholic prose which concentrates on rhetorical stratagem. See also George H. Tavard, *The Seventeenth-Century Tradition: A Study in Recusant Thought* (Leiden: Brill, 1978); John R. Roberts, *A Critical Anthology of English Recusant Devotional Prose, 1558–1603* (Pittsburgh: Duquesne University Press, 1966).

7 See G. A. M. Janssens and F. G. A. M. Aarts (eds.), *Studies in 17th-Century English Literature, History and Bibliography: Festschrift for Professor T. A. Birrell on the Occasion of His 60th Birthday* (Amsterdam: Rodopi, 1984); and, inter alia, his *Newsletter for Students of Recusant History* (1958–1970).
8 Nicholas Tyacke's comments in the introduction to *England's Long Reformation* (pp. 1–4), pointing out the similarity of Duffy's arguments to those in Aidan, Cardinal Gasquet's *The Eve of the Reformation* (1900), vividly demonstrate how long it has taken for the contentions of Catholic historiography to be addressed seriously in mainstream academic circles.
9 Two relatively recent summaries of developments in early modern English Catholic history are Martin Havran's chapter on the British Isles in John O'Malley (ed.), *Catholicism in Early Modern History: A Guide to Research* (St Louis: Centre for Reformation Research, 1988), and Lawrence Stone, *The Past and the Present Revisited* (London: Routledge, 1987), ch. 9. See also Alan Dures, *English Catholicism, 1558–1642: Continuity and Change* (Harlow: Longman, 1983); J. C. H. Aveling, *The Handle and the Axe: The Catholic Recusants in England from the Reformation to Emancipation* (London: Blond & Briggs, 1976).
10 *English Reformations* (Oxford: Clarendon Press, 1993), p. vii.
11 Virgil Nemoianu, 'Literary History: Some Roads Not (Yet) Taken', in Marshall Brown (ed.), *The Uses of Literary History* (Durham: Duke University Press, 1995), pp. 18–19 (citing Adorno, Bloch and Fredric Jameson as advocates and practitioners of the approach).
12 John Bossy, *The English Catholic Community, 1570–1850* (London: Darton, Longman & Todd, 1975), ch. 8 *et passim*, defines a Catholic as one having regular access to the sacraments.
13 See the introduction to D. George Boyce and Alan O'Day (eds.), *The Making of Modern Irish History* (London: Routledge, 1996) concerning the relationship between differing interpretations of Irish history and overt political commitment. Their comments engage with the controversy surrounding Brendan Bradshaw's attack on revisionist 'value-free' history, definitively expressed in 'Nationalism and Historical Scholarship in Northern Ireland', *Irish Historical Studies*, 26 (1988–9), pp. 329–51, repr. as ch. 12 in Ciaran Brady (ed.), *Interpreting Irish History* (Dublin: Irish Academic Press, 1994).
14 However, John Morrill rightly praises Hill's role in introducing the history of religious ideas to a wide audience: *The Nature of the English Revolution* (Harlow: Longman, 1993), p. 277.
15 However, it may have been a sign of sensitivity to anti-Catholic prejudice that Edward Said's comparable use of the term 'Protestant', in the oral version of his 1993 Reith Lectures, was edited out before they reached print: *Representations of the Intellectual* (London: Vintage, 1994). Information from Arnold Hunt.
16 Michael C. Questier, *Conversion, Politics and Religion in England, 1580–1625* (Cambridge University Press, 1996), pp. 28–31.

17 Haigh, *English Reformations*, esp. ch. 14.
18 See L. I. Guiney, *Recusant Poets*, vol. 1 (London: Sheed & Ward, 1938) under 'Myles Hogarde', 'William Forrest' and 'Poems of Mary I'.
19 Myles Hogarde, *A Treatise Declaring Howe Christ by Perverse Preachyng Was Banished Out of This Realme* (1554): quoted in Guiney, *Recusant Poets*, p. 128. See J. W. Martin, 'Miles Hogarde: Artisan and Aspiring Author in 16th-Century England', *Renaissance Quarterly*, 34:3 (1981), pp. 359–81.
20 *The Seconde Grisilde*, 'Oration Consolatorye' (Bod.MS.Wood empt.2), p. [3]. See *The History of Grisild the Second: A Narrative, in Verse, of the Divorce of Queen Katharine of Aragon*, ed. W. D. Macray (London: Roxburghe, 1875).
21 Haigh, *English Reformations*, p. 252.
22 Historians have been, perhaps, more at odds over how effectively survivalism was supplanted. John Bossy and Christopher Haigh, with others, have conducted a high-profile controversy dubbed 'The fall of a church or the rise of a sect?' after Haigh's review-article in *HJ*, 2:1 (1978), pp. 181–6. Haigh's view (first set out in *Reformation and Resistance in Tudor Lancashire* (Cambridge University Press, 1975), and elaborated in the above article; 'From Monopoly to Minority: Post-Reformation Catholicism in England', *Transactions of the Royal Historical Society*, 5th ser., 31 (1981), pp. 129–47; 'The Continuity of Catholicism in the English Reformation', *P & P*, 93 (1981), pp. 37–69; and *English Reformations*, ch. 16) is that post-Reformation Catholicism was doomed, though revived temporarily by an English Mission whose mistake was to concentrate almost exclusively on Catholic landowners; in *The English Catholic Community*, Bossy has argued instead that Catholics became a sectarian community dominated by the laity. Caroline Hibbard's is perhaps the most important further contribution to the debate, arguing for a more international perspective, and a greater emphasis on the Catholic presence in London: 'Early Stuart Catholicism: Revisions and Re-Revisions', *Journal of Modern History*, 52:1 (1980), pp. 1–34. Marie Rowlands's forthcoming volume for the Catholic Record Society, on Catholicism below gentry level in early modern England, will help future historians to look beyond the communities nurtured by the great Catholic houses.
23 R. Po-Chia Hsia, *The World of Catholic Renewal, 1540–1770* (Cambridge University Press, 1998), introduction, discusses recent uses of the term 'Counter-Reformation'.
24 NLW, Add.MS. 22250B; Bod, MS.Eng.th.b.1–2.; Folger, X.d.532 (information from Jan Rhodes). Some caution is necessary when approaching post-medieval manuscripts alluding to medieval precedent, as with early modern medievalising in general: medieval MSS were quite often used simply as binders' waste or to cover the boards of books; the antiquarian spirit was not confined to Catholics; and Protestants, Laudian and other, often appropriated the visual effects of medievalism.
25 In the library of Balliol College, Oxford, is a book of hours with an

early eighteenth-century annotation describing how the book was hidden by the Lovell family: R. A. B. Mynors, *Catalogue of the Manuscripts at Balliol College, Oxford* (Oxford: Clarendon Press, 1963), p. 362. See also Janet Backhouse, 'The Sale of the Luttrell Psalter', and T. A. Birrell, 'The Circle of John Gage (1786–1842), Director of the Society of Arts, and the Bibliography of Medievalism', both in Robin Myers and Michael Harris (eds.), *Antiquarians, Book Collectors and the Circles of Learning* (Winchester: St Paul's Bibliographies, 1996); Christopher de Hamel, 'The Dispersal of the Library of Christ Church, Canterbury, from the 14th to the 16th Century', in James P. Carley and Colin G. C. Tite (eds.), *Books and Collectors, 1200–1700: Essays Presented to Andrew Watson* (London: British Library Publications, 1997); the footnotes to Andrew Watson, 'The Manuscript Collections of Sir Walter Cope (d.1614)', *Bodleian Library Record*, 12:4 (1987), pp. 262–97, esp. p. 265.

26 For three case-studies of seventeenth-century Catholic antiquarians, see Theo Bongaerts (ed.), *The Correspondence of Thomas Blount (1618–1679): A Recusant Antiquary* (Amsterdam: APA, 1978); and (discussing William Blundell) D. R. Woolf, 'Little Crosby and the Horizons of Early Modern Historical Culture' in Donald R. Kelley and David Harris Sacks (eds.), *The Historical Imagination in Early Modern England* (Cambridge University Press, 1997); Dennis E. Rhodes, 'Richard White of Basingstoke: the erudite exile', in Susan Roach (ed.), *Across the Narrow Seas: Studies in the History and Bibliography of Britain and the Low Countries, Presented to Anna E. C. Simoni* (London: British Library, 1991), pp. 23–30. See also Graham Parry, *The Trophies of Time: English Antiquarians of the 17th Century* (Oxford University Press, 1995), ch. 2.

27 I have written elsewhere about the problematic relationship between Catholic texts and the mainstream book trade, which surfaced in censorship and censure, and operated more stealthily in the clandestine distribution of forbidden books: Alison Shell, 'Catholic Texts and Anti-Catholic Prejudice in the Seventeenth-Century Book Trade' in Robin Myers and Michael Harris (eds.), *Censorship and the Control of Print in England and France, 1600–1910* (Winchester: St Paul's Bibliographies, 1992), pp. 33–57. See also Alexandra Walsham's forthcoming article: '"Domme Preachers": Post-Reformation English Catholicism and the Culture of Print' (*Past and Present*), and Patrick Collinson, Arnold Hunt and Alexandra Walsham, 'Religious Publishing 1557–1640' in the *Cambridge History of the Book in Britain*, vol. 4 (1557–1695), forthcoming.

28 John Lilliat gives more of a clue to his beliefs than some compilers of MS miscellanies, in annotating his version of 'Why do I use my paper, ink and pen?', the ballad on Edmund Campion, as 'A good verse, upon a badd Matter': see Arthur Marotti, *Manuscript, Print and the English Renaissance Lyric* (Ithaca: Cornell University Press, 1995), p. 6.

29 BL MS Egerton 2403, ff. 2–32 (dateable ca. 1601) is a manuscript with the superscription 'IHS Maria', apparently compiled by Thomas

Wenman during a period of imprisonment for Catholicism: see Albert J. Loomie (ed.), *Spain and the Jacobean Catholics, Vol. II 1613–1624* (CRS 68, 1978), pp. 27–8. Among several signed original loyalist compositions, it includes a 'complaint' poem hostile to Mary Stuart and calling her followers 'popish' (e.g. in stanza 162). This has been taken as a sign of Protestant authorship by Phillips, *Images*, though it need only indicate an author unhappy with papalism; if so, one can probably accept the traditional attribution of this unsigned poem to Wenman on the grounds that several shorter pieces in the volume bear his signature (e.g. by John Fry in his 1810 edition, *The Legend of Mary, Queen of Scots*, the poem's only appearance in print). However, for the problems with such an assumption, cf. Henry Woudhuysen, *Sir Philip Sidney and the Circulation of Manuscripts, 1558–1640* (Oxford: Clarendon, 1996), p. 160. I differ from Marotti, *Manuscript, Print*, who sees the piece as criticising Elizabeth (pp. 182–4).

30 The Scolar Press series edited by D. M. Rogers between 1968 and 1979, *English Recusant Literature*, published many of these books in facsimile. *ARCR* has been supplemented by Thomas Clancy, *English Catholic Books, 1641–1700* (1974: rev. edn. Aldershot: Scolar, 1996); and F. Blom, J. Blom, F. Korsten & G. Scott, *English Catholic Books, 1701–1800* (Aldershot: Scolar, 1996).

31 This is despite the fact that Allison and Rogers were involved in the *New Short-Title Catalogue* at every stage: see T. A. Birrell's review article 'English Counter-Reformation Book Culture', *RH*, 22 (1994), pp. 113–22.

32 See D. M. Rogers, 'English Catholics and the Printing Press at Home and Abroad, 1558–1640. A Bibliographical Survey' (Oxford D.Phil. thesis, 1951), pp. 30–1 and 58–64, and ' "Popishe Thackwell" and Early Catholic Printing in Wales', *Biographical Studies, 1534–1829*, 2 (1953), pp. 37–54.

33 One has some sympathy for the Parisian compositors set to work on the thick Scottish dialect of John Colville's *The Paranaese* (1602). Colville remarks in his epistle to the reader that it is difficult 'to print any thing in our vulgar toung on this syid of the sea nanly in France vhar our langage and pronu[n]ciation seamit so strange, and vhar the prentars use seldome theis lettres k, y, and double VV' (f.ee1a). Typographical imprecision was such a recognised feature of Catholic printing that it was even used, like a false imprint, to conceal when printing had taken place at a secret press in England. Richard Bristow's *A Reply to Fulke* (1580), purportedly printed in Louvain, came from Greenstreet House in East Ham, and the printer's epistle to the reader elaborates on the fiction: 'my Compositor was a straunger and ignorant in our Englishe tongue and Orthographie'. Complaining that the printing lacks the 'varietie of letters' requisite in a book of this kind, he concludes with a proverb that can equally well be read as an apologia for having to lie:

'having these characters out of England, I could not joyne them together with any others ... Remember that when man can not do as he would, he must do as he may.' (f.Eee4b)

34 See my review of Blom, Blom, Korsten and Scott in *The Library*, 6th ser., 19:2 (1997), pp. 158–60; and Anthony Allison and David M. Rogers, 'Ten Years of *Recusant History*', *RH*, 6 (1961/2), pp. 2–11.

35 The term of 'Romanist' used by Peter Lake and Michael Questier would be possible, despite its potential anti-loyalist overtones: e.g. in 'Agency, Appropriation and Rhetoric Under the Gallows: Puritans, Romanists and the State in Early Modern England', *P & P*, 153 (1996), pp. 64–107.

36 See also David L. Smith, 'Catholic, Anglican or Puritan? Edward Sackville, 4th Earl of Dorset and the Ambiguities of Religion in Early Stuart England', in Donna B. Hamilton and Richard Strier (eds.), *Religion, Literature and Politics in Post-Reformation England, 1540–1688* (Cambridge University Press, 1996), pp. 115–37.

37 The work of two students currently completing their doctoral theses, Paul Arblaster of Brussels and Margaret Sena of Princeton, will clarify this topic; and I am grateful to them both for letting me see portions of their work in progress.

38 I shall address these topics in a follow-up study to this, dealing with Catholics and orality. John Austin's *Devotions* was first printed in 1668 after an extensive circulation in MS.

39 See Keith Wrightson, *English Society, 1580–1680* (London: Hutchinson, 1982), ch. 2; Ernest A. Strathmann, 'Robert Persons's Essay on Atheism', in James G. McManaway *et al.* (eds.), *Joseph Quincy Adams Memorial Studies* (Washington: Folger Shakespeare Library, 1948).

40 William Crashaw, *Manuale Catholicorum* (1611), ff.7b–8a; Luke Fawne/Francis Cheynell, *The Beacon Flameing With a Non Obstante* (1652), p. 20.

41 Carol Z. Weiner, 'The Beleaguered Isle: A Study of Elizabethan and Early Jacobean Anti-Catholicism', *P & P*, 51 (1971), pp. 27–62. See also Robin Clifton, 'The Popular Fear of Catholics During the English Revolution', *P & P*, 52 (1971), pp. 23–55; and Peter Lake, 'Anti-Popery: the Structure of a Prejudice', in Ann Cust and Richard Hughes (eds.), *Conflict in Early Stuart England* (Harlow: Longman, 1989); Paul Christianson, *Reformers and Babylon: English Apocalyptic Visions From the Reformation to the Eve of the Civil War* (University of Toronto Press, 1978); William Haller, *Foxe's Book of Martyrs and the Elect Nation* (London: Jonathan Cape, 1963); William M. Lamont, *Godly Rule: Politics and Religion, 1603–1660* (London, 1969); Helgerson, *Forms of Nationhood*, ch. 6; Claire McEachern, *The Poetics of English Nationhood, 1590–1612* (Cambridge University Press, 1996); and Julia Gasper, *The Dragon and the Dove: The Plays of Thomas Dekker* (Oxford: Clarendon, 1990). For its links to anti-Spanish sentiment, see William S. Maltby, *The Black Legend in England* (Durham: Duke University Press, 1971).

42 Questier, *Conversion*, ch. 2.
43 I am grateful to Raymond D. Tumbleson for allowing me to read, at proof stage, his monograph *Catholicism and the English Protestant Imagination: Nationalism, Religion and Literature, 1660–1745* (Cambridge University Press, 1998).
44 Examples of Catholic texts expurgated for use by Protestants are discussed in Victor Houliston, 'Why Robert Persons Would Not Be Pacified: Edmund Bunny's Theft of the *Book of Resolution*', in McCoog (ed.), *Reckoned Expense*; Shell, 'Catholic Texts', pp. 42, 56.
45 In Dyce MS 44.25.f.39 (National Art Library, London): see Robert F. Fleissner, *Resolved to Love: The 1592 Edition of Henry Constable's 'Diana'* (Salzburg: Salzburg Studies in English Literature, 1980), p. 72. Though Constable may not have been a Catholic at the time, he was concerned with convincing James I of the solidarity of the Roman church (p. xi).
46 Arthur Marotti of Wayne State University is currently writing a study of Catholicism and manuscript culture.

1 THE LIVID FLASH: DECADENCE, ANTI-CATHOLIC REVENGE TRAGEDY AND THE DEHISTORICISED CRITIC

1 Donna Tartt, *The Secret History* (London: Penguin, 1992), p. 646. The close association between revenge tragedy and the thriller is discussed in John Kerrigan, *Revenge Tragedy: Aeschylus to Armageddon* (Cambridge University Press, 1996), ch. 3. Ngaio Marsh, *Singing in the Shrouds* (1st edn., London: William Collins, 1958), illustrates how a taste for revenge tragedy is used as shorthand for criminal depravity; the character who prefers *The Duchess of Malfi* to Shakespeare turns out to be the murderer.
2 John Wilks, *The Idea of Conscience in Renaissance Tragedy* (London: Routledge, 1990), p. 194.
3 A recent discussion and checklist can be found in Ann Rosalind Jones, 'Italians and Others: *The White Devil* (1612)', in David Scott Kastan and Peter Stallybrass (eds.), *Staging the Renaissance* (New York: Routledge, 1991).
4 Davis J. Alpaugh, 'Emblem and Interpretation in *The Pilgrim's Progress*', *ELH*, 33 (1966), pp. 299–314 (quotation p. 300); Ronald Paulson, *Emblem and Expression* (London: Thames & Hudson, 1975) p. 53.
5 For a guide to the vast corpus of work on apocalyptic studies, see the bibliography to C. A. Patrides and Joseph Wittreich (eds.), *The Apocalypse in English Renaissance Thought and Literature* (Manchester University Press, 1984). See also Katherine Firth, *The Apocalyptic Tradition in Reformation Britain, 1530–1645* (Oxford University Press, 1979).
6 Bernard's commentary epitomises a number of apocalyptic anti-Catholic commonplaces and will be referred to extensively.
7 For a succinct account of the history of the interpretation of the Whore of Babylon, see Harold R. Willoughby and Juliette Renaud (eds.), *The*

Elizabeth Day McCormick Apocalypse. Volume 1 (University of Chicago Press, 1940), pp. 476–8.
8 Christopher Hill, *Antichrist in Seventeenth-Century England* (Oxford University Press, 1971), esp. ch. 1; Peter Lake, 'The Significance of the Elizabethan Identification of the Pope as Antichrist', *JEH*, 31 (1980), pp. 161–78.
9 See Henry Chadwick, 'Royal Ecclesiastical Supremacy', pp. 169–203 in Brendan Bradshaw and Eamon Duffy (eds.), *Humanism, Reform and Reformation* (Cambridge University Press, 1989).
10 See Tessa Watt, *Cheap Print and Popular Piety* (Cambridge University Press, 1991), ch. 4.
11 For the necessity to cover profane *fabulae* with the veil of Christian allegory, see Michael Camille, *The Gothic Idol* (Cambridge University Press, 1989), pp. 98–9. Nigel Smith, *Perfection Proclaimed* (Oxford: Clarendon, 1989), pp. 233–4, discusses the veil and links it to other metaphors of concealment.
12 Matthew 23.27: see also Acts 23.3. As with a number of anti-Catholic topoi, this can also be used for Puritans by conformists: the overlap comes because of the commonplaces associated with hypocrisy, because some conformists discerned popery in Puritanism, and – possibly – as a means of blackening Puritans by association. *Sphinx Lugduno-Genevensis* (1683) is an extended example of language normally anti-Catholic being transferred. John N. King, *English Reformation Literature* (Princeton University Press, 1982) discusses how hypocrisy became an epithet for Catholicism (pp. 157–60, 351).
13 In *Elizabethan Pamphleteers* (London: Athlone, 1983) Sandra Clark points out *apropos* the association of cosmetics and rich clothes with rotting flesh that the linking of commonplaces in a 'complex referential field' controlled the literary form of pamphlets (pp. 191–3, 211–14).
14 Ronald Paulson, *Breaking and Remaking* (New Brunswick: Rutgers University Press, 1989), p. 18.
15 Hill, *Antichrist*, p. 25, describes it as an almost universal corollary of Protestantism; for a more nuanced view, see Anthony Milton, *Catholic and Reformed* (Cambridge University Press, 1994).
16 Peter Lake, 'Anti-Popery: The Structure of a Prejudice', in Cust and Hughes (eds.), *Conflict in Early Stuart England*, pp. 73–5.
17 There will be no extended discussion of *A Game at Chess* in this chapter, since its anti-Catholic content has been well and frequently discussed. See Edgar C. Morris, 'The Allegory in Middleton's *A Game at Chess*', *Englische Studien*, 38 (1907), pp. 39–52; Edward M. Wilson and Olga Turner, 'The Spanish Protest against *A Game at Chesse*', *MLR*, 44 (1949), pp. 476–82 (printing and translating the shocked letter of the Spanish ambassador describing the production); G. Bullough, '*A Game at Chesse*. How it Struck a Contemporary', *MLR*, 49 (1954), pp. 156–8; Margot Heinemann, *Puritanism and Theatre: Thomas Middleton and Opposition Drama*

Under the Early Stuarts (Cambridge University Press, 1980), pp. 151–71 *et passim*; Jerzey Limon, *Dangerous Matter* (Cambridge University Press, 1986), ch. 4; Paul Yachnin, '*A Game at Chesse*: Thomas Middleton's Praise of Folly', *MLQ*, 48 (1987), pp. 107–23; Richard Dutton, *Mastering the Revels* (London: Macmillan, 1991), pp. 237–46. Quotations are taken from the edition by T. H. Howard-Hill (Manchester University Press, 1993). See also the introduction of Howard-Hill's facsimile edition (Oxford: Malone Society, 1990).

18 Cf. King, *English Reformation Literature*, p. 143, for comments on Latimer's observation that the lax preacher feeds his congregation on strawberries.
19 Cf. Thomas Middleton's pamphlets, discussed in Heinemann, *Puritanism*, ch. 3.
20 The unique copy was edited by J. P. Collier in 1841 (no imprint).
21 See R. D. Harley, *Artists' Pigments c. 1600–1835* (London: Butterworths, 1970). The use of monochrome is often characteristic of Protestant aesthetics: see Attilio Agnoletto, 'La "Cromoclastiá" Delle Riforme Protestanti', *Rassegna*, 23.3 (1985), pp. 21–31.
22 See Charles R. Forker, 'Webster and Barnes: The Source of the Cardinal's Arming in *The Duchess of Malfi* Once More', *Anglia*, 106:3–4 (1988), pp. 415–20.
23 See Katherine Eisamann Maus, 'Proof and Consequences: Inwardness and Exposure in the English Renaissance', *Representations*, 34 (1991), pp. 29–52, esp. pp. 36–7.
24 Bernard, *Key*, pp. 85–107.
25 King, *English Reformation Literature*, discusses the devotional importance of blinding light for the Protestant (p. 154).
26 This reference is taken from the reprint (London: E. Palmer, 1825).
27 This has an obvious similarity to the use of central curtained niches on Renaissance stages, behind which scenes were 'discovered'. More generally, a staging of this kind has its effect compounded by the ambiguity of the theatrical medium: see Jonas Barish, *The Antitheatrical Prejudice* (Berkeley: University of California Press, 1981), and Jonathan V. Crewe, 'The Theater of the Idols: Theatrical and Antitheatrical Discourse', in Kastan and Stallybrass (eds.), *Staging the Renaissance*.
28 Frances Yates, *The Art of Memory* (London: Routledge & Kegan Paul, 1966) is the classic discussion; see also Mary J. Carruthers, *The Book of Memory: A Study of Memory in Medieval Culture* (Cambridge University Press, 1990).
29 See Jan Ziolkowski, 'Avatars of Ugliness in Medieval Literature', *MLR*, 79 (1984), pp. 1–20.
30 Camille, *Gothic Idol*, p. 307.
31 See Mary Tom Osborne, *Advice-to-a-Painter Poems 1633–1856* (Austin: Texas University Press, 1949), nos. 24, 25, 27 and 31; Annette Drew-Bear, 'Face-Painting in Renaissance Tragedy', *Renaissance Drama*, 12

(1981), pp. 71–93; Shirley Nelson Garner, '"Let Her Paint an Inch Thick": Painted Ladies in Renaissance Drama and Society', *Renaissance Drama*, 20 (1989), pp. 123–139.

32 Laudians before the Civil Wars, and Anglicans after the Restoration, sometimes joined with those of more traditionally Calvinist affiliations to criticise Catholicism's cosmetic outside: *A Catholick Pill to Purge Popery* (1677) criticised fine churches as '*splendida peccata*, glittering dross, and beautiful deformities' (pp. 60–1).

33 See Carol Z. Weiner, 'The Beleaguered Isle: A Study of Elizabethan and Early Jacobean Anti-Catholicism', *P & P*, 51 (1971), pp. 27–62, esp. p. 46.

34 See Margaret Aston, *England's Iconoclasts. Volume 1. Laws Against Images* (Oxford University Press, 1988), p. 468; Robin Clifton, 'Fear of Popery', pp. 144–67 in Conrad Russell (ed.), *The Origins of the English Civil War* (London: Macmillan, 1973), p. 146.

35 Julia Gasper describes this as the 'definitive militant Protestant play': *The Dragon and the Dove*, p. 9.

36 Camille, *Gothic Idol*, pp. 18, 224, 346, 348. A summary of recent iconoclasm scholarship can be found in Linda Gregerson, *The Reformation of the Subject: Spenser, Milton, and the English Protestant Epic* (Cambridge University Press, 1995), introduction: commenting upon the perceived logocentricity of Protestantism, she says 'It was incumbent upon the verbal artifact at this period to register and guard its own referential states and its comparative *in*utility for idolatrous purposes' (p. 3).

37 Kenneth Clark, *Moments of Vision* (London: John Murray, 1981), p. 68.

38 Quoted from Cust and Hughes (eds.), *Conflict in Early Stuart England*, p. 82.

39 See Camille, *Gothic Idol*, pp. 63, 306.

40 See also *The Popes Great Year of Jubilee* (1675), and *Lambeth Faire* (1641). A twentieth-century example is Ernest Phillipps's *Papal Merchandise* (London: Chas. J. Thynne, 1911).

41 Cf. J. J. Scarisbrick, *The Reformation and the English People* (Oxford: Basil Blackwell, 1984), p. 141.

42 See Frederick F. Waage, *The White Devil Discover'd* (New York: Peter Lang, 1984): cf. John Raymond, *An Itinerary* (1648), f.A11b: 'Observe what machivillian unheard of Weapons they devise to surprize an enemy unawares. At Venice I saw a pocket Church Booke with a Pistoll hid in the binding, which turning to such a Page, discharges. A plot (I conceive) to entrap him you hate, whilst yon [sic] are at your devotions together, when there's least suspition.'

43 Walter Raleigh, 'The Lie', ll. 7–8. Taken from Emrys Jones (ed.), *The New Oxford Book of Sixteenth-Century Verse*, pp. 371–3.

44 Cf. *A Game at Chess*, III i, where the Black Knight says of the Fat Bishop, 'Here's a sweet paunch to propagate belief on, / Like the foundation of a chapel laid / Upon a quagmire.' (ll. 76–8)

45 See note 39.
46 Aston, *England's Iconoclasts*, p. 344. One must stress that medieval and Counter-Reformation Catholics also condemned idolatry.
47 Of those that have not, A. H. Bullen dismisses it as a 'damnable piece of flatness' and Margot Heinemann as a 'pious religious exercise' (*Puritanism*, pp. 51–2). Quotations and references are taken from the first edition of 1597, as A. H. Bullen's edition in *The Works of Thomas Middleton*, 8 vols (London: J. C. Nimmo, 1885–6), VIII, is inaccurate.
48 King, *English Reformation Literature*, pp. 130–1, comments on the paradox of how the Protestant insistence on Scriptural plainness combined with a need for exegeses.
49 Though the preponderant moralism of the Wisdom of Solomon would have made it unexceptionable, Protestants differed in the validity that they ascribed to the Apocrypha as a whole. See A. A. Bromham and Zara Bruzzi, '*The Changeling' and the Years of Crisis* (London: Pinter, 1990), pp. 138–41.
50 *The Complete Works of John Marston*, ed. A. H. Bullen, 3 vols (London: J. C. Nimmo, 1885–7), III, ll. 79–84. R. C. Horne comments of the poem that it exploits the ambivalence of a time when the word 'image' was widening its connotations to include statues that were not specifically religious: see 'Voices of Alienation: The Moral Significance of Marston's Satiric Strategy', *MLR*, 81 (1986), pp. 18–33. *The Scourge of Villainie* 8 also compares the language and actions of courtship to idolatry: see *The Poems of John Marston*, ed. Arnold Davenport (Liverpool University Press, 1961), pp. 150–7. For Marston's ideas on idolatry, see Philip J. Finkelpearl, *John Marston of the Inner Temple* (Cambridge, Mass.: Harvard University Press, 1969), pp. 98–9.
51 Quotations are taken from *The Works of Cyril Tourneur*, ed. Allardyce Nicoll (London: Fanfrolico Press, 1929).
52 See John N. King and Robin Smith, 'Recent Studies in Protestant Poetics', *ELR*, 21:2 (1991), pp. 283–307.
53 Cf. the title of E. Lee, *Legenda Lignea: With an Answer to Mr. Birchley's Moderator Pleading for the Toleration of Popery* (1653). The title puns on Voragine's popular compilation of saints' lives, *Legenda Aurea*.
54 Aston, *England's Iconoclasts*, pp. 406–7.
55 Camille, *Gothic Idol*, p. 117.
56 Samuel Harsnet, *A Declaration of Egregious Popish Impostures* (1603), p. 150: 'Our *Daemonopoiia*, or devil-fiction, is Tragico-Comoedia, a mixture of both ...' He defines the comedy as the cunning of Jesuits and the juggling of exorcism, and the tragedy as the winning of souls to Catholicism. Simon Shepherd, *Marlowe and the Politics of Elizabethan Theatre* (Brighton: Harvester, 1986) discusses the similar phenomenon in *Dr. Faustus* (p. 137). Stephen Greenblatt, 'Shakespeare and the Exorcists', in Geoffrey Hartman and Patricia Parker (eds.), *Shakespeare and the*

Question of Theory (London: Methuen, 1985), relates Harsnet's pamphlet to other public exposures of Catholicism.

57 Rupert Brooke, *John Webster and the Elizabethan Drama* (London: Sidgwick & Jackson, 1916), p. 158.
58 'The Democritean Universe in Webster's *White Devil*', in Clifford Davidson *et al.* (eds.), *Drama in the Renaissance* (New York: AMS, 1986).
59 The first complete English translation was not published till 1682 (Wing L3447). Lucretius's atheism would also have facilitated the polemical link with anti-popery.
60 H. A. J. Munro (trans.), *Lucretius: On the Nature of Things* (Chicago: William Benton, 1952), pp. 44, 46, 53.
61 Cf. *Revenger's Tragedy* I ii, ll. 4–10.
62 I am working on the assumption that Middleton wrote *The Revenger's Tragedy*, now the critical orthodoxy: see David J. Lake, *The Canon of Thomas Middleton's Plays: Internal Evidence for the Major Problems of Authorship* (London: Cambridge University Press, 1975); M. W. A. Smith, '*The Revenger's Tragedy*: The Derivation and Interpretation of Statistical Results for Resolving Disputed Authorship', *Computers and the Humanities*, 21 (1987), pp. 21–55 and 267, and 'The Authorship of *The Revenger's Tragedy*', *N & Q*, 236 (1991), pp. 508–13. A recent articulation of the opposing view occurs in Heinemann, *Puritanism*, pp. 104–5, 287–9. New evidence would, in any case, not greatly alter an argument based on the general anti-Catholic imaginative habits of Jacobean tragedians.
63 I have largely omitted Middleton's *Women Beware Women*, for reasons of space, and *The Changeling*, in which the language is less iconic. Bromham and Bruzzi, *Changeling*, discuss the anti-Catholic elements of the latter on pp. 19, 31–2, 45, 47–8, 120–3, 136, 152–4, 156–165, 169, 174–9, 184–5.
64 In 'Emblem and Antithesis in *The Duchess of Malfi*', *Renaissance Drama*, 11 (1980), pp. 115–34, Catherine Belsey argues that this play's structure shows a balance between formal iconographical representation and the narrative's dynamic moral evolution. Leslie T. Duer, 'The Painter and the Poet: Visual Design in *The Duchess of Malfi*', *Emblematica* 1:2 (1986), pp. 293–307, compares the visual effect of the emblem in the dramatic text to the moment when an anamorphic image becomes recognisable.
65 Muriel Bradbrook, *Themes and Conventions in Elizabethan Tragedy* (2nd edn. London: Cambridge University Press, 1980), p. 163. See also Nancy G. Wilds, '"Of Rare Fire Compact": Image and Rhetoric in *The Revenger's Tragedy*', *Texas Studies in Literature and Language*, 17.1 (1975), pp. 61–74, esp. pp. 61–2.
66 All quotations and line-references are taken from Lawrence J. Ross's edition of *The Revenger's Tragedy* (London: Edward Arnold, 1967).
67 E.g. in Ross's introduction (p. 65).
68 Cf. *Legenda Lignea*, discussing famous converts to Rome: '[Richard

Crashaw] is fallen in love with his own shadow, conversing with himself in verse, and admiring the birth of his own brains' (f.M5b).
69 For the apocalyptic associations of foul weather, see Joseph Wittreich, '"Image of That Horror": The Apocalypse in *King Lear*', Patrides and Weittreich (eds.), *The Apocalypse in English Renaissance Thought and Literature*, pp. 175–206.
70 E.g. II i, ll. 16–17; v iii, l. 27; v iii, l. 162 ff. See Bradbrook, *Themes*, pp. 183–8.
71 Bradbrook, *Themes*, p. 231.
72 All quotations and line-references are taken from *The White Devil*, ed. J. R. Mulryne (London: Edward Arnold, 1970).
73 William Rankins, *The Mirrour of Monsters* (1587), ff.21a–22b.
74 Turning infidel, and worshipping idols, was cant for becoming a prostitute. In support of his identification of the cant term, Ross (*The Revenger's Tragedy*, p. 42) cites 'pagan' in *2 Henry IV* II ii, l.168.
75 Trials are important loci of exposure, as Maus, 'Proof', has commented (pp. 39–41).
76 One of the few critics to notice this is H. B. Franklin, 'The Trial Scene of Webster's *The White Devil* Examined in Terms of Renaissance Rhetoric', *Studies in English Literature 1500–1900*, 1 (1961), pp. 35–51. For Webster's exploitation and transmutation of the topoi of his era, see Robert Ornstein, *The Moral Vision of Jacobean Tragedy* (Madison: University of Wisconsin Press, 1960), p. 6. Sandra Clark, *Elizabethan Pamphleteers* (London: Athlone, 1983), pp. 226–7, discusses the image-clusters by which pamphleteers evoked whores.
77 E.g. King, *English Reformation Literature*, p. 266, who discusses Luke Shepherd's *The Upchering of the Messe* [1548].
78 Anders Dallby, *The Anatomy of Evil: A Study of John Webster's 'The White Devil'* (Cwk Gleerup Lund: Lund Studies in English 48, 1974), p. 140: see also Floyd Lowell Goodwin Jnr., *Image Pattern and Moral Vision in John Webster* (Salzburg Studies in English Literature, 1977), pp. 16–33; Frederick F. Waage, *The White Devil Discover'd: Backgrounds and Foregrounds to Webster's Tragedy* (New York: Peter Lang, 1984), p. 54. For devils in crystal, see Barnabe Googe, *The Popish Kingdome*, ed. R. C. Hope (London: Chiswick, 1880), f.57b:
>Besides in glistering glasses fayre, or else in christall cleare
>They sprightes enclose...
79 This is one allusion to contemporary religious polemic that has been noticed. Waage, *White Devil*, ch. 9, discusses the common assumptions shared by Adams and Webster; see also George A. Aitken, 'John Webster and Thomas Adams', *Academy*, 35, pp. 133–4; Gustav Cross, 'A Note on *The White Devil*', *N & Q*, 201 (1956), pp. 99–100, who cites other uses of the phrase in contemporary texts; R. W. Dent, *Webster's Borrowing* (Berkeley: University of California Press, 1960), index under Thomas Adams.

80 Dallby, *Anatomy*, pp. 126–9: Waage, *White Devil*, p. 54. See also Muriel Bradbrook, *John Webster: Citizen and Dramatist* (London: Weidenfeld & Nicholson, 1980), p. 132.

81 Richard Bodtke, *Tragedy and the Jacobean Temper: the Major Plays of John Webster* (Salzburg Studies in English Literature, 1972), p. 198, comments that Ludovico in IV iii automatically paints a pejorative picture of woman when commenting on the dissimulation of the pope.

82 This identification seems more probable than either Sixtus V or Paul V, both of whom have been suggested in the past. Paul IV is the title that Monticelso takes at his election, while the real Paul IV had been well-known in England as Giampietro Caraffa, and Monticelso's Black Book in IV i can be seen as a parody of the Papal Index which Paul IV introduced. See also John Russell Brown, 'The Papal Election in Webster's *The White Devil* (1612)', *N & Q*, 202 (1957), pp. 490–4.

83 *Theatre Arts*, August 1955: quoted in *Webster: 'The White Devil' and 'The Duchess of Malfi'. A Casebook*, ed. Roger V. Holdsworth (London: Macmillan, 1975), p. 235; this volume, and *Webster: the Critical Heritage*, ed. Don D. Moore (London: Routledge & Kegan Paul, 1981), afford overviews of a vast literature. Sanford Sternlicht, in *John Webster's Imagery and the Webster Canon* (Salzburg Studies in English Literature, 1972) traces the critical history of Elizabethan and Jacobean dramatic imagery, identifying as most influential the opposed critical approaches of Caroline Spurgeon whose studies concentrated on iterated individual images, and Wilson Knight, who preferred to take images in context; he uses a cumulative definition of imagery as important in rhetorical economy, the presentation and exposition of character, the creation of mood, the structuring of the plot and the presentation of thematic lines. The following are significant individual articles: Una Ellis-Fermor, 'The imagery of *The Revengers Tragedie* and *The Atheists Tragedie*', *MLR*, 30 (1935), pp. 289–301; Hereward T. Price, 'The Function of Imagery in Webster', *PMLA*, 70 (1955), pp. 717–39; Inga-Stina Ekeblad (Ewbank), 'An Approach to Tourneur's Imagery', *MLR*, 54 (1959), pp. 489–98. See also Wilds, '"Of Rare Fire Compact"', pp. 61–74. But it may be a sign of weariness that the most recent edition of Webster, ed. David Gunby *et al.* (Cambridge University Press, 1995), hardly mentions imagery at all in its critical introduction. With these critics, as elsewhere in this chapter, one needs to bear in mind that the attribution of *The Revenger's Tragedy* to Middleton rather than Tourneur is of comparatively recent date.

84 De là tant de beautés difformes dans les oeuvres;
Le vers charmant
Est par la torsion subite des concleuvres
Pris brusquement;
A de certains moments toutes les jeunes flores
Dans la forêt
Ont peur, et sur le front des blanches métaphores
L'ombre apparaît . . .

See *Swinburne as Critic*, ed. Clyde K. Hyder (London: Routledge & Kegan Paul, 1972), pp. 286–311 (translation of Hugo in notes). See also Edmund W. Gosse's citation of Gautier with reference to the 'lurid' colours of Webster: *Seventeenth-Century Studies* (London: Heineman, 1914), p. 50.

85 T. S. Eliot, 'Cyril Tourneur' in *Elizabethan Essays* (London: Faber & Faber, 1934), pp. 128–9; cf. 'Whispers of Immortality', from *T. S. Eliot: Collected Poems 1909–1935* (London: Faber & Faber, 1954), pp. 53–4.

86 From *Vies Imaginaires* (Paris: Bibliotheque-Charpentier, 1896), p. 207 (essay pp. 207–15). Eliot condemned the phrase as 'hysterical' in the essay cited above.

87 '*The Revenger's Tragedy* (c. 1606): Providence, Parody and Black Camp', ch. 9 in Jonathan Dollimore, *Radical Tragedy* (Brighton: Harvester, 1984); see also p. 149.

88 Buggery was often deemed a characteristic popish sin: see Lake, in Cust and Hughes (eds.), *Conflict in Early Stuart England*, p. 75; King, *English Reformation Literature*, pp. 371–2, 384; Thomas Beard, *Theatre of Gods Judgements* (1st edn. 1597), p. 359. Marston criticises the Jesuit colleges of Douai and Valladolid for instilling homosexual habits in the young: *Scourge of Villainie*, 2, Marston, *Poems*, ed. Davenport (1961), pp. 112–13. John Carey, *John Donne: Life, Mind and Art* (1981, repr. London: Faber & Faber, 1990) discusses the imputation of buggery to Jesuits with reference to Donne's *Ignatius His Conclave* (pp. 20–1). See also Alan Bray, *Homosexuality in Renaissance England* (London: Gay Men's Press, 1982), pp. 19–21; Alan Stewart, *Close Readers: Humanism and Sodomy in Early Modern England* (Princeton University Press, 1997), ch. 2. I am grateful to Henry Woudhuysen for the latter reference.

89 See Roger MacGraw, 'Popular Anticlericalism in Nineteenth-Century Rural France', in J. Obelkevich *et al.* (eds.), *Disciplines of Faith* (London: Routledge, 1987), pp. 351–71.

90 Jean Pierrot (trans. Derek Coltman), *The Decadent Imagination 1880–1900* (University of Chicago Press, 1981), pp. 82, 85–9, 214–19, 224–32, 244. See also Jennifer Birkett, *The Sins of the Fathers: Decadence in France, 1870–1914* (London: Quartet, 1986; Ellis Hanson, *Decadence and Catholicism* (Cambridge, Mass.: Harvard University Press, 1997). The misogynistic implications of the connection are discussed briefly by Bram Dijkstra, *Idols of Perversity: Fantasies of Feminine Evil in Fin-de-Siecle Culture* (New York: Oxford University Press, 1986), pp. 210, 234, 363, 382, and, from the days before feminist criticism, by Mario Praz (trans. Angus Davidson), *The Romantic Agony* (1st edn. Oxford University Press, 1933), ch. 4.

91 Ronald Firbank, *The Artificial Princess*, pp. 32–3; *Vainglory*, p. 152: references from *The Complete Firbank* (London: Picador, 1988); cf. also the reference to Jacobean drama on p. 408, and the theme of relics in *Valmouth*. Thomas Pynchon, *The Crying of Lot 49* (London: Picador, this

edn. 1979), ch. 3, can be read as a post-modernist homage to the same fictional association.
92 Tourneur, *Works*, ed. Nicoll, pp. 44–5: on pp. 38–9 he says, unselfconsciously enough, that 'often purple passages roughly inspired by [Tourneur's] verse have done service for exact criticism'.
93 The snake in the Garden of Eden was often given a woman's face in medieval representations. See Camille, *Gothic Idol*, pp. 90–1.
94 A. C. Swinburne, *The Age of Shakespeare* (London: Chatto & Windus, 1908), p. 259, cf. also pp. 260, 266.
95 Ralph Berry, *The Art of John Webster* (Oxford: Clarendon, 1972), p. 107.
96 Cf. Christopher Ockland's *The Fountaine and Welspring of all Variance* (1589), on how Catholics undermine the state.
97 See Dror Wahrman, 'From Imaginary Drama to Dramatised Imagery: The *Mappe-Monde Nouvelle Papistique, 1566–67*', *Journal of the Warburg and Courtauld Institutes*, 54 (1991), pp. 186–205.
98 Wilks, *Idea of Conscience*, p. 194 (see also pp. 196, 198–9, 217, 219); L. L. Brodwin, *Elizabethan Love Tragedy, 1587–1625* (University of London Press, 1971), p. 269. Wilks is paraphrasing Webster, who in turn is alluding to *The Old Arcadia* (Oxford University Press edition, ed. Katherine Duncan-Jones, p. 333). I am grateful to Helen Hackett for pointing this out.
99 Bradbrook, *Themes*, p. 202; Roma Gill's edition of *Women Beware Women* (London: Ernest Benn, 1967), p. xxvi.
100 Margot Heinemann, 'Political Drama' in A. R. Braunmuller and Michael Hattaway (eds.) *The Cambridge Companion to Renaissance Drama* (Cambridge University Press, 1990), pp. 190–1.
101 David Farley-Hills summarises the two usual critical interpretations of the Websterian world, agnostic pathos versus theological scepticism: see *Jacobean Drama: A Critical Study of the Professional Drama, 1600–1625* (London: Macmillan, 1988), quotation p. 136. For the Calvinist worldview, see above. Charles R. Forker, *The Skull Beneath the Skin* (Carbondale: Southern Illinois University Press, 1986), p. 292, gives a critique of the nihilist approach. Yet another approach – that of ignoring religion almost entirely and attributing the evil of Jacobean tragedy to political unrest – is manifested by Molly Smith, *The Darker World Within: Evil in the Tragedies of Shakespeare and his Successors* (London: University of Delaware Press, 1991).
102 *Elizabethan Love Tragedy*, p. 273. Similarly, Isabel Damisch sees in Webster an equivocal attitude towards religion in the fact that profane references outweigh sacred in his imagery, and concludes from this that he is inveighing against a God he does not believe in: 'Analyse des motifs religieux dans les images de trois tragedies de Webster', *Caliban: Annales de l'Université de Toulouse*, 11 (1974), pp. 113–25.
103 G. Wilson Knight, *The Golden Labyrinth* (London: Phoenix, 1962), pp. 109–10. Also discussing *The Duchess of Malfi*, Nicholas Brooke has

referred to the dumb-show in the Catholic shrine at Loreto as a 'mockery of religion': *Horrid Laughter in Jacobean Tragedy* (London: Open Books, 1979), p. 55.

104 Jonathan Dollimore and Alan Sinfield (eds.), *The Selected Plays of John Webster* (Cambridge University Press, 1983) p. xvi, summarising key arguments in Dollimore's *Radical Tragedy* (1983) and Sinfield's *Literature in Protestant England* (1983).

105 See notes to Robert N. Watson, 'Tragedy', in Braunmuller and Hattaway (eds.), *Cambridge Companion to Renaissance Drama*.

2 CATHOLIC POETICS AND THE PROTESTANT CANON

1 Thomas F. Healy, *Richard Crashaw* (Leiden: E. J. Brill, 1986), introduction; John R. Roberts (ed.), *New Perspectives on the Life and Work of Richard Crashaw* (Columbia: University of Missouri Press, 1990). Healy's revisionist account downplays the continental elements of Crashaw's inheritance, while stressing his Anglicanism. See also Roberts's *Richard Crashaw, an Annotated Bibliography of Criticism, 1632–1980* (Columbia: University of Missouri Press, 1985: referred to as 'Roberts' below) and the essay by Anthony Low in Thomas N. Corns (ed.), *The Cambridge Companion to English Poetry: Donne to Marvell* (Cambridge University Press, 1993).

2 M. H. Abrams (general ed.), *The Norton Anthology of English Literature*, vol. I, 6th edition (New York: W. W. Norton, 1993), pp. 1,388–9. For other (perhaps more obviously outdated) comments on Crashaw in a widely available literary history, see D. J. Enright, 'George Herbert and the Devotional Poets', Boris Ford (ed.), *The New Pelican Guide to English Literature*, vol. III, 'From Donne to Marvell' (Harmondsworth: Penguin, 1954, rev. 1982), pp. 187–204.

3 Discussed in Murray Roston, *Milton and the Baroque* (London: Macmillan, 1980), ch. 1.

4 To borrow the title of a recent conference-paper given by Peter Davidson at the conference 'Papists Misrepresented and Represented' (University College London, June 1997), another heading for this chapter might be 'Why the English Don't Like the Baroque'. But Anthony Low's honesty in *Love's Architecture: Devotional Modes in 17th-Century English Poetry* (New York University Press, 1978), p. 158, is worth quoting: 'Personally, I find more strain in adjusting to Crashaw than to any other major seventeenth-century poet, religious or secular ... That is all the more reason to read him.' A microcosm of the scholarly debate on Englishness and baroque poetry can be found in *Modern Philology*, 61 (1963/4), where succeeding essays by Helen C. White ('Southwell – Metaphysical and Baroque') and Mario Praz ('Baroque in England') argue, respectively, for the Englishness of Southwell's verse and for the baroque being 'alien to the spirit of [England's] tradition' (pp. 159–68 and 169–79, quotation p. 179).

5 For Southwell's influence and importance as a theorist, see Louis Martz, *The Poetry of Meditation* (New Haven: Yale University Press, 1954, rev. edn. 1962), esp. ch. 5; and Pierre Janelle's indispensable *Robert Southwell the Writer* (London: Sheed & Ward, 1935, repr. 1971), esp. ch. 6; Brian Oxley, 'The Poetry of an Artificial Man: A Study of the Latin and English Verse of Robert Southwell' (University of St Andrews PhD, 1984). See Introduction for the definition of Catholicism used throughout this study.

6 Crashaw's debt to fourteenth-century mystics and Latin hymns (e.g. the Stabat Mater) has been recognised: see J. A. W. Bennett, *Poetry of the Passion* (Oxford: Clarendon Press, 1982), p. 146; Healy, *Richard Crashaw*, ch. 2.

7 Martz, *Poetry of Meditation*, pp. 199–210; Janelle, *Robert Southwell*, pp. 189–90, 205, 308–14; and (for a later period) Anne Vincent-Buffault, *The History of Tears* (English trans. Basingstoke: Macmillan, 1991). I am grateful to Lucy Newlyn for this reference, and to Ceri Sullivan of the University of Wales, Bangor, for letting me see her unpublished paper, 'The Physiology of Penance: Weeping Texts of the 1590s'.

8 The standard modern edition of Southwell's verse by James H. Macdonald and Nancy Pollard Brown (Oxford: Clarendon, 1967) has been used for all quotations. Otherwise, the most important studies are: Janelle, *Robert Southwell*; J. H. Macdonald, *The Poems and Prose Writings of Robert Southwell, S.J.: a Bibliographical Study* (Oxford: Roxburghe Club, 1937), referred to as 'Macdonald' hereafter; Christopher Devlin, *The Life of Robert Southwell, Poet and Martyr* (London: Watergate, 1967); Nancy Pollard Brown, 'Robert Southwell: The Mission of the Written Word', in Thomas M. McCoog, S.J. (ed.), *The Reckoned Expense* (Woodbridge: Boydell, 1996); *ibid.*, 'Paperchase: The Dissemination of Catholic Texts in Elizabethan England', *English Manuscript Studies 1100–1700*, 1 (1989), pp. 120–43. Vittorio F. Cavalli, 'St. Robert Southwell, S.J.: A Selective Bibliographic Supplement to the Studies of Pierre Janelle and James H. Macdonald', *RH*, 21:3 (1993), pp. 297–304, mostly lists theses and recent facsimile editions.

9 Martz, *Poetry of Meditation*, esp. pp. 184–97, and ch. 5, 'Robert Southwell and the 17th Century'. See also Anthony Raspa, *The Emotive Image: Jesuit Poetics in the English Renaissance* (Fort Worth: Texas Christian University Press, 1983); A. D. Cousins, *Catholic Religious Poets From Southwell to Crashaw* (London: Sheed & Ward, 1991)

10 Anne Lake Prescott, *French Poets and the English Renaissance: Studies in Fame and Transformation* (New Haven: Yale University Press, 1978) distinguishes between acknowledged and unacknowledged influences, and remarks: 'A stalwart like Jonson might scoff at du Bartas but not to praise a widely admired figure would have struck some of the writers I quote as violating... decorum' (p. xii).

11 E.g. p. 54, st. 26:
> See drouzie Peter, see whear Judas wakes,
> Whear Judas kisses him whom Peter flies:
> O kisse more deadly then the sting of snakes!
> False love more hurtfull then true injuries!
> Aye me! how deerly God his Servant buies?
> For God his man, at his owne blood doth hold,
> And Man his God, for thirtie pence hath sold.
> So tinne for silver goes, and dung-hill drosse for gold.

In *The Spenserian Poets* (London: Edward Arnold, 1969), pp. 194–5, Joan Grundy makes especial reference to Book III in discussing Fletcher's debt to Southwell and 'Counter-Reformation Poetics'; and Healy, *Richard Crashaw*, pp. 153–4, discusses Fletcher's influence on Crashaw.

12 Quoted from Alan Rudrum (ed.), *Henry Vaughan: The Complete Poems* (Harmondsworth: Penguin, rev. edn. 1983), p. 142.

13 Martz, *Poetry of Meditation*, p. 185, quotes the passage as an example of Southwell's diffused influence. See below for Southwell's influence on Herbert.

14 Quoted from the edition of *Hypercritica* in J. E. Spingarn (ed.), *Critical Essays of the 17th Century. Vol.I, 1605–1650* (Oxford: Clarendon, 1908), p. 110. For Bolton, see *DNB*.

15 'Conversations with William Drummond': quoted from George Parfitt (ed.), *Ben Jonson, the Complete Poems* (Harmondsworth: Penguin, 1975), 465.

16 To Anthony Bacon, 5 May [1601?]: printed in James Spedding (ed.), *The Letters and the Life of Sir Francis Bacon*, 7 vols (London: Longmans *et al.*, 1861–74), II (1862), p. 368. It is not clear whether Bacon knew the piece was Southwell's.

17 F.W., 'The Joyes of Heaven Delivered in Sonnetts … ', Bod. MS.Rawl.c.639, f.6b–7a.

18 See Brown, 'Robert Southwell', in McCoog (ed.), *Reckoned Expense*, pp. 193–213. I am grateful to Professor Brown for setting me right about many points to do with Southwell. See also Arthur F. Marotti, 'Southwell's Remains: Catholicism and Anti-Catholicism in Early Modern England', in Cedric C. Brown and Arthur F. Marotti (eds.), *Text and Cultural Change in Early Modern England* (Basingstoke: Macmillan, 1997).

19 See *STC* 22955–22955.5, 22955.7–22968. The Catholic editions are also described in ARCR II, nos. 718–20. For the contents of each edition, see Macdonald; Macdonald and Brown (eds.), textual introduction; and the bibliography in Janelle, *Robert Southwell*. In McCoog (ed.), *Reckoned Expense*, p. 200, Brown suggests that Wolfe may not have had a complete MS of the lyrics, or John Busby would not have published *Mœoniæ*; but it is also possible that the lyrics in *Mœoniæ* were deliberately left out of the first edition, or that it is a combination of progressive revelation and progressive tracking-down. Censorship may have been a factor: Martz, *Poetry of Meditation*, pp. 104–5, attributes the 'greater boldness of *Mœoniæ*

Notes to pages 62–3 247

to the success of the preceding publication'; a poetic sequence on the life of Mary was obviously Catholic in inspiration, and the poems on Christ's nativity and childhood from the sequence, the least objectionable to a Protestant, had appeared earlier in *Saint Peters Complaint*. Even so, *Mœoniæ* did not print the poems on Mary's death and assumption. See also note 25.

20 See Macdonald, pp. 4–5; Mario Praz, 'Robert Southwell's *Saint Peters Complaint* and its Italian Source', *MLR*, 19 (1924), 273–90.
21 Grundy, *Spenserian Poets*, p. 194.
22 Though he printed anti-Catholic material for Lord Burghley (see Denis B. Woodfield, *Surreptitious Printing in England, 1550–1640* (New York: Bibliographical Society of America, 1973), p. 25), John Wolfe also seems to have had a number of Catholic contacts. He had printed the only mainstream edition of any of Southwell's works to appear before 1595, the meditation *Mary Magdalen's Funeral Tears* (1st edn. 1591), and Brown ('Paperchase') has suggested that he may have been responsible for importing the paper used by clandestine Catholic printers and copyists; in *Elizabethan Impressions: John Wolfe and his Press* (New York: AMS, 1988), Clifford Chalmers Huffman argues that Wolfe was interested in the views on religious toleration held among the Italian emigré communities in London (pp. 19–27). See also Martz, *Poetry of Meditation*, pp. 12–13 and 104–5, for comments on the publication of Southwell's works.
23 See Macdonald and Brown (eds.), p. lv. In his earlier bibliography, Macdonald (pp. 73–5) conjectured that Wolfe was racing with Cawood and had a broken MS (hence some poems not appearing, despite their uncontroversial nature), and detected marks of hurried printing in the first Wolfe edition (pp. 70, 75). According to his account, Cawood's edition was set up from Wolfe's first edition – since Cawood had the right to the book, he could take Wolfe's copy and alter it – while the second Wolfe edition was probably printed after Cawood's first. However, both *STC* and Brown, 'Robert Southwell', put Cawood's first edition after Wolfe's second.
24 I discuss these tactics in Shell, 'Catholic Texts'.
25 For censorship of the obviously Catholic material, see Macdonald, p. 85; Macdonald and Brown (eds.), pp. xciv, 130–2, 143–4. The first edition printed in Scotland altered the text to suppress references to the Virgin Mary as intercessor, and other points of Catholic doctrine (Macdonald and Brown (eds.), p. lxvii). The contents of *Mœoniæ* are listed in Macdonald, no. 46, and accounts of the publishing history of individual poems are given in Macdonald and Brown (eds.).
26 Edward Arber (ed.), *A Transcript of the Registers of the Company of Stationers of London; 1554–1640*, 4 vols (London: privately printed, 1675–7), II, p. 131. Cawood had – in an early connection with Wolfe – published Southwell's *Mary Magdalen's Funeral Tears*, and may have had Catholic sympathies: see Brown in McCoog (ed.), *Reckoned Expense*, p. 200. In

1581 a member of the Cawood family, described as a bookbinder, was suspected of printing, binding and selling popish books: BL, MS Lansdowne 33, ff.148–9. Wolfe was beadle of the Stationers' Company from 1587.
27 Though entry was technically required before publication, it was not unusual for publishers to disregard the rule. See Macdonald and Brown (eds.), p. lxii.
28 CSPD, 1591–4, p. 467 (20 March 1594). Gabriel Cawood makes an appearance in the previous entry, where William Wiseman reveals in his examination that he bought a book entitled *Hieronymi Prelati de Societate Jesu* 'at Cawood's shop in Paul's Churchyard'. See *STC*, vol. 3, p. 38.
29 Southwell's full name first appears on the title-page of the St Omer edition of 1620 (Macdonald and Brown, p. lxxvii). The first title-page of a mainstream edition to incorporate Southwell's initials is *STC* 22965, published in 1620.
30 However, portions of the New Testament were occasionally versified: e.g. Christopher Tye's translation of Acts ca. 1553 (*STC* 2983.8 sqq).
31 This is one of the central arguments in Murray Roston, *Biblical Drama in England: From the Middle Ages Till the Present Day* (London: Faber & Faber, 1968).
32 Debora K. Shuger, *The Renaissance Bible* (Berkeley: University of California Press, 1994), ch. 3; J. A. W. Bennett, *Poetry of the Passion* (Oxford: Clarendon, 1982), chs. 6, 7 (whose study stretches over twelve centuries, rendering the de-emphasis particularly striking). However, Lily B. Campbell's contention that the wider availability of the Bible had a liberating effect on English poetry is obviously true in the long term: see her *Divine Poetry and Drama in Sixteenth-Century England* (1959, repr. New York: Gordian, 1972).
33 Campbell, *Divine Poetry*, chs. 3, 7–8. Roman R. Dubinski, *English Religious Poetry Printed 1477–1640: A Chronological Bibliography With Indexes* (Ontario: North Waterloo Academic Press, 1996) was seen too late to incorporate fully into this chapter; however, a preliminary study of his listings between the English Reformation and 1595 has tended to bear out the conclusions I have reached.
34 The Catholic William Forrest attempted some in a manuscript presented to the Duke of Somerset in the 1530s, and in a prefatory verse, praises Thomas Sternhold for versifying psalms to supplant 'songes and balades of veneryous kynde' (*The History of Grisild the Second*, ed. Macray (Roxburghe Club, 1875), p. 176). See also Rivkah Zim, *English Metrical Psalms: Poetry as Praise and Prayer* (Cambridge University Press, 1987); Campbell, *Divine Poetry*, chs. 5–6.
35 Hyder Rollins discusses Heywood's contribution in his edition of the work (Cambridge, Mass.: Harvard University Press, 1927), pp. li-lii. See also Martz, *Poetry of Meditation*, pp. 181–3 (though the greater scholarly

visibility that popular literature has attained since the publication of this study dilutes the claims for Southwell's novelty in ch. 5).

36 Holland is careful to emphasize his evangelical intention, conciliating readers who may dislike the story being in metre (f.A5b). Verses in commendation of the author show how Southwell's polarisation of love-poetry with religious verse was not the only way in which pagan or secular writing could be contrasted with Christian at this date: 'If Maro who did treate of Mars, / And Lucan civill warres, / If Naso for his wanton verse, / And change of men to stars, / Possest great praise and endlesse fame, / What then deserveth he, / That treats of him who brought us blisse, / And bond did make us free?' (f.A8b).

37 Tessa Watt, *Cheap Print and Popular Piety, 1550–1640* (Cambridge University Press, 1991), parts I, III.

38 See the introduction to the modern edition by G. D. Willcock and A. Walker (Cambridge University Press, 1936, repr. 1970).

39 Quoted from Katherine Duncan-Jones (ed.), *Sir Philip Sidney* (Oxford University Press, 1994), pp. 104–5. See also Campbell, *Divine Poetry*, pp. 47–9, 54, 85–7; Andrew D. Weiner, *Sir Philip Sidney and the Poetics of Protestantism* (Minneapolis: University of Minnesota Press, 1978), pp. 34–5. Campbell's discussion remains the best general account of how the Psalms and other biblical poetry became a means of displacing love poetry and pagan literature.

40 See Prescott, *French Poets*, ch. 5; Susan Snyder (ed.), *The Divine Weeks and Works of Guillaume de Saluste Sieur du Bartas, Translated by Josuah Sylvester*, 2 vols (Oxford: Clarendon Press, 1979). Snyder's account of du Bartas's influence is worth quoting: 'In England, the movement to create poetry out of the Bible had heretofore been rather tentative; some feared to contaminate sacred truth with poetic fiction, and all felt the lack of an established Protestant model. In the Divine Weeks the movement found its type and its sanction' (I, p. 82).

41 In *The Essayes of a Prentise* (1584). *His Majesties Poeticall Exercises* (1591) include translations of *Divine Weeks and Works* (II i 1, opening, and II i 3); and other translations remained in MS during James's life. See Snyder (ed.), *Divine Weeks and Works*, I, p. 70, and *The Poems of James VI of Scotland* (Edinburgh: Scottish Text Society, XX, 3rd ser., 1955), pp. 15–37, 106–11, 113–95. For a general account of du Bartas's influence, see Campbell, *Divine Poetry*, pp. 1–2 and chs. IX–X (not referring to Southwell).

42 Sylvester had previously published (in 1590) a translation of du Bartas's poem on Henri de Navarre's victory at Ivry, *Cantique de la Victoire* (1590), and was eventually to become du Bartas's most famous translator. His next du Bartas translation (*STC* 21661) was not published till 1598, though obviously undertaken much earlier: he had, in fact, promised the *Second Week* in *The Triumph of Faith* (Snyder (ed.), *Divine Weeks and Works*, I, pp. 12–13). Sylvester supported the work of anti-Catholic

polemicists like John Vicars and interpolated anti-Catholic material into his translations (*ibid.*, 1, pp. 30, 51–2).

43 See Katherine Duncan-Jones, *Sir Philip Sidney, Courtier Poet* (London: Hamish Hamilton, 1991), pp. 251–2; Snyder (ed.), *Divine Weeks and Works*, 1, p. 70. Snyder also mentions Churchyard's lost translation of 1 v, conclusion.

44 See Ernest A. Strathmann, 'The 1595 translation of Du Bartas's *First Day*', *HLQ*, 8 (1944/5), pp. 185–91; Snyder (ed.), *Divine Weeks and Works*, 1, p. 39 (and p. 71 for attributions).

45 The latter was not entered at Stationers' Hall.

46 One can guess that just as Southwell was read by Protestants, du Bartas would have been read by Catholics; and in a later generation, Thomas Lodge translated a commentary on du Bartas's work (published 1621).

47 First entered at Stationers' Hall in November 1594: for the publication history, see Woudhuysen, *Sir Philip Sidney*, pp. 232–5.

48 In *Protestant Poetics*, for instance, Barbara Lewalski describes English religious poets as 'rallying to the standard' of Du Bartas and Urania (p. 8). Southwell, together with such Southwellian pieces as *Christs Bloodie Sweat*, is relegated to a footnote.

49 The two exceptions are quoted below.

50 See Woudhuysen, *Sir Philip Sidney*, ch. 9, and Katherine Duncan-Jones, 'Sir Philip Sidney's Debt to Edmund Campion', in McCoog (ed.), *Reckoned Expense*, for Sidney's Catholic contacts and the circulation of his works in Catholic circles.

51 Cf. 'To the Reader', l. 15: 'With David verse to vertue I apply.' This tends to modify John Kerrigan's conclusion in *Motives*, p. 25, that David was generally a speaker of Protestant complaints.

52 See Anne Lake Prescott, 'King David as a "Right Poet": Sidney and the Psalmist', *ELR*, 19 (1989), pp. 131–51.

53 Pollard Brown, 'Robert Southwell', p. 199.

54 The term is Harold Bloom's, e.g. in *The Anxiety of Influence* (1st edn. New York: Oxford University Press, 1973); Bloom, however, does not list theological dissent among the reasons for poets to dissociate themselves from their predecessors.

55 E.g. Anthea Hume, *Edmund Spenser, Protestant Poet* (Cambridge University Press, 1981); Richard Helgerson, *Self-Crowned Laureates* (Berkeley: University of California Press, 1983); John N. King, *Spenser's Poetry and the Reformation Tradition* (Princeton University Press, 1990); Richard Rambuss, *Spenser's Secret Career* (Cambridge University Press, 1993); A. C. Hamilton (general ed.) *The Spenser Encyclopaedia* (University of Toronto Press, 1990), under Reformation, Religious controversies.

56 This passage from *The Shepherd's Calendar* is discussed in Patrick Cheney, *Spenser's Famous Flight* (University of Toronto Press, 1993), pp. 27–38. *The Tears of the Muses* is quoted from the edition of *Complaints* in William A. Oram *et al.* (eds.), *The Yale Edition of the Shorter Poems of Edmund Spenser* (New

Haven: Yale University Press, 1989). *The Tears of the Muses* was composed 1580–90 (the Editors speculate that the date is later rather than earlier), and *Complaints* was published in 1591. *Ruines of Rome* (also published in *Complaints*) refers to du Bartas's 'heavenly Muse' (Yale edn., l. 460).
57 It seems to have been largely written in April/May 1594 and entered in the Stationers' Company register on 19 November of the same year. See Yale edn., preface to *Amoretti*.
58 Poetic neoplatonism is discussed in Edgar Wind, *Pagan Mysteries of the Renaissance* (London: Faber & Faber, 1958), pp. 52–3; and T. Anthony Perry, *Erotic Spirituality* (University of Alabama Press, 1980). However, the Capuchin-inspired intellectual fashions of Henrietta Maria's court were later to link neoplatonic ideals with Catholic: Erica Veevers, *Images of Love and Religion: Queen Henrietta Maria and Court Entertainments* (Cambridge University Press, 1989), pp. 88–9.
59 Food for swine (*OED*).
60 Early 1596 also saw the first united appearance of Books 1–6 of *The Faerie Queene*; and the Mutabilitie cantos seem to have been written in 1595 (though not published until 1609). *Colin Clouts Come Home Againe* (1595) has a dedication dated 27 December 1591.
61 Cheney, *Spenser's Famous Flight*, ch. 5.
62 Campbell, *Divine Poetry*, ch. 10, sees it as part of the Du Bartas fashion. For discussion of the relationship of the hymns to each other, see references in *Edmund Spenser: Selected Shorter Poems*, ed. Douglas Brooks-Davies (London: Longman, 1995), pp. 320–1. Robert Ellrodt has discussed Burghley's criticism of *Colin Clout*, traditionally supposed to have stimulated the proem to Book IV of *The Faerie Queene* (also written at around this time and published in 1596) and assessed the internal evidence for the first two hymns being written or rewritten after the publication of the *Amoretti*: *Neoplatonism in the Poetry of Spenser* (Geneva: Droz, 1960), ch. 1.
63 Ellrodt, *Neoplatonism*, p. 14, points to similar conventional retractations.
64 Discussed in Martz, *Poetry of Meditation*, pp. 189–92.
65 For sacred parody and antigenres, see Alastair Fowler, *Kinds of Literature* (Oxford: Clarendon, 1982), pp. 174–6.
66 Cf. Janelle, *Robert Southwell*, ch. 6: 'From concettism to directness.'
67 See above, note 54, for the extensive recent critical interest in this topic.
68 Recent discussion is summarised in Cheney, *Spenser's Famous Flight*, p. 24 (see also pp. xi, 4–6, 45).
69 This conclusion is based on a search of the Chadwyck-Healey English Poetry Database, 'Tudor Poetry to 1603'. Fr Herbert Thurston (in 'Catholic Writers and Elizabethan Readers. II. Father Southwell the Euphuist', and '... III. Father Southwell the Popular Poet', *The Month*, 83 (Jan.-Apr. 1895), pp. 231–45 and 383–99) was the first to notice this reference (p. 392). One should emphasize that Spenser himself borrowed the epithet from Skelton.

70 See below, ch. 6.
71 Quoted from *The Complete Works of Thomas Lodge*, 4 (facsimile) vols (New York: Russell & Russell, 1963), III, 'Prosopopoeia', p. 10. For a more recent biography of Lodge than the *DNB*'s, see the biographical entry in Hamilton (ed.), *Spenser Encyclopaedia*.
72 Quoted from F. E. Hutchinson (ed.), *The Works of George Herbert* (Oxford: Clarendon Press, 1959 edn.), p. 206 (Southwell allusion noticed on p. 549). The poems were written around 1609 and sent to Herbert's mother. Hutchinson also prints an extract from the accompanying letter preserved in Walton's *Lives*: 'But I fear the heat of my late Ague hath dryed up those springs, by which Scholars say, the Muses use to take up their habitations. However, I need not their help, to reprove the vanity of those many Love-poems, that are daily writ and consecrated to Venus; nor to bewail that so few are writ, that look towards God and Heaven. For my own part, my meaning (dear Mother) is in these Sonnets, to declare my resolution to be, that my poor Abilities in Poetry, shall be all, and ever consecrated to Gods glory' (p. 363). Martz, *Poetry of Meditation*, pp. 185 and 264–5, sees the style of the sonnets as imitative of Donne and the sentiments of Southwell; Katherine Duncan-Jones's edition of Shakespeare's Sonnets in the Arden Shakespeare series (Thomson, 1998) suggests that Herbert's outrage was partly stimulated by their recent publication in 1609 (pp. 70–1). Moreover, the influence upon Herbert, Donne and the religious poets of the later 1590s of Henry Lok's holy sonnets, published in *Sundry Christian Passions* (1593) could bear further investigation. Barnabe Barnes's *A Divine Centurie of Spirituall Sonnets*, entered at Stationers' Hall on 26 August 1595 and with a dedication dated 30 August of that year, is both capitalising upon the trends of that year (alluding only to du Bartas in the prefatory material) and closely imitating Lok. The only critic I have found who discusses Lok and Barnes is P. M. Oliver, *Donne's Religious Writing: A Discourse of Feigned Devotion* (London: Longmans, 1997).
73 This bifurcated publication history is observable with other texts; Crashaw's Catholic collection *Carmen Deo Nostro* (1652) duplicates his mainstream *Steps to the Temple* (1st ed. 1646) in more respects than the two differ.
74 *The Teares of the Beloved* is initialled 'J.M.', as Markham often styled himself. *Marie Magdalens Lamentations*, though anonymous, is held to be Part II of the whole poem: see F. N. L. Poynter, *A Bibliography of Gervase Markham, 1568?-1637* (Oxford Bibliographical Society, 1962), nos. 4–5. The identification is strengthened by the Epistle to the Reader in Markham's *The Poem of Poems* ([1596]: Poynter 2), where he airs the Southwellian opposition of profane poetry to sacred. Thurston, 'Catholic Writers', pp. 394–6, also examines Markham's debt to Southwell's *Mary Magdalen's Funeral Tears*, 'only premising that Markham's poem contains no indication of indebtedness of any sort'.

Notes to pages 79–81   253

75 Part two was reprinted: *A Solemne Passion of the Soules Love* (1598). Jean Robertson consolidates the attribution in *Poems by Nicholas Breton (Not Hitherto Reprinted)* (Liverpool University Press, 1952), pp. lxi-lxvi. *Marie Magdalens Love* was entered on 24 July 1595 and *A Solemne Passion* on 20 September 1595 (the latter only ascribed to Breton), but the two were printed together. The printer, John Danter, was prepared to undertake Catholic printing; his press was seized in 1596 for printing the *Jesus Psalter*. Robertson points out that Grosart considered the poem was not by Breton because of its Southwellian influence (p. lxii). See also Suzanne Trill, 'Engendering Penitence: Nicholas Breton and the "Countesse of Penbrooke"', in Kate Chedgzoy, Melanie Hansen and Suzanne Trill (eds.), *Voicing Women* (Keele University Press, 1996). For the interpenetration of sacred complaint with secular, see Kerrigan (ed.), *Motives*, pp. 30–2.
76 Beinecke, Osborn MS b.89 (attributed to John Speed senior).
77 See Thomas George, 'Samuel Rowlands's "The Betrayal of Christ" and Guevara's "The Mount of Calvarie": An Example of Elizabethan Plagiarism', *N & Q*, 212 (1967), pp. 467–74.
78 Cf. the verse interludes in a later publication, *Mary Magdalen's Pilgrimage to Paradise* (1617). Thurston identifies many of these ('Catholic Writers', pp. 391–2).
79 Noticed by Thurston, 'Catholic Writers', p. 393; though Campbell, *Divine Poetry*, p. 91, without mentioning Southwell, quotes it to prove the wide influence of the du Bartas-Sidney-Spenser line of descent.
80 In 1632 it was possible to complain that the title of a book had been stolen by another bookseller (see notes to *STC* 5569). *Saint Peters Ten Teares* was reissued as *St Peters Tears* (1602).
81 Shuger, *Renaissance Bible*, p. 90.
82 The spiritual writers in question were both English and foreign: alongside Capuchin writers like Zacharie of Lisieux, author of *La Philosophie Chrestienne* (1639), can be found the Englishman William Fitch (Benet of Canfield), with *The Rule of Perfection* (1609). For the troubled bibliographical history of English editions of *The Rule of Perfection*, see notes to *ARCR*, II, no. 275; Fitch was imprisoned in England for three years from 1589 (*DNB*). See Patrick Grant, *Images and Ideas in the Literature of the English Renaissance* (London: Macmillan, 1979), ch. 4; Veevers, *Images*, pp. 92–3; Father Cyprien of Gamache, 'Memoirs of the Mission in England of the Capuchin Friars', translated in Robert Folkestone Williams (ed.), *The Court and Times of Charles I*, 2 vols (London: Henry Colburn, 1848), vol. II.
83 Martz, *Poetry of Meditation*.
84 Cf. remarks in Kerrigan (ed.), *Motives*, pp. 30–1. However, *Maries Exercise* (1597), a reformed equivalent of *Our Lady's Psalter*, incorporated prayers centred on a weeper's situation.
85 Janelle, *Robert Southwell*, ch. 8, discussing *inter alia* the Southwell MS at Stonyhurst which translates the beginnings of *Le Lagrime*.

86 Shuger, *Renaissance Bible*, ch. 5; Susan Haskins, *Mary Magdalen: Myth and Metaphor* (London: HarperCollins, 1993), *passim*.
87 Cf. Ellis, *Lamentation*, f.G3a. This is sometimes called the 'Venus and Adonis' stanza: see Paul Fussell, *Poetic Metre and Poetic Form* (rev. edn. New York: Random House, 1966), p. 152.
88
    Launche foorth my Soul into a maine of teares,
    Full fraught with grief the traffick of thy mind:
    Torne sailes will serve, thoughtes rent with guilty feares:
    Give care, the sterne: use sighes in lieu of wind:
    Remorse, the Pilot: thy misdeede, the Carde:
    Torment, thy Haven: Shipwracke, thy best reward. (*SPC*, ll. 1–6)
89 L. E. Stock *et al.*, (eds.), *The Nondramatic Works of John Ford* (New York: Medieval & Renaissance Texts & Studies 85, 1991). They are, however, incorrect in assuming that the author would not have seen Southwell's 'Christs bloody sweat' because it only existed in MS at the time (p. 137); lines 1–12 were printed in *Mœoniæ*, and it is entirely possible that the author might also have had access to a manuscript version of the whole poem.
90 The allusions are to three Shakespearian works: *The Rape of Lucrece* (1594), *Troilus and Cressida* (written and performed ca. 1601/2) and *Richard III* (first printed 1597): see C. M. Ingleby *et al.*, *The Shakespeare Allusion-Book*, 2 vols (London: Oxford University Press, 1932), 1, p. 125.
91 *Epitaphs* (1604), f.A4a. One can infer a question-mark at the end of line 4. Corydon = the shepherd in Virgil, *Eclogue* II; Silvanus = pastoral name denoting a dweller in the woods. For other Catholic repudiations of secular verse, see Verstegan, *Odes*, introduction; Walter Coleman, *La Dance Machabre or Deaths Duell* [1632?], ff.A3a–b, 4b; John Abbot, *Jesus Præfigured* (1635), p. 95 (voiced by John Lydgate); Philip Howard (trans.), *An Epistle in the Person of Christ to the Faithfull Soule, Written First by ... Lanspergius* (1595), prefatory material, esp. ff.A2b–4a. The last is particularly significant, given Southwell's close association with Philip Howard.
92 This seems never to have been published clandestinely. It was first entered to Gabriel Cawood in 1591, published the same year under the initials S.W., and ran through six editions before 1609. Prosopopoeia was a frequent point of confusion and controversy between Protestants and Catholics: a letter on the topic from a Welsh Catholic to his Protestant cousin explains how it is permissible to address the material Cross in this manner without idolatry (3 May 1625, Folger MS V.a.243, pp. [2–3]).
93 Cf. f.C4b, quoted in Macdonald, p. 133; but see also Harvey's *Pierces Supererogation* (1593), p. 191: 'Who can deny, but the Resolution, and Mary Magdalens funerall teares, are penned elegantly, and pathetically?' Sullivan, 'Physiology of Penance', suggests that Nashe's *Christ's Tears Over Jerusalem* satirises the genre.

94 See Virginia Stern, *Gabriel Harvey* (Oxford: Clarendon, 1979), pp. 110–12; Huffman, *Elizabethan Impressions*, p. 118.
95 I.e. 'Jewry'.
96 Hall is also punning on 'Bedlam' in l. 16. See Arnold Davenport (ed.), *The Collected Poems of Joseph Hall* (Liverpool University Press, 1949), pp. 19 (poem), 170–1 (notes); and cf. Hall's criticism of the complaint genre, I v (p. 17).
97 Hall also praised Spenser in 'To Camden' (Davenport (ed.), *Collected Poems*, p. 105); wrote a commendatory poem to Josuah Sylvester praising him and du Bartas (p. 144); published a metaphrase of selected psalms in 1607, with a dedicatory epistle giving an apologia (pp. 125–43); and wrote an epistle to Hugh Cholmley on the same topic, praising Sidney's psalms and Sylvester (pp. 270–1).
98 Arnold Davenport (ed.), *The Poems of John Marston* (Liverpool University Press, 1961), pp. 82–3 (poem), 244–5 (notes). Hall seems to have criticised a translator of du Bartas (Thomas Hudson) in the second *Returne from Parnassus* play (see F. L. Huntley, *Bishop Joseph Hall, 1574–1656* (Cambridge: D. S. Brewer, 1979), pp. 37–8) but his attitude towards du Bartas himself was favourable. Davenport's puzzlement can be resolved if one understands Marston's exclamation to be ironically prescriptive, rather than alluding to specific comments.
99 Folger, V a 399: [first part of poem apparently missing], f.1. This second part is itself in two parts.
100 See the autobiography of Davies's pupil Arthur Wilson in Francis Peck, *Desiderata Curiosa*, vols 1–2 (London; for Thomas Evans, 1779 edn.), p. 461; Woudhuysen, *Sir Philip Sidney*, p. 37. Alexander B. Grosart, *The Complete Works of John Davies of Hereford*, 2 vols (Edinburgh: for private circulation, 1878), I, pp. xviii–xix, sees internal evidence of Davies's Catholicism in passages against sectaries in *The Muses Sacrifice*, and comments on Mary and Elizabeth in *Microcosmos*.
101 Janelle, *Robert Southwell*, p. 189.
102 E.g. (Protestant) William Hunnis, *Seven Sobs of a Sorrowfull Soule* (1583); (Catholic) Richard Verstegan, *Odes* (1601).
103 *An Epithrene: Or Voice of Weeping: Bewailing the Want of Weeping* (1631), f.A6b: the Bellarmine reference is probably to *Gemitus Columbae*. William Holbrooke's St Paul's Cross sermon *Loves Complaint* (1610), however, emphasizes the efficacy of weeping exemplars (discussed in Kerrigan (ed.), *Motives*, p. 49), and other Protestant tears-sermons include William Whateley, 'Charitable Tears', in *A Cere-Cloth* (1624), dated 1623; Thomas Walkington, *Rabboni: Mary Magdalen's Teares, of Sorrow, Solace* (1620); Thomas Jackson, *Peter's Teares: A Sermon* (1612). Arnold Hunt's thesis, 'The Art of Hearing: English Preachers and their Audiences, 1590–1640' (Cambridge PhD, 1999), includes a discussion of weeping during sermons. Catholic-Protestant debate on the topic was not confined to England, and Hieronymus Osorius anticipates criticism in

An Epistle ... to ... Princesse Elizabeth (trans. Richard Shacklock, 1565): 'What (say they) doest thou put the holynes of our justifycation in weping and wayling, in sobbyng and syghing at the remembraunce of oure synnes? Yea surelye. And that I sholde so doo, I am not led with any lyght autoritie, but with the determination of holy scripture' (f.48b).

104   Henry Foley, S.J. *Records of the English Province of the Society of Jesus ... in the 16th and 17th Centuries*, 7 vols (London: Burns & Oates, 1875–83), I, p. 159.

105   V. E. C. Liber 1394: transcribed in Dana F. Sutton (ed.), *Unpublished Works by William Alabaster (1568–1640)* (Salzburg Studies in English Literature, no. 126, 1997), pp. 99–169 (quotation p. 114). See also Robert V. Caro, S.J., 'William Alabaster: Rhetor, Mediator, Devotional Poet – 1 (II)', *RH*, 19:1 and 19:2 (May & October 1988), pp. 62–79 and 155–70 (tears-poetry discussed on pp. 166–8). Martz, *Poetry of Meditation*, preface to 2nd edn., stresses Alabaster's influence on Donne's Holy Sonnets, composed about a decade later.

106   Ch. 4: quoted also in G. M. Story and Helen Gardner (eds.), *The Sonnets of William Alabaster* (Oxford University Press, 1959), p. xii. Surprisingly, this is all the use the editors make of it.

107   'To issue in a rapid stream; to gush or spurt' (*OED*).

108   I find this more convincing than the explanation offered by Story and Gardner (eds.), *Sonnets of William Alabaster*: 'probably "perspectives", that is pictures or figures constructed so as to appear distorted except from one point of view' (p. 61).

109   See also Sonnet 30, lines 1–4:
>   Before thy Cross, O Christ, I do present
>   My soul and body into love distilled,
>   As dewy clouds with equal moisture filled
>   Receive the tincture of the rainbow bent ...

110   Discussions of this can be found in (e.g.) Patrick Collinson, *From Iconoclasm to Iconophobia: The Cultural Impact of the Second English Reformation* (Reading University Press, 1986); Aston, *England's Iconoclasts*; and Ann Kibbey, *The Interpretation of Material Shapes in Puritanism* (Cambridge University Press, 1986), who discusses the Puritan usage of the classical concept of *figura*.

111   As printed in Story and Gardner (eds.), *Sonnets of William Alabaster*, the order of the sequence comprises Nos. 12–19, reflecting the order (with slight deviations recorded on pp. xlii-xliii) in their main manuscripts.

112   In the introduction to *Christs Bloodie Sweat* (ed. Stock *et al.*), Dennis Danielson discusses sweat as both signifier and signified: typologically to be identified with the river Jordan cleansing Naaman, but also liquid metaphors aiding meditation on Christ's agony, and the sinner's tears of repentance (pp. 146–7, 541–6).

113   All Crashaw quotations, unless otherwise stated, are taken from L. C. Martin's edition (Oxford: Clarendon Press, 1972).

114 Shelford claimed that though faith had primacy in spirituality, it was charity that converted the heart and will to God: see Thomas Healy, *Richard Crashaw: A Biography* (Leiden: E. G. Brill, 1986), pp. 67–71, 107 (and cf. his discussion of tears-literature in Cambridge, pp. 37–8). Low, *Love's Architecture*, pp. 138–41, 144–6, also discusses Crashaw's use of tears-poetry. It may be worth noting that Alabaster was an undergraduate contemporary of Richard's father, William Crashaw.

115 In post-1635 printed versions of the poem, the conclusion was deleted. See Martin (ed.), p. 139; and, more generally, Anthony Milton, *Catholic and Reformed: The Roman and Protestant Churches in English Protestant Thought, 1600–1640* (Cambridge University Press, 1995), p. 92.

116 From 'Votiva Domus Petrensis Pro Domo Dei'. 'You know yourself the wheel which revolves volatile wealth; therefore fix it here in the rock as the foundations of the eternal house of Peter; thus take away her wheel from Fortune.' Latin and translation (the latter slightly altered) from George Walton Williams (ed.), *The Complete Poetry of Richard Crashaw* (New York University Press, 1972), pp. 442–3. Healy, *Richard Crashaw*, describes Cambridge interest in Counter-Reformation aesthetics (p. 65); see also Hilton Kelliher, 'Crashaw at Cambridge', in Roberts (ed.), *New Perspectives*, pp. 180–214.

117 Bod.Ms.Rawl.poet.115, p. 49 (two translations, dated December 1635 and 2 December 1638): the MS's contents make up a liturgical year, and show an attempt to recover English medieval and Henrician traditions, supplemented by recent reprintings and illicit material. Huish lists his sources for non-original translations as: [John Cosin], 'Collection of private devotions, or houres of prayer, 1627' (see *STC* 5815.5–5816.4); 'Primer of Henry VIII, English and Latin, 1536' (see *STC* 15992–15993); 'English and Latin primer of King Henry VIII, 1546' (*STC* 16043.5–16047); 'English Primer of Our Lady, 1613' (no edition recorded with that date: but concerning this and the 1635 edition, see under 'Primer' in *ARCR* II); 'Primer, or office of the Blessed Virgin Mary in Latin and English, 1631' (probably not *STC* 16099–16100, which are in English only); 'Flowers of our Lady Engl. and Lat. ad usum Sarum, 1635' (no edition recorded in *STC* with that date); 'Ex antiquo manu-scripto Anglicano circa tempora Henrici 5'.

118 Bodleian, Walker MS C 7, ff.84, 86, 88, 90, 92 (testimonies); summarised in A. G. Matthews, *Walker Revised* (Oxford: Clarendon, 1948), p. 315. See also Somerset Record Office (Taunton), DD/LW.45; Journal of the House of Commons, 12–14 December 1640 and 2–4 January 1640/1 (petition against Huish); Calendar of the House of Lords, 20 June 1660 (petition of sequestered rectors).

119 For Lewgar, see *DNB*. He was Rector of Laverton, Somerset, and was converted by Chillingworth between 1627 and 1635.

120 Raspa, *Emotive Image*, p. 109. Questier, *Conversion*, p. 204, describes the convert's urge to progress in grace 'by moving about over all sorts of

boundaries'; David Trotter, *The Poetry of Abraham Cowley* (London: Macmillan, 1979), pp. 71–2, discusses the 'liminal moment' in Crashaw.

121 See note 1. In her conclusion, Lewalski calls for an exploration of the work of Southwell, Alabaster, Constable and Crashaw to 'examine more precisely just how Tridentine aesthetics relates to this Protestant poetics' (p. 427). Sullivan, *Dismembered Rhetoric*, discusses the Martz/Lewalski debate in her introduction.

122 Williams (ed.), *Complete Poetry of Richard Crashaw*, p. xv.

123 Sir Edward Sherburne, *The Poems and Translations*, ed. Franz Josef van Beeck (Assen: Van Gorcum, 1961), p. 116, ll. 1–2, 12–15 (notes p. 175). See also his version of Marino's 'Christo Smarrito' (pp. 97–9).

124 Folger V.a.137, 'An exortation to pennance' (pp. 70–83).

125 Eldred Revett, *Poems* (1657), pp. 116–117. Raspa, *Emotive Image*, is the only critic I have found who discusses Revett's work.

126 Greek for 'Red Sea'.

127 Arthur Clifford (ed.), *Tixall Poetry* (Edinburgh: Longman, Hurst, Rees, & Orme, 1813), pp. 3–5.

128 *Ibid.*, p. 40; see Kenneth J. Larsen, 'The Religious Sources of Crashaw's Sacred Poetry', (Cambridge PhD, 1969), pp. 299–300. For Crashaw's period in Rome, see Edward Chaney, *The Grand Tour and the Great Rebellion: Richard Lassels and the 'Voyage of Italy' in the 17th Century* (Geneva: Slatkine, 1985), appendix II; N. W. Bawcutt, 'A 17th-Century Allusion to Crashaw', *N & Q*, 207 (1962), pp. 215–16; P. G. Stanwood, 'Crawshaw [sic] at Rome', *N & Q*, 211 (1966), pp. 256–7; Hilton Kelliher, 'Crashaw at Cambridge and Rome', *N & Q*, 217 (1972), pp. 18–19, and 'Cowley and "Orinda". Autograph Fair Copies', *British Library Journal*, 2:2 (1976), pp. 102–8 (giving a text of Cowley's elegy 'On the death of Mr. Crashaw').

129 Frank J. Warnke, 'Metaphysical Poetry and the European Context', in *Metaphysical Poetry*, Stratford-upon-Avon Studies, 11 (1970), p. 265. For the comments in this section, cf. Lorraine M. Roberts and John R. Roberts, 'Crashavian Criticism: A Brief Interpretative History', in Roberts (ed.), *New Perspectives*.

130 E.g. Roberts 934, 1,041, 1,079, 1,142, 1,143, 1,150, 1,151. However, an article by Graham Hamill ('Stepping to the Temple', *South Atlantic Quarterly*, 88:4 (1989), pp. 933–59) suggests that a Lacanian approach could prove more fruitful.

131 Though the critical language used for baroque poetics ensures that this is sometimes unintentionally done: the *Norton Anthology* relates how Marino and the Jesuit epigrammatists pushed Crashaw towards the exploitation of 'far-fetched, almost perverse parallels in which familiar physical objects not only stood for but were sometimes distorted by extravagant spiritual pressures' (p. 1,389).

132 George Williamson, *A Reader's Guide to the Metaphysical Poets* (London: Thames & Hudson, 1968), pp. 119–20.

133 Joan Bennett, *Four Metaphysical Poets: Donne, Herbert, Vaughan, Crashaw* (Cambridge University Press, 1934), pp. 27, 56.
134 Williams (ed.), *Complete Poetry of Richard Crashaw*, p. xxii.
135 Thurston, 'Catholic Writers' (cited in full at note 69).

3 CATHOLIC LOYALISM: I. ELIZABETHAN WRITERS

1 David Mathew, *Sir Tobie Mathew* (London: Max Parrish, 1950), pp. 44–9; A. H. Mathew (ed.), *A True Historical Relation of the Conversion of Sir Tobie Mathew* (London: Burns & Oates, 1904), pp. viii-x, 75–83.
2 The poet may be alluding to a passage in one of Constable's own sonnets to the Queen, written ca. 1585–8:
> Thine eye hath made a thousand eyes to weepe
> And every eye [a] thousand seas hath made
> And each sea shall thyne Ile in saftie keepe.   (ll. 12–14).

All quotations and biographical details come from *The Poems of Henry Constable*, ed. Joan Grundy (Liverpool University Press, 1960), pp. 33–5 (poem originally from NAL, MS Dyce 44 (D.25.F.39), f.44, also known as the Todd MS) and pp. 84–5, 98–100, 109–10, 112, 137; see also p. 231.
3 See comments in introduction; Judith Doolin Spikes, 'The Jacobean History Play and the Myth of the Elect Nation', *Renaissance Drama*, n.s., 8 (1977), pp. 117–48; Gasper, *The Dragon and the Dove*.
4 Milward, *Religious Controversies*, I & II, and Thomas Clancy, *Papist Pamphleteers: the Allen-Persons Party and the Political Thought of the Counter-Reformation in England, 1572–1715* (Chicago: Loyola University Press, 1964), are two excellent guides to the Elizabethan and Jacobean controversies over allegiance, which this chapter has exploited but does not aim to supplant.
5 Quentin Skinner, *The Foundations of Modern Political Thought*, 2 vols (Cambridge University Press, 1978), II, pp. 345 ff. For the interdependence of Catholic and radical Calvinist resistance theory, see Skinner's 'The Origins of the Calvinist Theory of Revolution', in Barbara C. Malament (ed.), *After the Reformation* (Manchester University Press, 1980), pp. 309–30. See also J. H. M. Salmon, 'Catholic Resistance Theory, Ultramontanism and the Royalist Response, 1580–1620', ch. 8 in J. H. Burns and Mark Goldie (eds.), *The Cambridge History of Political Thought, 1450–1700* (Cambridge University Press, 1991).
6 Leo Hicks, 'Father Robert Persons, S.J., and *The Book of Succession*', *RH*, 4:3 (1957–8), pp. 104–37, describes its early misrepresentation in Catholic circles. See also Peter Holmes, 'The Authorship and Early Reception of *A Conference About the Next Succession to the Crown of England*', *HJ*, 23:2 (1980), pp. 415–29. Where Hicks asserts that Persons always considered it a necessary and opportune book, but never acknowledged sole authorship, Holmes believes that Persons half-disowned the text some years after writing. Though the date given on the title-page is 1594, the

volume was not actually published until 1595. J. H. M. Salmon, in *Renaissance and Revolt: Essays in the Intellectual and Social History of Early Modern France* (Cambridge University Press, 1987), pp. 165–7, sees the English Catholic opposition as papalist during the 1560s and 1570s, shifting to the stress on visible loyalism characteristic of Allen and Persons.

7 Munday, *The English Roman Life*, ed. Philip Ayres (Oxford: Clarendon, 1980), pp. 24–8, 44.

8 Thomas Clancy, 'English Catholics and the Papal Deposing Power, 1570–1640', 2 parts, *RH*, 6:3 (1961–2), pp. 114–40, and 6:5 (1961–2), pp. 205–27, enlarged upon in *Papist Pamphleteers*. See also Peter Holmes, *Resistance and Compromise: The Political Thought of the Elizabethan Catholics* (Cambridge University Press, 1982); Arnold Pritchard, *Catholic Loyalism in Elizabethan England* (London: Scolar, 1979). An account for the whole period is given in Edward Norman, *Roman Catholicism in England from the Elizabethan Settlement to the Second Vatican Council* (pbk, Oxford University Press, 1986), chs. 2–3.

9 For Campion's trial, see *Cobbett's Complete Collection of State Trials* (London: R. Bagshaw *et al.*, 1809–26, vol. I (1809), cols. 1,050–84.

10 Westminster Diocesan Archives, MSS Archiv. Westmon., vol. III, item 89. The account is said to be written by a Protestant.

11 Alastair Macintyre, *After Virtue: A Study in Moral Theory* (London: Duckworth, 1981), p. 8.

12 'Loyalty, Religion and State Power in Early Modern England: English Romanism and the Jacobean Oath of Allegiance', *HJ*, 40:2 (1997), pp. 311–29. For a Benedictine who defended the Oath and so was placed under government protection, see W. K. L. Webb, S.J., 'Thomas Preston OSB, Alias Roger Widdrington (1567–1640)', *Biographical Studies*, 2 (1954), pp. 216–68.

13 E.g. in Suzanne Gossett (ed.), *Hierarchomachia: Or, the Anti-Bishop* (London: Bucknell University Press, 1982).

14 Transcribed in Dorothy Latz, *Glow-Worm Light: Writings of 17th-Century English Recusant Women From Original Manuscripts* (Salzburg: Institut für Anglistik und Amerikanistick, 1989), pp. 71–7 (prayer before martyrdom on reverse of paper). There seems no especial reason to ascribe it, as there, to a woman author.

15 Northampton's co-author was Robert Cotton. See Linda Levy Peck, 'The Mentality of a Jacobean Grandee', in *The Mental World of the Jacobean Court*, ed. L. L. Peck (Cambridge University Press, 1991); and her biography *Northampton: Patronage and Policy at the Court of James I* (London: George Allen & Unwin, 1982), pp. 111–13. The reference is to CSP Venetian 1603–1607, pp. 438–9, 7 December 1606.

16 It should be remembered that texts dedicated – or even sent – to monarchs might never have been seen by them.

17 Pritchard, *Catholic Loyalism*, ch. 10.

18 Michael Lynch (ed.), *Mary Stuart: Queen in Three Kingdoms* (Oxford: Blackwell, 1988), introduction (quotation p. 1). See also P. J. Holmes's essay 'Mary Stewart in England' in the same volume; Patrick Collinson, *The English Captivity of Mary, Queen of Scots* (Sheffield: Sheffield History Pamphlets, 1987); Helen Smailes and Duncan Thomson, *The Queen's Image: A Celebration of Mary, Queen of Scots* (Edinburgh: Scottish National Portrait Gallery, 1987). I am grateful to Helen Hackett for the last reference.
19 BL, Tresham Papers (Add. MS. 39829, ff.119–24) and HMC, Salisbury, ii, p. 74: both discussed in Holmes, 'Mary Stewart', pp. 119–200.
20 Mary Stuart's agent Thomas Morgan was, however, implicated in Parry's plot: see Antonia Fraser, *Mary, Queen of Scots* (London: Weidenfeld & Nicolson, this edn. 1994), pp. 472–3; Holmes, 'Mary Stewart', pp. 204–5. James Emerson Phillips claims that even in propagandist pamphlets printed after Parry's execution, Mary was rarely mentioned and never attacked: *Images of a Queen: Mary Stuart in 16th-Century Literature* (Berkeley: University of California Press, 1964), pp. 76–8. A general account of Mary's own involvement in plots is given in Jenny Wormald, *Mary, Queen of Scots: A Study in Failure* (London: George Philip, 1988), ch. 7.
21 Robert Southwell declared that Parry had never professed himself a Catholic (R. C. Bald (ed.), An Humble Supplication to Her Majestie (Cambridge University Press, 1953), p. 17) and in 'The Strange Case of William Parry', *Studies: an Irish Quarterly Review*, 37 (1948), pp. 343–62, Leo Hicks claims that Parry was a government agent paid to infiltrate Catholic communities overseas, who was then deserted. However, this does not alter the fact that most Englishmen, Catholic and Protestant, believed him to be a Catholic at the time.
22 HMC.Var. Coll.III, 37, 39 (quoted in W. R. Trimble, *The Catholic Laity in Elizabethan England, 1558–1603* (Cambridge, Mass.: Harvard University Press, 1964), p. 133). The reference is to the Cardinal of Como. Parry's confession – possibly doctored – is printed in *A True and Plaine Declaration of the Horrible Treasons, Practised by William Parry* [1585], pp. 11–19.
23 Bod. MS Lyell empt.13.
24 See David Cressy, *Bonfires and Bells: National Memory and the Protestant Calendar in Elizabethan and Stuart England* (London: Weidenfeld & Nicolson, 1989), ch. 4.
25 Though the beginning of the poem is lost, the pope is suggested by lines such as 'his words provoke to workes, his workes are parchments; thei turne swords' (f.2b).
26 Biographical data is given at f.12b in the poem.
27 This was a letter expressing general approval for Parry's intentions, which, though without specific reference to the conspiracy, was taken as referring to it when made public in England.
28 Probably Cardinal William Allen's *A True Sincere and Modest Defence of English Catholiques* [1584], which answers Lord Burghley's *The Execution of*

Justice in England (1583) and was answered, together with Allen's *An Apologie ... of the Institution of the Two English Colleges* (1581) by Thomas Bilson's *The True Difference Betweene Christian Subjection and Unchristian Rebellion* (1585). Allen's and Burghley's books have been edited by Robert M. Kingdom (Ithaca: Folger Shakespeare Library/Cornell University Press, 1965), who discusses the disingenuousness of Allen's rhetoric; Allen was involved in a number of international plots to invade England, though he kept these separate from the English mission. Burghley's book does not mention Mary Stuart; it argues that punitive action taken against Catholics was not because of their religious beliefs *per se*, but occurred when their activities constituted treason against the state in the form of altering the government, removing Elizabeth or tampering with the succession. See Phillips, *Images of a Queen*, p. 76. Nevell's confession only refers to 'Allens booke': see *A True and Plaine Declaration*, pp. 8, 17 (which this passage paraphrases).

29 E.g. Crum W1003 (two examples); three examples in BL in-house first-line index (both pre- and post-1894), one being from the Tresham papers (Add. MS. 39829, f.93). For MS occurrences, see Peter Beal (comp.), *Index of English Literary Manuscripts*, vol. 1, part 2, 1450–1625 (London: Mansell, 1980), HrJ 303–14.

30 Quoted from N. E. McClure (ed.), *The Letters and Epigrams of Sir John Harington* (Philadelphia: University of Pennsylvania Press, 1930). See Jason Scott-Warren, 'Sir John Harington As A Giver of Books', (Cambridge PhD, 1996), pp. 133–4; Phillips, *Images of a Queen*, pp. 209–10.

31 A variant – and less subversive – reading is 'judgement' (Crum).

32 Mary Stuart's executioner struck twice before the head was severed (Phillips, *Images of a Queen*, p. 139).

33 Full accounts of early literature on Mary Stuart are given in Phillips, *Images of a Queen*, and John Scott, *A Bibliography of Works Relating to Mary Queen of Scots, 1544–1700* (Edinburgh Bibliographical Society, 1896). Eighteenth- to twentieth-century material is covered in Samuel A. Tannenbaum and Dorothy R. Tannenbaum in *Marie Stuart Queen of Scots: A Concise Bibliography*, 3 vols (New York: Tannenbaum, 1944–6).

34 Phillips, *Images of a Queen*, pp. 162–70 (Blackwood), pp. 61–68 (Buchanan). Buchanan's view that the people had the right to repudiate a legitimate prince is discussed in Skinner, *Foundations*, II, pp. 339–345.

35 The traditional identification of the poem's speaker with Mary Stuart, necessitating the name 'Marie' in l. 14, has been consolidated by David Rogers's discovery of the sole contemporary printed version in *Epitaphs* (1604): see Alan G. R. Smith (ed.), *The Last Years of Mary Queen of Scots* (London: Roxburghe Club, 1990), pp. 88–94. This version was not set up from any of the surviving MSS. Macdonald & Brown (eds.), *Poems of Robert Southwell*, pp. 47 and 143, list MS variants; see also Guiney's account (*Recusant Poets*, pp. 247–8) of LPL MS 655. Phillips, *Images of a*

Queen, pp. 165–6, 183–4, discusses anagrams deriving 'martyr' from Mary's name.

36 Beinecke, Osborn b.33, pp. 2–3. The author was living in Paris at the time of writing (just after Charles I's marriage to Henrietta Maria), and appears to be addressing both a French and an English audience.

37 See introduction, note 24.

38 Grundy (ed.), *Poems of Henry Constable*, Introduction, p. 16. All quotations are taken from this edition, with biographical details also from George Wickes's article 'Henry Constable, Poet and Courtier (1562–1613)', *Biographical Studies*, 2: 4 (1954), pp. 272–300. The discussion below also draws, in part, from the comments on Constable in Marotti, *Manuscript, Print*, p. 47, and Hackett, *Virgin Mother*, pp. 136–9. See also W. B. Patterson, *King James VI and I and the Reunion of Christendom* (Cambridge University Press, 1997), p. 51. I am writing an article on three previously unpublished sonnets by Constable on Mary Stuart, which came to light too late for inclusion in this study.

39 Cf. Constable's sonnet 'To the Q: upon occasion of a booke he wrote in an answer to certayne objections against her proceeding in the Low countryes' (Grundy (ed.), *Poems of Henry Constable*, pp. 139 and 232, where she speculates that this may have been in response to a libel of Thomas Throgmorton's).

40 Wickes suggests that Constable may not have wanted to be associated with the pamphlet after his conversion. The English translation was issued in 1623 by a mainstream publisher, Nathaniel Butter, and co-opted into anti-Catholic polemic by means of its prefatory material. W.W., the translator, points to Constable's subsequent Catholicism as a controversial advantage to Protestants 'which will give us as much advantage as we can desire from one man, which is to answer them by one of their owne' (ff.¶1b–2a). David Rogers calls the pamphlet 'typical of the state of mind of a near-convert': '"The Catholic Moderator": A French Reply to Bellarmine and Its English Author, Henry Constable', *RH*, 5 (1960), pp. 224–35 (quotation p. 229). This article is supplemented by John Bossy, 'A propos of Henry Constable', *RH*, 6:5 (1962), pp. 228–37.

41 See Healy, *Richard Crashaw*, p. 3; Martz, *Poetry of Meditation*, pp. 101–5 (pointing out that a poem on the Assumption may have been suppressed from Southwell's *Mæoniæ*).

42 Mary Talbot (née Cavendish) became Countess of Shrewsbury on 10 November 1590: Grundy (ed.), *Poems*, pp. 84, 235, and Arthur Collins, *Historical Collections* (1752). The poem survives only in the Todd MS, probably compiled in the early 1590s, and is headed 'To the Countesse of Shrewsburye'; none of this, however, gives any indication of the *original* date of composition. I am grateful to Martin Butler for discussion on the reading of this sonnet.

43 Constable was strongly anti-Jesuit all his life, a position which usually

accompanied anti-Spanish feeling: writing to Essex, he explained 'Though I am passionately affectionated to my Religio[n], yet am I not in the nomber of those w[hi]ch wish th[e] restitution thereof w[i]t[h] the servitude of my country to a forrein Tyranny' (Hatfield House MSS, vol. xxxv, f.50).

44 College of Arms, Talbot MS O.f.94: quoted by Grundy (ed.), *Poems of Henry Constable*, p. 55.

45 *Ibid.*, pp. 55–6.

46 Hackett, *Virgin Mother*, argues that Marian-inspired panegyric is most characteristic of the latter years of Elizabeth's reign, a time when 'Catholic' vocabulary began to be extensively redeployed to love-poetry.

47 Both men were part of the circle round Essex and Anthony Bacon: see Wickes, 'Henry Constable', esp. pp. 279–80. A third Catholic poet who had Essex as patron was William Alabaster, with whom Wright is alleged to have collaborated for a lost tragedy condemning the Church of England. See Theodore A. Stroud, 'Father Thomas Wright: A Test Case for Toleration', *Biographical Studies*, 1:3 (1951), pp. 189–219, esp. p. 215; and Robert V. Caro, S.J., 'William Alabaster: Rhetor, Mediator, Devotional Poet – 1', *RH*, 19:1 (1988), pp. 62–79. A recent description of Jesuit emblematic theory and practice, which may have influenced Wright, can be found in Karel Porteman *et al.*, *Emblematic Exhibitions ('Affixiones') at the Brussels Jesuit College 1630–1685* (Brepols: Royal Library, Brussels, 1996), pp. 10–11, 18, 20, 22–3. I am most grateful to Michael Bath and Alan Young for last-minute help with this section, and several references.

48 Roy Strong, *The Cult of Elizabeth* (London: Thames & Hudson, 1977), pp. 126–7. See also R. C. McCoy, *The Rites of Knighthood: The Literature and Politics of Elizabethan Chivalry* (Berkeley: University of California Press, 1989), esp. pp. 79–86; Alan R. Young, 'The English Tournament Imprese', in Peter M. Daly (ed.), *The English Emblem and the Continental Tradition* (New York: AMS, 1988).

49 Paul Hammer makes the distinction between Bacon's role as Essex's 'special friend' and the membership of Essex's secretariat: 'The Uses of Scholarship: The Secretariat of Robert Devereux, Second Earl of Essex, c.1585–1601', *EHR*, 109:430 (1994), pp. 26–51 (quotation, p. 50). The only extended study of Anthony Bacon remains Daphne du Maurier's romantic *Golden Lads: A Study of Anthony Bacon, Francis and their Friends* (London: Gollancz, 1975).

50 For Wright's biography, see Stroud, 'Father Thomas Wright'; B. Fitzgibbon, S.J., 'Addition to the Biography of Thomas Wright', *Biographical Studies*, 1:4, pp. 261–2; D. M. Rogers, 'A Bibliography of the Published Works of Thomas Wright (1561–1623)', *ibid.*, pp. 262–280.

51 Anthony Standen, a Catholic attached to Essex's household, wrote a verse on the French wars (LPL MS 653, ff.197–8: parallel texts in Spanish and English).

52 Lilian M. Ruff and Arnold Wilson, 'The Madrigal, the Lute Song and Elizabethan Politics', *P & P*, 44 (1969), pp. 3–51. See also Paul Hammer, '"The Bright Shininge Sparke": The Political Career of Robert Devereux, 2nd Earl of Essex, c.1585–1597' (Cambridge PhD, 1991), pp. 140–4. See also Mervyn James, 'At a Crossroads: The Political Culture of the Essex Revolt, 1601', in M. James (ed.), *Society, Politics and Culture: Studies in Early Modern England* (Cambridge University Press, 1986).
53 Hammer, '"Bright Shininge Sparke"', ch. 5; R. C. McCoy, '"A Dangerous Image": The Earl of Essex and Elizabethan Chivalry', *Journal of Medieval and Renaissance Studies*, 13:2 (1983), pp. 313–29.
54 There are multiple (and variant) copies of all three texts in LPL MS 652, in different hands, but all endorsed as being by 'Mr Wright' or 'Mr W' in at least one copy, and dated 1595 or November 1595. The pictures are described, not drawn. Remarkably, they have never been previously discussed.
55 I.e. Spain's.
56 Henri IV had largely overcome opposition from the Catholic League in the mid-1590s. See Mack P. Holt, *The French Wars of Religion, 1562–1629* (Cambridge University Press, 1995), ch. 6, for events between 1593 and 1610. Essex was a supporter of Henri IV, and in late 1595 was under pressure to make the Queen change her mind about her discontinuation of English support for France: see Hammer, '"Bright Shininge Sparke"', pp. 48, 188–94. See also R.B. Wernham, *After The Armada: Elizabethan England and the Struggle for Western Europe, 1588–1595* (Oxford: Clarendon, 1984), and *The Return of the Armadas: The Last Years of the English War Against Spain, 1595–1603* (Oxford: Clarendon, 1994).
57 From LPL MS 652, ff.217a–218a, with another copy of nos. 1–5 at ff.332a–b. Nos 1–5 (not in that order) are differently explicated at ff.327–8a and 329a–b, in Latin epigrams of which the English verses are a translation, with long explanations of the meaning: the explication of the above verse, for instance, begins 'Now we see a præparatione as it wear to a dilu<d>ge, for the warres betwixt us and the Spainyeardes, the dissention of relligion betwixt us at home, the likehood of variannce betwixt us and Fraunce, but as ... the rainbow appearinge signifiethe that there is a peace made betwixt god and man heaven and earthe: so ... the sight of this noble man ... dothe undoubtedly pronosticate unto us a future peace, bothe at home and abrode yf his noble procedinges bee not crossed' (f.329a). At f.328a: 'Illustrissimo comiti de Essexia / Tho. Wr. S.P.D. / Dant alij nummos, numeros pro munere forma[m?] / Ast ego virtutes, accepe (sic) quæso tuas.' There are other panegyrical verses by Wright at ff.309–10a (dated 20 December 1595: copy at ff.335–6). F.331a appears to be notes for displaying a large quantity of *imprese* at once (nos. 2 and 4–6 corresponding to nos. 9, 11, 7 and 8 in the set of verses at ff.217–18a).

58 Descriptions and quotations from the copy at ff.205–6a, headed as to Elizabeth: other copies at f.204a (of nos. 3, 5–6, differently numbered), f.207b (of nos. 1, 4 differently numbered), f.214 a–b (of nos. 1–2, 8, 4, 9, 11), 215 a–b (of nos. 1–2, 8, 4, 9, 11). The last two are referred to as (2) and (3) below.
59 Reading taken from (2).
60 A lioness in (2) and (3).
61 There may, however, have been an opportunity to display others. Strong, *Cult of Elizabeth*, p. 145, suggests that the device of Philautia or Self-Love illustrated by Henry Peacham in *Minerva Britanna* (1612) may have been Essex's eventual emblem for the occasion.
62 Unicorns had a proverbial ability to negotiate traps, while their horns were efficacious against poison.
63 Hammer, ' "Bright Shininge Sparke" ', pp. 189, 192. However, Spanish troops had landed in Cornwall in July 1595, and intelligence reports had news of a restored Armada.
64 (2) and (3) read 'circumspicit'.
65 (2) reads: 'no[n] poterit'.
66 There was no French Dauphin at the time; Louis XIII was born in 1601. But as well as having implications of succession, the dolphin was a standard Renaissance attribute of Water and Fortune.
67   *Est ponti dominus quo non velocior alter*
        Delphinus, terram roscida serta docent.
        Albion imperium est, debentur Gallica regna
        Insula hybernorum, vastus & Oceanus.
'Debentur' could also be translated as 'there is owed to her'.
68 See Hammer, ' "Bright Shininge Sparke" ', pp. 190–3 (pointing out that Essex tried to force Elizabeth's hand by arranging for reports exaggerating the French plight), 205–7, 267.
69 Hermit iconography was not an exclusive Cecil perquisite – it is also associated, for instance, with Sir Henry Lee – but Lord Burghley had acted the part of a hermit when Elizabeth was received at Theobalds in 1591, and again in 1594; his younger son, Robert Cecil, was at this stage the favoured candidate for the Secretaryship, and *de facto* holder of the office, with Essex as his rival. See Alan Young, *Tudor and Jacobean Tournaments* (London: George Philip, 1987), pp. 172–5; Strong, *Cult of Elizabeth*, pp. 140–1; Hammer, ' "Bright Shininge Sparke" ', p. 95 (and ch. 7, Section ii, for comments on Essex's relationship with both Cecils). The soldier is usually taken to suggest Sir Roger Williams. Roy Strong, *Artists of the Tudor Court: The Portrait Miniature Rediscovered, 1510–1620* (London: Victoria & Albert Museum, 1983), pp. 136–7, reproduces a painting of Essex with a diamond *impresa*, which may record his costume at the 1595 tournament; see also Young, 'English Tournament Imprese', p. 72, on the contemporary accounts of the diamond impresa used on this occasion and its attribution to Essex; and Young's *The*

English Tournament Imprese (New York: AMS, 1988), pp. 26–7, 58 (*impresa* no. 95). One of the *impresa* verses which Wright addresses to Essex takes the diamond as its theme.

70 McCoy, '"Dangerous Image"', pp. 314–15, 321–3, argues that Francis Bacon was using the event to heal divisions between Essex and Elizabeth, as well as to commend Essex for high office.

71 Writing to Sir Robert Sidney on 5 November, Rowland Whyte mentions that Essex first saw the book 'on Monday last': HMC, *Report on the Manuscripts of Lord De L'Isle and Dudley Reserved at Penshurst Place*, II (1934), pp. 182–4. 5 November was a Wednesday (assumed Old Style). Most of the Wright papers are dated 'November 1595' or similar, but this could relate to when they were filed, or the occasion itself, as easily as to the date of copying. Hicks, 'Robert Persons', suggests that Burghley or Robert Cecil may have shown Elizabeth the book (pp. 122–3).

72 James Spedding (ed.), *The Letters and the Life of Francis Bacon*, 7 vols (London: Longmans *et al.*, 1861–74), I, pp. 374–92.

73 Spedding (*ibid.*, I, p. 386) believes the speeches were written by Essex, but Hammer, '"Bright Shininge Sparke"', p. 96, suggests that Francis Bacon – perhaps also Sir Edward Reynoldes, and others – may have composed some of them. Young, *Tudor and Jacobean Tournaments*, p. 172, points to the problem of distinguishing drafts from what was really used.

74 Letter to Sir Robert Sidney, transcribed in Arthur Collins, *Letters and Memorials of State* (1746), and quoted in Spedding (ed.), *Letters and the Life of Francis Bacon*, I, pp. 374–5.

75 Young, *Tudor and Jacobean Tournaments*, p. 175.

76 'Wenche' is a substitute for 'Q–e' ('Queene') in f.207a, from which the above transcription is taken (explanatory verses only); other copies at f.210a–b (explanatory verses only), f.212a–b (both devices and verses), f.224a–b (devices only). All copies have eight items; the explanatory verses have marginalia. For a different reworking of the ass emblem, originally from Alciato and copied in Whitney's *Emblemes* (1586), see Peter M. Daly and Barri Hooper, 'John Harvey's Carved Mantel-Piece (ca. 1570): An Early Instance of the Use of Alciato Emblems in England', in Peter M. Daly (ed.), *Andrea Alciato and the Emblem Tradition* (New York: AMS, 1988), pp. 177–204.

77 Quoted from the copy at f.212.

78 This in turn may have alluded to a Cecil entertainment where a postboy with letters from the Emperor of China asks for Secretary Cecil: see Young, *Tudor and Jacobean Tournaments*, p. 175.

79 Stroud, 'Thomas Wright', pp. 203–5. Hammer, '"Bright Shininge Sparke"', suggests that the two sides disavowed 'possible causes of private animosity' (p. 291) but since the Tilt itself was a jibe, it is not impossible that Essex approved the pasquinade.

80 Despite his passionate support of Elizabeth, Copley was imprisoned several times during her reign: *DNB*. Around the time of James I's

accession, he was involved in a plot to secure the throne for Arbella Stuart. See Pritchard, *Catholic Loyalism*, pp. 78–118; Salmon, *Renaissance and Revolt*, pp. 176–88 (discussing the assimilation of Gallican principles by some English Catholics).

81 Jeffrey Kemp, *An Empire Nowhere: England, America, and Literature from 'Utopia' to 'The Tempest'* (Berkeley: University of California Press, 1992), p. 83. His discussion of *A Fig For Fortune* (pp. 85–6, 94–5) suffers from an assumption that Copley, as a Catholic, must be using the term negatively. But in stanzas such as the following, Copley is consoling the Catholic exile without impugning either Elizabeth or England.

> But such her glories are but eare-delightes
> And lip-sweets only to our far awayes,
> For we are no Elizium-bred wightes
> Nor have we any such like merrie dayes;
> Wee have our joyes in another kind
> Ghostly innated in our soule and mind. (p. 59)

82 For the Catholic contribution to English neo-stoicism, see J. H. M. Salmon, 'Seneca and Tacitus in Jacobean England', in Peck (ed.), *Mental World*, esp. pp. 184–6.

83 Copley may have published the book himself (*STC*); no reference to the ban has been found in the Stationers' Company records.

84 Copley goes on: 'as also in regard of (the herrings taile) which what stuff it is the title shews, and yet they highly esteeme and give it countenance for being penned by a lay disciple of theirs'. The reference is to *A Herrings Tayle*, an allegorical poem of 1598 which can be interpreted as satirising the conflict between Jesuits and Appellants by a retelling of the proverb 'The slow snail climbeth the tower at last', in which the Appellant side, cast as the snail, challenges St. Peter's weathercock on the top of a church spire. Though the episode ends with the discomfiture of the Appellant, Copley is wrong in supposing the poem to be pro-Jesuit; the poem's author was of conformist sympathies, which would be in keeping with its traditional attribution to Richard Carew of Anthony. (I plan to write an article which will give a more detailed account of the poem.)

85 Sometimes attributed to Robert Chambers: *ARCR* II, no. 112.

86 Maureen Quilligan, *The Language of Allegory: Defining the Genre* (Ithaca: Cornell University Press, this edn. 1992), pp. 26–33, 41 (commenting on the doctrinal significance of Spenser's onomastic wordplay).

4 CATHOLIC LOYALISM: II. STUART WRITERS

1 E.g. in Joseph Stevenson, S.J. (ed.), *Henry Clifford. The Life of Jane Dormer, Duchess of Feria* (London: Burns & Oates, 1887), p. 94; Clifford himself, however, believed her last hours were anguished and devoid of prayer (pp. 98–100).

2 Clancy, *Papist Pamphleteers*, p. 2.

3 The most recent narration of Catholic loyalism and extremism in early Jacobean England is Antonia Fraser's *The Gunpowder Plot: Terror and Faith in 1605* (London: Weidenfeld & Nicolson, this edn. 1997). See also Francis Edwards, S.J. (ed.), *The Gunpowder Plot. The Narrative of Oswald Tesimond Alias Greenway* (London: Folio Society, 1973), p. 21. For the mood of optimism at James I's accession, see Philip Caraman, S.J., *Henry Garnet, 1555–1606, and the Gunpowder Plot* (London: Longmans, 1964), pp. 305, 315, and *William Weston: the autobiography of an Elizabethan* (London: Longmans, 1955), pp. 222–4.
4 See Gary Wills, *Witches and Jesuits: Shakespeare's 'Macbeth'* (New York: Oxford University Press, 1995). B. N. de Luna, *Jonson's Romish Plot: A Study of 'Catiline' and its Historical Context* (Oxford: Clarendon Press, 1967). Brought before the Consistory Court on charges of recusancy in January 1606, Jonson confessed to 'having heretofore been of some other opinion in religion, which now upon better advisement he is determined to alter' (p. 135).
5 'Quid iuvat occultæ tot semina condere flammæ? / Ah miseri prohibete minas. Sua Numina novit / Fulmen, & in magnum nescit peccare Tonantem' (f.C3a).
6 Questier, 'Loyalty, Religion', and Patterson, *King James VI and I*, ch. 3, are the two most extended studies of the Oath. I know of no hostile poetic reactions to the Oath of Allegiance comparable to those elicited later in the century by the Test Act (first embodied in legislation in 1661, extended to cover all public offices in 1673): e.g. Dryden in Part III of *The Hind and the Panther*, or Jane Barker in her versified conversion-narrative (Magdalen College, Oxford, MS 343, pp. 21–2): but cf. the satirical poem 'The Reformers Oath of Alleageance' in I.B., *Epigrammes* [1627–34], pp. 41–5, followed by a poem to Charles I where the writer swears that Reformers are the true traitors (p. 46).
7 D. M. Rogers, 'John Abbot (1588?-1650)', *Biographical Studies 1534–1829*, 1:1 (1951), pp. 22–33.
8 It was a Catholic belief that the spiritual merits of Mary Stuart's martyrdom would bring about the grace of James's conversion. See Fraser, *Gunpowder Plot*, p. xxix.
9 Gordon Albion, *Charles I and the Court of Rome* (London: Burns, Oates & Washbourne, 1935), ch. 1 (part 2) describes Lope de Vega's song of welcome to Charles (p. 27), and, more generally, the Spaniards' attempts to convert Charles during his stay.
10 Though he does write that the poem was begun 'for your royall sakes' (p. 109). Puzzlingly, the poem is dated from Antwerp on 12 November 1623 (from what Rogers thinks may have been a fictitious address to conceal Abbot's real whereabouts) even though Charles had returned unmarried to England on 5 October. Abbot may not have known this; or have received the news while the poem was in the press; or it might have been published from a manuscript that had been sent to the royal

addressees some months earlier, with Abbot's letter redated and left in as a plea for reconsideration. However, misleading reportage seems most likely: *Nieuwe Tijdinghen*, no. 131 (10/11), 1623, carries a letter from London dated 17 October (old style) claiming that the Infanta would travel to England in the spring. (I am grateful to Paul Arblaster for this reference.) The printing was done abroad (*ARCR* II, no. 3).

11 Joseph Meade to Sir Martin Stuteville, 24 May 1623 BL, Harleian MS 389, f.33a1. (I am grateful to Arnold Hunt for this reference.)

12 Bodleian, MS.Eng. poet.c.61, ff.52b–53a, 'Uppon Prince Charles his going to Spaigne' (attr. 'John Brereley'). A fragment in the same manuscript (slip guarded in before p. 45) gestures towards allegory in its imaginative rendition of the workings of Providence. Britannia leaves heaven, and God calls an angel to him, to whom he conveys his desire that Prince Charles should be married to the Infanta. The angel flies to Whitehall, where the king, 'still carefull of his country' and puzzling over the question of the Spanish match, becomes tired and falls asleep. The angel appears to him in a vision, and tells him to send Charles into Spain. Waking, the king is plagued by doubts until he submits to God's will.

13 See Thomas Cogswell, *The Blessed Revolution: English Politics and the Coming of War, 1621–1624* (Cambridge University Press, 1989), prologue, and C. F. Main, 'Poems on the "Spanish Marriage" of Prince Charles', *N & Q*, 200 (1955), pp. 336–40.

14 See the introductions to the two most recent editions of *A Game At Chesse*, both edited by T. H. Howard-Hill (Oxford: Malone Society, 1990, and Manchester University Press, 1993) for summaries of recent scholarship. See ch. 1, note 17.

15 Explanations of the allegory were appended to Robert le Grys's translation in 1628 (2nd edn. 1629) and the second edition of Kingsmill Long's in 1636. All quotations come from the second edition of Long.

16 Annabel Patterson, *Censorship and Interpretation: The Conditions of Writing and Reading in Early Modern England* (Madison: University of Wisconsin Press, 1984), pp. 180–5, speculates that le Grys's edition, which emphasizes how it has been done at royal command, may be related to Charles's difficulties with the passage of the Petition of Right through Parliament in 1628. The Petition asserted the illegality of taxation without parliamentary consent, while *Argenis* has a debate which concludes that the right of taxation belongs to kings.

17 See Gordon Albion, *Charles I and the Court of Rome: A Study in Seventeenth-Century Diplomacy* (London: Burns, Oates & Washbourne, 1935); Caroline Hibbard, *Charles I and the Popish Plot* (Chapel Hill: University of North Carolina Press, 1983); R. Malcolm Smuts, *Court Culture and the Origins of a Royalist Tradition in Early Stuart England* (Philadelphia: University of Pennsylvania Press, 1987), esp. ch. 8, and (ed.) *The Stuart Court and Europe: Essays in Politics and Political Culture* (Cambridge University Press, 1996), chs. 4–8. The most recent biography of Barclay is contained in

the introduction to David A. Fleming (ed.), *John Barclay Euphormionis Lushini Satyricon* (Nieuwkoop: B. de Graaf, 1973).
18 See Paul Salzman, *English Prose Fiction, 1558–1700: A Critical History* (Oxford: Clarendon, 1985), pp. 149–55; Potter, *Secret Rites*, pp. 74–7.
19 E.g. Racan's *Artenice* in 1626: see Stephen Orgel and Roy Strong, *Inigo Jones: The Theatre of the Stuart Court*, 2 vols (London: Sotheby Parke Bernet/University of California Press, 1973), I, pp. 383–8. All quotations from the masques are taken from this edition.
20 *Chloridia* (1631); *Tempe Restored* (1632); *The Temple of Love* (1635); *Luminalia* (1638). *Salmacida Spolia* (1640) was presented jointly with Charles.
21 David Lindley (ed.), *The Court Masque* (Manchester University Press, 1984); Martin Butler, *Theatre and Crisis, 1632–1642* (Cambridge University Press, 1984), esp. chs. 2–4; Kevin Sharpe, *Criticism and Compliment: The Politics of Literature in the England of Charles I* (Cambridge University Press, 1987). Further discussion of the political context of individual masques can be found in Martin Butler, 'Politics and the Masque: *Salmacida Spolia*', in Thomas Healy and Jonathan Sawday (eds.), *Literature and the English Civil War* (Cambridge University Press, 1990); Stephen Kogan, *The Hieroglyphic King: Wisdom and Idolatry in the Seventeenth-Century Masque* (London: Associated University Presses, 1986); David Norbrook, '"The Masque of Truth": Court Entertainments and International Protestant Politics in the Early Stuart Period', *The Seventeenth Century*, 1:2 (1986), 81–110; Martin Butler, 'The Politics of the Caroline Masque', in J. R. Mulryne and Margaret Shewring (eds.), *Theatre and Government Under the Early Stuarts* (Cambridge University Press, 1993). A study of the Catholic literature of Charles I's reign is currently being undertaken by Victoria James of Merton College, Oxford.
22 Stephen Orgel has commented that 'royal patrons should be considered full collaborators in these productions': 'Plato, the Magi, and Caroline Politics: A Reading of *The Temple of Love*', *Word and Image*, 4:3/4 (1988), pp. 663–77 (quotation p. 669). Jerzy Limon's distinction between the pre-text, existing as part of the scenario for the dramatic performance, and the printed text may be helpful in establishing the stage at which royal ideas were most likely to have been incorporated: *The Masque of Stuart Culture* (Newark: University of Delaware Press, 1990), pp. 26–8.
23 Veevers's book is indispensable reading to anyone interested in the subject, and the discussion below is indebted to her, though my readings of the Queen's masques modify hers in some respects.
24 Veevers, *Images*, pp. 84, 135–42; Albion, *Charles I*, ch. 6.
25 Veevers, *Images*, pp. 138, 147–8; and see also Martin Butler's important response to Veevers's reading of *The Temple of Love* in his review of *Images in History*, 75 (1990), p. 321. For evidence of Inigo Jones's Catholic sympathies, see Chaney, *Grand Tour*, pp. 343–4.
26 Davenant was pro-Catholic at the time, and officially converted in the

late 1640s. See Mary Edmond, *Rare Sir William Davenant* (Manchester University Press, 1987), pp. 88, 103.
27 Veevers, *Images*, pp. 93–109, 122–33 (comparing the iconography with recusant devotional books such as Henry Hawkins's *Parthenia Sacra*).
28 Butler, *Theatre and Crisis*, chs. 3–4, discusses the Queen's 'politicisation of love'. For her political allegiances before 1637, see R. Malcolm Smuts, 'The Puritan Followers of Henrietta Maria in the 1630s', *EHR*, 93 (1978), pp. 26–45. Though Sharpe argues that the masque criticises the 'unnaturalness and sterility' of platonic love (*Criticism and Compliment*, p. 245), Henrietta Maria had imbued a high doctrine of marriage from the writings of St Francis de Sales and held that marriage could potentially be a realisation of neoplatonic ideals; both Davenant and the Queen may simply have intended to satirise misconceptions of platonic love. See Veevers, *Images*, ch. 1 generally and pp. 44–7 (*Shepherd's Paradise*), 88–9, 134–5 (*Temple of Love*).
29 Veevers, *Images*, ch. 1 and p. 88.
30 The anti-puritan satire is discussed by Martin Butler, 'Politics of the Caroline Masque', pp. 142–6.
31 In *Salmacida Spolia*, Intellectual Appetite is dressed in changeable silk: 'while she embraceth Reason, all the actions of men are rightly governed' (Orgel and Strong (eds.), *Inigo Jones*, II, p. 730).
32 Veevers, *Images*, pp. 83, 183.
33 Martin Butler places *The Temple of Love* in the context of the revival of the Queen's political activities in the mid-1630s: *Theatre and Crisis*, p. 30.
34 Kevin Sharpe has recently commented that Charles's 'attitudes to government and authority often read like an extension to the commonweal of the government of the family', and, of later in the reign, 'it was the happy circumstances and practice of domestic government ... that empowered the representation with reality': *The Personal Rule of Charles I* (New Haven: Yale University Press, 1992), p. 188. Sir Robert Filmer's *Patriarcha*, maintaining that rulers had a fatherly power over their subjects rather than power derived from those subjects' consent, was written in the 1620s and early 1630s: but as J. P. Sommerville comments in the introduction to his edition of *Patriarcha and Other Writings* (Cambridge University Press, 1991), it was also possible to argue in favour of an authoritarian and patriarchal family and against an authoritarian state.
35 E.g. James Daly, *Sir Robert Filmer and English Political Thought* (University of Toronto Press, 1979) ch. 3, esp. pp. 63–7; J. P. Sommerville, *Politics and Ideology in England, 1603–1640* (London: Longman, 1988), pp. 27–34. Margaret J. M. Ezell, *The Patriarch's Wife: Literary Evidence and the History of the Family* (Chapel Hill: University of North Carolina Press, 1987), discusses Filmer's emphasis on a wife's participation in domestic government.
36 E.g. *Tempe Restored*, l. 250 ff.; *Luminalia*, l. 39 ff.

37 Butler, 'Politics of the Caroline Masque', has commented that Charles I's own masques were focused more immediately than James I's on the person of the king (p. 125).
38 Albion, *Charles I*, pp. 67, 78.
39 See *The Letters of Queen Henrietta Maria*, ed. Mary Anne Everett Green (London: Richard Bentley, 1857), pp. 7–8; discussed in Veevers, *Images*, ch. 3. These are exemplars from a common Catholic stock. Nicolas Caussin's *The Holy Court*, a devotional work dedicated to the Queen and popular at the Caroline court, refers to the evangelical efforts of Helena, Clotilde and Inegondis; John Abbot in the dedication to *Jesus Praefigured* compares the Spanish Infanta to Clotilde, Theodolinda and Inegondis.
40 After the failure of the Spanish marriage negotiations, which had involved a daringly pro-Catholic marriage treaty, Parliament had been promised on 23 April 1624 that English Catholics would be given no concessions in any subsequent ones: Martin Havran, *The Catholics in Caroline England* (Stanford University Press, 1962), pp. 20–3.
41 *Ibid.*, p. 35.
42 E.g. the letter of 12 July 1626 printed in Sir Charles Petrie (ed.), *Letters, Speeches and Proclamations of King Charles I* (London: Cassell, 1968), pp. 42–5 (cf. pp. 40–1).
43 *Cabala. Mysteries of State* (1654), pp. 198, 301. This account is synthesised from Havran, *Catholics*, chs. 2–3; Albion, *Charles I*, chs. 2–3; and Henrietta Maria's two most recent biographers: Quentin Bone, *Henrietta Maria: Queen of the Cavaliers* (London: Peter Owen, 1973), ch. 2; and Elizabeth Hamilton, *Henrietta Maria* (London: Hamish Hamilton, 1976), chs. 6–8. Henrietta Maria's later correspondence with Charles and others sometimes reveals her criticising him, or combining protestations of obedience with an assumption that she will be given an active role in decision-making (*Letters*, ed. Everett Green, pp. 112–18, 124–7, 224–5): cf. the case-studies of marital correspondence in Anthony Fletcher, *Gender, Sex and Subordination in England, 1500–1800* (New Haven: Yale University Press, 1995), ch. 8.
44 Jonathan Goldberg has discussed the politicisation of the Stuart marriages: 'the private sphere ... is mystified, politicised, made into an ideological construct' (*James I and the Politics of Literature: Jonson, Shakespeare, Donne and Their Contemporaries* (Baltimore: Johns Hopkins University Press, 1983), pp. 94–7).
45 From the *Mémoires inédits* of the French ambassador, Conte Leveneur de Tillières, ed. M. C. Hippeau (Paris: Poulet-Malassis, 1862), pp. 118–22.
46 Butler, 'Politics of the Caroline Masque', p. 121 (cf. pp. 127, 152).
47 1 Peter 3.1–2.
48 Veevers, *Images*, introduction; Sophie Tomlinson, 'She That Plays the King: Henrietta Maria and the Threat of the Actress in Caroline Culture', in Gordon McMullen and Jonathan Hope (eds.), *The Politics of Tragicomedy: Shakespeare and After* (London: Routledge, 1992).

49 Elizabeth Cary, Lady Falkland, *The Tragedy of Mariam, Fair Queen of Jewry. With The Lady Falkland Her Life*, ed. Barry Weller and Margaret W. Ferguson (Berkeley: University of California Press, 1994), 'Life', p. 195. It may not be a coincidence that matters came to a head between Cary and her husband in the first years of Charles's and Henrietta Maria's marriage.
50 In fact, the succession devolved to the son of Mariam's son (also called Aristobolos) by Herod.
51 *Mariam* was printed in 1613 and may have been written up to ten years earlier. Marta Straznicky has argued against a 'biographical and mimetic orientation' on the grounds that dates are too vague to permit life-art connections ('Profane Stoical Paradoxes': *The Tragedie of Mariam* and Sidnean Closet Drama', *ELR*, 24:1 (1994), pp. 104–34). In the same issue of the journal, Laurie J. Shannon censures the use of the biography as a hermeneutical tool ('*The Tragedie of Mariam*: Cary's Critique of the Terms of Founding Social Discourses', pp. 135–53). See also Stephanie Wright, 'The Canonization of Elizabeth Cary', in Kate Chedgzoy, Melanie Hansen and Suzanne Trill (eds.), *Voicing Women: Gender and Sexuality in Early Modern Writing* (Keele University Press, 1996); and Dympna Callaghan, 'Re-Reading Elizabeth Cary's *Tragedy of Mariam, Fair Queen of Jewry*', in Margo Hendricks and Patricia Parker (eds.), *Women, 'Race', and Sexuality in the Early Modern Period* (London: Routledge, 1994), esp. pp. 165–7. I have discussed the literary effects of prolonged conversion, and of experimentation with conversion, in chapter two, and do not consider the chronologies given by any of these scholars to militate against an autodidactic interpretation of the play. There would, as well, have been no particular *hagiographical* reason for claiming, as the 'Life' does, that Cary had Catholic sympathies for most of her married life before 1626.
52 Alison Shell, 'Autodidacticism and Authority: Elizabeth Cary's *Mariam*' (forthcoming).
53 However, Catholic households frequently consisted of recusant wives married to occasional conformists, since recusant heads of households faced much severer penalties than their wives: Walsham, *Church-Papists*, p. 78. On the related phenomenon of Catholic matriarchalism, see Bossy, *English Catholic Community*, pp. 153–60. Patricia Crawford argues that both Catholic and Protestant women married to husbands not of their faith were invited to put the demands of their conscience before the wish of their spouses, where these conflicted; but she also points out that as Protestantism became the established faith, its commentators grew less radical: 'Public Duty, Conscience, and Women in Early Modern England', in John Morrill, Paul Slack and Daniel Woolf (eds.), *Public Duty and Private Conscience in Seventeenth-Century England* (Oxford: Clarendon Press, 1993), ch. 5, esp. pp. 67 ff. Trimble, *Catholic Laity*, pp. 151–3, comments on the inconsistency of legal practice relating to female recusancy.

54 George Hakewill's MS treatise 'The Wedding Robe' (Bod MS Jones 14, ff.305–14) claims in its subtitle to be written to address 'the unlawfullnes of Protestants marriages with Papists', but actually designs itself to exclude any comment on couples already married – though he quotes, without comment, the opinion of the 'Civilians and Canonists' that disparity of worship or *cultus disparitus* is 'a sufficient stop, not only to hinder marriage to bee made; but of force to inforce a nullity, and to reave it asunder beeing made' (p. 306). Hakewill's treatise, which would reward further research, dates from around the time of the proposed marriage of Prince Charles with the Spanish Infanta, and is probably that which caused his dismissal from the post of chaplain to the Prince (*DNB*). This crisis also affected William Gouge's treatise *Of Domesticall Duties*; it seems to have been censored in 1622, with the section advising against Protestants marrying papists being cut to four lines.

55 The usual assumption of a male addressee tends to leave the question unanswered, e.g. in John Dod and Robert Cleaver, *A Godlie Form of Household Government*, 1617 edn., p. 313.

56 The problem is sometimes addressed *via* the question of correct behaviour for Protestant wives married to Catholic husbands: Dod and Cleaver, *ibid.*, 1617 edn., f.F3b–4. William Perkins, MS notes on marriage quoted in Peter Lake, 'Feminine Piety and Personal Potency: the "Emancipation" of Mrs Jane Ratcliffe', *The Seventeenth Century*, 2:2 (1987), pp. 143–65, esp. p. 152; William Gouge, *Of Domesticall Duties* (1634 ed.), p. 329; and (from the heroic early stages of Protestantism) John Bale, *Select Works*, ed. Henry Christmas (Cambridge: Parker Society, 1849), p. 199. See also Thomas Becon, *A New Catechism*, in John Ayre (ed.), *The Catechism of Thomas Becon* (Cambridge: Parker Society, 1844), p. 341, suggesting that if a wife was encouraged by a husband to commit idolatry she should forsake him.

57 The few Catholic commentators on the subject appear more uniformly radical: Gregory Martin, *A Treatise of Schisme* (1578), f.B6b; Henry Garnet, *Treatise of Christian Renunciation*, pp. 145–6 (discussed in Walsham, *Church Papists*, p. 35). The Catholic martyr Margaret Clitheroe defied her Protestant husband with the priest John Mush's support (see Mush's biography in John Morris, *The Troubles of Our Catholic Forefathers*, 3 vols. (London: Burns & Oates, 1872–7), pp. 381–2). Other writers (e.g. John Radford, *Directorie Teaching the Way to the Truth* (1605), p. 522, and Thomas Hide, *Consolatorie Epistle to the Afflicted Catholikes* (1580 edn.), f.Bi-iia), assume a male addressee but stress the limited claims of familial duty as against duty to God.

58 See Rebecca W. Bushnell, *Tragedies of Tyrants: Political Thought and Theatre in the English Renaissance* (Ithaca: Cornell University Press, 1990); Maurice J. Valency, *The Tragedies of Herod and Mariamne* (New York: AMS, 1966, first published 1940). Catholics at this time could go out of their way to endorse tyranny, stressing personal dissociation from the resistance

theorists of the recent past: Edmund Bolton stated in *Nero Caesar* [ca. 1621], that 'No Prince is so bad as not to make monarckie seeme the best forme of government' (f.A2b, quoted from 2nd edn. of 1627).

59 Thomas Gataker, *Certaine Sermons* (1637), f.3R4b.
60 See also Foley, *Records of the English Province of the Society of Jesus*, I, pp. 210–11, for a letter written to Henrietta Maria by an anonymous Jesuit commending Esther as exemplar [22 March, ca. 1641–4].
61 Huntington Library, MS HM 120, dedicated to Sir Anthony Cage and wife. For other copies cited in library catalogues, and their dedicatees, see Leota Snider Willis, 'Francis Lenton, Queen's Poet', PhD thesis (printed), University of Pennsylvania, 1931. William Carew Hazlitt, the only person to have compared them all, writes that there are few points of divergence between the MSS except in the titles, dates and patrons to whom each is addressed: *Collections and Notes* (London: Reeves & Turner, 1876), p. 255. The poem is briefly discussed by Veevers, *Images*, pp. 82–3.
62 A contemporary reader has annotated the end of the MS with adjurations and biblical texts forbidding frowardness, 'a sine as well to be strove against as other grosser ons'.
63 Paraphrasing Esther 1.16–18.
64 McClure (ed.), *Letters and Epigrams*, Epigram 401. For a less ironical instance of Esther as Catholic exemplar, see Robert Southwell, *An Humble Supplication to Her Majestie*, ed. R. C. Bald (Cambridge University Press, 1953), p. 9. Francis Quarles's *Hadassa: Or the History of Queen Ester* (1621) is addressed to James I, and uses the story to reflect upon governance.
65 ARCR II, no. 524, describing the Bodleian copy of Gregory Martin's *A Treatise of Schisme* (1578), in which Catholic women are recommended to emulate Judith, who refused even to eat with Holofernes. At the trial of the printer William Carter, this was interpreted as an incitement to Elizabeth's assassination.
66 I.e. tinsel-cloth.
67 The two main costume-designs for *Luminalia* reproduced by Orgel and Strong (*Inigo Jones*, II, pp. 718–23) have a number of comparable details, though it is not clear whether either was intended for the Queen. The light-giving carbuncle may allude to the central image of *Luminalia* (though a date of 1637, even old-style, argues against the poem's having been begun after the actual performance on 6 February 1638). Esther was traditionally costumed in a richly seductive manner (cf. portrait in Thomas Heywood, *The Exemplary Lives ... of Nine [sic] the Most Worthy Women* (1640)), though, as Pierre Merlin commented in *A Most Plaine and Profitable Exposition of the Booke of Ester* (1599), 'they who are delighted with the noveltie and vanitie of sumptuous and most luxurious apparell ... are nothing holpen by this example' (pp. 256–7).
68 Veevers, *Images*, pp. 146–7.

69 Cf. the versified Litany of Loreto in I.B., *Virginalia* (1632), pp. 30, 36.
70 Cressy, *Bonfires and Bells*, argues that this encouraged the mythical construction of Elizabeth's reign as a golden age.
71 Trinity College, Dublin, TCD MS 1194, pp. 50–7.
72 Keith Lindley, 'The Part Played by the Catholics', in Brian Manning (ed.), *Politics, Religion and the English Civil War* (London: Edward Arnold, 1973), pp. 127–78 (quotation from editor's introductory comments).
73 The introduction to John Morrill (ed.), *Reactions to the English Civil War, 1642–1649* (London: Macmillan, 1982) argues that few English writers of any persuasion proclaimed the right of resistance to tyrants in the early Stuart period, and that passive disobedience had always been more characteristic of the Puritan party, with theories of resistance being evolved in an *ad hoc* manner as hostilities began.
74 Nor, as J. C. H. Aveling has commented, the claims made by most Catholic peers and gentry around 1660 that they had been royalists all along: *The Handle and the Axe: the Catholic Recusants in England from Reformation to Emancipation* (London: Blond & Briggs, 1976), ch. 7. The Christopher Hill quotation comes from *The Century of Revolution, 1603–1714* (1961: this edn. London: Abacus, 1978), p. 60. B. G. Blackwood, *The Lancashire Gentry and the Great Rebellion, 1640–1660* (Manchester: Chetham Society, 1978), while emphasizing the strong Royalist commitment among recusant gentry in this county, comments that up to one hundred of them may have been neutral (pp. 63–4). See also J. T. Cliffe, *The Yorkshire Gentry From the Reformation to the Civil War* (London: Athlone, 1969), p. 345; and David F. Mosler, 'The Warwickshire Catholics in the Civil War', *RH*, 15 (1980), pp. 259–64, who argues for large-scale neutralism on grounds of poverty. Margaret Blundell (ed.), *Cavalier: The Letters of William Blundell to His Friends, 1620–1698* (London: Longmans, Green & Co., 1933) provides a case-study of one Catholic Royalist.
75 Quoted in Sir George Duckett, 'Civil War Proceedings in Yorkshire', *Yorkshire Archaeological and Topographical Journal*, 7 (1881–2), pp. 63–79. For the statistically negligible, individually interesting Catholics who supported Parliament, see Cliffe, *Yorkshire Gentry*, p. 345; Ivan Roots, *The Great Rebellion, 1642–1660* (London: Batsford, 1966), pp. 63, 66.
76 P. R. Newman, 'Catholic Royalist Activists in the North, 1642–1646', *RH*, 14:1 (1977), pp. 26–38, and 'Catholic Royalists of Northern England, 1642–1645', *Northern History*, 15 (1979), pp. 88–95, both articles engaging with the neutralist model set out in Lindley, 'Part Played by the Catholics'. C. B. Phillips argues for a lesser (though still significant) correlation between Catholicism and Royalism in two other Northern counties, offset by a high degree of neutralism: 'The Royalist North: The Cumberland and Westmorland Gentry, 1642–1660', *Northern History*, 14 (1978), pp. 169–192. See also B. G. Blackwood, 'Parties and Issues in the Civil War in Lancashire and East Anglia', *Northern History*,

29 (1993), pp. 99–125; Cliffe, *Yorkshire Gentry*, pp. 343–8 (royalists). In *Lancashire Gentry*, Blackwood also offers brief comments on the promising, and under-researched, topic of divided Catholic families and individual side-changers (pp. 65, 71).

77 For anti-popery, see Brian Manning, *The English People and the English Revolution, 1640–1649* (London: Heinemann, 1976), ch. 2; and ch. 3 in Manning (ed.), *Politics, Religion*. Clifton, 'Fear of Popery', discusses disquiet over Catholic loyalty to the Crown at this date; G. E. Aylmer, *The Struggle For the Constitution* (London: Blandford, 1963), p. 118, suggests that some Catholics were driven from neutralism to royalism by the anti-popery of Parliament. The frequent invisibility of Catholics to the historian is particularly noticeable in discussions of initial recruitment, and such formulations as the following: 'just as the royalist clergy had recruited for the king so the Puritan divines did so for Parliament. . . . It was not so much men's belief in rival sets of political principles which distinguished the two armies as the sharp contrast between their religious attitudes' (Anthony Fletcher, *The Outbreak of the English Civil War* (London: Edward Arnold, 1981), p. 346). Fletcher himself, however, points towards a more nuanced picture when describing the difficulties inherent in Catholic support for a king who declared himself to be fighting in defence of the Protestant religion (pp. 328–9).

78 See also John Austin (William Birchley), *The Christian Moderator* (1st edn. 1651: see Clancy, *English Catholic Books, 1641–1700*, 50–5).

79 The two most recent studies of Blackloism are Beverley C. Southgate, '*Covetous of Truth': The Life and Work of Thomas White, 1593–1676*, Archives Internationales d'Histoire des Idées, 134 (Dordrecht: Kluwer, 1993), esp. chs. 5–7, commenting on divisions among Catholics in the mid-1650s on the subjects of regicide and religious toleration; and Dorothea Krook, *John Sergeant and His Circle: A Study of the Seventeenth-Century English Aristoteleans* (Leiden: E. G. Brill, 1993). See also Robert I. Bradley, S.J., 'Blacklo and the Counter-Reformation: An Enquiry Into the Strange Death of Catholic England', in Charles H. Carter (ed.), *From the Renaissance to the Counter-Reformation: Essays in Honour of Garrett Mattingly* (London: Jonathan Cape, 1966), pp. 348–70; T. A. Birrell, 'English Catholics Without a Bishop, 1655–1672', *RH*, 4 (1958), pp. 142–78, and his introduction to Robert Pugh, *Blacklo's Cabal (1680)* (Farnborough: Gregg, 1970); Chaney, *Grand Tour*, p. 91.

80 I.e. King or Parliament.

81 Cf. the reference to Philo the Jew by the writer of an anonymous prefatory verse to John Abbot's later volume *Devout Rhapsodies* [1647: published under the name of J. A. Rivers], f.A4a.

82 For (e.g.) Sir Percy Herbert's *The Princess Chloria*, see Nigel Smith, *Literature and Revolution in England, 1640–1660* (New Haven: Yale University Press, 1994, repr. 1997), pp. 237–9.

83 NLW, Peniarth MS 375B.

5 THE SUBJECT OF EXILE: I

1 The poem is probably dateable to mid-late 1651, when Cowley was living in the Louvre as secretary to Henry, Lord Jermyn. See Hilton Kelliher, 'Cowley and "Orinda": Autograph Fair Copies', *British Library Journal*, 2:2 (1976), pp. 102–8 (from which the above transcription is also taken); and David Trotter, *The Poetry of Abraham Cowley* (London: Macmillan, 1979), pp. 59–60, 72–82 (for the friendship between Cowley and Crashaw).
2 Oldisworth's verse is preserved in Bod. MS Don.c.24, f.25.
3 Anthony G. Petti, 'Unknown sonnets by Sir Toby Matthew', *RH*, 9:3 (1967), pp. 123–58 (transcription taken from this source). As surviving in Huntington Library MS 198, Part II, they begin with a sonnet to the poet's friend and end with one entitled 'Upon the Expectacon of a friends Cominge to me', and may originally have been grouped together thus as a gift. The subjects combine protestations of friendship with Catholic hagiological topics.
4 John P. Feil, 'Sir Tobie Matthew and His Collection of Letters' (Chicago University PhD thesis, 1962), Part I, is the most recent biography.
5 Designated as George Gage I in the biographical account by Philippa Revill and Francis W. Steer, 'George Gage I and George Gage II', *Bulletin of the Institute of Historical Research*, 31 (1958), pp. 141–158 (correcting *DNB* account). Gage was involved in the negotiations in Rome for the Spanish marriage treaty; an account of these is attributed to him (Bod. MS. Rawl. B.488). However, D. M. Rogers believed this was forged (p. 153).
6 David Howarth, *Lord Arundel and His Circle* (New Haven: Yale University Press, 1985), pp. 66–7, 156–8.
7 Chaney, *Grand Tour*. Chaney's more recent *The Evolution of the Grand Tour: Anglo-Italian Cultural Relations Since the Renaissance* (London: Frank Cass, 1998) may well give a wider currency to his interpretation of the topic, and I am grateful to him for letting me see proofs of his book as this study was about to go to press. See also the discussion of Catholic travellers and exiles in John Stoye, *English Travellers Abroad, 1604–1667: Their Influence on English Society and Politics* (London: Jonathan Cape, 1952), pp. 265–7, 272–6, 353–5, 379–81. Stoye's 'The Grand Tour in the 17th Century', *Journal of Anglo-Italian Studies*, 1 (1991), pp. 62–73, distinguishes between English tourism and English residence abroad.
8 See Jeremy Black, *The British Abroad: The Grand Tour in the 18th Century* (Stroud: Alan Sutton, 1992), p. 3. This useful study is marred by a tendency to take Whiggish prejudice as a benchmark of how all Englishmen thought, in observations like 'tourism in the 17th century was different in kind from that of the mid-18th, when Jacobitism had been crushed and Britain appeared less threatened, at home by Catholicism and autocracy, abroad by Spain and France'. The intro-

duction to Christopher Hibbert, *The Grand Tour* (London: Spring Books, this edn. 1974) is more inclusive. But the continuing predisposition towards the eighteenth century has recently been reinforced by John Ingamells (comp.), *A Dictionary of British and Irish Travellers in Italy, 1701–1800* (New Haven: Yale University Press, for Paul Mellon Centre, 1997), reflecting the emphases of its source, the Brinsley Ford archive.

9 Black, *Grand Tour*, p. 3; R. S. Pine-Coffin, *Bibliography of British and American Travel in Italy to 1860* (Florence: Leo S. Olschki, 1974), pp. 24–6.

10 Richard Lassels, 'An apologie for the Roman Catholicks' [1652–3], Oscott MS 44, pp. i–ii.

11 A. C. F. Beales, *Education Under Penalty: English Catholic Education From the Reformation to the Fall of James II* (London: Athlone, 1963), describes the various educational possibilities at home and abroad. In Barclay's *Argenis* (see ch. 4), Iburranes describes how the king of Sicily, or France, is seeking to wipe out Huguenots from his realm by the peaceable method of having their children removed and educated in the national religion. Barclay himself left England in 1615, and in his preface to *Paraenesis ad Sectarios* (1617), he claimed that this was in order that his children born in England could be brought up as Catholics; the discrepancy demonstrates both Barclay's ideal of unquestioning obedience to absolutism, and absolutism's limited territorial sway. Cf. Annabel Patterson, *Censorship and Interpretation: The Conditions of Writing and Reading in Early Modern England* (Madison: University of Wisconsin Press, 1984), pp. 180–185.

12 No. 448 in the *Oxford Book of Local Verse* (from the version given in G. C. Miller, *Hoghton Tower* (1954), pp. 29–32), where the author is tentatively identified as Roger Anderson, butler to Thomas Hoghton. For the Continental exiles, see Peter Guilday, *The English Catholic Refugees on the Continent, 1558–1795, Vol. I. The English Colleges and Convents in the Catholic Low Countries, 1558–1795* (no Vol. II) (London: Longmans, 1914); Adrian Morey, *The Catholic Subjects of Elizabeth I* (London: George Allen & Unwin, 1978), chs. 6–7; John Bossy, 'Rome and the Elizabethan Catholics: A Question of Geography', *HJ*, 7:1 (1964), pp. 135–49 (mostly tracking the routes used): Christian Coppens (ed.), *Reading in Exile: The Libraries of John Ramridge (d. 1568), Thomas Harding (d. 1572) and Henry Joliffe (d. 1573), Recusants in Louvain* (Cambridge: Libri Pertinentes, no. 2, 1993), introduction; Beales, *Education Under Penalty*, ch. 3.

13 Translated in Philip Caraman, *The Other Face: Catholic Life Under Elizabeth I* (London: Longmans, 1960), p. 141 (ch. 17 anthologises reflections on exile from contemporary writers). In his description of how he sought the opportunity to go abroad after his conversion to Catholicism, Henry Piers uses contemporary, perhaps Jesuit-inspired meditational terminology to connect the experiences of conversion and travel. 'I made use of my outward sences whoe havinge found her posted messengers unto the inward sences and imagination whoe presented

her unto my understandinge will and memorie, which are the pouers of the soule. The which eternall substance beinge then in desperatt estate, and meetinge soe necessarie a guide was right glade to be carried unto the place in the which the shipp wherein shee sayled might be newly trymmed and rigged and hir pilate well instructed to direct hir unto the haven of everlastinge happines, Nowe for as muche as noe motion can be without a place from the which and to the which it should be lymitted I made choise of Dublin [to be the one and Rome the other ...] ... and so not without many difficulties then occurringe leauvinge behinde me, my parents, wife and children, Lands and an office of creditt, I undertooke my Jornye'. Transcription, checked against original, from Thomas Frank (ed.), 'An edition of A Discourse of HP his travelles (MS Rawlinson D 83) With an Introduction on English Travellers in Rome During the Age of Elizabeth', B.Litt thesis, Oxford, 1954, p. 111. For the distinction between memory, understanding and will, see Martz, *Poetry of Meditation*.

14 Dures, *English Catholicism*, p. 30; Morey, *Catholic Subjects*, pp. 96–8; Hibbert, *Grand Tour*, introduction.

15 Pine-Coffin, *British and American Travel*, introduction. As he also points out, travel-literature provides a barometer of softening attitudes towards Catholicism in later periods.

16 The literature on English Jesuit drama is still small, but this chapter draws on the following general studies: William M. MacCabe, 'The Play-List of the English College of St Omers, 1592–1762', *Revue de Litterature Comparée*, 66 (1937), pp. 355–75, 'Notes on the St Omers College Theatre', *PQ*, 17.3 (1938), pp. 225–239, and *An Introduction to the English Jesuit Theatre* (St Louis: Institute of Jesuit Sources, 1983); Suzanne Gossett, 'Drama in the English College, Rome, 1591–1660', *ELR*, 3 (1973), pp. 60–93. My doctoral thesis, 'English Catholicism and Drama, 1578–1688' (Oxford D.Phil., 1992), has a more extensive discussion of the topic than it has been possible to include here. For continental Jesuit drama, see Johannes Muller, *Das Jesuitendrama in den Landern Deutscher zunge vom Aufang (1555) bis zum Hochbarock (1665)*, 2 vols (Augsburg: Benno Filser, 1930); Jean-Marie Valentin, *Le Théâtre des Jesuites de Langue Allemande* (Benn: Peter Lang, 1978), and *Le Théâtre des Jesuites Dans les Pays de Langue Allemande: Repertoire Chronologique des Pièces Representées et des Documents Conservées (1555–1773)*, 2 vols (Stuttgart: Hiersemann, 1983–4).

17 E.g. the dramatist William Drury (see below, note 41).

18 Randolph Starn, *Contrary Commonwealth: The Theme of Exile in Medieval and Renaissance Italy* (Berkeley: University of California Press, 1982), p. 7.

19 A. Bartlett Giamatti, *Exile and Change in Renaissance Literature* (New Haven: Yale University Press, 1984), pp. 13–14; Dolora Wojciehowski, 'Petrarch's Temporal Exile and the Wounds of History', in James Whitlark and Wendell Aycock (eds.), *The Literature of Emigration and Exile* (Lubbock: Texas Tech University Press, 1992), pp. 11–21. However,

Michael Seidel, *Exile and the Narrative Imagination* (New Haven: Yale University Press, 1986), introduction, calls the use of exile as a metaphor for the alienated and marginalized consciousness 'post-Romantic'.

20 I am grateful to Anna Kasket for letting me consult her undergraduate dissertation: ' "How Like a Widow?": *Lamentations* in English Literature of the 1640s'.

21 Starn, *Contrary Commonwealth*, p. 24, remarks on the use of the genres of elegy and *consolatio* by exiles.

22 Quotations are taken from the MS (BL Egerton 2402) identified as the author's in Richard S. Sylvester (ed.), *The Life and Death of Cardinal Wolsey, by George Cavendish* (Oxford University Press, for EETS, 1959). The transcription of the *envoi* is emended from that on pp. x–xi. See also the edition of *Metrical Visions* by A. S. G. Edwards (Columbia, S.C.: University of South Carolina Press for Newberry Library, 1980); Emrys Jones prints the elegy on Mary in *The New Oxford Book of 16th-Century Verse*, pp. 131–4. As John Kerrigan remarks in *Motives*, p. 25, it obviously imitates the *Mirror for Magistrates*, despite the fact that this was suppressed under Mary.

23 As John Kerrigan has pointed out in his discussion of lamentation, topics of bereavement, family betrayal and loss of state 'shadow but do not coincide with the shapes of love lament': *Motives*, p. 55.

24 Catholics had no monopoly on this: see also *The Answere of a Mother Unto Her Seduced Sonnes Letter* (1627), printing a Catholic text re-titled 'A letter written from Doway 6. of March 1627. By a seduced sonne unto his mother', together with a response which, though described as a letter, breaks into dialogue between mother and son at one point. This is recognised in the re-titling of the enlarged second edition: *A Mothers Teares Over Hir Seduced Sonne: Or a Dissuasive From Idolatry* (1627).

25 Quoted from Katherine Duncan-Jones (ed.), *Sir Philip Sidney* (Oxford University Press, 1989), p. 229.

26 Abbie Potts, *The Elegiac Mode* (Ithaca: Cornell University Press, 1967), p. 37.

27 W. David Shaw, 'Elegy and Theory – Is Historical and Critical Knowledge Possible?', *MLQ*, 55:1 (1994), pp. 1–16 (quotation p. 14).

28 *Versibus impariter iunctis querimonia primum, / post etiam inclusa est voti sententia compos* (ll. 75–6): quoted from the edition and translation by H. Rushton Fairclough in the Loeb Classical Library series (Cambridge, Mass.: Harvard University Press, this edn. 1978), pp. 456–7.

29 See H. L. Bennett, 'The Principal Historical Conventions in the Renaissance Personal Elegy', *Studies in Philology*, 51 (1954), pp. 107–26. Francis White Weitzmann, 'Notes on the Elizabethan Elegie', *PMLA*, 50 (1935), pp. 435–43, points out that the Elizabethans could use the term to mean a didactic poem.

30 Barbara Lewalski, *Donne's 'Anniversaries' and the Poetry of Praise: The Creation of a Symbolic Mode* (Princeton University Press, 1973).

31 Quoted from *The Complete Works of Thomas Lodge*, facsimile edn., 4 vols (New York: Russell & Russell, 1963), I, f.37a.
32 The change of direction which Lodge's conversion brought about in his literary career was briefly discussed in chapter two.
33 There is a recent summary of the evidence in George Alan Clugston's edition of Lodge and Greene's *A Looking Glasse for London and England* (New York: Garland, 1980), introduction. Guiney (pp. 229-39) and Thurston, 'Catholic Writers', have previously discussed the Catholic content of the poem.
34 Drayton illustrates the connection between the two: 'For now as Elegiack I bewaile / These poore base times; then suddainly I raile / And am Satirick' ('To Master William Jeffreys', in *Works*, ed. J. William Hebel, 5 vols (Oxford: Basil Blackwell, 1931-41), III, p. 240). Another poem of Drayton's, 'On the noble lady Aston's departure for Spain' (p. 105, ll. 1-6), has the term 'elegy' used for departure.
35 Two similar poems by Catholic authors – published, unlike Lodge's, outside the mainstream – are *Holy Churches Complaint* [c.1598-1601] and Verstegan, *Odes*, pp. 94-7. Two uses of the trope in manuscript Latin Catholic poetry can be found in CSPD, Addenda (15) 28, 58 (v); and Trinity College, Cambridge, O.3.53, 'De Calamitate Britannica Ode'.
36 Hackett, *Virgin Mother*, p. 28.
37 Quoted from Jones (ed.), *New Oxford Book of 16th-Century Verse*, pp. 550-1.
38 Margaret Aston, 'English Ruins and English History: The Dissolution and the Sense of the Past', *JWCI*, 36 (1973), pp. 232-55.
39 Gothic survival and revival is a topic that needs a full-length interdisciplinary reconsideration. Standard histories of the Gothic revival, even Michael McCarthy's recent *The Origins of the Gothic Revival* (New Haven: Yale University Press, 1987), tend to start from the mid-eighteenth century, and draw their evidence largely from surviving buildings and elite architectural theorists. Kenneth Clark's often-reprinted *The Gothic Revival* (1928: this edn. 1970, repr. London: John Murray, 1995), while acknowledging that Gothic was maintained in early modern England by vernacular builders and recorded by antiquarians, calls their efforts a 'tiny brackish stream' (p. 11).
40 Whereas most statues of the Virgin portray her standing, the statue of Our Lady of Walsingham shows her sitting on a throne with the infant Jesus in her arms. The visual image suggested by this verse may be intended as a Protestantised travesty of this, with Satan in the arms of Sin.
41 Quotations taken from Robert Knightley, *Alfrede or Right Reinthron'd*, ed. Albert H. Tricomi (New York: Medieval and Renaissance Texts and Studies 99, 1993), pp. 154-5. See also Arthur Freeman, 'William Drury, Dramatist', *RH*, 8:5 (1966), pp. 293-7.
42 *ARCR* I, no. 1,011. In his edition of the play (Austin: University of Texas

Press, 1964), from which the Latin and English quotations are taken, Louis A. Schuster describes how it was inspired by Sander's *De Origine ac Progressu Schismatis Anglicani*; Sander had lived for a time in Louvain. Vernulaeus treats the story of Thomas Becket in an analogous manner in *S. Thomas Cantuariensis* [1625] (pp. 547–614 in his *Tragœdiae Decem* (Louvain, 1631), not in *ARCR* 1).

43   *Delubra iacent obruta flammis,*
     Sacros rapiunt cineres venti,
     Destruit aras impius ignis,
     Christusque suis pellitur aris,
     Multum in templis perplacet aurum,
     Aurumque reas efficit aras.
     Populator amat quicquid ditat ...
     Pars Belgiacas incolet oras,
     Pars Italicos incolet agros,
     Pars Occiduos viset Iberos.
     Sparsi toto protinus Orbe
     Miseri latebimus exules. (f.E2)

I am grateful to Julia Griffin for this reference.

44 Quoted from the translation in Victor Houliston, '*Breuis Dialogismus*', *ELR*, 23.3 (1993), pp. 382–427 (see also his article 'St Thomas Becket in the Propaganda of the English Counter-Reformation', *Renaissance Studies*, 7:1 (1993), pp. 43–70). I am grateful to Dr Houliston for letting me see a copy of the translation before publication.
45 See Alastair Fowler, *Kinds of Literature* (Oxford: Clarendon, 1982), pp. 136–7, 174.
46 Quoted from Jones (ed.), *New Oxford Book of 16th-Century Verse*, pp. 332–7.
47 Catholic Ireland yielded a number of weeping Irelands around this date, mainly connected with the Irish Rebellion in 1641. Some are plays, like *Colas Furie or Lirenda's Miserie*,'Lirenda' being a transparent anagram of 'Ireland' (see Patricia Coughlan, '"Enter Revenge": Henry Burkhead and *Cola's Furie*', *Theatre Research International*, 15.1 (1990), pp. 1–17); or *Landgartha* (1640), in which Ireland is personified as a Norwegian princess (see Catherine Shaw, '*Landgartha* and the Irish Dilemma', *Eire-Ireland*, 13 (1968), pp. 26–39). Woodcuts of Ireland bemoaning her dismembered sons can be found in pamphlets, e.g. *A Prospect of Bleeding Irelands Miseries* (1647).
48 See Daniel Woolf, 'Conscience, Constancy and Ambition in the Career and Writings of James Howell', in John Morrill, Paul Slack and Daniel Woolf (eds.), *Public Duty and Private Conscience in 17th-Century England* (Oxford: Clarendon Press, 1993).
49 Cf. Seidel, *Exile*, p. 13.
50 *Ratio Discendi et Docendi* (1685), discussed by Diana de Marly Batsford, *Costume on the Stage 1600–1940* (London: Batsford, 1982), p. 12. For a later (eighteenth-century) description of Jesuit costumes for Comoedia and Tragoedia, see Alexander Rudin (ed.), *Franz Lang: Abhandlung über die Schauspielkunst (Dissertatio de Actione Scenica)*, (Berne: A. Francke, 1975),

pp. 112, 150 (see also the costumes for Haeresis, Hypocrisis and Idololatria, pp. 124, 127).
51 V.E.C. MS 321 (ff.123a–176b) (3); V.E.C. Scritt. 33 (3) (frag.) All transcriptions are taken from the former.
52 COMOEDIA *Nec alarum remigio.*
TRAGOEDIA *Nec pedum talaribus.*
COM *Nec velorum pennis.*
TRAG *Nec essedorum currubus*
    Vecti.
COM *Londinum appulistis.*
AMBO *Spectatissimi.*
COM *Hîc, portus rostratis statio est fida puppibus.*
TRAG *Dulcis hîc amoenas allambit ripas Thamesis.*
COM *Pontem en sacris martyrum stellantem comis.*
TRAG *Hic, carcer aerumnis Romanae alumnos premit*
    Fidei.
COM *Captiva hîc Religio.*
TRAG *Malis*
    Gravatur asperis. (f.123b)
Talaribus has been emended from *talariis* (of or belonging to dice). Robert Carver has pointed out to me the allusions to Virgil, *Aeneid*, I, 301, & VI, 19, in this passage.
53 COMOEDIA *Reliqua nunc auribus,*
TRAGOEDIA *Et oculis, benigne.*
COM *Haurienda. linquimus.*
TRA *Qui Prologi ad vos ornatu venimus.*
COM *Unicum*
    Vos erga indultum accepimus:
TRA *Tragi-*
COM *Comoedia*
    In scenam prodit:
TRA *Risus nil moror, malo*
    Suspiria.
COM *Risus malo, nil moror suspiria.*
TRA *Lugubris Angliam fletus squalentem decet.*
COM *Ludicris squalentem solari decet Angliam.*
TRA *Eheu!*
COM *Vah!*
TRA *Hei mihi!*
COM *O festum diem!*
TRA *Lachrymae,*
COM *Adeste ioci.*
TRA *Flete.*
COM *Ridete.*
TRA *Placet, Angliae modo[.]*
AMBO *Spectatores, benevolis vacetis mentibus.* (f.123b)
54 State Papers Foreign, Italian states and Rome: 85/4/101. Summarised in Feil, 'Sir Tobie Matthew', p. 78.
55 He is not, unfortunately, identifiable from the (imperfectly surviving) *Responsa Scholarum* of the English College, Rome, ed. Anthony Kenny,

Part 1, 1598–1621 ([London]: CRS, no. 54, 1962), or from John Doran, *The History of Court Fools* (London: Richard Bentley, 1858), or Enid Welsford, *The Fool* (London: Faber & Faber, 1935). Archibald Armstrong, a fool to James I, travelled to the court of Spain, and a letter survives in which he invokes the Virgin, perhaps facetiously (28 April 1623: BL Add.MS. 19,402, f.159).

56 Helgerson, *Forms of Nationhood*, p. 219.
57 See Chapter six.
58 L. E. Whatmore, 'William Somers, Henry VIII's Jester', *Biographical Studies, 1534–1829*, 1:2 (1951), pp. 128–30.
59 Bod. MS Rawl. Poet. 171, ff.60–82. First identified in G. C. Moore Smith, 'Notes on Some English University Plays', *MLR*, 3 (1908), pp. 143–6.
60   *Elpis evasit manus cruenti Mysi*
    Sic haeresis rabiem pauci qui Bootim modo
    Tyberim aut Pysuerga[m] bibunt. det illis numen faciles
    In Angliam reditus . . .

The above translation is Moore Smith's; punctuation emended from the MS. The Venerable English College, Rome, stands near the Tiber; 'Baetis' is the Guadalquivir, on which stands Seville, where an English College was established in 1592. Moore Smith inferred a local significance from the non-classical name of Pisuerga, the river upon which Valladolid stands, and suggested that the play came from the English College at Valladolid. He may be right, though not for this reason – Valladolid would not have had a monopoly among the English Colleges in referring to itself or its own river. If the identification is correct, then it may be the (highly unsuccessful) play performed at Valladolid to entertain Philip III of Spain in June 1615: see Valladolid, *Registers*, ed. Henson, p. xxiv (translated). MacCabe, *Introduction to the English Jesuit Theatre*, p. 235, accepts Moore Smith's identification, having formerly queried it (in MacCabe, 'Notes', p. 368, where he reports that Moore Smith himself had suggested to him that *Psyche et Filii Eius*, described in the Bodleian catalogue as a play *de lugentis Angliae facie*, can possibly be identified with a *declamatio de statu calamitoso Angliae* performed at St Omer on 30 October 1643). But given that *declamatio* generally signifies a debate rather than a play, it seems unlikely that *Psyche et Filii Eius* could be so described; and the subject itself is commonplace.

61 See Lewis and Short under 'Pæstum'.
62   *Ænigma solvitur, nam huc miseriae appulimus*
    Non nisi ænigmate licitum est vera loqui.
    Sub Psyches nomine Anglia exoptat rosam
    Florem avitæ fidei, qui quondam eius
    Erroribus aetas auras multiplici germine
    Alia in regna fuderat. ah pudet dicere
    Qualis nunc foetor est ubi dulces olim halitus.
    Hoc novit Anglia, luget, ingemiscit, dolet . . .
    Erotis schemate omnes Catholici latent

      Hos Mysus premit, Mysus quem haeresim nuncupo
      Proteo mobiliorem haeresim, omnes haec figuras subiens
      Non turpe putat e monstri fari faucibus
      Dummodo sententiam capitis in Catholicum ferat.
      'Erroribus' is an emendation from 'Erratis [?]'.

63   *O si quis Hercules hydrae pullulantia capita*
      Fidei contunderet clava, et liberaret Angliam[.]
(*Clava* (club) is an emendation from *clavo* (nail or rudder, though cf. the quotation at fn 65 below). In addition, Jane Stevenson has pointed out to me the pun on *clavis* (implying St Peter's keys) in the last line.) Cf. G. E. Varey, 'Minor Dramatic Forms in Spain With Special Reference to Puppets', 2 vols (Cambridge PhD thesis, 1950), 1, p. 154, for a description of the battle between Hercules and the hydra, depicted in fireworks, at Segovia in 1613.

64 Nigel Griffin, 'Some Aspects of Jesuit School Drama, 1550–1600, With Particular Reference to Spain and Portugal', 2 vols (Oxford D.Phil thesis, 1975), p. 49. I am grateful to Dr Griffin for his help with my thesis.

65   *Psyches vidistis lachrymas! mysterium habent.*
      Mysterium quod melius lachrymae, quam lingua doceat.
      Psyche (iam nostis Angliae quod vices gerat.)
      Volvitur curarum æstu naufragium timens
      Nec vanus terror, haeresis cum clavum regit.
      O Anglia, Anglia . . .

66 Though no key survives to *Antipaelargesis* (St Omer, n.d.) its theme of filial sacrifice may have a similar relevance to England. The play has been edited by Charles Burnett and Masahiro Takenaka: *Jesuit Plays on Japan and English Recusancy* (Tokyo: Sophia University (Renaissance Monographs 21), 1995). I am grateful to both editors for an advance copy of the translation, and much information on Jesuit drama. See also Valentin, *Théâtre des Jésuites* (1983–4), II, subject-index under *Amour des Parents* and *Père et Fils*.

6 THE SUBJECT OF EXILE : II

1 Starn, *Contrary Commonwealth*, p. 125.
2 Paul Tabori, *The Anatomy of Exile: A Semantic and Historical Study* (London: Harrap, 1972), pp. 32 ff.
3 E.g. in Hebrews 11. 13–16. See Josephine Evetts-Secker, '*Fuga Sæculi* or Holy Hatred of the World: John Donne and Henry Hawkins', *RH*, 14:1 (1977), pp. 40–52, on the notion of England as an island adrift from the united Catholic continent in 'Treatise of the Holy Hatred of the World', the versified preface to Hawkins's translation of Giovanni Pietro Maffei's *Fuga Sæculi* (1632).
4 H. E. Rollins, *Old English Ballads, 1553–1625, Chiefly From Manuscript* (Cambridge University Press, 1920), no. 24 (all poems in this section are transcribed from Rollins, unless otherwise stated). Another version of 'Jerusalem, my happy home', together with a version of 'Jerusalem, thy

joys divine' (Rollins, no. 25), appears in *The Song of Mary the Mother of Christ* (1601), an anthology probably taken from a Catholic MS. See also under title in John Julian, *A Dictionary of Hymnology* (London: John Murray, 1907).

5   Rollins, *Old English Ballads*, p. 169, for variants.
6   This is probably echoed (or *vice versa*) in 'Amount, my soul', Rollins, no. 23 st.19:

> Good Magdalene hath lefte her mone,
> her sighs and sobes doe cease;
> And since her teares and plaintes are gone,
> she lives in endlesse peace.

7   This hymn was sometimes attributed to Augustine at this date, and may be alluded to by his singing in 'Jerusalem, my happy home'. The visions of heaven in the two ballads have similarities, though partly because they both paraphrase descriptions of the new Jerusalem from the Book of Revelation.
8   A translation of the hymn can be found in J. M. Neale (ed. and trans.), *Collected Hymns, Sequences and Carols* (London: Hodder & Stoughton, 1914), pp. 162–5. I am grateful to Jeremy Maule for these references.
9   A more literal translation of the Latin (ll. 3–4 below) is Neale's 'Lead me, when my warfare's girdle / I shall cast away from me'.
10

> Christe, Palma bellatorum,
> Hoc in Municipium
> Introduc me, post solutum
> Militare cingulum;
> Fac consortem donativi
> Beatorum civium.
>
> Præbe vires inexhausto
> Laboranti prœlio;
> Ut quietem post præcinctum
> Debeas emerito;
> Teque merear potiri
> Sine fine præmio.   (p. 15)

11   A currently – or hitherto – obsolete term (*OED*): 'Resting in hope or expectation.'
12   Alluding to Revelation 21. 21.
13   There were a few mainstream printed versions: see Rollins, *Old English Ballads*, pp. 163–4 (noting variants).
14   Macdonald and Brown (eds.), *Poems of Robert Southwell*, pp. 47–8.
15   David Crystal, *The Cambridge Encyclopaedia of the English Language* (Cambridge University Press, 1995), p. 403; Paul van Buren, *The Edges of Language: An Essay in the Logic of a Religion* (London: SCM, 1972).
16   *OED*.
17   On the assumption that the burden was sung at the close of each stanza, or after short groups of stanzas.
18   Rollins, *Old English Ballads*, p. 169.

19 For the *Salve Regina*, see *New Catholic Encyclopædia*, 15 vols (New York: McGraw-Hill, 1967), XII, p. 1,002. Tabori, *Anatomy*, p. 31, links it with the *contemptus mundi* commonplace.
20 See Michael E. Williams, *St. Alban's College, Valladolid: Four Centuries of English Catholic Presence in Spain* (London: C. Hurst, 1986), ch. 5; Bede Camm, *In the Brave Days of Old: Historical Sketches of the Elizabethan Persecution* (London: Art & Book Co., 1899) pp. 177ff.: the personification continues in Camm's use of the Vulnerata as a frontispiece. The Vulnerata is central to a complex iconographical programme in the chapel featuring the portraits of English martyrs, and I am grateful to Harriet Hawkes for letting me see her photographs of these.
21 Camille, *Gothic Idol*, p. xxvi, discusses how new meanings can be superimposed on to old images as they decay.
22 Ann Kibbey, *The Interpretation of Material Shapes in Puritanism* (Cambridge University Press, 1986), comments on Ely (pp. 47–8). For the characteristic mutilation of iconoclasm, cf. J. R. Phillips, *The Reformation of Images: Destruction of Art in England, 1535–1660* (Los Angeles: University of California Press, 1973), figs. 16–21, 36–8; from the practical point of view, these appendages are usually the portions of a statue it is easiest to break. The miracles performed by the Virgin for dismembered suppliants were satirised in anti-Catholic pamphlets, e.g. in London's pope-burning procession of 1673, when the pope's scaffold-speech included an anecdote about a Damascene who had his right hand restored in this manner: *The Last Speech and Confession of the Whore of Babylon* (1673), p. 4.
23 Stephen Greenblatt, *Learning to Curse: Essays in Early Modern Culture* (New York: Routledge, 1989), p. 172.
24 For details of the manuscript, see note 26.
25 Kevin Sharpe, *Politics and Ideas in Early Stuart England. Essays and Studies* (London: Pinter, 1989), p. 49.
26 The main contemporary account is Antonio Ortiz, *Relacion de la Venida de los Reyes Catolicos, al Colegio Ingles de Valladolid* (1600). It is divided into two parts, the first describing the reception of the Royal couple and the second that of the Vulnerata. It is partially translated by Francis Rivers as *A Relation of the Solemnetie Wherewith the Catholike Princes K. Phillip the III and Quene Margaret Were Receyued in the Inglish Colledge of Valladolid* (1601); the account of the Vulnerata's reception, and a few other passages, are omitted, possibly to enhance the conciliatory nature of a publication which – if one is to take Rivers's dedication of the book to the Lord Chamberlain of England at face value – may have aimed to demonstrate continued Spanish goodwill towards England at a time when the two countries were still at war. V.E.C. Liber 1422, ff.49a–61a (and eight unnumbered pp. of hieroglyphics) is a translation of the second part of Ortiz which complements Rivers; all quotations are taken from this. See also Williams, *St. Alban's College, Valladolid*, pp. 62–3; Albert J. Loomie, *The Spanish Elizabethans: The English Exiles at the Court of Philip II*

(London: Burns & Oates, 1963), pp. 214–15; [Mgr Ronald Hishon], *College of Saints and Martyrs: The English College, Valladolid. 1589–1989* (London: Catholic Truth Society, 1989); [Robert Persons], *A Relation of the King of Spaines Receiving in Valliodolid* (1592), an account of an earlier visit which also details the emblems for the occasion (pp. 23–4, 52–3); *Registers of the English College at Valladolid*, ed. Edwin Henson (London: CRS, 1930), pp. xx, xxxii (for an account of the statue's temporary deposition in Valladolid Cathedral in 1679).
27 Hackett, *Virgin Mother*.
28 Triangular brackets, selected erasures of first hand; round brackets, insertions in second hand.
29 See Peter Holmes, *Resistance and Compromise: The Political Thought of the Elizabethan Catholics* (Cambridge University Press, 1982), pp. 64, 81. Anthony Munday describes how Elizabeth was sometimes referred to by the epithet of Jezebel at Rome, and how she and her councillors were railed against: *The English Roman Life*, ed. Philip Ayres (Oxford: Clarendon, 1982), pp. 25, 28, 92.
30 Litt. Ann. 1609/1610; Cardwell Collections, Farm Street, London, vol. III, ff.37–38a.
31 In Granada on 13 September 1635, her triumph over heretics was celebrated by a pyrotechnical display in which a castle of fireworks, representing her chastity, was shown with heretics burning and giants lobbing rockets and crackers from it. See Varey, 'Minor Dramatic Forms', I, p. 155. Varey also describes (II, p. 153) a presentation at Salamanca in 1658 utilising Marian symbolism, showing a tower on which heretics are consumed by flames and Faith stands forth triumphant.
32 See Jacques Lafaye (trans. Benjamin Keen), *Quetzalcoatl and Guadalupe: The Formation of Mexican National Consciousness, 1531–1813* (University of Chicago Press, 1976); references to the Virgin of Guadalupe in Octavio Paz, *Sor Juana: Her Life and Her World* (London: Faber & Faber, 1988) pp. 40–1; Jean Franco, *Plotting Women: Gender and Representation in Mexico* (London: Verso, 1989).
33 Poets too were sometimes incautious in their language: see the acrostic poem in BL Add.MS. 23, 229, f.39a, which calls Mary a 'powerfull Goddesse'.
34 E.g. in Verstegan, *Odes*, pp. 55–6, 'A reprehension of the reprehending of our ladies praise':

> And let performance of her woorthy praise,
> Of her praise-yeilding race remaine the signe,
> That so the blame that for it others raise,
> Become the marck of their dissenting lyne. (p. 56)

Some polemical works address the point, e.g. *Maria Triumphans* (1635), in which Mariadulus, an imprisoned Catholic priest, and Mariamastix, described as an 'Imaginary Precisian, and a Minister', debate the validity of Marian veneration. Analogues can be found in the defiant triumphalism of nineteenth-century Catholicism: e.g.

> O teach me, holy Mary,
> A loving song to frame,
> *When wicked men blaspheme thee,*
> *I'll love and bless thy name.*

(From first verse and chorus to Hymn 112, Westminster Hymnal (London: Burns, Oates & Washbourne, 1912)).

35 For the Marian devotion of the English Jesuit colleges, see also C.N., *Our Ladie Hath a New Sonne* (1595); for the personification of the True Church, see *The Holy Churches Complaint* [c. 1598–1601] (facs. Ilkley: Scolar Press, 1975).

36 Tapestries (*panos* or *tapices*) were used extensively by Spanish Jesuits to create an effect of *ornatus*, as often for the walls of a theatre or a stage: cf. Griffin, 'Aspects', pp. 51–3.

37 Griffin, 'Aspects', p. 54; see also pp. 53, 56, and Griffin's article, 'Miguel Venegas and the 16th-Century Jesuit School Drama', *MLR*, 68 (1973), pp. 796–806; Jennifer Montagu, 'The Painted Enigma and French 17th-Century Art', *JWCI*, 31 (1968), pp. 307–5.

38
> *Umbra fovet Platani nimio siccata calore*
> *Corpora; et hæc, vafros fronde fugat colubros.*
> *Tu platanus (pia Virgo) æstus Syriumque repellens;*
> *Hac recubans umbra, tutus ab hoste manet.*
> *Ergo salutifera Mariæ requiesce sub umbra*
> *Qui nocuas flammas, hæreticosque fugis.*

Like many of the emblems below, this alludes in part to one of the titles of the Virgin in the Litany of Loreto: 'Quasi Platanus'. Cf. Verstegan, *Odes*, p. 48.

39 Cf. Henry Hawkins, *Parthenia Sacra* (1633), pp. 151–61; the frontispiece of *Eikon Basilike* (1649) where it is emblematic of Charles I as confessor and martyr. See Rosemary Freeman, *English Emblem Books* (London: Chatto & Windus, 1948), pp. 50, 77, 150–1, 184, 228; index of emblems to Mario Praz, *Studies in 17th-Century Imagery*, 2 vols (2nd edn. Rome: Edizioni di Storia e Letteratura, 1964); J. M. Diaz de Bustamente, '*Onerata Resurgit*. Notas a la Tradicion Simbolica y Emblematica de la Palmera', *Helmantica*, 31, nos. 94–6 (1980), pp. 27–88; Pedro A. Galera Andreu, 'La Palmera, *Arbor Victoriae*. Reflexiones Sobre un Tema Emblematico', *Goya*, nos. 187–8, (1985), pp. 63–7; Peter Davidson, *The Vocal Forest: A Study of the Context of Three Low Countries Printers' Devices of the 17th Century* (Leiden: Academic Press, 1996), pp. 11–14.

40 Freeman, *English Emblem Books*, p. 93.

41 For other Marian hieroglyphs see Jacques Callot, *Vita Beatae Mariae Virginis Matris Dei Emblematibus Delineata* (1646); Appendix Z to Pedro F. Campa, *Emblemata Hispanica: An Annotated Bibliography of Spanish Emblem Literature to the Year 1700* (Durham: Duke University Press, 1990) has a short-title bibliography to fete, royal entry and funeral books of the Spanish Golden Age containing emblematic material.

42 Mary was the subject or dedicatee of a number of Jesuit dramas: see

Muller, *Jesuitendrama*, II, p. 119; Valentin, *Théâtre des Jesuites*, II, subject-index.

43 Act II ii (pp. 458–460). Quoted from Simons's *Tragœdiæ Quinque* (1st edn., 1656). Simons's plays have been translated by Louis J. Oldani and Philip C. Fischer as *Jesuit Theatre Englished: Five Tragedies of Joseph Simons* (St. Louis: Institute of Jesuit Sources, 1989), from which the following translations come. (Starred translations have been slightly emended.)

44 *O turpe spectrum! Coelitum vanus colis*
 Simulacra? Caesar, jussa proculcat tua.

45 THEOPHILUS *O mater! O lux orbis! O rerum salus!*
 Quam per pericla, perque Carnificum metus
 Servavit usque natus illaesam tuus.
 Da pauca tecum corde sollicito loquar.
 SABATIUS *Puelle vecors, verba simulacro facis?*

46 This point is not brought out in the translation from *Jesuit Theater Englished*: 'In his impiety he venerates a mere picture of a saint.'

47 However, Tarasius the Patriarch, a character who has died in exile, appears in a dream to Leo in I ii: *Jesuit Theater Englished*, p. 330.

48 T *Dic mater, unde tantus Eoum furor*
 Divexet orbem? Rara perpetuum fides
 Servat tenorem. Fas jacet, floret nefas.
 S *Per te patremque, fas jacet, floret nefas.*
 T *Quin & tuorum castus occumbit chorus:*
 Pars ense, pars squalore, pars fuga perit.
 Qui te Sabaea nube genitricem colat,
 (O digna thure mater aeterno coli.)
 Rarus per orbem superest.
 S *Exsuperet licet;*
 Rerum potitus impios dedam neci.

49 The stage direction *Imagine[m], qua[m] nequit per vim extorquere, pugione in os vulnerat, & exit*, which appears after *Potens Maria* in the 1656 text, ought probably to appear after *Chalybe rescindam manum* or *O facinus!* in Theophilus's next speech.

50 *cerno? Nec suos latent*
 Retroacta in orbes lumina, & tantum nefas
 Pati recusant? Prome singultus dolor,
 Oculosq[ue] densa conde lacrymarum vice . . .
 Quo fulgor oris, dulce quo frontis jubar,
 Quo luminum recessit Augustus decor? . . .
 Fuscate radios astra: Virgineos latro
 Radios abegit. Conde sol oris decus:
 En majus oris periit erasum decus.
 Perite flores: Laesa jam florum est parens.
 Marcescite rosae, Coelitum elanguet rosa.
 Pix atra canum liliis turpet caput:
 En liliatum spina labefecit caput . . .
 Assertor orbis, Virginis magnae parens,

Idemque nate: non ut iratum vibres
Ab axe fulmen, matris ulturus probrum,
Rogo: scelestum poena non dubia premet.
Impune Matrem nemo violavit tuam.
Da, da Mariam foedere aeterno colam:
Cujusq[ue] pictam laesit effigiem Leo;
Da, non movendum corde simulacrum geram.
Haec summa voti, Mater orantem juva.

51 Probably William Cecil, Lord Burleigh. For these plays, see Martin Murphy, *St. Gregory's College, Seville, 1592–1767* (London: CRS 73, 1992), pp. 19–20. I am grateful to Dr Murphy for information on Jesuit drama.

52 V.E.C., Liber 321 (2), ff.61a–121a; see Gossett, 'Drama', pp. 60–93; and Houliston, 'St Thomas Becket'. This was well before the first German use of the theme, at Constanz in 1626: Valentin, *Théâtre des Jésuites* (1983–1984), I, no. 958, p. 112.

53   *Salvator tuis*
Obtemperavi vicibus, dedi fidem
Tuam Brytannis: . . .
                    sanguinis non est datum
Nostri rigare rore; martyrii decus
Nondum Brytannae mellis est merces data,
Dabitur deinde, fusus aperiet cruor
Coelum Brytannis: astra penitrabit frequens
Et purpuratus Anglus: adopertas fores
Albanus illas vidit, et alii suas
Meruere sanguine laureas tingi suo:
Aspirat et nunc Purpurae clarum caput
Thomas, potentum proterens Regum impia
Mandata, vobis ille spectetur: dabit
Hoc approbatum: facilis a terris via
Ad astra fortibus: viam Thomas docet . . .   (scene 1)

The reading 'vicibus' in line 2 is emended from 'vocibus(?)'.

54 A post-Reformation Catholic account of this is given in Richard Brown, *S. Thomas Cantuariensis et Henrici II Illustris. Anglorum Regis Monomachia* (1626).

55   *Non ficta gerimus sceptra, non plausu tenus*
Occupo theatrum fictus ad ludos breves
Iners Tyrannus . . .   (I iv)

56   *. . . pondus ac decus dabit*
Rei theatrum, principes inter viros
Rex ipse primas [vices] sustinet: . . .
Notetque quisque lege quis vestra Chori
Leges tenebit melius ut dignam ferat
Quam quisque palmam meruit . . .   (II i)

57 Chaney, *Grand Tour*, p. 39 (and n. 85) discusses *The Life or the Ecclesiasticall Historie of S. Thomas Archbishope of Canterbury*, trans. and adapt. A.B., from

Baronius's *Annales*, 1,163–74 (1639) which praises Thomas Becket in its dedication for knowing God's part from Caesar's; he further suggests of the figures in the frontispiece that their placement was inspired by dramatic prototypes.

58 Jos Simons (ed. and trans.), *'Ambrosia': A Neo-Latin Drama* (Assen: Van Gorcum, 1970).

59 Alison Shell, ' "We Are Made a Spectacle": Campion's Dramas', in McCoog (ed.), *Reckoned Expense*.

60 The speech is transcribed and translated in *ibid.*, pp. 116–17.

61 V.E.C., MS 321 (1) and (4), ff.2b–60a, 179a–232b (incomplete). 'Roffensis' is Fisher's Latin title as Bishop of Rochester.

62 Houliston, 'St Thomas Becket', pp. 44 ff.

63 MS. Stonyhurst B VII. 23 (1), fourth item. No evidence survives as to when it was performed: see MacCabe, *Introduction*, p. 102; Muller, *Jesuitendrama*, II, p. 127; and cf. Thomas Carleton's lost play *Henrico 8o* (Douai, 1623).

64 *Morus* cites William Roper's life of More, *The Mirror of Vertue* (1626) and Nicholas Sander's *De Origine ac Progressu Schismatis Anglicani* (1585) at the end of its *argumentum*. Sander's was by far the most influential and widely translated of the English Catholic histories of the schism: see *ARCR* I, nos. 972–1,011. The translation used here has been David Lewis's (London: Burns & Oates 1877). See also Nicholas Harpsfield, *Historia Anglicana Ecclesiastica* (1622); David Chalmers, *De Ortu & Progressu Haeresis in Regnis Scotiae & Angliae* (1631); John Pits, *Relationum Historiarum de Rebus Anglicis* (1619).

65 It is the longest of the Lives, 261 pages in comparison to the Life of the apostle (twenty-six pages) and that of Thomas Becket (141 pages). See *The Life and Illustrious Martyrdom of Sir Thomas More, by Thomas Stapleton*, trans. Philip E. Hallett, intro. and notes, E. E. Reynolds (London: Burns & Oates, 1928, repr. 1966) pp. xi–xii. Stapleton's most important sources were the brief manuscript memoir of More written by More's son-in-law William Roper, possibly the longer biography by Nicholas Harpsfield which was based on Roper's account and enjoyed an international circulation in manuscript in the late sixteenth and early seventeenth centuries, and a series of letters formerly belonging to John Harris, More's one-time secretary (pp. xii–xiii). See also *The Life and Death of Sr Thomas Moore . . . Written . . . by Nicholas Harpsfield*, ed. Elsie Vaughan Hitchcock (London: E.E.T.S., 1932), with an introduction describing the eight Harpsfield MSS in detail; *William Roper and Nicholas Harpsfield: Lives of St. Thomas More*, ed. E. E. Reynolds (London: Dent, 1963), introduction. Richard Marius, *Thomas More: A Biography* (London: Collins, 1986) is the standard modern life, while R. W. Chambers, *Thomas More* (Brighton: Harvester, 1982) deals with More's posthumous history in detail. More's life, in various versions, was available in other European languages: see Denis Rhodes, 'Il

Moro: Italian Lives of Sir Thomas More', in Edward Chaney and Peter Mack (eds.), *England and the Continental Renaissance. Essays in Honour of J. B. Trapp* (Woodbridge: Boydell, 1990). Lastly, there was oral anecdote; Cresacre More and other descendants were prominent members of various Catholic communities on the Continent, and the More family were zealous guardians of his memory. See James K. McConica, 'The Recusant Reputation of Thomas More', reprinted in R. S. Sylvester and G. P. Marc'hadour (eds.), *Essential Articles For the Study of Thomas More* (Hamden, Connecticut: Archon, 1977); Mark Robson, 'Posthumous Reputations of Thomas More: Critical Readings' Leeds University PhD, 1997.

66 There is probably an obscene pun on *iuris*, which also means 'broth' or 'stock', and hence 'semen' (Lewis and Short).
67 It was believed by some Catholics that Anne Boleyn was Henry's daughter: see Sander, *De Origine*, ed. Lewis (1877), preface and Book I, ch. xiv.
68 *Suscipies eandem filium istum, quam per tot flagitia, perque effusas in omni intemperantia sibi dires [sic: possibly a contraction of 'diritates'] tantopere concupisces; sed filium eius modi qui e matris suae visceribus crudeli ferro efossus, prius Parentem a qua vitam hausit, lucis usura privabit, quam lucem ipse aspiciat; filium sui iuris numquam futurum, sed venenato poculo ab illis ipsis viperis, quas tu iam sinu foves, illi propinato, praematura morte extinguendum, ultimamque prolem seu marem seu foeminam ex pestifero tuo semine procreandam ... Tertio post Patrem loco Tyrannidem occupabit postrema ex nefanda tua stirpe proles, ex tetranima illa Lupa pro incestos amores suscipienda: Filia, quae totum Patrem, totamque Matrem una induet; ... Et hic terminus esto abominandae prosapiae tuae.*
69 Cf. the Cacodaemon in the Praeludium of *Sanguinem Sanguis Sive Constans Fratricida* (St Omer, ca. 1600: Bodleian, MS Rawlinson poet. 215). Though precedence is uncertain, *Furor Impius Sive Constans Fratricida* (St Omer, n.d.: Stonyhurst MS. A VII 50 (2), item 8) is probably an adaptation of this play.
70   *Sic sic agendum, fusus extinguat cruor*
       Inimicā lumina lampadum; iniectus cruor
       Pretiosus ille sit licet Mori ...   (I iv)
71 Though More's son John takes the historical place of his daughter Margaret Roper in visiting him in prison and accompanying him on the way to the scaffold (III iv–vi, v ii–iii). Cf. Stanley Morison, *The likeness of Thomas More: An Iconographical Survey of Three Centuries* (London: Burns & Oates, 1963), p. 45 (for reductionism operating on More's character) and p. 20 (for an account of the play *Heroica in Adverssi* (sic) *Constantia Thomae Mori* put on by Jesuits at Olmutz in April 1727, where – in contrast – several of the *dramatis personae* were taken from Holbein's family group of the More family).
72 *DNB*, under Hall.
73 See Gossett, 'Drama', p. 66.
74 But a revisionist approach to Fisher has begun: see Brendan Bradshaw and Eamon Duffy (eds.), *Humanism, Reform and Reformation: The Career of*

Bishop John Fisher (Cambridge University Press, 1989); Richard Rex, *The Theology of John Fisher* (Cambridge University Press, 1991).

75 The Jesuit John Percy took the name of John Fisher for his controversial pamphlets: see Milward, II, p. 143.

76 Probably intended for Anne's father, Thomas Boleyn; but the list of *dramatis personae* is missing.

77 ROMA *Cecidit, cecidit Regina throno*
Et desertis quaeritur thalamis
Praeponitos pellicis amplexus.
Quid non audet violentus amor,
Et cum imperio iuncta libido? . . .
HISPANIA *En nova nostrae principis intrat*
Pellex thalamos. Quid sancta illi
Prodest pietas? quid magnorum
Gloria patrum? . . .
Iacet, iacet, heu, tanta
Ingloria virtus, et regum
Inclyta proles procul a regis
Pellitur aula.   (Ist chorus)

Cf. Vernulaeus's *Henricus Octavus*, above. *Praeponitos* (line 3) may be a mistake for *praepositos*.

78 Julia Gasper, 'The Reformation plays on the Public Stage', in J. R. Mulryne and Margaret Shewring (eds.), *Theatre and Government Under the Early Stuarts* (Cambridge University Press, 1993).

79 Quoted from the edition by John Margeson (Cambridge University Press, 1990).

80 Probably the most famous crux in *Henry VIII* – as in Henry VIII's life – is whether his conscientious qualms about his marriage to Catherine should be read as hypocritical or not. The substantial critical literature on *Henry VIII* tends to disagree on the extent to which the play should be read as having controversial, topical or allegorical significance, suggesting above all that the playwrights – like, in another context, the authors of the Book of Common Prayer – were deliberately creating a text that was interpretible in a number of ways, and so could be endorsed by the majority of its audience. For recent summaries and re-statements, see Gordon McMullan, 'Shakespeare and the End of History', *Essays and Studies*, 48 (1995), pp. 16–37; Joseph Candido, 'Fashioning Henry VIII: What Shakespeare Saw in *When You See Me, You Know Me*', *Cahiers Elisabethains*, 23 (1983), pp. 47–59; Paul Dean, 'Dramatic Mode and Historical Vision in *Henry VIII*', *Shakespeare Quarterly*, 37.2 (1986), pp. 175–89; Stuart M. Karland, '*Henry VIII* and James I: Shakespeare and Jacobean Politics', *Shakespeare Studies*, 19 (1987), pp. 203–17; Peter L. Rudnytsky, '*Henry VIII* and the Deconstruction of History', *Shakespeare Survey*, 43 (1991), pp. 43–57 (arguing for a Catholic perspective on the divorce); Camille Wells Slights, 'The Politics of Conscience in *All Is True* (or *Henry VIII*)', *Shakespeare Survey*, 43 (1991),

pp. 59–68; Ivo Kamps, 'Possible Pasts: Historiography and Legitimation in *Henry VIII*', *College English*, 58.2 (1996), pp. 192–215; Judith Anderson, *Biographical Truth: The Representation of Historical Persons in Tudor-Stuart Writing* (New Haven: Yale University Press, 1984), suggesting Cavendish's *Life of Wolsey* as a possible source (see above, chapter 5). Annabel Patterson, ' "All Is True": Negotiating the Past in *Henry VIII*', in R. B. Parker and S. P. Zitner (eds.), *Elizabethan Theater: Essays in Honor of S. Schoenbaum* (Newark: University of Delaware Press, 1996), pp. 147–66, suggests that the play critiques the possibility of telling the historical truth on stage.

81 Though identification of the hands is only a partial solution to the question of division of labour: see Vittorio Gabrieli and Giorgio Melchiori (eds.), *Sir Thomas More* (Manchester University Press, 1990), introduction, section 2:4. Quotations below are taken from this edition.

82 Gabrieli and Melchiori emphasise its domestic nature, and in particular the informal presentation of the trial seen through the eyes of More's humblest dependants (p. 6). See also Richard Dutton, *Mastering the Revels: The Regulation and Censorship of English Renaissance Drama* (London: Macmillan, 1991), ch. 3.

83 However, this never happened. See Gabrieli and Melchiori (eds.), *Sir Thomas More*, pp. 18, 27.

84 This point is made at length in *ibid.*, p. 31, though the editors are mistaken in attributing Shrewsbury's line at IV i, l. 110, to Surrey.

85 Gabrieli and Melchiori suggest that this speech may contain an oblique reference to the apocryphal anti-Protestant Erasmian poem *D. Erasmi Rotterdami Carmen Heroicum in Mortem Thomae Mori* (1536).

86 Probably meaning in this context 'unhealthy' rather than 'improvident' (*OED*). The life of the poet was traditionally held to be the antithesis of the public career: see Charles Segal, 'Catullan *Otiosi*: The Lover and the Poet', *Greece and Rome*, n.s. 17 (1970), pp. 25–31.

87 See Gabrieli and Melchiori (eds.), *Sir Thomas More*, pp. 1, 12–16; Sir Edward Maunde Thompson, 'The Autograph Manuscripts of Anthony Mundy', *Library*, n.s. 14 (1915–17), pp. 325–53.

88 Gabrieli and Melchiori (eds.), *Sir Thomas More*, p. 15, point out that the name of Sherwin listed by Holinshed among the May Day rioters must have struck Munday, since Campion's companion Ralph Sherwin led a rebellion against the College Rector, Dr Morris, at the time when Munday was there. They also postulate, rather less convincingly, that the retention of the name Morris for Cranmer's secretary is a reference to the Rector himself.

89 *Ibid.*, pp. 8, 43–4 *et passim*.

90 Critical consensus places the first version not later than 1593; see *ibid.*, p. 12.

91 Critics have often compared the two plays, with articles by A. A. Parker, 'Henry VIII in Shakespeare and Calderón: An Appreciation of *La*

'Cisma de Ingalaterra [sic]', *MLR*, 43 (1948), pp. 327–52, and John Loftis, 'Henry VIII and Calderón's *La Cisma de Inglaterra*', *Comparative Literature*, 34.3 (1982), pp. 208–22, proving especially influential. For a summary of critical findings, see George Mariscal, 'Calderón and Shakespeare: The Subject of Henry VIII', *Bulletin of the Comediantes*, 39.2 (1987), pp. 189–213. The most recent study is Gregory Peter Andrachuk, 'Calderón's View of the English Schism', in Louise and Peter Fothergill-Payne (eds.), *Parallel Lives: Spanish and English National Drama, 1580–1680* (Lewisburg: Bucknell University Press, 1991), pp. 224–38.

92 See Kenneth Muir and Ann L. Mackenzie (eds.), *The Schism in England* (Warminster: Aris & Phillips, 1990), introduction, esp. p. 25. All quotations and translations are taken from this.

93
Si fuero lícito dar
al sueño interpretación,
vieras que estas cartas son
lo que acabo de soñar.
La mano con que escribía
era la derecha, y era
la doctrina verdadera,
que celoso defendía;
aquesto la carta muestra
del Pontífice, y querer
deslucir y deshacer
yo con la mano siniestra
su luz, bien dice que lleno
de confusiones vería
juntos la noche y el día,
la triaca y el veneno.
Mas por decir mi grandeza
cuya la victoria es,
baje Lutero a mis pies,
y León suba a mi cabeza.
Por arrojar la carta de Lutero a sus pies, y poner la del Pontífice sobre la
cabeza, las trueca.
(Act I, ll. 141–60)

94 See Parker, 'Henry VIII'. Gongora is said to have referred to Anne Boleyn as a she-wolf: see Varey, 'Minor Dramatic Forms', II, p. 205.

CONCLUSION

1 Hibbard, *Charles I*; Veevers, *Images*. Recent studies of Jacobitism emphasizing the Catholic factor include Paul Kléber Monod, *Jacobitism and the English People, 1688–1788* (Cambridge University Press, 1989); Leo Gooch, *The Desperate Faction? The Jacobites of North-East England, 1688–1745* (University of Hull Press, 1995). See also Daniel Szechi, *The Jacobites: Britain and Europe, 1688–1788* (Manchester University Press, 1994), pp. 18–20, 126–9.

2 Bossy, *English Catholic Community*, introduction. Jeremy Gregory, 'The

Making of a Protestant Nation: "Success" and "Failure" in England's Long Reformation', in Nicholas Tyacke (ed.), *England's Long Reformation, 1500–1800* (London: UCL Press, 1998) evaluates differing recent historiographical models of the 'success' of the Reformation.
3 See introduction; and, for a recent critique of this approach, Questier, *Conversion*, pp. 200–2.
4 See Peter Lake and Michael Questier, 'Prisons, Priests and People', in Tyacke (ed.), *England's Long Reformation*.
5 Anne Dillon of Selwyn College, Cambridge, is completing a thesis which will discuss *Ecclesiae Anglicanae Trophæa*, the widely disseminated and frequently copied martyrological engravings taken from the frescoes of the Venerable English College, Rome. Other Catholic martyrological material includes William Allen, *A Briefe Historie of the Glorious Martyrdom of XII. Reverend Priests* (1582); John Gibbons, *Concertatio Ecclesiæ Catholicæ in Anglia* (1st edn. 1583); Robert Persons, *De Persecutione Anglicana* (1582); Pedro de Ribadenyra, *Historia Ecclesiastica del Scisma* (1st edn. 1588); Nicholas Sander, *De Origine ac Progressu* (1st edn. 1585); Richard Verstegan, *Theatrum Crudelitatum Hæreticorum Nostri Temporis* (1st edn. 1587) and *Præsentis Ecclesiæ Anglicanæ Typus* (1582); John Wilson, *The English Martyrologe* (1st edn. 1608); Thomas Worthington, *A Relation of Sixtene Martyrs* (1601) and *A Catalogue of Martyrs in England* [1608]; Diego de Yepes, *Historia Particular de la Persecucion de Inglaterra* (1599). See J. T. Rhodes, 'English Books of Martyrs and Saints of the Late 16th and Early 17th centuries', *RH*, 22 (1994), pp. 7–25; A. G. Petti, 'Richard Verstegan and Catholic Martyrologies of the Later Elizabethan Period', *RH*, 5 (1959–60), pp. 64–90; Nicholas Roscarrock, ed. Nicholas Orme, *Lives of the Saints: Cornwall & Devon*, Devon and Cornwall Record Society, n.s., 35 (Exeter, DCRS, 1992); Sullivan, *Dismembered Rhetoric*, ch. 5; G. F. Nuttall, 'The English Martyrs, 1535–1680: A Statistical Review', *JEH*, 22 (1971), pp. 191–7. M. J. Rodriguez-Salgado and Simon Adams, *England, Spain and the Gran Armada, 1585–1604* (Edinburgh: John Donald, 1991), pp. 274–8, discuss Ribadeneyra's work, heavily influenced by Sander.
6 Shell, ' "We Are Made a Spectacle" '.
7 Shell, 'English Catholicism', chs. 3–4.
8 Lake and Questier, 'Agency, Appropriation and Rhetoric Under the Gallows'.

Works frequently cited

In a wide-ranging study limited in length, it has, sadly, not been possible to include a full bibliography. The vast majority of book and manuscript sources are referred to in one chapter only (for this purpose, Chapters 3–4 and 5–6 are taken together) and full bibliographical details are given at the first citation. The following list is of works cited in more than one chapter.

Arber, Edward (ed.), *A Transcript of the Registers of the Company of Stationers of London; 1554–1640*. 4 vols. London: privately printed, 1875–7; and Birmingham: 1894.

Allison, Anthony and Rogers, D. M., *The Contemporary Printed Literature of the English Counter-Reformation Between 1558 and 1640*. Volume I: works in languages other than English; Volume II: works in English. Aldershot: Scolar Press, 1989–94.

Aston, Margaret, *England's Iconoclasts. Volume I. Laws Against Images*. Oxford University Press, 1988.

Camille, Michael, *The Gothic Idol*. Cambridge University Press, 1989.

Chaney, Edward, *The Grand Tour and the Great Rebellion: Richard Lassels and the 'Voyage of Italy' in the 17th Century*. Geneva: Slatkine, 1985.

Clancy, Thomas H., S.J., *English Catholic Books, 1641–1700: A Bibliography*. Revised edition. Aldershot: Scolar, 1996.

Papist Pamphleteers. Chicago: Loyola University Press, 1964.

Clifton, Robin, 'The Popular Fear of Catholics During the English Revolution', *Past and Present*, 52 (1971), pp. 23–55.

Crum, Margaret (ed.), *First-Line Index of English Poetry, 1500–1800, in Manuscripts of the Bodleian Library, Oxford*. 2 vols. Oxford: Clarendon, 1969.

Cust, Ann and Hughes, Richard (eds.), *Conflict in Early Stuart England*. Harlow: Longman, 1989.

Davenport, Arnold (ed.), *The Poems of John Marston*. Liverpool University Press, 1961.

Dures, Alan, *English Catholicism, 1558–1642: Continuity and Change*. Harlow: Longman, 1983.

Foley, Henry, S.J., *Records of the English Province of the Society of Jesus ... in the*

Sixteenth and Seventeenth Centuries. 7 vols. London: Burns & Oates, 1875–83.
Fowler, Alastair, *Kinds of Literature.* Oxford: Clarendon, 1982.
Gasper, Julia, *The Dragon and the Dove: The Plays of Thomas Dekker.* Oxford: Clarendon, 1990.
Guiney, L. I., *Recusant Poets.* Volume 1 (no vol. II). London: Sheed & Ward, 1938.
Hackett, Helen, *Virgin Mother, Maiden Queen: Elizabeth I and the Cult of the Virgin Mary.* Basingstoke: Macmillan, 1995.
Healy, Thomas, *Richard Crashaw: A Biography.* Leiden: E. G. Brill, 1986.
Helgerson, Richard, *Forms of Nationhood: The Elizabethan Writing of England.* University of Chicago Press, 1992.
Holmes, Peter, *Resistance and Compromise: The Political Thought of the Elizabethan Catholics.* Cambridge University Press, 1982.
Janelle, Pierre, *Robert Southwell the Writer.* London: Sheed and Ward, 1935.
Kerrigan, John (ed.), *Motives of Woe: Shakespeare and the Tradition of Female Complaint.* Oxford: Clarendon, 1991.
Kibbey, Ann, *The Interpretation of Material Shapes in Puritanism.* Cambridge University Press, 1986.
Lake, Peter and Questier, Michael, 'Agency, Appropriation and Rhetoric Under the Gallows: Puritans, Romanists and the State in Early Modern England', *Past and Present* 153 (1996), pp. 64–107.
Macdonald, James H., S.J., and Brown, Nancy Pollard (eds.), *The Poems of Robert Southwell S.J.* Oxford: Clarendon, 1967.
McCoog, Thomas M., S.J. (ed.), *The Reckoned Expense: Edmund Campion and the Early English Jesuits. Essays in Celebration of the First Centenary of Campion Hall, Oxford.* Woodbridge: Boydell, 1996.
Marotti, Arthur, *Manuscript, Print and the English Renaissance Lyric.* Ithaca: Cornell University Press, 1995.
Martz, Louis, *The Poetry of Meditation.* New Haven: Yale University Press, 1954, rev. edn. 1962.
Milton, Anthony, *Catholic and Reformed: the Roman and Protestant Churches in English Protestant Thought, 1600–1640.* Cambridge University Press, 1995.
Morrill, John, *The Nature of the English Revolution.* Harlow: Longman, 1993.
Myers, Robin and Harris, Michael (eds.), *Censorship and the Control of Print in England and France, 1600–1910.* Winchester: St Paul's Bibliographies, 1992.
Jones, Emrys (ed.), *The New Oxford Book of 16th-Century Verse.* Oxford University Press, 1991.
Parry, Graham, *The Trophies of Time: English Antiquarians of the 17th Century.* Oxford University Press, 1995.
Phillips, James Emerson, *Images of a Queen: Mary Stuart in 16th-Century Literature.* Berkeley: University of California Press, 1964.
Phillips, J. R., *The Reformation of Images: Destruction of Art in England, 1535–1660.* Los Angeles: University of California Press, 1973.

Pollard, A. W. and Redgrave, G. R. comp., *A Short-Title Catalogue of Books Printed in England, Scotland, and Ireland, and of English Books Printed Abroad, 1475–1640*. Second edition, revised by W. A. Jackson, F. S. Ferguson and Katharine F. Pantzer. London: The Bibliographical Society, 1976–91.

Potter, Lois, *Secret Rites and Secret Writing: Royalist Literature, 1641–1660*. Cambridge University Press, 1989.

Questier, Michael C., *Conversion, Politics and Religion in England, 1580–1625*. Cambridge University Press, 1996.

Rollins, H. E., *Old English Ballads, 1553–1625, Chiefly From Manuscripts*. Cambridge University Press, 1st edn. 1920.

Shell, Alison, 'Catholic Texts and Anti-Catholic Prejudice in the Seventeenth-Century Book Trade', in Robin Myers and Michael Harris (eds.), *Censorship and the Control of Print* (see above), pp. 33–57.

Sullivan, Ceri, *Dismembered Rhetoric: English Recusant Writing, 1580 to 1603* (London: Associated University Presses, 1995).

Thurston, Fr Herbert, 'Catholic Writers and Elizabethan Readers. II. Father Southwell the Euphuist', and '... III. Father Southwell the Popular Poet', *The Month*, 83 (Jan.–Apr. 1895), pp. 231–45 and 383–99.

Tyacke, Nicholas (ed.), *England's Long Reformation, 1500–1800*. London: UCL Press, 1998.

Veevers, Erica, *Images of Love and Religion: Queen Henrietta Maria and Court Entertainments*. Cambridge University Press, 1989.

Verstegan (*alias* Rowlands), Richard, *Odes* (1601).

Walsham, Alexandra, *Church Papists: Catholicism, Conformity and Confessional Polemic in Early Modern England* (London: Royal Historical Society/Boydell Press, 1993.

Watt, Tessa, *Cheap Print and Popular Piety, 1550–1640*. Cambridge University Press, 1991.

Weiner, Carol Z., 'The Beleaguered Isle: A Study of Elizabethan and Early Jacobean Anti-Catholicism,' *Past and Present*, 51 (1971), pp. 27–62.

Wing, Donald, comp., *Short-Title Catalogue of Books Printed in England, Scotland, Ireland, Wales, and British America and of English Books Printed in Other Countries, 1641–1700*. Second edition, revised and edited by John R. Morrison, Carolyn W. Nelson *et al*. 3 vols. New York: Modern Language Association of America, 1982–94.

Woudhuysen, Henry, *Sir Philip Sidney and the Circulation of Manuscripts, 1558–1640*. Oxford: Clarendon, 1996.

All references to Shakespeare, unless otherwise stated, are from Stanley Wells and Gary Taylor (eds.), *William Shakespeare: The Complete Works*, Oxford University Press, 1st ed. 1988.

For the reader's convenience, all references to the Bible are from the Authorised Version – though some of them, at least, should have been from the much less widely available Douai/Rheims translation.

Index

Abbot, John, 142–4, 166
  Jesus Praefigured, 142–4, 166
  The Sad Condition of a Distracted Kingdom, 166
absolutism, royal, chapter 4 *passim*
Accession Day Tilt, 127–33
Act of Uniformity, 10
Adams, Thomas, 48
advice-to-a-painter poems, 30
agnosticism in critical discourse, introduction
  passim, 55, 101
Ahasuerus, 159–60
Alabaster, William, 14, 58, 88–94, 98
  sonnets, 88–94
Aldiberga, queen of Britain, 152
Alexander VI, Pope, 29
Alfred the Great, 181
allegory, 25–6, 34, 66, 72, 127, 142, 148, 188–93
Allen, William, cardinal, 117, 119
Allison, Anthony, 13–14
Alpaugh, Davis J., 24
Ambrose, St, 196, 213
Anglicanism: see Church of England
Anglo-Catholicism, 95
anti-Catholicism, 16–19, chapter 1 *passim*, 56, 64, 72, 82, 165; *daemonopoiia*, 40
  Catholics as mountebanks, 33–4
anticlericalism, 42, 48–9
anti-Puritanism, 11
antiquarianism, 12
apocalypse, chapter 1 *passim*
  Book of the Apocalypse, see Bible: Revelation
Apostles, the, 142
Appellants, 109, 115, 133–5
Apples of Sodom, 27, 34, 47
Aquinas, St Thomas, 2
aristocracy, Catholic, 67
Armada, 115
Arundel, Earl of: see Howard, Thomas
Arundell, Charles, 167

Aston, Margaret, 36, 40
Astraea, 179
Audley, Thomas, baron Audley of Walden, 215–16
Augustine of Hippo, St, 143, 196, 197
autodidacticism, 157, 226
Austin, John, 16
Aveling, Hugh, 3, 4

Babington Conspiracy, 117
Bacon, Anthony, 127
Bacon, Francis, 60
Bacon, George, 170
Bale, John, 37
ballads, 16, 64, 163–4, 195–9
Bansley, Charles, 27
Barclay, John, 115, 142–6
  Argenis, 115, 145–6
  Euphormio, 145
  Series Patefacti, 142
Barnes, Barnabe, 28–30
baroque in England, 56, 103
Bartas, Guillaume Salluste du, see du Bartas, Guillaume Salluste
Bassompierre, Marshal de, 153
Bathsheba, 70
Beast of Revelations, 25
Bellarmine, St Robert, cardinal, 87
Bennett, Joan, 102
Bernard, Richard, 25, 28
Bible:
  Old Testament, 64
  Psalms, 64, 96; penitential psalms, 87
  Jeremiah, 177
  Lamentations of Jeremiah, 69, 177, 184, 195
  New Testament, 64
  Gospels, 64, 68, 89
  Book of Revelation, 24–38, 195, 198
  Apocrypha, 37, 64, 161
  Biblical paraphrases, 37, 39, 64, 73

303

Birrell, T.A., 4
Blacklo, Thomas, see White, Thomas
Blackwell, George, 113, 133
Blackwood, Adam, 121
Blainville, Sieur de, 153
Bloody Questions, 111, 113
Bodye, John, 112
Boleyn, Anne, queen of England, 190, 216–17, 221–3
Bolt, John, 63
Bolton, Edmund, 60
Borgia, Lucretia, 28
Bossy, John, 15, 108, 224
Bradbrook, Muriel, 54
Bradshaw, Brendan, 4
Breton, Nicholas, 79–80, 84
Breton, Richard de, 211
Brewer, Thomas, 185
Brevis Dialoguismus, 183, 211
Briant, Alexander, 221
Brodwin, L.L., 54
Brooke, Rupert, 41
Brooks-Davies, Douglas, 75
Broxup, W., 79
Buchanan, George, 121
Buckland, Ralph, 142
Busby, John, 62
Butler, Martin, 155
Byrd, William, 96
Byzantium, 174, 208

C., I., author of *St Mary Magdalen's Conversion*, 83
C., R., author of *Palestina*, 137–40, 157
Calderón de la Barca, Pedro, 221–3
California, Huntington Library, 170
Calvin, John, 145
Calvinism, 54, 64, 80
Cambridge, Peterhouse, 95
Camm, Bede, 4
Campion, Edmund, 111, 184–5, 221; *Ambrosia*, 213
canonicity, 24, chapter 2 *passim*
Captiva Religio, 187–90, 210
Capucins, 80
Caraman, Philip, 4
Carpenter, Richard, 27
Cary, Sir Henry, 1st viscount Falkland, 157–8
Cary, Elizabeth, Lady Falkland, 156–9; *Mariam*, 156–60
Catherine of Aragon, 182, 217
Catholic Record Society, 4
Catholics:
    'angry' Catholics, 19
    catacomb culture, 16

church-papists, 14–15, 111, 225
Catholic communities, 107–9, 121, 172–3
deracination of Catholics, 19, 56, 97, chapters 5–6 *passim*, 224–5
Catholics in exile, 19, 108–9, chapters 5–6 *passim*, 224
as expatriates, 108–9, 121
historiography and Catholics, Introduction *passim*;
paralleled with Jews, 137–40, 156–62, 174
recusancy, 14–16, 67, 152, 225
Catholic revival, 11
Catholic seepage, 17–19, chapter 2 *passim*, esp. 63
Catholic texts, 12–13, 225–6
Cato, 134–6
Cavendish, George, 175
Cawood, Gabriel, 62–3
Cecil, Robert, earl of Salisbury, 116, 131
Cecil, William, Lord Burghley, 210
censorship, 63, 223
    expurgation, 17
Champernoun, Sir Arthur, 116
Chaney, Edward, 171
chapbooks, 64
Chapel Royal, Dean of, 95
Charles I, 141, 143–60, 165
Cheney, Patrick, 74
Church of England, 3, 39, 101, 136–7, 169, 195
    episcopal visitations, 10
    ideologies fostered by Anglicanism, 3, 101
Churchyard, Thomas, 87
Clancy, Thomas, 4, 111
Clark, Kenneth, 32
Clifford, Margaret, countess of Cumberland, 74
clothes, sinfulness of fine, 27–8
Clotilde, queen of France, 152
'Colin Clout', 76–7
Collingwood family, 98
comedy, 188–90
complaint, 87–8, chapter 5 *passim*
Como, Cardinal, 118
Constable, Henry, 17, 107–8, 122–6, 150, 163, 169–70
    Diana, 108
    Catholic Moderator, 123
    sonnets, 122–6
conversion, 15, 19, 88–97
Copley, Anthony, 114, 134–7, 195
Corpus Christi, 11
cosmetics, 26–30
Counter-Reformation, Continental and English, 11, 60, 80, 97, 100, 201, 208

Index

Cowley, Abraham, 169–70
Cranmer, Thomas, 215–16, 218
Crashaw, Richard, 2, 15, 19, chapter 2 *passim*, 169
Crashaw, William, 16
Cromwell, Thomas, 215–16
Cuthbert, St, 181

Dante, 174, 188
Davenant, Sir William, 146, 148
David the Psalmist, 65, 69–70
Davies, John, of Hereford, 86
Decadents, 30–1, 49–51
deceit, chapter 1 *passim*
deconstruction, 17
dedications, 115, 137–8
Dekker, Thomas, 31
Devereux, Robert, 2nd earl of Essex, 127–33, 201
disputations, public, 89
Dissolution of the Monasteries, 181
Dodd, Charles, 4
Dollimore, Jonathan, 49–50, 55
Donne, John, 2, 56, 59, 100–2
  Pseudo-Martyr, 135
Douai, English College at, 173, 181–2
drapery, 40, 206
Drury, William, 181–2
du Bartas, Guillaume Salluste, 59, 65–7, 73, 78, 85, 147–8
Dudley, Anne, countess of Warwick, 74
Dudley, Robert, earl of Leicester, 212
Duffy, Eamon, 4, 7
Dyer, Edward, 75

ecumenism, 150
Edward VI, king of England, 10, 176, 214–15
Edwards, Francis, 4
Egan, Anthony, 33
Eisenstein, Elizabeth, 13
elegy, 175–87, 197–8
Eliot, John, 65
Eliot, T.S., 49, 101
Elizabeth, mother of John the Baptist, 138
Elizabeth I, 10–11, 39, 110–12, 116–23, 128–41, 146, 163, 176, 179, 184, 190, 203–5, 214–15, 218
Elizabethan Settlement, 10–11
Ellis, G., 79
emblematics, 19, 44, 127–133, 171, 206–7
eschatology, 24; see also apocalypse
Esther, 70, 152, 159–63
Eve, 138
exemplarity, 14

Fawne, Luke, 16
Feilding, Susan, Countess of Denbigh, 96–7
feminist criticism, 17–18
Finson, Mr, 190
Firbank, Ronald, 50
Fisher, John, St, 194; *Roffensis*, 214, 216–19
Fitzurse, Reginald, 212
Fletcher, John, 217
Fletcher, Giles, 59
Fletcher, Phineas, *The Purple Island*, 34–6
Foley, Henry, 4
Fonseca, Jeronimo Osorio da, 138
Ford, John, 2; *The Broken Heart*, 23; *Christ's Bloody Sweat*, 82
Forrest, William, 10
Foucault, Michel, 103
Foxe, John, 226
free will, 149; see also predestination
French Revolution, 50

Gage, George, 171
Gardner, Helen, 101
Garlick, Nicholas, 83
Garnet, Henry, 114, 213
Gataker, Thomas, 159
Gautier, Théophile, 50
Gee, John, 53
gender-roles, blurring of, 49
Genesis, 66
Giametti, A. Bartlett, 174
Gill, Roma, 54
Gillow, Joseph, 4
Godfrey, Sir Edmund Berry, 27
Gotardi, Federico, 190
Greenblatt, Stephen, 201
Grene, Christopher, 4
Griffin, Nigel, 192, 206
Grundy, Joan, 62, 107, 125
Guiney, L. I., 2
Gunpowder Plot, 110, 115, 142

Habsburgs, 118, 130
Hackett, Helen, 203
hagiography, 8, 14, 225–7
Haigh, Christopher, 5
Hall, Joseph, 78, 84–6, 169
Hall, Richard, 216
Haman, 160
Hammer, Paul, 127
Harington, Sir John, 120, 161
Harpsfield, Nicholas, 221
Harsnet, Samuel, 40, 47
Harvey, Gabriel, 84
Healy, Thomas, 97
Heimann, Mary, 5

Helgerson, Richard, 190
Henri III of France, 121
Henri IV of France, 125
Henrietta Maria, queen of England, 19, 80, 107, 146–63
Henry II of England, 211–14
Henry VIII of England, 176, 180, 190, 214–23
Heraclitus, 177
Herbert, George, 56, 58–60, 78–9, 100–2
Herbert, Mary, Countess of Pembroke, 64
heresy, 34, 85, 178, 182, 207
hermeneutics of suspicion, 17
Herod, 139, 156–60
Heywood, Jasper, 64
hieroglyphics, see emblematics
Hill, Christopher, 8–9, 165
Hodgetts, Michael, 4
Hogarde, Myles, 10
Hoghton, Thomas, 172
Holland, Robert, 64
Holofernes, 161
Horace, 177–8
Howard, Henry, Earl of Northampton, 114–15
Howard, Henry, Earl of Surrey, 219–20
Howard, Thomas, 2nd earl of Arundel, 171
Howell, Thomas, 168, 186–87
Hudson, Thomas, 65
Hugo, Hermann, author of *Pia Desideria*, 81
Hugo, Victor, 49
Huguenots, 145
Huish, Alexander, 95
Hutchinson, F.E., 78
Huysmans, J.K., 50
hymns, 74–76
hypocrisy, 26–36

iconoclasm, 28–32, 174, 201–3, 207–10
iconodulia, 40, 207–10
iconography, 30–3, 44
idolatry, chapter 1 *passim*, 73, 85, 110
ignis fatuus, 29, 35
imagery, chapter 1 *passim*, 192
images, chapter 1 *passim*, 74
imprese, 127–33
imprisonment, 89
information networks, 15
Inquisition, 167, 173
interludes, 31, 188
Isaac, 159
Isabella, Infanta, of Spain, 110

Jacobitism, 168, 171, 224
James VI of Scotland and I of England, 59, 65, 85, 123, 125–26, 141–6, 152, 190

Janelle, Pierre, 57
Jerusalem, 177, 195; hymns on, 173, 195–200
Jesuits, 9, 109, 113–15, 117–18, 127, 135, 165, 172, 192, 206
Jesuit drama, 19, 109, 173–4, 183, 187–193; chapter 6 *passim*, 226
jewels, 29, 34
Jews: see Catholics, paralleled with Jews
Jollet, Thomas, 12
John, St, the apostle, 80–1
John the Baptist, St, 138
Jones, Inigo, 146–7
Jonson, Ben, 2, 60; *Catiline*, 142; translation of *Argenis*, 146
Joseph of Arimathaea, St, 211–12
Josephus, 157–9
Jouvancy, Joseph, 188
Judas, 79
Judith, 65, 70, 161

Kingsmell, Sir William, 112
Knight, G. Wilson, 55
Knightley, Robert, 181–2
Kroll, Norma, 41–2

Lake, Peter, 27, 32
lamentation, see complaint
Landau, Jack, 49
Lassels, Richard, 171–2
Laudianism, 94–6, 165
Le Grys, Robert, 146
Lenton, Francis, 160–3; *Queen Esther's Halleluiahs*, 160–2; *Great Britain's Beauties*, 162–3
Lesly, John, 87
Lewalski, Barbara, 97, 178
Lewgar, John, 95
Lille: Benedictine convent, 114
Lindley, Keith, 165
Lisbon, 29
liturgy, 16, 24, 26
  use of incense, 198
  liturgy of the Madonna Vulnerata, 203
  Magnificat, 205
  the Mass, 179, 198, 201
  use of monstrances, 40
  Prayer Book, 10, 204
Lodge, Thomas, 77, 84, 93, 157, 186
  edition of Josephus, 157
  Prosopopoeia, 77, 84
  'Truth's Complaint over England', 178–80, 184
London:
  Covent Garden, 48
  Lambeth Palace Library, 121

Index

Somerset House Chapel, 147–8
Stationers' Hall, 80
Long, Kingsmill, 146
Loreto, 85, 169–70; Litany of Loreto, 163, 205
Louis XIII of France, 152
Louvain, Porc College, 182
loyalism, Catholic, 10, 19, chapters 3–4 *passim*
Lucretius, 42
Ludlam, Robert, 83
Luna, B.N. da, 142
Luther, Martin, 164
Lynch, Michael, 116

Machiavellianism, 24
Macintyre, Alastair, 112
Madonna Vulnerata, 195, 201–7
madrigals, 87
manuscript culture, 12
Margaret, queen of Spain, 203–4
Maria, Infanta, of Spain, 143
Marie de Medici, queen of France, 153
Marino, Giovanni Battista, 98
Markham, Gervase, 79–80
marriage, 141–2, 150–64
Marston, John, *Malcontent*, 23; *Metamorphosis of Pygmalion's Image*, 38; *Certain Satires*, 85–6
martyrologies, 19, 112, 183, 226–7
Martz, Louis, 2, 57–9
Mary, the Blessed Virgin, 10, 11, 123–6, 148, 151, 163, 170, 180–1, 186–7, 196, 203–6 (see also *Madonna Vulnerata*)
Mary Magdalen, St, chapter 2 *passim*, 193, 196
Mary Stuart of Scotland, 115–22, 124, 142, 152
Mary I of England, 9–10, 112, 117, 175–6
masques, 147–51, 155–63
  Chloridia, 148
  Luminalia, 147, 150–1
  Salmacida Spolia, 151
  Tempe Restored, 148
  The Temple of Love, 147–51
Mathew, Toby, 107, 170–1
Mavericke, Radford, 26
Mayo, John, 29
McCoog, Thomas, 4
medievalising, 12
meditational practice, 80–1
  Ignatian meditation, 58, 198
memento mori, 30, 44
metaphorical clusters, 23, 46
Middleton, Thomas, 18, chapter 1 *passim*

The Changeling, 53
A Game at Chess, 27, 144–5
The Revenger's Tragedy, 23–4, 43–6, 49–52
The Wisdom of Solomon Paraphrased, 37–44, 52, 79
Women Beware Women, 46, 54
Milton, John, 9, 56, 172
  Paradise Lost, 166
Milward, Peter, 4
misogyny, 30, 78
monarchy, chapters 3–4 *passim*
Monica, St, 143
Montague, Walter, 146–7
moralistic verse, 64, 73, 87
More, Thomas, St, 194
  S. Thomas Morus and *Morus*, 214–21
Morris, John, 4
Morville, Hugh de, 212
Munday, Anthony,
  Discovery of Edmund Campion, 221
  English Roman Life, 110, 220–1
  Sir Thomas More, 218–21

Narcissus, 44
Nashe, Thomas, 84
nationalism, 109, 195
  Englishness, 101
Nemoianu, Virgil, 6
neo-Latin writing, 56, chapters 5–6 *passim*
neoplatonism, 73, 148, 151
neutralism, 165
Nevell, Edmund, 119
Nicoll, Allardyce, 49–52
Niobe, 175
Northern Rising, 117, 172

Oates, Titus, 33
Oath of Allegiance, 113, 142
Oath of Succession, 218–19
obedience, chapter 4 *passim*
Oldisworth, Nicholas, 170
orality, 11, 20
ornament, 26, 34, 192
Orpheus, 147
Osorius: see Fonseca, Jeronimo Osorio da
othering, 55, 100
Ovid, 174
Owen, John, 29
Owen, Lewis, 206
Oxford, Bodleian Library, 191–2

Pallotta, Giovanni Battista, Cardinal, 99
Palmer, Sir Thomas, 218
pamphlet debates, 109
Panzani, Gregorio, 147–8

papacy, 8, 25–7, 36, 40, 49, 87, 94–5, 110–15, 147–52
Parliament, 95, 153, 165–8
parody, sacred, 75, 99
Parr, Catherine, queen of England, 82
Parry, William, 117–19
Paul, St, 141, 155
Paul IV, pope, 49
Paulson, Ronald, 24
Peckham, Robert, 173
Perron, Cardinal, 13
Persons, Robert, 88, 110, 117, 137, 210, 213
Peter, St, chapter 2 *passim*, 193
Peter Damian, St, 196
Petrarch, 174
Petrarchan sonnet, 122–6
Petti, Anthony G., 170
Philip II of Spain, 117–18, 124
Philip III of Spain, 203
Pine-Coffin, R.S., 173
Pius V, pope, 111
pigmentation, 28–30
Pilgrimage of Grace, 10
Plaidy, Jean, 154
polemic, 16–18, chapter 1 *passim*, 73, 82, 95, 110, 188
Potter, Lois, 146
Potts, Abbie, 177
Poulton, Thomas, 88
predestination, 40, 54, 149: see also free will
Pritchard, Arnold, 115
prostitutes, chapter 1 *passim*, esp. 43–9
Protestantism, 8–9, 16–17, 80; Protestant poetics, 54–5, chapter 2 *passim*; visual imagination of Protestant, 32; Protestant readers of Catholic poetry, 63
Proteus, 191
Prynne, William, 146, 163
Psyche et Filii Eius, 187–8, 191–5, 200–1, 210
psychoanalytical criticism, 100
Puritanism, 8–9, 24, 30
Puttenham, George and Richard, 65

Questier, Michael, 15, 113
Quilligan, Maureen, 139

Raleigh, Walter, 35
Rebecca, 159
religious orders, 12: see also Jesuits; Capucins
resistance theory, 165
revenge tragedy, 18, chapter 1 *passim*
Revett, Eldred, 98
Rex, Richard, 4
Rheims, 173
Rich, Penelope, 68–70

Ridolfi Plot, 117
Robinson, Thomas, 29
Rogers, D.M., 13–14
Roman Catholicism: see Catholicism
Rome, 33, 38, 173
  Venerable English College, 88, 188–90, 211–17, 220–1
Roper, Margaret, 219
Rops, Felicien, 50
rosaries, 34, 81
Rowlands, Richard: see Verstegan, Richard
Rowland, Samuel, 79
royalists, 165–8, 171, 175, 186

St Omer, English College at, 173, 205
Sackville, Lady Margaret, 70
Salluste du Bartas, Guillaume: see du Bartas, Guillaume Salluste
Salve Regina, 187, 200
Samson, 71
Sander, Nicholas, 121
Santa Gadea, Count and Countess of, 201
Scarisbrick, J. J., 4, 7
Schwob, Marcel, 49
secular priests, 113, 133, 172
sermons, 87, 183
Seville, English College at, 173
Shacklock, Richard, 138
Shakespeare, William, 2
  Henry VIII, 217–18, 223
  Macbeth, 142
  associated with *Sir Thomas More*, 221
  The Taming of the Shrew, 154
Sharpe, Kevin, 203
Shaw, W. David, 177
Sherburne, Sir Edward, 98
Sherwin, Ralph, 221
Shirley, James, 2
Short-Title Catalogue, 13
shrines, 180–1
Sidney, Lady Mary, see Herbert
Sidney, Sir Philip, 59, 64–5, 67–70, 72
  Astrophil and Stella, 68
  Defence of Poetry, 65, 67, 177
similitudes, 25
Silvester, Josuah, 65
Simeon, 196
Simons, Joseph, 207–10
Sinfield, Alan, 55
Sixtus V, pope, 49
Smith, Richard, 133, 166
Smyth, Richard, 108
Society of Jesus: see Jesuits
Solomon, Wisdom of: see Middleton, Thomas

Index

Somers, William, 190
Southern, A. C., 4
Southwell, St Robert, 2, 14, 17, 19, chapter 2 *passim*, 121–2, 147–8, 193, 195, 199, 213
Spenser, Edmund, 37, 56, 59, 67, 72–7, 84–5, 135–6, 139
  Amoretti, 73
  Faerie Queene, 135–6
  Four Hymns, 74–6
  Tears of the Muses, 72
speratory verse, 197
Stabat Mater, 81, 86
Stafford, Anthony, 162
Stapleton, Thomas, 214
Starn, Randolph, 174, 194
Sternhold, Thomas, 85
Strong, Roy, 127
survivalism, 11
Swinburne, A. C., 49, 52
Sympson, Richard, 83

Tabori, Paul, 194
Talbot, George, 4th earl of Shrewsbury, 219
Talbot, Mary, countess of Shrewsbury, 123–5
Tansillo, Luigi, 62, 81, 98
Tartt, Donna, 23
Taylor, Jeremy, 186
tears-poetry, chapter 2 *passim*
Tertullian, 30
Theodosius, emperor, 213
Thimelby, Edward, 98–100
Thomas Becket, St, 194, *St Thomas Cantuar*, 211–14
Thompson, E.P., 17
Thurston, Herbert, 103
Tilney, Sir Edmund, 219, 221
Tootell, Hugh: see Dodd, Charles
Topcliffe, Richard, 221
Tourneur, Cyril, chapter 1 *passim*, esp. 38–9, 49, 52 (see also Middleton, Thomas)
Tracy, William de, 212
tragedy, chapter 1 *passim*, 187–90
tragicomedy, 187–93
Traherne, Thomas, 56
Trent, Council of, 97
Tresham, Thomas, 116–17

Urania, the heavenly muse, 65–7, 72, 147
Urban VIII, pope, 145, 160

Valladolid, English College at, 173, 191, 195, 200–7
Vanitas, 30
Vashti, 160–1
Vaughan, Henry, 56, 59–60
Vautrollier, T., 65
Veevers, Erica, 147, 150–1
Verstegan, Richard, 2, 15, 79, 121
Vernulaeus, Nicholas, 182
vestments, 26, 34
Villiers, George, 1st duke of Buckingham, 143, 153
Villiers, Mary, countess of Buckingham, 154
Virgil, 76, *The Aeneid*, 84; *Eclogue IV*, 214
virgins, 45, 182, 196
virtuosi, 171–2

W. F., author of a poem on heaven, 60
Walpole, St Henry, 213
Walsham, Alexandra, 15
'Walsingham', 173, 180–1
Walton, Isaac, 78
Warnke, Frank J., 100
Watson, Robert N., 55
Weber, Max, 3
Webster, John, 18, chapter 1 *passim*
  The Duchess of Malfi, 34, 50, 53–5
  The White Devil, 24, 34, 36, 46–9, 54–5, 223
Weiner, Carol, 31
Wentworth, Thomas, 1st earl of Strafford, 165
Weston, William, 142
White, Rowland, 132–3
White, Thomas, 166
Whore of Babylon, 25, 31–2, 38–42, 47–9
'Why do I use my paper, ink and pen?', 184–5
Wilde, Oscar, 50
Wilks, John, 53
Williams, George Walton, 97
Williamson, George, 101
Wisbech Stirs, 133
witchcraft, 34, 47
Wolfe, John, 62, 65, 84
Wolsey, Thomas, cardinal, 175
Wright, Thomas, 122, 126–33

Zachary, 196